D0310316

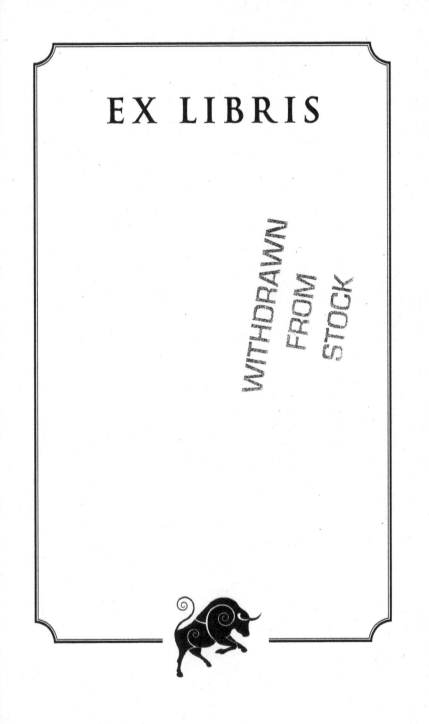

EX LIBRIS

The MURDERER of WARREN STREET

The True Story of a Nineteenth-Century Revolutionary

MARC MULHOLLAND

HUTCHINSON
LONDON

1 3 5 7 9 10 8 6 4 2

Hutchinson
20 Vauxhall Bridge Road
London SW1V 2SA

Hutchinson is part of the Penguin Random House group of companies
whose addresses can be found at global.penguinrandomhouse.com

Penguin
Random House
UK

Copyright © Marc Mulholland, 2018

Marc Mulholland has asserted his right under the Copyright, Designs
and Patents Act, 1988, to be identified as the author of this work.

First published in the United Kingdom by Hutchinson in 2018

www.penguin.co.uk

A CIP catalogue record for this book is available from the British Library.

ISBN 9781786331137

Typeset in 11.5/15 pt Sabon MT Pro
by Integra Software Services Pvt. Ltd, Pondicherry

Printed and bound in Great Britain by Clays Ltd, St Ives plc

Penguin Random House is committed to a sustainable future
for our business, our readers and our planet. This book is
made from Forest Stewardship Council® certified paper.

MIX
Paper from
responsible sources
FSC® C018179

To my mother, Ita, and in memory of my father, Dominic

'Suddenly Barthélemy aimed a pistol and fired. Moore dropped dead as the maid ran screaming out of the front door.' *Brisbane Telegraph*, 5 July 1854.

CONTENTS

PREFACE

'One cannot imagine how entirely different everything is just across the Channel from what it is in France. London, which is only a few hours distant from Paris, might be on the other side of the globe.' So wrote Francis Wey, a cultivated French art connoisseur who visited London in the early 1850s. His Paris was a city of eight-storey apartment buildings, each with its own porter or '*concierge*', fronted by shops. Streets were methodically numbered, odd on one side, even on the other. The sun shone through the faint smoke of wood fires on to lively public entertainments. At night cheerful cafés sparkled with light, while armed troops policed its turbulent streets. The Parisians he knew were vain, chivalrous, loud, demonstrative and fanatical. In London, by contrast, Wey found a sprawling metropolis of sturdy three-storey terraced houses, bustling docks, belching chimneys, and rain blackened by coal soot. The streets brimmed with advertising posters. The few street signs made little sense but policemen would politely offer directions. Rich men dined at home, or in about sixty grand 'Clubs', while the poor gathered in dreary and uninviting public houses. Londoners were proud, businesslike, taciturn and discreet. To the French ear, the English language was 'a mere murmur punctuated by soft, hissing sounds'. Modern readers might be surprised at the differences between the two cities Wey described.

Parisians would patiently queue, Londoners would rush and barge. Young Frenchwomen were repressed, their English counterparts flirtatious.

Francis Wey knew Paris and London because he wandered their streets. His pavement-level '*flâneur*' view of society had become fashionable by the 1840s. The *flâneur* is the casual wanderer who saunters about, led by no plan other than their own restless curiosity, observing what is happening in streets and alleyways. He sees what most people fail to see because they are rushing by, intent on business.

For Charles Baudelaire, the nineteenth-century poet and essayist, the *flâneur* was the detached observer, the 'botanist of the sidewalk'. Baudelaire advises us to take a seat at the pavement café and to watch passers-by. When one particular unknown face piques our interest – perhaps he looks troubled or distracted, or she is a beauty in rags, or his eyes blaze with a criminal intent – we rise and hurl ourselves 'headlong into the midst of the throng' in pursuit of the 'unknown, half-glimpsed countenance'. We leave the familiar routes of respectable workaday life for the mysterious, overlooked, crowded passageways and haunts of the underworld. Baudelaire certainly appealed to artists and bohemians. As a rule, however, historical writers – a sober lot – prefer to know where they are going. The great English historian of the nineteenth century, Lord Acton, advised scholars to 'choose a problem' before beginning their historical researches. This is good advice. But it is also possible to write history as a *flâneur*. Rather than focusing on a problem, we might choose one character from history – neither a great man nor a great woman – and decide to follow them. What might we then see that otherwise would remain overlooked?

In this book the reader will track the unknown, half-glimpsed Emmanuel Barthélemy: nineteenth-century revolutionary, conspirator, gaol-breaker, duellist, inventor and murderer. In pursuing Barthélemy we not only uncover an extraordinary life, but travel the world through which he moved. This was a world that crossed national borders and its richness is best appreciated from multiple angles. We learn how Barthélemy saw society and how society saw him. As we make our way, we look about ourselves and see a world in transformation, in the midst of revolution and counter-revolution, becoming modern. Much of what we see is surprising and unfamiliar. But we find also much that is strikingly relevant to our own times.

In 1827 an Irish actress, Harriet Smithson, took Paris by storm when she played Ophelia in a touring performance of Shakespeare's *Hamlet*. Her Irish accent had not gone down well in London, but the literary 'Romantics' of France, first among them the writer Victor Hugo, were entranced. They found in Smithson's performance and Shakespeare's art a commingling of tragedy and comedy, violence and lyricism, high politics and low life, which seemed to speak to a dawning age of popular passions. Eighteen years later, Hugo wrote the first draft of his great novel on revolution, *Les Misérables*. His story of Jean Valjean, the redeemed galley convict and barricade fighter, was interrupted in 1848 by the reality of revolution and counter-revolution. When Hugo, now an exile, returned to his novel in January 1861, he began in a completely different register, with a meditation on the 'June Days', a doomed workers' rebellion, and its enigmatic leader, Emmanuel Barthélemy. Revolutionary romanticism had come to life. This is a book about that life and the world it reveals.

1

'THE MAN I NOW SEE IS THE MAN WHO SHOT ME'

When Emmanuel Barthélemy visited George Moore for the last time, he was not in a good mood. Perhaps few of us would be: it was a dank, freezing cold, wet night. Barthélemy was footsore and weary, and he had plenty on his mind. In his pocket a ticket for travel to the Continent: his plan, to assassinate the Emperor of the French.

Tying up loose ends in London was proving to be a complex business and Barthélemy had decided to work off his frustration by practising his pistol-shooting at the 'Gun Tavern' at Westminster, near Buckingham Palace. But on his way he met with a mysterious woman and between them they concocted a plan to visit George Moore, Barthélemy's former employer.

When they arrived at Warren Street it was just gone eight in the evening. The overture was playing at Her Majesty's Theatre in the Haymarket and the elegant audience there, 'glorious with beauties and with riches', was settling in for the evening's opera performance. At the same time, in the teeming slum streets, workers emerging from a day's labour were crowding round shabby stalls and shops. Under the three golden balls identifying the pawnbroker's establishment they presented their scanty possessions and in return 'the capitalist' lent them housekeeping money. This is how the rich lived and the poor survived. It was the bustling, energetic, often desperate face of London.

The date was 8 December 1854. England, in alliance with France, had been at war with Russia since March. Florence Nightingale was nursing the diseased British expeditionary force at Scutari on the Crimean peninsula. British public opinion had scorned Napoleon III, ruler of France, as a despotic upstart. But now they celebrated him as a stout and faithful ally. Crude portraits of Louis Napoleon Bonaparte and his Empress, Eugénie, were on display all over London. For a revolutionary like Barthélemy, vehemently opposed to the Bonapartist dictatorship, this vexed him almost to wildness. Never had he felt more of a foreigner in England.

Only a few years earlier, in 1848, revolution had swept the Continent, and Barthélemy's dreams had appeared to be on the brink of fulfilment. But now 'reaction' was inexorably rolling back the radical wave. Cities across Europe had risen in revolt against their monarchs in 1848, only to be suppressed by armies based on peasant recruitment. Now, in its aftermath, the religious, the conservative, and the revolutionary contended for the ear of the people. As a revolutionary, Barthélemy knew that the influence of his party was diminishing.

Barthélemy stopped at 73 Warren Street, a large townhouse and workplace near the juncture with Tottenham Court Road. He was in Fitzrovia, close to the centre of radical London. Barthélemy knew the area well.

Barthélemy was a familiar figure in London's radical community, both natives and exiles from European countries. But he was little known outside its ranks. For London was not just a centre of political agitation or a bolthole for revolutionaries. It was, primarily, the beating heart of the most extraordinary economic transformation to date. Only three years earlier the Great Exhibition had showcased Britain's world-beating

industrial might. London's docks were crowded with commercial shipping and fragranced by cotton, preserved fruits, spices,
dyes, spirits, perfumes and drugs, all piled high in warehouses
or, if unsold, burnt in a huge furnace known as the 'Queen's
Pipe'. The railways had tied together the country. In 1829 the
first railway passenger service opened between Liverpool and
Manchester. By the middle of the century railways criss-crossed
the United Kingdom. For *The Economist* newspaper this was
a transformation putting London at the centre of national life
as never before:

> In the days of Adam the average speed of travel, if Adam
> ever did such things, was four miles an hour ... in the year
> 1828, or 4000 years afterwards, it was still only 10 miles ...
> in 1850, it is habitually forty miles an hour, and seventy for
> those who like .... The railroad is the Magna Carta of ...
> motive freedom. How few among the last generation ever
> stirred beyond their own village? How few among the pre-
> sent will die without visiting London?

In the middle of the nineteenth century, London was expanding
at a dizzying rate, and new comfortable middle-class houses
were springing up. The house of George Moore on Warren
Street was in many respects typical of the prosperous middle-
class merchant. These were large houses, though as land in
London was expensive they were also narrow, with rooms
arranged one on top of the other. Steps brought the visitor up
to a front door which opened into a hallway. Below this level
were the servants' quarters, where could be found the kitchens,
pantries, larders and perhaps a cramped sitting room. The front
room was typically a dining room, behind this a study or occasional room. Upstairs on the first floor was a large fine drawing
room, the best in the house. Up another flight of stairs was the
'front bedroom', occupied by the master and mistress, and

another bedroom. The one or two floors above this were shared by children and servants. 'Pure undiluted gentility did not rise above the second floor.' It was the acme of the 'class-consciousness house'.

Inside this particular address was its master, George Moore; the maid, Charlotte Bennett; and innocently sleeping upstairs, Moore's grandson aged eight. At 8.30 p.m., Charlotte heard an impatient knocking and ringing at the door. She hurried to answer. The hallway had no lighting and she carried a tallow candle in a passageway otherwise illuminated only by the glow of street lamps coming through the glass fanlight over the front door. By the dim radiance of the flickering wick she peered at her visitors. Barthélemy was certainly a handsome man, standing five foot seven inches, of lithe and muscular build, with jet-black curling hair over a well-proportioned face. He had high cheekbones, a firm chin, a straight nose, defined lips, and striking, penetrating eyes. Charlotte had met him on previous occasions, when Barthélemy had come to the house to do mechanical work at the factory in the rear, but he had shaved off his large black moustache, and she did not recognise him. A hat, perhaps the common top hat or the recently invented bowler sported by working men, was pulled low over his face.

Barthélemy was accompanied by a woman who Charlotte did not know. She later described the mysterious lady as about thirty years of age, rather shorter than herself, dressed in dark clothing, and upon her head a straw bonnet. Covering her face was a 'fall', or a thick veil, and she wore a cloak of dark brown merino cloth, trimmed with black satin ribbon and small black satin buttons. Barthélemy was dressed in a rough blue overcoat with large bell sleeves. Sewn into the lining of his undercoat was a dagger. Also hidden were two pistols, and in his pocket twenty-four cartridges, a quantity of loose firing-caps, and that ticket for the boat to Hamburg.

Barthélemy asked Charlotte if Mr Moore was at home. Charlotte said he was. She walked the visitors down the long hallway to the back parlour. Here George Moore appeared, a large, stout and confident figure, the very model of a successful businessman. He had made a good living by the manufacture of fizzy drinks, for which there was a healthy market. Moore welcomed the visitors as friends, but he brought them into his second-best room. Her duty done, Charlotte left them to it, going through the kitchen and downstairs to her basement quarters.

Barthélemy and the woman followed Moore into the well-appointed parlour of tables, chairs and sideboard: a crowding together of walnut, rosewood and mahogany all richly decorated with carvings; plush curtains, thick carpet, rugs and Staffordshire figurines – the proud furnishings typical of a prosperous early to mid-Victorian gentleman. 'Hideous solidity was the characteristic,' as Charles Dickens wrote of such 'Podsnappery'. 'Everything was made to look as heavy as it could, and to take up as much room as possible.' Amid this self-congratulatory display of comfortable living, George Moore and his guests remained together for about twenty minutes.

At first the meeting went well. Moore was proud of his manufactory and his wares were displayed on the sideboard. He took down bottles of carbonated waters, drew chairs around the table and showed off an item of his trade: a kind of mallet used for tapping corks into pressurised bottles. With a corkscrew, Moore opened three bottles. Soda water and lemonade were provided for his guests. Barthélemy and his lady companion sipped at their drinks. Moore poured himself a ginger beer in a third tumbler, drained it, and started on another. He felt himself very much the gregarious patron.

From this congenial beginning, however, the meeting turned sour. The woman took a letter out of her pocket and began to read from it. She had reached nearly the bottom of the first page when Moore rose from his chair in a fury and lunged to snatch the letter out of her hand. Barthélemy jumped from his chair and flung Moore back with his arm. Caught off guard, Moore stumbled and partly fell. Barthélemy snatched up the weighty mallet, and in a fury smashed at a heavy mahogany chair with such force that both mallet and chair disintegrated. He did not, however, draw the dagger he was carrying.

Barthélemy swung at Moore with the mallet handle, dealing him a glancing blow to the head, which whipped back and cracked sharply off the wall. Moore's blood splashed on the wallpaper, the sofa cushions and the corkscrew. From her room downstairs, the maid heard a voice cry, 'Murder!' Moore was a big man, injured but outraged, and in fear for his life. He advanced on his now unwelcome guests, striking at Barthélemy and pushing him towards the door. Behind him he trailed blood through the room.

Charlotte heard the scuffle in the parlour from her servants' quarters. As she listened, the racket grew in volume and finally she summoned her courage and crept upstairs. Coming in view of the back parlour she saw her master and Barthélemy tumble out of its door, engaged in what appeared to be a deadly struggle in the passage. The mysterious woman followed closely behind. All was confusion and shadows as Charlotte's small tallow candle, the only light source illuminating the scene, danced and flickered.

As Barthélemy reached the front door, pursued by Moore, he attempted to stop Charlotte calling for help by clamping his hand over her mouth. Charlotte dropped her candle and it guttered out on the floor. Moore was still pushing at Barthélemy. As the two men grappled, Barthélemy swivelled round. Moore had his hand up and fixed on Barthélemy. 'I do not know whether he was pushing him or whether he was holding him back – he had his hand upon him, and he was doing either one or the other,' said Charlotte later. As the two men locked eyes, Barthélemy raised his pistol breast-high and tilted it at Moore's head. He pulled the trigger and the dark hallway was suddenly lit by a flash. Moore was hit full in the face.

Mr Richard Slaughter Carter, a surgeon who was called to the crime scene later, 'found a man lying in the passage on his back, quite dead'. With that lack of squeamishness characteristic of Victorian newspapers, the press quoted his report.

> A large quantity of blood was around about his head as he lay on the floor. I first saw a wound just above the eyebrow, about half an inch from the root of the nose. I found that the wound reached into the brain, and some brain was oozing out of the wound. On further examination I discovered two jagged wounds on the top of the head, penetrating to the skull bone. There was likewise a wound at the back of the head, exactly opposite.

The post-mortem examination showed that the bullet had entered the orbit of the eye, completely traversed the brain, and fractured the occipital bone at the back of the skull, from where it had rebounded. It had ended up lodged in the centre of the cerebellum. Death had been instantaneous.

Terrified by the flash and bang of gunfire and by the sight of her collapsed master, Charlotte tore open the front door, calling out in alarm to those gathering out on the pavement. Curious as to the noise, three people had already stopped by the house. Barthélemy and the maid stumbled out together, but Charlotte fell against the iron wicket-gate at the front of the steps, preventing Barthélemy making a quick getaway on to the street. He ran back into the house, slamming and bolting the door behind him. Charlotte was now locked outside.

Barthélemy rushed down the hallway, past the parlour, to the back door. He wrestled down the bar that went across it, and quickly hustled his female companion outside. In the back yard, she collapsed, distraught over Moore's death, and begged Barthélemy to shoot her too. 'I had not the heart to do so,' said Barthélemy later. 'I was anxious she should escape.' From the deep pocket of his overcoat he removed his purse, containing a gold sovereign and some silver coins, and pressed it into her hand. The woman had brought with her another cloak and hat. She donned these as a disguise and Barthélemy hoisted her over the wall into the neighbouring back yard, from whence she disappeared into the night. After she was clear, Barthélemy took a different route to draw off any pursuers. With a gun clamped in one hand he climbed up the high back gate and fell into the New Road – the artery renamed the Euston Road a few years later.

At the front of the house, meanwhile, someone shouted, 'Break open the door!' Charlotte, who had been unable to speak for a few moments, now found her voice and loudly urged the crowd: 'Go round into the New Road, or he will get out that way.' Hearing the noise, Charles Collard, a greengrocer aged thirty-six, emerged from his premises at 74 Warren Street. Collard had formerly been a soldier in the service of the East India Company, and then for two or three years a constable in the E (Holborn) Division of the police. He was still well known to the force, having a contract to supply a number of police stations with vegetables. With a passing house painter, William Moseley, bringing up the rear, Collard dashed to the back of the Moore residence. The two men came round the other side to see Barthélemy falling from railings some six foot high. Collard was also joined by William Beetleson, a waterman at the hackney coach stand on the New Road. Beetleson had been alerted, he recalled, by 'a person [coming] towards me crying "Police!" and "Murder!"' He saw Barthélemy 'falling from the palings' as 'his hat fell off and bounded on the pavement'.

Collard and Beetleson closed in on Barthélemy. Moseley saw confused grappling in the night and heard Collard cry out, 'For God's sake lay hold of him, as he has something in his hand. Take care, or he will shoot someone!' The two men pinioned Barthélemy in a stooping position, Moseley holding his right arm and Collard his left. Suddenly Barthélemy's pistol went off. Collard fell to the ground, crying out, 'Good God, I am shot!' Beetleson wrested the remains of the shattered mallet from Barthélemy's hands, but Barthélemy used his pistol to land a blow on his head. As Beetleson reeled back, Barthélemy broke free, stumbled over a low wall and was set upon by another man attracted by the furore. William Henry Madden, a woodcarver living on Tottenham Court Road, was returning home from work and passing by the back premises of Moore's soda-water manufactory. He spied the scuffle and chased Barthélemy for nearly a hundred yards. Barthélemy stopped running, spun round, switched his pistol from one hand to the other, and struck Madden twice on the head, knocking his hat off, cutting through his left eyelid, slicing a piece off his ear, and tearing through to the bone behind his left ear.

Having gouged Madden in the face, Barthélemy dropped his pistol behind him. Once again he broke free and ran a further twenty or thirty yards. But his furious flight was nearing its end. He was finally brought down by George Cope, an organ-pipe maker, who had seen a man running with a group of persons following him, and heard a cry of 'Stop him!' Cope was a strong and powerful young man, and as he intercepted Barthélemy he threw him violently against a garden wall. Then seizing Barthélemy, he wrestled him to the ground. Men gathered around him and pummelled his hunched body. Exhausted, Barthélemy put up no more resistance. (Madden was afterwards hailed as a hero, and awarded £10. The unfortunate George Cope received nothing, and over the next three years peppered the press with letters of complaint.) Police Constable John Mundy – carrying his truncheon, lamp and rattle – presently reached the scene.

Moseley said to him, 'Take him in charge, he has shot a man further down.' Barthélemy was now a prisoner.

Barthélemy refused to answer any questions from his captors. As he was being marched to the police station on Tottenham Court Road, he and his escort were followed by a crowd hooting the captive. Fearful that he was about to be lynched, Barthélemy asked for a transport to bring him in safety. Mundy suspected a ruse: 'He asked me if I would let him have a cab; I said "No, there is no cab allowed for you".' Once arrived at the station, Barthélemy was searched.

Collard, who had been shot in the struggle outside Moore's house, was brought into University College Hospital at about 8.45 p.m. He was suffering great pain. The house surgeon, Mr Henry Kiallmark, found a circular wound on the wall of the belly at the left side of the navel. Collard complained of numbness in the left thigh and leg. Kiallmark concluded that his spine had been damaged. The bullet was lodged just beneath the skin, and he cut it out. He called for Mr John Erichsen, the hospital surgeon, who on his arrival expressed no hopes for Collard's recovery. 'My good man,' he told Collard, 'you are in a dying state.'

Barthélemy was brought into Collard's presence. The stricken man, though too weak to point at him, immediately identified Barthélemy as his killer: 'That is the man who shot me,' he whispered through his pain. Barthélemy made no reply and showed no emotion. The wounded Collard turned away, saying, 'Oh, you cruel man!'

Collard was able to make a sworn statement to Inspector Checkley of the E Division:

I, Charles Collard, of number 74, Warren Street, say that at a quarter to nine PM this day I heard a cry of 'Murder' in 73, Warren Street. I went there, and found a man attempting to escape. I prevented him. He then re-entered the house, and fastened the door in Warren Street, and got out at the back. I ran into the New Road, and caught hold of him as he was getting over the garden wall, when he pulled a pistol from his pocket and shot me through, and I fell. The man ran away. Another man was standing near me at the time, who tried to hold him; but he got away. The man I now see is the man who shot me. I am certain of that. I have made this statement believing that I am dying. – (Signed) CHARLES COLLARD, his mark. Witness, RICHARD CHECKLEY, HENRY KIALLMARK.

All the time Barthélemy looked on expressionless, unmoving and seemingly unmoved.

The immediate cause of Collard's death, which came after several hours of extreme agony, was inflammation. He left behind him two children and a pregnant widow. Barthélemy, when told of Collard's death, 'wept bitterly, wrung his hands, and stated that, bearing no ill will to Collard, he never intended to do him any injury'.

What was in the letter that so enraged George Moore and led to his death? Who was the mysterious woman? What *had* Emmanuel Barthélemy intended to do that night? Who was this 'cruel man' – this murderer of Warren Street – and why was he there? Why did he plan to assassinate Napoleon III? To find out we must travel to France, and to the revolutionary Paris that shaped him.

2

THE CRIME OF BEING
A KING

Emmanuel Barthélemy was born in 1823, eight years after the restoration of the French monarchy, and thirty-four years after the outbreak of the French Revolution. It is clear that his family was of no great elevated position, but we know little else of his forebears. His father, François, was described as a 'very honest, obliging and worthy man'. From what Barthélemy told people later in life, he was the son of poor parents and was himself 'a simple worker from hot-blooded Marseille'. In 1839 his birthplace was given as Sceaux, a town just south of Paris. It may be that his family had moved from Marseille in the far south. At any rate, Barthélemy's people hailed from that part of France where religious observance was low and anti-clericalism strong.

A leading militant in Marseille during the turmoil of the French Revolution had been one Louis Barthélemy. Louis, who worked as a foreman in a soap manufactory, was poorly educated but 'with a strong mind and fiery speech'. For him, popular violence was a regrettable necessity, not to be celebrated, but not to be ducked either. 'The people will rise up in a terrible way,' he had said when criticised for his incendiary attacks on the wealthy. 'What saddens me is that many innocent people will die.' There was no doubt that Louis was prepared to countenance such innocent deaths as a price well worth paying for the greater good. When the moderate local government of Marseille rose in rebellion against the radical dictatorship of Paris, Louis Barthélemy was arrested, accused of inciting violence and sentenced to death by guillotine. It was recorded that he strode out firmly on to the scaffold, acknowledged the crowd and addressed his guards: 'I die for our country.' Then he kissed the revolutionary tricolour flag and gave himself up to the executioner. He 'died an atheist ... with unmatched fearlessness'. Marseille was reconquered by the central government shortly afterwards, just too late to save his life. Was Louis Barthélemy an ancestor of Emmanuel? We cannot know for sure, but it seems likely. At any rate, as a local legend it is easy to see how his ideals and honour could have influenced a young Emmanuel Barthélemy.

Barthélemy's family migrated from Sceaux to Paris in about 1833, when Barthélemy was aged nine. The great writer Honoré de Balzac remarked that the rustic scenery of Sceaux was much admired, perhaps beyond its merits, by city folk buried in their 'stony abyss'. It could certainly be a shock for anyone migrating to swollen Paris from the countryside. 'How ugly Paris seems after one has been away for a year,' exclaimed an aristocrat, the Vicomte de Launay, in the 1830s. 'How one stifles in those dark, damp, narrow corridors which you are pleased to call the streets of Paris! One would think this is an underground city, so sluggish is the air ... And the thousands of people live, bustle, throng in the liquid darkness, like reptiles in a marsh.' Paris, with a population approaching 900,000, was the second largest city in Europe, though much smaller than London where over 2.5 million people would be living by the early 1850s. No doubt the cram and busy activity of Parisians was head-spinning for new arrivals. But the capital was also a place of excitement and adventure for the newcomer, as Frances Trollope, the English travel writer, found:

> It is true, that there is something most exceedingly exhilarating to the spirits in the mere external novelty and cheerfulness of the objects which surround a stranger on first entering Paris. That indescribable air of gaiety which makes every sunshiny day look like a fête; the light hilarity of spirit that seems to pervade all ranks; the cheerful tone of voice, the sparkling glances of the numberless bright eyes; the gardens, flowers, the statues of Paris, – all together produce an effect very like enchantment.

The wide rivers, magnificent bridges, extensive *trottoirs* (pavements) and noble *hôtels* were interlaced, however, with the world of the 'dangerous class', those living in crowded tenements barely eking out a life in the shadow of crime. As the city had yet to become residentially segregated, the 'dangerous classes' were 'scattered more or less in all quarters of Paris', wrote H. A. Frégier, a political economist and civil servant. 'The richest and most thickly populated are not exempt, since it is rare for even the handsomest quarters not to contain some narrow alley, lined with old houses, ill-looking and badly kept. It is in such places that the doss houses are set up, and the prostitutes, pimps, thieves and rogues congregate. Around them collect the gamblers, vagabonds, and all the rest who have no means of livelihood.' In 1840 there were at least 85,000 residents of Paris subsisting on meagre relief.

Life was a struggle too for the working poor. A carpenter's family of four, for example, could earn 1,200 francs if they were able to find work for 300 days in the year. It required 1,050 to 1,300 francs for a family to live decently. Barthélemy's father was one of these working poor, and ultimately he took up employment as a concierge at a business establishment. The concierge, a Paris institution, was a door porter, security guard, receptionist and general dogsbody, rolled into one, usually housed in a small apartment on the ground floor, called *la loge*. It was a somewhat anomalous position, being of the working class but in close contact with the wealthy. 'Paris porters have a knowing eye,' wrote Balzac. 'They do not stop men who wear a decoration, are dressed in a blue uniform, and have a heavy gait. In short, they recognise the rich.' Concierges were generally distrusted by radicals as being servile to the elites, and they were a fruitful source of information for the police. It was just as possible, however, for those in close contact with the privileged to grow contemptuous.

Barthélemy was sent for some time to an '*École d'enseignement mutuel*' – a school of mutual instruction. This was one of about 2,000 non-denominational schools for the children of the poor. Large numbers of pupils – often more than 800 – would be accommodated in one building run by a single schoolmaster. Pupils would be seated in groups of ten to a dozen at large desks. As the name suggests, education was mostly conveyed by older pupils, who acted as monitors. This was education on the cheap, but it also may well have fostered Barthélemy's confidence that roughly egalitarian enterprises could run quite as well as hierarchical institutions while allowing more freedom and autonomy for the ordinary people who comprised them. They were, in many respects, models of the 'social workshops' dreamt of by French socialists in the 1830s. They were certainly identified with socialist ideas, and specifically with those of the famous Welsh socialist, Robert Owen.

Owen, who never suffered from self-doubt, tirelessly promoted his ideas which caused a stir in England and made their way over to France. He was convinced that human nature was entirely malleable. If industrial workers were treated brutally, as nothing more than 'work hands', it was no surprise if they turned out to be a degenerate, demoralised and violent class.

Instead Owen wished for pleasant, clean, well-paying enterprises that could mould upstanding and respectable workers. He had a paternalistic theory of human psychology, believing that close direction could radically reshape human nature: 'Man may be trained to acquire any sentiments and habits, or any character.' For young men like Barthélemy, who saw so many of their class sink into despair and degradation, it was a resonant message.

The desire for learning was strong in France's urban working class. Yet Barthélemy's own formal education was brief. He was taken out of school by his father so he could contribute to family income from home. Here his father taught him to make what were known as '*Chaussons de lisière*': slippers fashioned from strips of cloth torn from old bed sheets and hangings. This was the most unskilled of labour, considered to be a fit occupation only for gaol inmates or residents of institutions for the blind. Emmanuel was a quick learner, however, and his dexterity was evident. He was already forming these simple objects in accordance with a certain idea of beauty. He had a craft sensibility, in which skill, dexterity and imagination impressed themselves on raw materials. Seeing potential, his father found for his son a position as an apprentice with artisan carpenters. Here he was to learn a trade. But Barthélemy was showing his ornery streak. Without seeking permission, he walked out of the job and took employment in a '*sertisseur*' workshop, at 34 rue de la Marche, 'because I found it the more convenient position, less painful and more lucrative'.

This street was in the heart of the Marais, the old and gloomy area of ancient Paris on the Right Bank of the Seine. Historically, this district had been the aristocratic centre of the city and highly skilled craftworkers had gathered there to produce and sell luxury goods. As the aristocrats moved away, to follow the court or flee revolution, many of their private mansions were taken over by the master craftsmen who divided and subdivided them into small workshops. They employed often migrant labour from the provinces and abroad. The jewellers' craft was increasingly 'proletarianised': masters would subcontract jobs to multiple competing workshops, and artisans were given specific and limited tasks. The goldsmith and the chiseller could expect to earn about 4 francs a day, the jeweller and the engraver 5 francs, and the gem-setter (*sertisseur*) 6 francs. The Marais became crowded, with workshops on every floor from basement to attic. It was bordered on the west by Les Halles, the infamously raucous food market, and on the east by the Faubourgs Temple and Saint-Antoine, where hand-loom workers wove textiles and craftsmen carved and assembled furniture.

In these decades before the 1848 revolution, Paris became 'the world's greatest manufacturing city'. But though there was some heavy industry beginning in the 1840s, most manufactories remained small-scale, especially those along the River Bièvre, the industrial artery of Paris since the Middle Ages. By 1847, there were some 330,000 industrial workers of Paris mostly scattered in small workshops: some 89 per cent of firms employed fewer than ten workers. Barthélemy, therefore, was a typical French industrial worker, carrying out skilled labour for wages in an artisanal manufactory. Yet his extraordinary aptitude soon caught the eye. From early youth he showed ample evidence of being 'endowed with a very remarkable mechanical genius'.

Barthélemy would have been trained up by his fellow workers. In France, the characteristic workshop was a tall room with windows high on the walls, or on the roof, to let in light. Those inside could see little outside other than a patch of sky and the tops of poplar trees. Men, women and children worked at tables and tools. It was human-sized, and massive machinery was uncommon. Capitalists provided little actual direction to the workshop. A carpenter called Agricol Perdiguier, who wrote a memoir of his working life in the 1820s and 1830s, recalled how his employer 'never taught me to lay out or assemble; I never had any theoretical or practical training. Nevertheless I did all the work that was given to me without any trouble.' Employees thought of the workplace as belonging to them, not to the boss. Paris tailors, when they went on strike in 1833, demanded the right to smoke, to read newspapers, and for masters to take their hats off when entering the workshop. As the boss was probably a subcontractor, the capitalist financer of the enterprise would have seemed even more distant from the workshop.

A particular mode of capitalism produces its own mode of socialism. Most workplaces and communities were contained and the workers knew each other well. Association, cooperation and 'harmony' were not romantically abstract concepts, but 'derived directly from the actual experiences of men in small-scale groups'. A rather moderate working-class journal of the early 1840s, *L'Atelier*, gave advice on how workers might advance:

> You may form small societies of six, eight, or ten members as the case may be. Each society shall choose its most trustworthy member to act as an intermediary with the contractor. He will take the place of the old subcontractor or jobber, but then it will be to the advantage of all his associates, since the profits will be divided among them according to the amount of work done by each.

Not every socialist would agree with this in detail, but it encapsulates the socialism of the small workshop characteristic of the period. The ideal was not state ownership of the means of production, nor even state welfarism, but the cooperative workshop and the division of people into self-governing communes. Indeed, the very concept of socialist *republicanism* implied a free workshop. 'The socialism which would make the State ... the director and dictator of labour ... such socialism would not be republican,' English radicals wrote in the same period. That Barthélemy, himself employed in one of many small metalworking shops, was attracted to such ideals should not surprise us. It would be wrong to say that Barthélemy was typical of his working-class background, but he was certainly characteristic of it.

This was not an age of large factories, which would only really characterise capitalist society from the time of the First World War to the 1960s. In many respects the emergent capitalist society of the 1830s and 1840s was rather closer to our own: a 'gig economy' based upon plutocratic providers of capital contracting out business to quite small enterprises and taking as little responsibility as possible for the workers at the point of production.

Barthélemy's work as a *sertisseur* suited his personality – intelligent, precise but single-minded. It also gave him an opportunity to focus on his burgeoning politics. Having got hold of an old medal struck to commemorate the Fête de la Fédération of 14 July 1790, celebrating the first anniversary of the storming of the Bastille, he decorated it with an emerald-coloured stone. Working on his medal, carefully fixing green translucence in finely wrought filigree, it may well be that Barthélemy's young mind escaped the rigid class order of 1830s France, returning to the myths and glory of the revolutionary era a generation before his own. Only in France could men of Barthélemy's humble station feel that they, once, had stormed heaven, burst the bounds of servitude immemorial, and made world history.

In 1789, an 'estates general', a kind of parliament representing aristocracy, clergy and everyone else – the 'third estate' – had been called to Paris by King Louis XVI in an attempt to generate support for reforms to save the state from bankruptcy. The 'third estate' insisted that they represented the true will of the nation. Defying the King, they established a National Assembly and demanded government responsible to the representatives of the people. The armed forces of the Crown began manoeuvring in order to strike back. It was feared that the Bastille, a huge prison and arms depot in Paris, would form the pivot of a military counter-revolution. This was a building of eight towers linked by walls eighty feet high. Inside was a meagre garrison of only 114 soldiers. An enormous crowd surged outside, loudly demanding to be allowed in. A small party clambered over the rampart wall, dashed into the guardhouse and cut the ropes holding the drawbridge. It crashed down, crushing one of the besiegers. Masses of people, waving muskets and pikes, swarmed into the outer courtyard. The defenders began firing from the towers, and a deafening battle was soon raging. Only after the crowd dragged cannon into the courtyard did the garrison surrender. About a hundred had died in the battle.

The storming of the Bastille in July 1789, predominantly by artisans – particularly furniture workers from the Faubourg Saint-Antoine – pinched out the immediate threat of a *coup d'état*, but triggered five years of acute turmoil. These artisan 'sans-culottes' became revolutionary legends in their own time, and for the generations that followed.

The National Assembly was dominated by bourgeois lawyers and officials, but they relied upon the sans-culottes – small masters, tradesmen, apprentices and wage-earning journeymen in workshops – as a militant and popular force to keep the threat of counter-revolution in check. Gwyn A. Williams, a historian of popular passions, remarked that 'a central feature of sans-culottes psychology was its permanent anticipation of betrayal and treachery'. This is true, but this mentality also gave them great energy.

Again and again, the labouring people of Paris rose up in insurrection to prevent counter-revolutionary backsliding. The workmen of the faubourgs – 'covered with rags', carrying guns, pikes, axes and knives, and followed by female 'furies' – would march behind banners emblazoned with the words, 'Tremble tyrants! The sans-culottes are here!' They would burst into the Tuileries Palace, where the nation's elected representatives sat in deliberation, and 'show them these pikes which overthrew the Bastille', as one of their leaders put it. This was mass intimidation with the aim of dictating to the government: a kind of 'popular sovereignty' by riot. These '*journées*' – or days of insurrection – were inscribed on the memory of all subsequent nineteenth-century revolutionaries.

Prussian and Austrian armies invaded France with the aim of overthrowing the revolution: they declared their opponents not to be soldiers but rebels against rightful authority liable to summary execution. By August 1792, they were rapidly closing in on the capital. The 'sections' of the city dominated by the sans-culottes seized control of Paris, and raised the red flag. Until this point, the crimson flag had been flown by authority to show that martial law had been declared. The sans-culottes' red flag declared a people's martial law, a seizure of legal right into revolutionary hands. So began the long history of the red flag as the standard of revolution. The royal family, conspiring with the counter-revolutionary armies of invasion, were taken into custody and the Republic was declared.

A murderous suspicion grew in the popular masses. What if foreign armies reached Paris and opened the prisons to unleash the recently incarcerated royalists and brutalised criminals upon the sans-culottes? In September 1792, fanatical crowds descended upon the Parisian gaols, dragging out royalist and Catholic clerical prisoners, and slaughtering them. About 3,000 were killed, many with brutal indignity before jeering onlookers. It was a horrible outrage, but the revolutionary leaders held aloof, refusing to intervene. Marie-Victoire Monnard, then a thirteen-year-old apprentice, in retrospect captured the complex psychology of the mob. 'Like everybody else, I was shaking with terror lest royalists be permitted to escape from prisons and arrive to murder me for having no holy pictures to show them .... While shuddering with horror, we regarded the deeds as more or less justified.'

A new revolutionary parliament, or Convention, debated what to do with the deposed king. The youngest member of the Convention was Antoine Saint-Just, a leader of the radical 'Jacobin' faction committed to waging war to the knife against any threat to the revolution. In his youth, his determination, and his cold-bloodedness, Barthélemy would later often be compared to Saint-Just. Both men prided themselves on their spartan simplicity and terse realism. Having read deeply of the ancient Greek Tacitus and the eighteenth-century French philosopher Montesquieu – both exemplars of clarity in prose – Saint-Just adopted their epigrammatic, economical style. Grandiloquence and verbosity he condemned as aristocratic inauthenticity and obfuscation. 'Republican children must be strictly trained to speak laconically, which suits the nature of the French language,' he wrote. Barthélemy too would later be noted for his precise and clear language. Saint-Just dressed with neat precision, eschewed flamboyance, and bore himself with steadfast control. He carried his head like a 'sacred sacrament'. Barthélemy was likewise always neatly dressed and strove to maintain an implacable self-possession.

For Saint-Just, the aim of a virtuous Republic warranted violence and terror against its enemies. In the Convention debates, on 13 November 1791, he argued for immediate execution rather than a trial for Louis XVI. The King's very existence, he argued with a remorseless logic, was itself a threat to liberty. A monarch could not be allowed to benefit from the normal processes of law.

And I say that the King must be judged as an enemy ... we have less to judge him than to combat him .... A king should be tried not for the crimes of his administration, but for the crime of having been king ... an eternal crime against which every man has the right to rise up and arm himself.

With clinical certitude Saint-Just argued that lethal force against kings was legitimate at all times and in all circumstances. Barthélemy would come to think in very similar terms. But in 1792 most revolutionaries baulked at Saint-Just's merciless reasoning. They wanted to justify themselves to history, and for the former king to be made an example of. This was all the more tempting when they found a mass of correspondence incriminating him hidden in an iron box. Louis Capet was placed on trial for treason and, his guilt hardly in doubt, he was guillotined on 21 January 1793.

Barthélemy, like Saint-Just, saw the greatest threat to revolution not in its outright enemies, but in those faint hearts and traitors who would blanch at necessary deeds. Saint-Just found a kindred soul in Maximilian Robespierre, the elegant, pallid and deeply serious 'sea-green incorruptible' of the revolution. Saint-Just, Robespierre and their zealous followers organised in the Jacobin Club were convinced that the leadership of the revolutionary government, provided by the Girondin Club, lacked that iron in the soul required to defeat counter-revolution both internal and external. In this they had the support of the radical sans-culottes.

On 31 May 1793 and again on 2 June, the sans-culottes of Paris rose in insurrection to secure the expulsion from the Convention of thirty-one Girondin leaders. The commune of Paris was now in 'permanent session', seeking to apply continuous revolutionary pressure on the national government. A new constitution was drawn up, the Constitution of 1793, which was avowedly democratic, being based upon universal male suffrage. Saint-Just was its principal architect. A revolutionary calendar replaced the old.

In Paris the emergency Committee of Public Safety was taken over by Robespierre and Saint-Just. It was now the government of France. In October Saint-Just decreed that the government would be 'revolutionary until the peace', meaning that the 1793 constitution was suspended and that emergency dictatorial government would be in place until the end of the war. Only ruthless dictatorship, he argued, could save the revolution. The Girondin leaders were guillotined the same month.

Determined to secure centralised control, the Jacobins turned on the sans-culottes leaders. They would tolerate no more insurrections. On the other hand, they introduced price controls to try and save the labouring masses of the cities from destitution. Executions became frequent, and extended to the radical representatives of the Paris commune: the followers of the foul-mouthed tribune of the sans-culottes, Jacques Hébert and the expressively named *Enragés*. In 1794, the sans-culottes-controlled commune of Paris was suppressed and their most direct political representatives guillotined as dangerous extremists. Revolutionary discipline, exercised through the most extreme means, had triumphed over popular energy. Then the regime turned on the Jacobin 'Indulgents' who wished to moderate the Terror. They were led by Georges Danton, a hulking orator, darling of the people, endearingly ugly, and endlessly wily. To relax tension now, Robespierre and Saint-Just feared, would be to risk a catastrophic collapse just on the eve of victory. As Saint-Just put it, 'Those who only half make revolutions dig their own grave.' The 'Indulgents' were executed.

In the spiralling mind of Robespierre, there seemed no way back from Terror. But with the destruction of organised political opposition, Terror could now only take the form of a universal threat of destruction hanging over all potential enemies. The line between 'innocence' and 'guilt' blurred and disappeared.

Heads fell by the hundred. But as victory over the invaders at the frontiers of the nation was finally secured, the Convention turned against Robespierre and his colleagues. On 27 July 1794 (9 Thermidor by the new revolutionary calendar), Saint-Just rose in the Convention to make a speech. He was immediately and violently interrupted by restive deputies who feared that they must be next for the chop. Robespierre and his comrades were shouted down. Against the hubbub and din, only Saint-Just remained calm and imperturbable. The Jacobin Terrorists were taken prisoner. As Saint-Just was being removed from the Conciergerie prison to the guillotine, he pointed to a copy of the 1793 constitution hanging on display and said with proud dignity: '*C'est pourtant moi qui ai fait cela*' (Yet it was I who made that). With Robespierre and the others, he was guillotined before a jeering crowd. The Jacobins went down blood-grimed and reeking of arbitrary violence. Yet they had extended a hand to the unregarded masses, and saved France from counter-revolution both domestic and foreign.

After the collapse of the Jacobin dictatorship, a new constitution was drawn up, abolishing universal male suffrage, and vesting executive authority in a Directory of Twelve. Boissey d'Anglas, a lawyer and politician, was tasked with drafting a new constitution. He made clear the principle underlying it: 'We must be governed by the best, the best are the most educated, and you will only find such men among those who own property.' The democratic ideals of the revolution were definitively abandoned. But for revolutionaries of Barthélemy's generation the example of the French Revolution – when the sans-culottes dicated to their masters – could never be forgotten or effaced.

3

THE REPUBLIC IN THE WORKSHOP

As Barthélemy contemplated his medal decorated with a green gemstone, the larger-than-life figures of the Great Revolution lived in his mind. But of course he was just as influenced by the city in which he lived. In the seventeenth and eighteenth centuries, wide straight streets had been opened inside and beyond the city walls. Nevertheless, much of the mediaeval city still survived.

Great sights still familiar to us – Notre-Dame Cathedral, the Panthéon, the Louvre – made 1830s Paris one of the most grandiloquently magnificent cities in the world. Long elegant arcades had been built on the rue de Rivoli, remodelling royal and religious establishments seized in the revolution. The Arc de Triomphe, a towering monument to French militarism at the end of the Avenue des Champs-Élysées, was finally completed in 1836, when Barthélemy was aged thirteen. The pleasant Jardin du Luxembourg – here sat the magnificent Chamber of Peers, surrounded by artfully cultivated roses – provided relief from the pungent smell of the streets. The Place de la Révolution, scene of so many guillotine executions during the Jacobin dictatorship, had hopefully reverted to its original (and current) name of Place de la Concorde. In the 1850s and 1860s, Napoleon

III and his Prefect for the Seine district, Baron Haussmann, would drastically remodel the city by radiating boulevards out from important squares and public buildings. These criss-crossed the city, binding it together, expanding its reach and absorbing villages and towns into the suburbs. As any visitor knows, this beautified the city, but they were built with the intention of demolishing twisting streets ready-made for effective barricade fighting. They facilitated the movement and concentration of troops against insurrection. In the 1830s, however, much of the ancient city centre of higgledy-piggledy housing and narrow streets remained. The 'People's Paris' covered the Île de la Cité, Montmartre and the rue Saint-Denis, pushing right up against the Louvre, the Tuileries Palace and Notre-Dame. It heaved with the working poor and destitute, surrounding and intimidating the gardens and palaces where the notables nervously enjoyed the precarious delights of wealth and power.

The city had not yet become divided between a prettified centre of conspicuous consumption surrounded by and excluding a proletarian 'red belt' of suburbs. Rich and poor mingled in the historic heart of the city. The stately boulevards were lined by shabby stalls where old women sold metal oddments, pastries and children's toys. There was the incessant cry of 'Messieurs!' from men attracting custom to their games of chance or displays of gymnastics and mime. For the theorist Walter Benjamin, writing in the 1930s, the middle of the nineteenth century was the true age of the bohemian *flâneur*. Even the famous 'arcades' of Paris – glass-covered walkways between shops that had proliferated since the early years of the century – facilitated curious wanderers by protecting them from the rain. They could easily witness all social life by exploring the city-centre streets. In a few decades, Benjamin remarked sadly, there would be only the grand department store left as 'the last promenade for the *flâneur*'.

It's certainly true that the centre of Paris in Barthélemy's time was a complete and curiously intimate social world in itself. Unlike the North of England – heartland of the emerging factory system, where employers confronted sullen workers across a chasm – the classes mixed in the centre of Paris. Pauperised 'dangerous classes', wage-earning journeymen, apprentices, masters, students, professionals, capitalists and even aristocrats – all passed each other in the streets. This did not necessarily make for amity between the classes, but it does seem to have broadened the cultural horizons of workers. 'Everything was new and interesting to me in Paris in the manners and habits of the masses,' wrote Robert Lowery, a Chartist tailor from Tyneside, of his visit to France in 1839:

> I was at once struck with the obvious superiority of the working people to ours in courtesy and politeness. I saw very few people intoxicated during the four weeks I was there. What pleased me most was that the politeness was not mere deference to superiors, but the dignified courtesy of self-respect; where the working man felt himself a gentleman, acted as such, and was treated as such in return.

Benjamin Haydon, an English painter, was equally impressed: 'Nothing struck us English more in the manners of the French than the sweetness of address in all classes.'

In the Paris of the 1830s, Barthélemy had employment in his workshop and digs at a lodging, but he was out and about in this most lively of cities, picking up political ideas from the famous café culture. Countless small wine shops and *cabarets*, 'more cheerful, more fraternal than the family hovel', allowed workers to meet, read newspapers, play cards or bowls, sing, and chat about life. Employers huffed and puffed, but they could not keep their employees away from the heady swirl of subversion that roiled the city. In particular taverns, men and occasionally women would gather in back rooms to discuss politics and plot revolution: 'There was smoking and drinking, gambling and laughter,' as Victor Hugo wrote. 'There was talking in very loud voices about all sorts of things, and in very low voices about other things.' Socialists, republicans, Bonapartists, even dissident Royalists would meet up, argue and grumble at the upstart King, installed after a revolution in 1830, which seemed so '*bourgeois*'. There were also regular republican demonstrations of students and artisans at the Porte St Martin. Young urchins, known as *gamins*, would dart through the crowd, carrying banners, shouting slogans and taunting the police at these '*petits spectacles*'. Perhaps this is where Barthélemy first came into contact with the revolution. Certainly a change was seen to overcome him at the *sertisseur* workshop where he worked. According to his employer, Monsieur Loigelot, Barthélemy was an uppity employee, 'concerned about political things and ... talking freely'.

Loigelot thought too that Barthélemy was rather contemptuous of his fellow workers. He misunderstood him. Certainly he made a particular effort to dress more elegantly and neatly than his workshop companions. But this was quite characteristic of the self-respect felt by those youths who had adopted republican ideals. For Barthélemy was now in revolt against the easygoing, rather decadent monarchy that ruled France. He had joined the 'Society of Seasons', a revolutionary organisation with about 1,000 members in Paris. Barthélemy was brought before a conclave of this secret society – probably in the back room of a tavern, in the presence of some thirty or so members – blindfolded, and asked a series of questions for which he had the expected replies:

- What do you think of royalty and kings?
- *That they are as dangerous to mankind as the tiger is to other animals.*

- Who are now the aristocrats?
- *The aristocracy of birth was abolished in July 1830. It has been replaced by the aristocracy of money, which is as voracious as the former.*

- Will the people be able to govern themselves immediately after the revolution?
- *The social state being gangrenous, heroic remedies are needed to return to a state of health. For a period of time the people will need a revolutionary power.*

- In short, what then are your principles?
- *We must exterminate the monarchy and all aristocrats, and replace them with a Republic, that is, a government of equality. But, in order to bring about this government, we must employ a revolutionary power to assure that the people exercise their rights.*

Having gone through this catechism, Barthélemy swore an oath of eternal hatred to all kings. A dagger was placed in his hand as a symbol that should he ever break his oath he would be punished with a traitor's death. It would have been traditional in such circles for the leader, probably Auguste Blanqui himself, to plant on Barthélemy the kiss of brotherhood.

At the young age of fifteen or sixteen, Barthélemy was already a dedicated revolutionary. He had grown his hair to shoulder length, in the 'republican mode'. When arrested in 1839, Barthélemy refused to divulge any information about the political underground, but he made abundantly clear that 'I have served the cause, and I will always serve.'

The 'Society of Seasons' drew on Jacobin sensibilities, but was determined to learn the lessons of the 1790s. Organisation, discipline and an iron will was all. The next revolution would liberate the workers, but only after a revolutionary elite had reshaped society.

The Society of Seasons, under the firm leadership of Blanqui and Armand Barbès, was a relatively new organisation, formed only in 1838 – Barthélemy was perhaps a charter member – but it built upon a tradition extending back to the 1790s.

The Jacobin dictatorship of Robespierre and Saint-Just, as we have seen, had been overthrown in the 'Thermidorian Reaction' of 1794. A new Directory of twelve men, representing revolutionaries who wanted to finally end the process of radicalisation, had taken over. They abandoned the Terror, but the new government also became notorious for its hostility to popular mobilisation – suppressing not only insurrection but even demonstrations – and its rampant corruption. As so often after episodes of revolutionary puritanism, the surviving elites revelled in their displays of wealth. The Directory became a symbol of the nouveau riche betraying revolutionary ideals and the poor.

In retrospect, the 'heroic' period of Jacobin dictatorship came to be seen by radicals like Étienne Cabet, the socialist propagandist most popular with ordinary French workers in the 1830s and 1840s, as an alliance between the radical bourgeoisie and the working-class sans-culottes. With the sans-culottes defeated and excluded, the French Revolution was defined as irredeemably bourgeois. The next revolution, it was determined, would be for the workers.

Socialists of Barthélemy's generation, therefore, looked back on a long and dismal retreat from revolution since the heroic days of the sans-culottes Paris Commune. Exhausted by its own cynicism, the Directory fell in 1799. But this only opened the door to the military men. In 1804, General Napoleon made himself Emperor of the French. The seemingly permanent revolution of the 1790s was replaced by permanent war for imperial expansion. This in turn came to an end in 1815 when the Bourbon monarchy, in the person of Louis XVIII, returned in the baggage train of the British, Austrian, Prussian and Russian conquerors of Napoleon. In 1825, the pragmatic Louis was succeeded by the nostalgic reactionary, Charles X. Charles believed in the holy charisma of monarchy, but for the French nation such happy faith was no longer possible after the mystique-shattering events of the 1790s. Monarchs now were only men; virile at their best, no doubt, but with advancing years growing dumpy, dull and indifferent, as is the common lot of mankind.

On 19 December 1827, after a gap of nearly two centuries, barricades reappeared in Paris, in the vicinity of the Hôtel de Ville. Barricades had never been a feature of the French Revolution, but now they mushroomed in the working-class districts. They prevented the free movement of government troops and gave insurgents protection from fire. Ensconced behind makeshift fortifications, crowds could not be easily dispersed, and republicans had the opportunity to organise themselves into armed detachments. The idea was that barri-caded streets would link up, secure the insurgent rear and encircle their goal. In Paris, this was always the Hôtel de Ville, capture of which generally meant command of the city. Barricades were just as much symbolic as practical, however. It meant the ordinary folk of the 'People's Paris' asserting ownership of their streets – though in fact it was always a minority of rebels who first took the initiative in building a barricade – and shouting defiance at authority. It was, for so long as the barricades survived, a declaration of independence from the state. The 1827 rebellion failed to stir the masses – barricade fighting was hopeless unless it spread like wildfire – and was easily put down, but it was the first blooding of a man who would have enormous influence on Barthélemy: Auguste Blanqui.

Blanqui, a man of respectable birth and good education, was a dedicated revolutionary from his youth. Thin, pallid, wiry, Blanqui was an ascetic, spurning material comforts, a lifelong vegetarian and a teetotaller. He listened more than he spoke, but when he did speak it was in terse, cutting phrases. He was determined to make revolution happen not through flamboyance and instinct, but by organisation and discipline. He was Robespierre to Barthélemy's Saint-Just, and Barthélemy was devoted to him.

Blanqui first rose to a revolutionary command in 1830, when Barthélemy was still a young boy. He actively organised street fighting in the 'Three Glorious Days' of July that year, when the republicans took control of the east of Paris. Liberal royalists, who favoured a constitutional monarchy on the British model rather than a republic, were quick to seize the Hôtel de Ville and present to the nation Louis Philippe, heir of the Orléans branch of the royal family, as the new liberal monarch. There would be no radicalisation this time. Republicanism was squashed before it could even articulate itself. The bourgeoisie, middle-class professionals and businessmen, were armed and organised into a National Guard to keep order.

Victor Hugo, the romantic writer, switched his loyalty to the new regime, but in retrospect saw the 1830 revolution as a half-made job:

Who stops revolutions in mid-course? The bourgeoisie. Why? Because the bourgeoisie is satisfied self-interest. Yesterday it represented appetite, today it represents repletion, tomorrow it will represent surfeit .... Some people have wanted wrongly to identify the bourgeoisie as a class. The bourgeoisie is simply the contented section of the people. The bourgeois is the man who now has time to sit down .... But the very progress of the human race may be halted because of a desire to sit down too soon. This has often been the failing of the bourgeoisie.

The new royalist regime seemed to represent this middle-class complacency. Louis Philippe, who ascended to the throne, dressed like a bourgeois gentlemen, carried his own umbrella, and sniggered at the piety of Catholic fanatics. His ministers, notably Adolphe Thiers and François Guizot, were practical-minded, money-orientated, and without lofty ideals or much compassion for the poor. Only five Frenchmen in every thousand had the vote. Many workers were disillusioned with the new order and were attracted by a vague Christian socialism. These *démoc-socs* (democratic socialists) 'liked to imagine that if Jesus returned to earth, he would be on their side'.

Unlike Hugo, those on the emerging socialist left increasingly identified the bourgeoisie as a very definite class: those who owned and profited from the very instruments of production workers needed to live. Proletarians, on the other hand, were obliged to work for wages, bound to their capitalist employers, without hope of ever owning their own farm or workshop. For other classes, these new proletarians were demoralised, turbulent and drink-sodden. The great novelist, Honoré de Balzac, brooded on 'the repulsive mask of pauperism in revolt, ready to take its revenge for all its past sufferings on some day of sedition'. Wage-earners themselves, however, were proud, often rejecting the term 'proletarian' as offensive, a condition they were resisting or seeking to escape, and preferring to think of themselves as 'working men' or '*ouvriers*'. While most no longer aspired to the proprietorship of a farm or workshop, they did yearn for a regular wage that would give them an independence based upon their own labour as property. 'We are all,' wrote Jem Devlin, a shoemaker, 'in quest of the golden apple of security.' The next revolution, it was hoped, would destroy their dependence on capitalists, and re-establish the ideal of independent workmen on a new basis of cooperative production.

That these hopes and fears concerned something more than shadows became evident with the *Révoltes des canuts*. In 1831, the struggling silk weavers of Lyon – the canuts – rioted in an attempt to enforce a fixed price for silk goods. This turned into an insurrection during which the workers held the city for ten days. There were republicans among them, but most of the workers and their leaders disavowed any attempt to undermine the existing authorities. In an even larger rebellion in Lyon in April 1834, however, workers and republicans operated in harness. Though massively outnumbered by government forces, the insurgents rooted themselves in their narrow streets and workshops. One of the poorest districts of Lyon, the Guillotière quarter, was almost entirely gutted by artillery fire to root out 150 rebels, many armed only with pitchforks. Finally the canuts' stronghold, La Croix-Rousse, a hill overlooking the city centre, was taken by storm on the third attempt. The novelist Stendhal described the entry of solidiers into conquered Lyon:

> At last the regiment came out into the main business street of the town; all the shops were shut, there was no face at the windows, and a silence of the grave .... The laundry spread out at the windows to dry was horrifying in its poverty, its raggedness and its dirt. The windowpanes were grimy and small, and many windows had, instead of glass, old writing paper soaked in oil. Everywhere there was a living image of poverty that gripped one's heart, though not the hearts of those who hoped to win medals by dealing sabre-cuts in this poor little town.

Stendhal sympathised with the workers, but worried that they were infected by unrealistic ambitions dating from the French revolutionary and Napoleonic eras. Then it had seemed that

any common man might become an army marshal or an entre-
preneur. 'The heads of the workers caught fire ... because of
that unhappy thirst for pleasure and speedy fortune, which is
the madness of all young Frenchmen.'

Others were less dismissive. The slogan of the canuts, emblazoned upon a black flag, was *'vivre en travaillant ou mourir en
combattant'* ('live by working or die fighting'). An 1835 article
introducing a romantic novel on the Lyon silk workers, under
the pen name L. S., identified the slogan as a harbinger of the
future: 'This formula will go down in history: it was written
with the blood of the Lyonnais on the flag of the proletariat ...
it is destined to reappear at each future crisis of our industrial
society.' For the author, it was the characteristic cry of the
wage-earner. It would underpin social conflict until 'the great
final revolt of the proletariat'. This great final revolt was thought
to be by no means distant.

The canut slogan may seem like little more than a cry of
desperation. It was, in fact, far more prophetic than that.
Hitherto, popular rebellions had focused on the desire for
possession of private property, whether it be a plot of land for
the peasant, a workshop and guaranteed market for the artisan,
or simply bread for the starving. But this new slogan seemed
to point to something different. Now the demand was for a
guaranteed job, the right to work. The implications of this were
profound. The Lyon rebels, through a glass dimly, were contem-
plating themselves as the very basis of modern commercial
production, the hands turning the wheels of industry. Society
should be organised so as to guarantee the right to work.

No one stated this more clearly than the great French socialist
and feminist, Flora Tristan. Herself a victim of persecution by a
bitter ex-husband and a misogynistic society, Tristan identified
with the cause of disregarded and oppressed labourers. Tristan
was evidently a woman of great energy and tenacity. On a visit
to London in 1841 she was determined to watch parliamentary

debates. Women were not admitted to Westminster and English male friends refused to lend her men's clothing as a disguise. 'Woe to him who creates a scandal,' declaimed a friendly Tory MP. 'Woe to him who lets himself be scandalised,' retorted Tristan. A Turkish diplomat, however, was pleased to offer a disguise of colourful robes and a turban. Tristan stole into the 'strangers' gallery' from where she saw the great Irish radical Daniel O'Connell – 'a short fat man, thickset and common looking; his face … ugly, all wrinkled red and pimply' – making the English oppressor quake with his superb parliamentary oratory.

Inspired by O'Connell's 'Association' – a mass organisation of the Irish resting on the penny subscription of ordinary people – Tristan returned to France and campaigned furiously for a 'Workers' Union' on the same lines. What defined the workers, in her view, was not their poverty but their 'usefulness' as labourers:

> … for the poor worker who possesses neither land nor houses, nor capital, nor absolutely anything except his arms … the right to live is the right to work, the only one that can give him the possibility of eating, and consequently of living …. What, in fact, does the working-class demand? … Its own property, the only one that it can ever possess, is its arms … the only instruments of labour in its possession …. Now the actual free use of this property would consist, for the working-class, in being able to make use of its arms, whenever and however it wished, and to make this possible it must possess the right to work. And as for the guarantee of this property, it consists of a wise and equitable ORGANIZATION OF LABOUR.

The 'organisation of labour', to protect workers from the vagaries of the capitalist market, was by far the most popular slogan of the socialist left in France in the 1840s.

This 'social question' was no mere talking point for academic seminars: it reshaped the nature of politics in France. There had emerged after the 1830 revolution, according to a survey by the socialist intellectual, Louis Blanc, sharp divisions of opinion between those unreconciled to the new government. This opposition to the increasingly conservative 'bourgeois monarchy' was a 'vast whirlwind of interests, thoughts, and principles'. It comprised bourgeois republicans, state-socialists, Christian Socialists, and finally a 'small number of Republican Democrats, already taking as their motto the abolition of the proletariat'. One of their leaders, Martin Bernard, a worker and typographer, explained that theirs was a struggle against the rising capitalist 'industrial feudalism' and for the cooperative 'republic in the workshop'. They wanted to destroy proletarian wage-slavery and replace it with secure labour organised in self-governing communes. Most workers were rather wary of extravagant schemes for insurrection, but a minority were attracted to the 'republican democrats'. Numbered among them was the young Emmanuel Barthélemy.

Blanqui was the most striking representative of these neo-Jacobin 'republican democrats'. Blanqui believed that the revolt of the poorest of society came from more than crude economic or social interests. For him, the masses were motivated not by 'low monetary interests but the nobler passions of the soul, the aspirations of elevated morality'. This noble simplicity, however, meant that workers were easily misled:

> The poor man does not know the source of his ills. Igno-rance, the daughter of subjection, makes him into the docile instrument of the privileged. Crushed by toil, a stranger to the intellectual life, what can he know about these social phenomena in which he plays the beast of burden?

He believed that it was the duty of dedicated revolutionaries –
like him – to give leadership to this willing and moral but fickle
mass. Blanqui was, with Armand Barbès, leader and organiser
of secret conspiracies geared towards preparation for the insurrection: first the Society of Friends, later the Society of Seasons,
where Barthélemy, his loyal protégé, joined him. Often imprisoned – he was incarcerated for some thirty years of his life –
Blanqui accrued a semi-mythical reputation as an indomitable,
unyielding revolutionist.

In 1817, not long after the restoration of the monarchy, a police
bulletin had observed with satisfaction that the working class
'have no opinions beyond those which result from consciousness
of their needs'. In other words, workers were concerned with
nothing more than securing their next meal.

> Beyond this they are more or less resigned to their discom-
> forts. The time is gone when would one need fear that they
> will take to crime. They scarcely even talk of it, and if talk
> should go beyond the sort of back-chat left over from the
> Revolution and army life anyone indulging it is looked
> upon as a police agent. The populace has learnt the mean-
> ing of fear, and there is more reserve on the streets than in
> the fashionable drawing rooms.

Such complacency was impossible by the late 1830s. Revolutionary
republicanism had profoundly shifted its social orientation. In
1838, a police spy reported to his superiors on the changing
nature of the revolutionary underground in France. 'The recruitment among the ill conditioned members of the bourgeoisie
[has been] replaced entirely by recruiting from the scum of the
popular class.' Revolutionary conspiracy became a working-
class affair as 'the bourgeois element altogether abandoned
illegal means'. Two years later another high official in the

prefecture of police declared that in Paris's population of 1 million inhabitants no fewer than 60,000 had declared war on society. Paris was a cauldron, boiling and churning, bringing to the surface a new kind of working class. The very idea of revolution was changing – and Barthélemy was amongst the first of this new generation of working-class revolutionaries.

4

'ANGER DOES NOT CALCULATE'

The English were proud of their freedoms, their prosperity, and their plain-speaking. John Bull, the national stereotype, was a plump yeoman of cheerful demeanour, candid expression, red cheeks and unshorn chin. The French, in contrast, were caricatured as skinny, malnourished and forever conspiring to overthrow their mildly oppressive if inefficient government. The bohemian fashion for facial hair in Paris seemed to suggest a kind of mask behind which revolutionary ideas lurked. 'As for the beards, there is no end to them,' wrote William Makepeace Thackeray of the French, 'and Nature, though she has rather stinted the bodies and limbs of the French nation, has been very liberal to them of hair.'

The new regime could see behind the mask. Having been made by revolution, Louis Philippe's government knew it could be unmade by one. That sombre respect for national institutions that characterised English public opinion could hardly be found in France. Thackeray, visiting theatres in Paris, was struck by the audiences. 'They laugh at religion, they laugh at chastity, they laugh at royalty.' There was little positive enthusiasm for Louis Philippe's monarchy. Governmental ministers, aware of popular discontent in Paris, established a Municipal Guard in the capital, 3,200 strong. Though gorgeously attired, wearing bronze helmets embossed with the Gallic rooster, decorated with leopard skin and finished off with a crimson plume tufted on the front and a horsehair mane at the back, the Municipal Guard soon developed a vile reputation for violence and thuggery in working-class districts.

By 1839, the rank-and-file of the Society of Seasons, established the year before, was pressing hard for an insurrection to be launched as soon as possible. Barthélemy, aged sixteen, was no doubt one of these militants. As an outlet for their enthusiasm, and to test the political water, the Seasons leadership of Blanqui, Armand Barbès and Bernard authorised a protest outside the parliamentary Chamber on 4 April. When the republicans gathered to harass Louis Philippe's legislators, however, they were set upon by the police. The notorious Municipal Guard led the charge. Barthélemy endured a savage thrashing. 'A policeman, who was with his comrades including several dressed in plain clothes, grabbed me and beat me with his baton.' Years later he still bore scars from the attack and was seen to be missing a finger.

As Alexander Herzen, a Russian who would befriend Barthélemy, later heard the story, Barthélemy had been stopped by a gendarme 'and as he began to say something the gendarme gave him a punch in the face with his fist. Barthélemy, who was being held by a *municipal*, tore himself away, but could do nothing. This blow awakened the tiger in him. Barthélemy – an eager, good-humoured young working lad – got up the next day transformed.' We may doubt that Barthélemy was quite so naive before this encounter. Members of the Society of Seasons, after all, saw themselves as part of a dedicated revolutionary elite. It was not in Barthélemy's nature to endure a humiliating assault without bearing a grudge.

Barthélemy was certainly not dissuaded from his revolutionism by the police beating he had endured. Preparation for a rising was now taking up much of his time, and the metal workshop took distant second place. On 4 May, his master, Monsieur Loigelot, finally lost patience and, due to yet another absence from work, dismissed Barthélemy. Barthélemy did not return to his parents but instead lodged at number 11, rue Michel-le-Comte, with Prosper Dufour, a fellow *sertisseur*. This was a very narrow street, only eighteen or nineteen feet wide, with houses looming on either side. As he lay in bed, Barthélemy could see no more than a yard or two of sky. But he had things on his mind, dreaming of overthrowing the king and re-establishing the glorious Republic.

The signal for action was finally given on 12 May 1839. About 500 answered Blanqui's summons, including some foreigners resident in Paris, mostly German, organised in the sympathising League of the Just. At about 2.30 p.m. that afternoon, a detachment of rebels led by Martin Bernard and Blanqui occupied the Hôtel de Ville, that traditional focal point of insurrection, and disarmed the small guard there. Their call of 'To arms!' was greeted mostly with confusion by the public, and only a few hundred fell in with the rebels. Barricade fighting broke out, but the cause was hopeless from the outset. By the end of the day government troops had recovered full control. In all, about a hundred were either killed in action or subsequently died of wounds, thirty of them soldiers.

Just under three hundred rebels were put on trial. Many of them were men like Barthélemy: nearly 87 per cent were working class, mostly artisan; 54.5 per cent were born outside Paris, usually from neighbouring districts; 37 per cent worked in the high-quality metalworking trades. Those members of the League of the Just who had fought with the rebels fled abroad, many winding up in London, where in 1840 they organised a Workers Educational Society. They were to become the Communist League, for which Karl Marx and Frederick Engels would write their famous *Communist Manifesto* in 1848.

By the time the insurrection had broken out, however, Barthélemy was already in police custody. At about 9.30 a.m. on the day of the rising, a sergent-de-ville of the Municipal Guard, a fifty-eight-year-old ex-soldier called Zôphirin Beudet, was patrolling the Boulevard Saint-Martin, a thoroughfare in the north of the city where raised pavements showed where the city ramparts used to be. He saw a young man approaching him with what appeared to be a firearm in his hand. Before Beudet knew what was happening, the gunman had raised his weapon and fired at him from point-blank range. Most of the shot was taken by Beudet's left arm and absorbed by the folds of his heavy cloak and overcoat. Beudet was stunned, and it fell to civilians to chase after and overpower the assailant.

Monsieur Duprat, an upholsterer living in the Faubourg du Temple, was passing by on the boulevard when he heard a gunshot. He turned and saw a policeman shouting that he had been wounded and a young man fleeing the scene. He ran after Barthélemy, for it was he, and grabbed him. Monsieur Touzelin, a tailor, heard the cry, 'Stop the murderer!' and grabbed Barthélemy's gun arm. A dagger, with a shortened serrated blade, tumbled to the ground from under Barthélemy's workman's blouse. Barthélemy was 'pale but calm'. He did not actively resist but tried to shake off their hands. Both witnesses recalled his words: 'Do not abase me!'

When Gabet, the police commissioner, arrived on the scene, he found on Barthélemy three cartridges, similar to those with which the gun was loaded, containing large lead shot. This was buckshot rather than bullets and unlikely ammunition for an assassination attempt. Gabet asked Barthélemy if he really thought that these cartridges would kill. 'No doubt!' replied Barthélemy, 'had I not fired a blank as I did.'

Also found on Barthélemy was a fragment of the *Vieux Cordelier* newspaper – published by Camille Desmoulins during

the French Revolution to criticise the Terror – and paper placards written in his own hand. The first read, 'People, arm
yourselves with daggers to punish your executioners! Strike
without fear – blood calls out for blood, and they have shed
yours without pity.' On the second piece of paper, King Louis
Philippe's father – who had gone so far as to change his name
so as to win the favour of radicals during the revolution – was
berated. 'Philippe Egalité was a wretch, his son is a perjurer
and a murderer. The history of his reign is written with the
blood of victims of Pont d'Arcole, Place de la Bourse and rue
Transnonain.'

These were referring to notorious episodes of police repression. On 29 July 1832, early-morning commuters had been
horrified to see long trails of blood and a scrabble of footprints
on the Pont d'Arcole, a bridge over the river Seine. Neighbours
had been awakened, between midnight and one o'clock, by
screams. Looking through their windows they made out a scene
of sergents-de-ville on the bridge savagely beating people and
then, allegedly, rolling the corpses of those they had killed into
the river. The truth eventually emerged out of the confused and
terrified reports of eyewitnesses. The day before, young people
had been visiting the graves of street fighters who had fallen in
the revolution of July 1830. To round off their republican
stations, they visited the Pont d'Arcole, associated with the
heroic death of a young revolutionary hero, and stood about
in pairs on the bridge singing the republican 'Marseillaise'.
Within minutes, both sides of the bridge were sealed off by the
police. The young republicans, now trapped, were ferociously
set upon, suffering heavy blows from police batons, swords and
bayonets. Certainly they were very badly beaten, though there
was never sure evidence that anyone had been murdered and
thrown off the bridge.

The second episode referred to on Barthélemy's placard
had taken place in March 1834. Republicans – including

Blanqui – had defied the new government press laws by publicly selling their newspapers on the Place de la Bourse. When the authorities moved in, bloody clashes ensued, with rioting continuing until mounted police arrived. Police force was heavy-handed, and one worker appears to have been killed.

The third episode was the most infamous of all. In April 1834, the massive rebellion of silk workers in Lyon triggered rioting across the country and a formidable republican rebellion in Paris. On 14 April, near a barricade in the street of Transnonain, an infantry captain was wounded by a shot fired from a window. In response, all the inhabitants of number 12 Transnonain, from where it was assumed that the shot had been fired, were massacred by the military. This slaying of twelve men, women, children and infants was immortalised in Honoré Daumier's stark and compelling lithograph depicting a slaughtered family. The *Massacre de la rue Transnonain* entered into popular memory as an indictment against the forces of order. These were the horrors which infuriated Barthélemy, and which he was sure would encourage the people of Paris to join the insurrection of that May. Martyrology and iconic art probably are necessities for any successful insurrection; but this time there were not enough to tip the balance.

After his arrest, Barthélemy was held in the Conciergerie, a Parisian version of the Tower of London, located in the middle of Paris on the Île de la Cité. This had been a mediaeval Royal Palace in the Gothic style, before being converted into a prison. It was a large and sombre building, 'sullen-looking, dark, and grey, pierced by iron-grated windows'. During the French Revolution it held prisoners awaiting the guillotine, including Danton, Robespierre and Saint-Just. Now those due for trial lay in underground cells, or paced about a prison yard located below ground level. It was considered to be the most insalubrious prison in Paris. When the river rose, the prison floor would flood with black mud, and the walls continuously streamed with condensation. Prisoners had to pay eighteen francs for the privilege of a bed, and even then had to wait a fortnight for one. The Conciergerie was located just beside the courts of justice and the writer Honoré de Balzac described the procedure when inmates were required for court appearance. 'When the hour of trial strikes, the sheriffs call the roll of the prisoners, the gendarmes go down, one for each prisoner, and each gendarme takes a criminal by the arm; and thus, in couples, they mount the stairs, cross the guardroom, and are led along passages to a room … where sits the … Assize Court.' On 20 December 1839, it was Barthélemy's turn.

He faced three judges, one of whom, Monsieur Férey, presided. Férey would himself question the defendant and any witnesses. The defence and prosecution lawyers, in their robes, would present closing statements. A jury had been gathered to hear not only Barthélemy's case, but all cases that came before the court's quarterly session. They would have the power to declare him innocent or guilty. Barthélemy stood in the dock with a policeman on either side. Close by him were benches for the public. Barthélemy's family, no doubt distraught, sat amongst them.

The trial attracted international attention because it was thought to be the first instance of an attempt at assassinating a police officer in France. The defendant appeared with his hair cut in republican fashion – shoulder length – though still too young to sport either a beard or moustache. He was wearing the clothes in which he had been arrested: a dark and heavy coat and a bright white linen necktie over a working man's blouse. As ever, he was immaculately tidy.

Barthélemy, who was defended by Monsieur Paillet of the Bar Association, was quick and ready with his replies during the Président's examination. He showed no fear and cast a cold eye across the court. He denied that the shooting had been a calculated assassination attempt. 'I am neither disruptive nor criminal,' he insisted, but he would certainly defend the republican cause come the day of danger. Barthélemy explained that he had been carrying arms on behalf of a secret society from one hiding place to another. It seems more likely that he was on his way to an insurrectionary muster in preparation for the uprising planned for later that afternoon. Barthélemy, however, was not going to give too much information away. When instructed by the Président of the court, Monsieur Férey, to 'make known the person to whom [the weapons] belong', he replied, 'No one will know that but myself.' Barthélemy would be no *mouchard*, no informer.

Barthélemy claimed that when carrying out his mission he had chanced across Zôphirin Beudet, whom he recognised as the policeman who had beaten him on 12 May. Barthélemy explained that he had been overcome with sudden fury. He darted behind one of the stone sentry boxes on the boulevard. 'Recognising the man who had hit me I felt beside myself, and yielding to a first impulse, I loaded the gun and I shot him.' Barthélemy admitted that there had been no immediate provocation, though he dismissed the prosecution's assertion that Beudet could hardly have been the man responsible for assaulting him with a cane because he lacked two fingers. 'I do not think a man who is missing two fingers is unable to handle a cane with his remaining three fingers,' responded Barthélemy wryly. 'I could use a cane perfectly with three fingers; let alone someone who has a long history [of doing so].'

Barthélemy was anxious not to have his secret society implicated in a tawdry assassination campaign against policemen. It was not republican ideals, he said, that had made him carry out the attack. 'I would not do anything that may dishonour a cause that I believe in too much to want to degrade.' Nor was Barthélemy carrying out a vendetta against policemen in general. 'Certainly I would not have the madness to go alone to declare war on all sergents-de-ville who are in Paris.' He had only been seeking to vent his fury as an individual on an individual. Pointing out that his pistol had been loaded not with bullets but rather with lead shot, Barthélemy claimed, 'I did not intend to kill him, but only to punish him.' It was put to him that he had in fact fired towards Beudet's heart. Barthélemy denied this: 'I fired at random .... Anger does not calculate.'

Barthélemy may have confessed to the attack, but he was far from being apologetic, despite the splenetic outbursts of the court president:

> Président. – You dare to arrogate to yourself punishment of law on the agents of authority? You belong to a secret society but you refuse to divulge the source of your weapons, which consists not only a gun, but a dagger. You tell coldly and with an inexplicable impassivity what happened, showing neither repentance nor remorse, not even regret.
>
> Barthélemy. – I have nothing with which to reproach myself.

There were gasps in the audience at Barthélemy's imperturbable retort.

In summing up the case, the prosecuting Avocat-Général addressed the court on the nature of the revolutionary societies. At certain times, he instructed his audience, the revolutionaries thought themselves strong enough to descend en masse in public and engage the state in a sort of general battle. This had been the case in June 1832 and April 1834, when there had been insurrections in Lyon and in Paris. In May 1839, there had been another such attempt, though already weakened and reduced in its chances of success by the growing indifference of the country. Revolutionaries, therefore, were being driven to undertake acts of terror alone.

The Avocat-Général reminded the court of recent assassination attempts. Guiseppe Fieschi in July 1835 had attempted to kill Louis Philippe by firing an 'infernal machine' of twenty-five gun barrels, bound by a steel band, primed to go off simultaneously as the King passed in a procession along the Boulevard du Temple. The King was merely grazed but all around him, 'the pavement and roadway were strewn with men and horses dead and dying'. Eighteen people were killed in the onslaught – including women and children – and forty-two were wounded. Louis Alibaud the same year lunged into Louis Philippe's carriage and fired at him from point-blank range with a newly invented 'cane gun'. The King escaped death only because he was bowing his head to acknowledge a guard. There had been no fewer than six assassination attempts in total, but all had failed. (Never let it be thought that nineteenth-century heads of state lacked courage; or, at any rate, they had need of it.) Now, the Avocat-Général continued, the focus of the revolutionaries was in the opposite direction. Instead of attacking the elites, they were targeting their subalterns. In his view, therefore, Barthélemy's attack was part of an orchestrated campaign against the agents of the Crown.

We may doubt this proffered argument whilst admiring the cogency of its presentation. Blanqui, Barthélemy's leader, was opposed to regicide and terrorism. As we have seen, it is much more likely that Barthélemy had been on his way to a gathering for the insurrection when he came across the policeman who had assaulted him so brutally, and that he reacted in a passion. Young men in their teens are not remarkable for their self-control.

The Avocat-Général went on to address Barthélemy's age: he would be seventeen by Christmas. That such a youthful man should be charged with so a serious crime was reflective of the times. 'We always hear talk of progress,' he remarked sardonically, 'we are concerned that this is a progress in evil.' Adolescents were being drawn into political crime. 'Today we see children of thirteen and fourteen years old engaging in acts that seem placed at the extreme limit of despair. We also see the most serious crimes against persons committed by young people. We see them led astray by a republican ideal of maniacal and impractical equality to attack anything that may put obstacles to their disordered passions.' These were 'individuals in whom respect for all things is lost; they first defy their fathers, then their masters. Difficult apprentices become bad citizens. They move from being insolent with their masters to insulting their King. Ultimately we arrive at this point; they see in a police officer a man must be killed because he is a symbol of repression, the image of the law to which they refuse to submit.' The Avocat-Général wound up by calling for Barthélemy to be found guilty, with the aggravating circumstance that he had attacked a policeman carrying out his legal duties.

Barthélemy's defence lawyer, Monsieur Paillet, denied any premeditation and urged indulgence 'towards a child led astray by fanaticism'. He pointed to Barthélemy, 'an industrious and honest worker, a model worker … next to him a perfectly respectable family'. The court should keep their severity for those 'who ferment such dangerous doctrines in young heads'.

Monsieur Ferey, Président of the Court, then summed up, and the jury – all male and respectable property owners – retired to deliberate. When they returned they found Barthélemy guilty of attempted murder on the person of Zôphirin Beudet, but dismissed the question of premeditation and the aggravating circumstance. It was hardly a ringing endorsement of the police. The Avocat-Général asked that Articles 2 and 504 of the Penal Code be applied, meaning that Barthélemy be sentenced to death. Given his youth and the jury's verdict, however, he was sentenced to exposure on the pillory – which would see him being chained to a post on the street to invite the derision of passers-by – before being bound to forced labour for life. Barthélemy 'listened to this judgment with an unalterable composure' and 'calmly took up his hat on the bench behind him, and followed the gendarmes below to the Conciergerie'. A few months later, in February 1840, Barthélemy's sentence of public humiliation was lifted, and he was sent directly to the galleys.

Barthélemy had managed to convince the Assize Court of the Seine that his attack on Beudet was a personally motivated outburst. Later, when talking to fellow revolutionaries, he was to change his story. The shooting, he claimed ten years afterwards in 1849, had indeed been an attempted assassination. Zôphirin Beudet had been deliberately targeted because he was an ex-member of a republican secret society and as such was condemned to death by the Blanquist revolutionaries as an agent provocateur. The designated assassin had been chosen by lot, and quite by chance it had fallen to Barthélemy.

We may doubt the story. Why would such an assassination, motivated by revenge, be carried out on the morning of a planned insurrection? It ran the risk of revealing the plans of the Society of Seasons. His original story seems much more likely, though. We can see why Barthélemy, who wished to be taken as a self-disciplined revolutionary, may have been tempted to rewrite his past. Barthélemy was, indeed, a focused revolutionary, but one with a fiery temper. He would not tolerate those who would lay hands upon him to do him violence. 'Do not abase me,' he had said to those passers-by who had seized him after the shooting. There is perhaps no better insight into this young worker's psychology.

5

GALLEY CONVICT

It was a chill February morning that Barthélemy was taken from his cell for transportation to the galleys – a life of hard labour ahead of him. Barthélemy and his fellow convicts were told to wait at the low doors leading out into the prison court. At midday, they heard a large gate being opened, and the trundling of a cart, escorted by soldiers and rattling with chains. In an instant, both the prisoners assembled for transport and those watching from their cells burst into mocking raillery and loud laughter. The galley sergeants threw down the chains from the top of the cart and stretched them across the yard, testing each link as they went. When all was ready, the inner doors were thrown open, and the galley convicts pushed out before the cart. Shouting from the prison cells swelled, echoing around the walls, and we can imagine Barthélemy – a young rebel already made famous by his well-publicised trial – being saluted by his comrades: 'Farewell, citzen!'

The convicts were called out by name alphabetically, and put in pairs. They exchanged their worn-out prison clothes for thin linen uniforms, shivering in the cold weather of midwinter, as in groups of twenty or so they were led to the corner of the yard where the chains, attached to the cart, were laid out in wait. Every two feet along there hung another short chain which ended in a heavy hinged iron collar. The prisoners were ordered to sit on the ground, as two prison blacksmiths, with portable anvils, riveted 'hard, unheated metal with heavy iron hammers' around their necks. This was 'a frightful operation, and even the most hardy turned pale! Each stroke of the hammer, aimed on the anvil resting on their backs, makes the whole form yield; the failure of its aim, or the least movement of the head, might launch them into eternity.'

The men were then loaded on to the wagons, sitting back to back with their feet dangling over the side. Escorted by mounted gendarmes and guards on foot they passed through Paris, gazing bitterly at abusive crowds who jeered at them as they went by. With heavy wheels turning and fetters clanking, Barthélemy began his long journey – three or four weeks of travelling – to the galleys.

Barthélemy was to spend nearly the next nine years in the Breton port of Brest as a 'galley convict'. As the name suggests, galley prisoners had originally been press-ganged into the navy. Though they no longer put to sea, they were still under the navy's authority, imprisoned in 'bagnes' – decommissioned hulks or, in the case of Brest, an old building in the port town.

The bagnes were profit-making institutions and convicts were paid a small stipend for their labour. These prisoners, amounting to about 3,200 in Brest, were required to work for a certain number of hours, but otherwise they were more or less left to themselves by the naval guards, who acted only as sentinels on the perimeter to prevent escape. All prisoners – the forçats – had their heads shaved and were branded on the right shoulder for ease of identification. Barthélemy would always carry his mark: the letter T for 'forced labour' – travaux forcés – and P for a life sentence – à perpétuité. They wore a loose-fitting jacket of dirty red serge, yellow trousers, and a cap, the colour of which designated the severity of the offence. Condemned as he was to life imprisonment, Barthélemy's was green. The most fractious convicts were heavily loaded with shackles fastened to a ring riveted around the leg. However, most prisoners were left relatively free. As soon as they had completed their allotted task for the day they were allowed to return to their cell to do what they wanted. Some had writing desks; others employed themselves in handicrafts, making toys out of coconuts and horsehair. They could sell these to earn a little extra money. The daily food allowance included a pint of wine, a measure of biscuit, or half a loaf of brown bread. *Forçats* were daily marched out to work in the town, and were a well-known sight around Brest, even itemised as an entertaining diversion in a holiday guide published for English tourists. The *Hand-Book for Travellers in France* noticed with equable interest that the prison wings featured cannons loaded with grapeshot pointing inwards. In the event of 'tumult or rebellion' the cannon 'would enfilade the chamber, and sweep it from end to end'. Close supervision was thereby rather unnecessary.

Despite these small freedoms, Victor Hugo imagined the galley prisoner's grim life: 'to be shown no respect by anyone, to be searched by the warder, beaten by the galley-sergeant, to wear hobnailed shoes on his bare feet and allow the shackles on his leg to be checked morning and night by the guard on patrol with his hammer, to endure the curiosity of strangers ... Oh, what misery!' And survival for prisoners was no straightforward matter: the annual mortality rate by the 1840s ran at about 3 per cent per year.

Nonetheless, the *bagnes* can justly be thought of as brutal but roughly egalitarian colonies. Prisoners were not under micro-control; they could chat, went out to labour in the docks or surrounding factories during the day, and sometimes were even allowed to stay outside the prison overnight. The naval administrator, Maurice Alhoy, claimed in the 1840s that prisoners in the *bagnes* ate better than free men and enjoyed the 'relative tranquillity' of 'happy criminality [in] an establishment of charity in favour of thieves and assassins'. The left-wing author, Eugène Sue, even surmised that hardened criminals would commit murder to secure transfer from the central prisons to the *bagnes* because of 'the riotous life they lead' there. This of course was exaggerated, but in its rough and coercive cooperation, the *bagne* in some respects must have reminded Barthélemy of his schooling. Curiously enough, it was probably the closest he ever came to working in something like a large-scale industrial enterprise; not much less appealing a place of work than the grim factory mills of early industrial England.

We know very little of Barthélemy's time in the *bagne*, but the records that do exist suggest that his conduct was considered to be good. It seems likely that it was here that he educated himself – he would later be a ready writer able to read sophisticated literature – and perhaps practised his noted oratorical skills. It must also have been during these years that he gained his skills as an 'engineer-mechanic', as he would be described thereafter. Probably he worked in the naval armoury in Brest and picked up a good deal of military art, in particular an expertise with firearms.

Monsieur Masse, a captain in the navy, was willing to speak well of Barthélemy's character during his years of incarceration. In future years, when his reputation was being traduced by political rivals, Masse spoke up for him:

Since the condemnation of Barthélemy, in 1839, I have made enquiries about his conduct of the authorities of Brest, and I am bound to say they agreed to a man that he was gifted with an admirable temper, a heroic bravery, and the utmost straightforwardness. When I was holding a situation there, I heard from M. Severain, a commissioner in the Navy, a very respectable man, as can be easily ascertained, that Barthélemy, on December 18, 1842, threw himself in the sea to save the life of one of the port officers, whose name is M. Barthe.

Barthélemy not only took lives, he saved at least one, with coolness and courage in the face of danger.

With convicts, including political offenders, organised as labourers in large-scale factory work, it is not surprising that some revolutionaries saw in the prisoners promising material for making revolution. In the 1840s, the idea of the convict-as-revolutionary was most associated with the German artisan communist, a tailor called Wilhelm Weitling. 'Every person who is sorely oppressed and who has the courage to take from the superfluity of others for his basic needs and who is prepared to defend his action proudly and publicly before the courts, and before the people, I call a communist,' he wrote in 1842. For Weitling, the proletarian thief was an instinctive revolutionary: 'Their communism is from the heart, and they are committed to it.'

Weitling was a rarity in being a socialist writer of genuine working-class background. In contrast to Barthélemy, who was a thoroughgoing rationalist, Weitling was mystical in his beliefs, but he was nonetheless a hard-bitten veteran of struggle. When Heinrich Heine, the German poet, democrat and socialist sympathiser, met with Weitling, he was disconcerted by his sense of revulsion. Heine had expected to find a modern-day version of John of Leydon, a tailor and fanatically radical Protestant who had been barbarously martyred by the German aristocracy in 1536. But he was guiltily irritated when his condescension to this proletarian hero was not reciprocated by appreciation of his own cultural and educational superiority:

What particularly offended my pride was the fellow's utter lack of respect while he conversed with me. He did not remove his cap and, while I was standing before him, he remained sitting .... I, who had made an exalted cult of the dead tailor, now felt an insurmountable aversion for this living tailor, Wilhelm Weitling, though both were apostles and martyrs in the same cause.

Barthélemy would also disconcert democrats who idealised the working class in principle but found them difficult to deal with in person. This is not an uncommon characteristic of the middle-class radical, nor is it one we should be too hard on, for it can be difficult to connect with those distant from us, no matter how much we may respect or admire them. Heine, as always, was refreshing in his candour.

Weitling was temporarily a hero for those German comrades of Blanqui and Barthélemy in the League of the Just who had escaped to London after the failure of the 1839 rising. Exposure to the relatively free political conditions of Britain and the mass working-class movement there of the semi-legal Chartists – who since 1838 had been campaigning for the male working classes to have the vote – gradually pushed these German communists away from the methods of secret society conspiracy. This was accelerated by their coming into contact with two German communist intellectuals, friends and admirers of Heine, Karl Marx and Frederick Engels.

Karl Marx, born in the Rhineland in 1818, was a powerfully built, barrel-chested man of unusual intellectual ability, boasting thick black hair and a full beard. After a carousing youth, he had settled down into married life, but remained fully committed to radical journalistic activity. At first sceptical of socialist ideas, he had come to believe that only common ownership of the means of production could allow individuals real autonomy and freedom. 'Modern universal intercourse can be controlled by individuals ... only when controlled by all.' Marx was converted to this socialism primarily by French thinkers, but he looked to industrial Britain with its modern working class as the society with the greatest potential for socialist transformation. Marx brought a rigorous academic philosophy to his thinking. Frederick Engels, who had lived in Manchester in the early 1840s, contributed an intimate knowledge of the industrial proletariat. (Unusually for middle-class radicals Engels did not find genuinely working-class comrades at all abject; indeed, he took two of them as common-law wives, Lizzie Burns and then her sister Mary. Marx and his wife Jenny, however, were always rather snooty towards the Burns sisters.) Engels was slightly younger than Marx, having been born in Bremen in 1820. A tall, lithe man with fair hair and a military bearing, Engels was a lover of women, song and wine. Supremely self-confident, he deferred to no one but Marx, and could rather aggravate colleagues by his unwillingness to listen. His boundless good humour and zest carried him above any grumblings, however. Not just politics but common liking for sometimes rather laborious parody and jest bound the two men in partnership. Together they came to think of themselves as not just the leaders of a party, but virtually a party in themselves. It need hardly be said that these two men were to become the unrivalled giants of the international socialist movement.

Marx and Engels, however, were rather hostile to mainstream socialist thinking at the time, which was based upon the cooperative workshop. They saw this, not inaccurately, as an artisan style of socialism. Being well-versed in political economy, they were convinced that attempts by worker-run cooperatives to exchange their products equitably with one another would simply lead to the re-emergence of trading, market relations, profiteering, and ultimately the whole panoply of exploitative capitalism. Instead, Marx and Engels put their faith not in the artisan, who ultimately wanted to secure the workshop as a small-scale property, but in the proletariat, those who had no possession other than their ability to work for wages. As this proletariat was not chained down by individual property it could escape narrow horizons. For wage-workers, their hunger for possession extended far beyond the isolated workshop or farm, and extended to society as a whole, as only a complete reordering of society could free them from their bondage to the capitalist employers. Proletarian revolution, in the first instance, would mean the state taking over broad swathes of productive property – certainly large factories and landed estates – to smash the power of the capitalist class. Where it would go from there was left opaque by Marx and Engels, though they seemed to think that large-scale nationalisation was the logical way forward.

The French socialist Louis Blanc was much more definite that state intervention would be a limited phase. Blanc proposed that the state would establish and in the first instance finance worker-run 'social workshops', but that these would become self-supporting and effectively independent within a year or two. 'Someday, if the dearest hope of our heart is not mistaken,' Blanc predicted, 'a day will come when a strong and active government is no longer needed, because there will no longer be inferior and subordinate classes in society. Until then, the establishment of a tutelary authority is essential.' He meant by 'tutelary authority' a temporary state authority over workers to educate them in the ways of self-reliance.

Marx and Engels were not unsympathetic to Blanc's point of view, but they did not like the idea of the state educating society. Only *revolutionary practice* – the process of struggle and self-organisation – would develop working-class capacities. Moreover, they believed that cooperatives could only be transitional to a nationally and even internationally planned economy. Refusing to peer too far into the future, however, they emphasised the necessity of suppressing bourgeois power and forming the proletariat as a self-conscious class able to dominate society. They called this the 'dictatorship of the proletariat'.

Impressed by Marx and Engels' learning and commitment, the German revolutionaries in London, led by Karl Schapper, in 1847 agreed to convert their League of the Just into the Communist League, and they formally abandoned 'hankering after conspiracy', becoming instead 'a pure propaganda society'. They invited Marx and Engels to write a manifesto for this new organisation. The *Manifesto of the Communist Party* – now better known as the *Communist Manifesto* – was published in early 1848, focusing on the proletariat and class struggle. When it finally appeared, after much prevaricating by Marx, the *Manifesto* made relatively little impact. It was to become, however, one of the most famous publications of the modern age.

In France itself, the secret societies seemed to have been definitively defeated. Inside the prison of Mont St Michel, Blanqui and Barbès fell out acrimoniously, ensuring the dissolution of what was left of the 'Society of Seasons'. The leading socialists now were Étienne Cabet, who disavowed politics altogether, arguing that workers should establish communist colonies on the open frontier of the American West, and Louis Blanc, who favoured public agitation for a democratic 'social Republic' – though he thought that women were too much under the influence of priests to have the vote – and won a considerable reputation with his 1839 work, *The Organisation of Labour*. Just as Blanqui provided Barthélemy with his model for revolution, so too would Blanc inspire him with a vision for the future. Blanc and other democratic socialists established a newspaper called *La Réforme*. This had connections with secret society veterans, but its focus was on open propaganda and education in favour of socialism. They had a sympathiser in the French parliament in the person of Alexandre Auguste Ledru-Rollin, who would occasionally speak up for their cause. Even Marx and Engels, in the *Communist Manifesto*, declared their own tendency to be allied to these French Social Democrats. The liberal republicans in France, on the other hand, were sympathetic to the plight of the workers, but determinedly favoured the inviolability of individual private property and rejected common ownership. They gathered around the *National* newspaper and their leader was the romantic poet, Alphonse de Lamartine. For now, however, both liberals and socialists could work together in opposition to the French monarchy. The failure of the potato crop in 1846 and a poor grain harvest in 1847 spread misery, and the shaky foundations of order began to crumble away. Revolution loomed.

6

BARRICADES PILED LIKE MOUNTAINS

As Barthélemy sweated in the *bagne*, discontent with the policies of the Guizot government in France was growing. The moderate and pro-monarchy opposition, led by Odilon Barrot, wanted to see the right to vote extended beyond the small portion of property owners who already held the privilege. To this end they attempted to mobilise non-voters while largely ignoring the republican and socialist propaganda of Ledru-Rollin and Louis Blanc. Banquets were organised in large cities and towns: Colmar, Strasbourg, Soissons, St Quentin and Mascon. Here political speeches could be made without breaking legal prohibitions on public meetings. The elegant soirées also had the advantage of excluding the poor. But when a banquet was planned for Paris in February 1848, republican leaders organised unofficial meetings in all quarters of working-class Paris. The public places were filled with anxious crowds. Government proclamations were posted on every wall in the city prohibiting the banquet. People collected round them in large knots, while one man read out the contents. They were then torn down and trampled underfoot. Republican activists moved silently from group to group, 'sounding the disposition of the people, who, artisans, shopkeepers, professional men, all showed but one desire – that of resistance'. The nervous filled the trains leaving Paris.

The moderate opposition decided to call off the banquet themselves, but too late – already people were taking to the streets. Cannon and ammunition wagons trundled through the streets. The Municipal Guard, cavalry and troops of the line were mobilised. As Monday morning dawned, on 22 February, the weather was damp and dismal. But crowds of workers and of shopkeepers milled on the streets. Many had swords, daggers and pistols hidden under their *blouses*. As processions formed, the army attempted to disperse them, but they were half-hearted. The despised Municipal Guard, however, showed little mercy or pity, charging repeatedly into the multitude. One old woman was kicked to death by a police horse. As rumours spread, large numbers of workmen left their workshops and join the crowds. Many were wearing red bonnets. In the working-class Faubourg Saint-Antoine a man was pointed out as a sergent de ville in disguise and was lynched. Barricades sprang up and spread across the city. These improvised fortifications were constructed from street paving, benches, railings, heaped cobblestones, unhitched carriages, water carts, uprooted trees, barrels, furniture, rubble, even *pissoirs* (public urinals). Broken bottles and coils of wire were scattered to impede cavalry. Street gas-lamps were torn down and overturned.

At first collisions were tentative, but when the army massacred about thirty-five people in a mishandled engagement, it suddenly became wild. The corpses of the dead were carried around Paris in a large cart lighted by torches. As it passed by, what had been contempt turned to fury. 'They have been struck by assassins! We will avenge them! Give us arms! – arms!' The following morning, the city was full of armed and angry crowds. They tore up over a million cobblestones and cut down several thousand trees to construct over 1,500 barricades. First the

National Guard retired from fighting the insurgents, many joining the protesters instead, and then the regular soldiers made themselves scarce. Finally even the Municipal Guards bowed to the people. Louis Philippe, who had always felt his throne to be uncertain given its revolutionary origin, threw in the towel. On 24 February he fled to England in disguise.

The liberals in France hoped to establish a new constitution and retain the monarchy, but the republicans remembered 1830 and this time were quick to seize that centre of people's power, the Hôtel de Ville. An enormous crowd had gathered round this imposing building when suddenly the doors 'flew open, and Louis Blanc came forth upon the steps':

> Never stepped forth so small a man to perform so mighty an office; but loudly was he greeted by the thousands who awaited .... In another minute all doubt was at an end, for the Republic was proclaimed by Louis Blanc amid a profound silence.
>
> No one can imagine the scene which followed. After a terrific shout, that shook the very welkin [heavens], the delighted masses began to dance from very joy; they waved their arms, they embraced perfect strangers, they shook hands with one another, exclaiming, in an ecstasy of delight, 'La République! Nous avons la République!'

The monarchy had been abolished and the French Second Republic, following that of the 1790s, had come into existence. It had been an extraordinary moment of mass mobilisation. The ailing political poet, Heinrich Heine, had been quite deafened – his brain 'nearly split' – by the incessant beating of drums, firing of shots, and singing of the 'Marseillaise'. Arriving from abroad, the Russian revolutionary Mikhail Bakunin described the scene three days after the fall of the monarchy:

> ... on every street, almost everywhere, barricades have been piled up like mountains, reaching roofs, and on them, among rocks and broken furniture ... workers in their colourful blouses, black from powder and armed head to foot .... And the dandies, young and old, all the hated social lions with their walking sticks and lorgnettes [hand-held spectacles], had disappeared, and in their place MY NOBLE OUVRIERS in rejoicing, exalting crowds, with red banners and patriotic songs, revelling in their victory!

Even in the countryside there was a cautious welcome for the revolution. The overthrown 'July Monarchy', after all, had been suspiciously indifferent to religion, and across France parish priests now supervised the planting of 'liberty trees' – usually poles with a red cap on top.

Once more the Gallic cock had crowed; and, this time, all of Europe woke up. Revolutionary outbreaks leapt from capital city to capital city – Berlin, Frankfurt, Kassel, Munich, Vienna, Budapest, Milan, Venice, Rome – wherever students and artisans waved a French-style tricolour flag in their own national colours. Thrones tottered or even fell in the German states, the Italian states and the Austrian Habsburg Empire. It was not so much a case of the ruling elites losing their nerve; they simply couldn't rely upon their urban garrisons to suppress insurrection. It was the springtime of peoples and an astonishing concentration of revolution.

In France, meanwhile, a Provisional Government formed itself, led by the liberal republican Alphonse de Lamartine. Lamartine was not himself a socialist, favouring only such reform as was 'compatible with the liberty of capital and the security of property'. He would not countenance any interference with capitalist ownership. Lamartine believed, however, that it was crucial to have representation of the *Réforme* faction in his government. These *démoc-socs* – or 'social republicans' – were in a minority, but they did secure some important positions. Their nominee, Marc Caussidière, a former member of the secret societies, took charge of the Prefecture of Police. Louis Blanc was given a post in the government itself. At his side was Alexandre Martin – known as *Citoyen Albert, ouvrier* (Citizen Albert, worker) – a locksmith and a veteran of the 'Seasons' Society. The presence of a minister like Albert – who was not just a socialist but unquestionably of the working class – was something startlingly new. It appeared to signal a new era of social emancipation. The *démoc-socs* could also rely upon the occasional support of the democrats, Ferdinand Flocon and Ledru-Rollin.

With the overthrow of the monarchy, the new government was under pressure to concede even more to the radical and socialist-minded working class of Paris. With considerable courage and skill, Lamartine persuaded an armed crowd of workers that the new Republic should fly the *tricoleur* rather than the red flag. He promised to distribute 1 million francs to labouring men and the government passed a decree pledging to furnish every Frenchman with work. General Louis-Eugène Cavaignac, a stern republican, took over command of the armed forces.

Lamartine, the effective head of the government, was a poet and a historian. He was of aristocratic background but genuinely committed to the democratic cause. An eloquent if flowery speaker, Lamartine basked in the adoration of the crowd. Few politicians could match his skill in reasoning with and persuading tumultuous mobs seeking to impose demands. He had a self-confidence in dealing with his social inferiors born of his pride of caste. Lamartine's undoubted ability at inspiring the masses, however, was tempered by a fear of the people going too far. He smiled at the illusions entertained by the left about the goodness and wisdom of the people. But he did not wish to be a prisoner of his right-wing ministers, so he cultivated the *démoc-socs* as a balance. Still, Lamartine was never a social democrat himself, and he was ironical about their tendency to idealise the common people of Paris. 'Fundamentally, whatever they may say,' he told Louis Blanc and Marc Caussidière, while pointing at the crowd, 'all these people want law and order and they are relying on me to provide them with both.' No doubt this was not entirely wrong, but it smacks of that shallow cynicism typical of the politician without conviction. Lamartine had poise, but his confidence was brittle. Through the torrid months of the 1848 revolution he was on an emotional rollercoaster, diffidence and conceit succeeding each other in rapid oscillations. He found strength in being above and independent of narrow political groups, which allowed him to keep the government in some sort of balance until June 1848. But this was also his weakness. Lamartine had no solid base for his own political point of view, whatever that might have been.

Ledru-Rollin, the Minister of the Interior in the Provisional Government, was a tall, striking, rather fleshy man. A literary lion, fine speaker and sincere republican, he was more flamboyant than consistent. What political skills he possessed he had honed in long years of opposition and they were little adapted to government. This did not prevent him working actively to reconstruct the administration of France to the advantage of republicans as soon as he was in position. He lacked the decisive instinct, however, and was a poor judge of politics as the art of the possible. He had a tendency to take his own goodwill and lofty rhetoric for reality, and soon found that his parliamentary support was much less than he had imagined. Never one to treat his own occasionally super-revolutionary rhetoric too seriously, he was disconcerted to find others taking him at his word. Conservative hostility amongst elected representatives focused on his person. He was seen as the dangerous radical in the government. But, in reality, Ledru-Rollin was not at all as one with the revolutionary crowd. When confronted with street demonstrations, he sided with Lamartine against them.

With acute psychological insight, the moderate liberal Alexis de Tocqueville described Ledru-Rollin as fearsome in reputation but vacillating in reality:

> At that time, the nation saw Ledru-Rollin as the bloody image of the Terror. They regarded him as the evil and Lamartine as the good genius, mistakenly in both cases. Ledru was nothing but a great sensual sanguine boy, with no principles and hardly any ideas; he had no true courage of mind or heart, but he was also free of malice, for by nature he wished all the world well and was incapable of cutting an enemy's throat, except perhaps as an historical reminiscence or to please his friends.

These were not entirely unattractive men. But neither Lamartine nor Ledru-Rollin matched up to Barthélemy's concept of the hard-bitten revolutionary.

Louis Blanc was the leading socialist intellectual of the Provisional Government, and the minister most prepared to appeal to the Paris crowd. Though he abhorred political violence and was genuinely committed to democracy, Blanc was quite prepared to postpone elections if he thought they would go against him and to call on the armed crowds to intimidate political opponents. Blanc relied upon his intellectual authority and moral courage to command respect. He lacked the common touch, however. 'I believe he has a mind more rich than his heart,' a friend said of him. Though there are many rue Blancs in France today, it is rather striking how little an impression he left in the collective left-wing mythology.

Blanc was a believer in the 'great man' view of history and so it is all the more tragic that he lacked that spark of greatness in himself. In 1844 he had written that: 'It is the nature of superior statesmen to give an impulse to things, to ennoble each situation ... Great men fecundate the present; they elevate history.' It was the role of intellectuals, he believed, to develop ideas which slowly permeate society until there comes a man who finds the formula which expresses the ideas of the masses. Blanc felt he had done this himself, with his famous call for the 'organisation of labour', but in fact he was rather poor at reading the popular mood and showed little skill at reacting to it.

Nature had been cruel. Blanc lacked the physical presence of his rivals, being of strikingly small stature, standing barely five foot in his socks, slim with it, and needing to climb on a stool to address meetings. He was, moreover, very young looking, and was vain about his appearance, dressing himself with pernickety care. This was not a man to sway the masses. He had little of the natural rapport with the crowd enjoyed by Lamartine. While Lamartine was elegantly sentimental in his speechifying, Blanc was terse, efficient and rather abrupt. He had no time for social niceties, and he allowed his political rivalries to turn into personal grudges. Blanc was often depicted as a kind of latter-day Robespierre – a man he admired. They shared the same fastidious love of humanity which did not seem to extend to familiarity with actual people.

These were the leading political figures of the 1848 revolution in France. In the tumultuous times to come they would find themselves encountering a young man still serving a life sentence in the *bagne* at Brest: Emmanuel Barthélemy.

It was one thing to have republicans in the government. It was another thing to republicanise the sprawling administration of France. It made sense, therefore, to scour the prisons for incarcerated republicans who could now be put to good work in support of the revolution. Days after the Provisional Government came to power, the new director of the admirably titled Department of Crimes and Mercy, Faustin Helie, a humanitarian lawyer, recommended to the minister of justice, Adolphe Crémieux, that Emmanuel Barthélemy be released. Republicans remembered his steadfast courage before the court in 1839 and knew that he had been unbroken by the galleys. On 19 March, just under a month after Louis Philippe's abdication, and eight years and ten months after his incarceration, Barthélemy duly regained his freedom. As Crémieux later explained, 'In my eyes, and in the eyes of the members of the *Gouvernement Provisoire*, Barthélemy had acted [in 1839], not as a murderer who deliberately commits a crime, but as a young man blinded by political enthusiasm and struck with the idea he is avenging his friends slaughtered in the streets by the hands of the *sergents de ville*. It is as a man condemned for a political offence, at the age of 17 [he was actually 16], and for no other reason, that he was liberated.' This reasoning was no doubt in their minds, but the republicans were seeking able loyalists, for in truth their followers were limited still to a minority of the population. There was an enormous premium on tested and zealous republican activists, and Louis Blanc was able to get Barthélemy a job as an Overseer in the Department of Forests and Waterways. This was no more than a cover, however. The republicans were looking for enforcers and Barthélemy, with his newly acquired knowledge of armaments and his unwavering revolutionary zeal, fitted the bill. He plunged straight into political activity. According to Wilhelm Liebknecht, at this time active as a student in the German revolution but afterwards a fellow refugee, Barthélemy in 1848 'took part in all the movements and demonstrations of the proletariat'.

The socialists were strong in Paris itself. They operated mainly through the political clubs, organising about 100,000 people. These clubs primarily saw their role as defending the revolution. Probably the most significant was the Central

Republican Society, dedicated to the destruction of the tyranny of capital. This was led by Auguste Blanqui, the revolutionary chief who had been held under lock and key since the 1839 insurrection, but who had also been released from prison. Blanqui had no desire to recreate the old Society of Seasons. Conspirators have a habit of falling out, and he was now in bitter enmity with his former co-leader, Armand Barbès, who had established his own Club of the Revolution.

Blanqui's line was clearly neo-Jacobin: 'Behind us we have the people and the clubs in which we shall organise ourselves for revolution as once the Jacobins did. What we need for our support is the mass of the people, the faubourgs in insurrection, a new August 10th [1792]. Then we should at least have the prestige of a revolutionary force.' This implied not an uprising to overthrow the Provisional Government, but a kind of dual power, a working-class organisation in permanent session able to place pressure on the government and to counter reactionary influences. For Blanqui, the arming of the workers would act as a bulwark of revolution, preventing the standing army from turning against the Republic. His aim, therefore, was to maximise the organisational capabilities of the working class. He demanded complete freedom of the press, a secure right for workers to form in associations, and a thorough purging of the old judiciary inherited from the monarchy.

Like most clubs, Blanqui's had considerable influence within Paris itself, but relatively few activist members. Blanqui was content with this situation for he always favoured a revolutionary vanguard working as a disciplined elite. The Central Republican Society had a maximum attendance of about 500, with actual workers in the minority. As he had long argued, the working class would be led by an educated elite.

Other clubs proliferated. Indeed, Paris had been converted into one vast club, or network of clubs. The Palais Royal, Tuileries Gardens, boulevards and the corners of thoroughfares and alleyways, hummed with street democracy, as groups congregated, talked and listened. Political placards, urging vigilance against counter-revolution, plastered the walls. The barricades had come down within three days of the overthrow of the monarchy, and the clubs were seen by its leaders as an alternative mode of popular mobilisation. They were to act not just as a 'crucible of opinion' for workers, but as a 'second National Assembly', permanently applying pressure on the government. They were 'the living barricades of Democracy'.

Upon his release, Barthélemy founded his own club. This did not attempt, however, to formulate a particular viewpoint. It was entirely turned to practical revolutionary requirements, more of an adjunct to Blanqui's Central Republican Society. Barthélemy, as a veteran of secret society armed struggle and the quasi-military discipline of the *bagnes*, quickly asserted himself as a leading specialist on revolutionary combat. He was to teach men how to fight: Barthélemy was under no illusion that the days of combat were over. His Club des barricades du 24 février, set up in March, was named after the date of the insurrection that had overthrown the King. Its purpose was to 'study the formation of barricades, military disposition, their inclination, strategic points where they were to rise and interconnect in every street, on every square, and at every city wall'. This was street fighting as an art and a science. Barthélemy kept membership limited; most initiates were already veterans of street battles. At this time, street-fighting manoeuvres and training could be openly conducted in Paris, an entertaining diversion for passers-by. In accordance with Blanqui's strategy, Barthélemy was preparing the organisation of the armed working class as a revolutionary pressure on the government and as a counterweight to royalist or conservative reaction.

The prefect of police in Paris, Marc Caussidière, and his lieutenant, Joseph Sobrier, a fellow veteran comrade of the 'Seasons', were also attempting to bolster the armed power of the Parisian republican working class. They had created a

People's Guard made up of former political detainees, basing them in barracks taken over from the disbanded Municipal Guard. The People's Guard comprised four companies, one of which was called the Compagnie Saint-Just, after the Jacobin hero. We do not know what association Barthélemy had with this organisation, if any, but it would be surprising if he was not involved. Certainly Blanquists were insinuating themselves into police headquarters.

Much more substantial, and far less politicised, were the twenty-four battalions of Gardes Mobiles organised on the initiative of the right wing of the Provisional Government, which was drawn from 'the most turbulent superfluity of the young population of Paris', as Lamartine put it. This was certainly a working-class military organisation, but it lacked much political consciousness and was disdained by socialist republicans as a 'lumpenproletariat' – a bunch of mercenaries. From the outset it was evidently a potential shock force in the service of counter-revolution.

On 17 March, Blanqui led an armed procession seeking an audience with the government. Fearing an attempt at insurrection, the ministers sent out Louis Blanc to quiet the crowd. Backed up by the National Guard, Blanc succeeded in having the demonstration dispersed. So far at least, Blanqui's armed regiments of workers could not dictate to the government. Never a man to lose patience, he bided his time. At the end of the month, however, there came a shattering blow to his prestige. From shady sources came the publication of the 'Taschereau Documents', seeming to prove that Blanqui had informed on fellow revolutionaries while in prison. Blanqui condemned these revelations as forgeries, but only after allowing them to fester for a few days, and his influence was much damaged. Most republicans, even those sympathetic to Blanqui's sacrifices, were inclined to believe that the documents were genuine, and that Blanqui had indeed 'named names'. Even Louis Blanc regretfully concluded that the documents were most likely authentic. Ledru-Rollin, in contrast, was glad to see a dangerous radical compromised before the public, and Barbès was positively jubilant at his old rival's discomfiture. Barthélemy, however, vehemently rejected any such accusation as a base slander and libel. He was furious at this 'ganging up' on an austere and heroic revolutionary. For Barthélemy, honour was worth dying for, and worth killing for.

The scandal blew apart the covert collaboration unsteadily established between Caussidière's prefecture of police and the Blanquist secret society operatives. Believing that he was heavily involved in promoting the calumnies of the Taschereau document, Blanqui nursed a particular hatred for Caussidière. Blanquists infiltrated within the police Prefecture now plotted his downfall. As Caussidière recalled:

> I soon discovered that this band of traitors had hatched a plot, which was to break out during the night. They were to enter my chamber while I was asleep and murder me in bed; they were then to seize upon the arms in the Prefecture; and counting upon friends outside, were to proclaim an insurrection .... As I always retired very late to rest, it was agreed that a deputation should wait upon me during the night, and put me to death with their daggers.

Caussidière pre-empted any such plot by purging his police force of the conspiring Blanquists, incurring the wrath of the revolutionary hard-liners. He received a supportive letter from Ledru-Rollin, who signed off, 'Good night, – as usual, not to sleep. – Ah! Saint-Just was right!'

What did Ledru-Rollin mean by this? He told the story in his own history of the Girondins. During the French Revolution, Saint-Just had once been rebuked by Robespierre for retiring placidly to bed while the September Massacres raged outside:

'Alas!' replied Saint-Just, 'I know well that murder will be done in this night; I deplore it, and wish I were sufficiently powerful to moderate these convulsions of society, struggling between life and death; but what am I? And, after all, those who perished this night are not the friends of our ideas. Adieu!' And with those words he fell fast asleep.

Ledru-Rollin feared men such as Barthélemy as modern incarnations of Saint-Just: young, ruthless, prepared to countenance any perfidy in defence of their vision of revolution.

We can be sure that Barthélemy was one of these Blanquist infiltrators in the police prefecture. Caussidière had described them as including former *forçats* (convicts), and his Préfet de Police described Barthélemy as '*ex-forçat, la terreur de Caussidière*'. There is evidence, indeed, that Barthélemy did try to terrorise the police chief directly. He was reported to have challenged Caussidière to a duel, which Caussidière refused. This seems entirely plausible. In the following years, when Napoleon III was Emperor, his policemen gave their own version of what happened: 'Barthélemy then proposed that they should place in a hat, or ballot box, two pieces of paper – the one white and the other black – and that whoever drew the black should blow out his own brains in the presence of his opponent!'

Caussidière, who did not suffer from an overdeveloped sense of personal honour, quite justifiably evaded this unnecessary contretemps with death. Circumstances, however, would give Barthélemy a far nobler cause for which to fight.

7

BLOOD AND SAND
IN THE STREETS

We do well to remember that the French government established by the February revolution of 1848 was the very first ever to include a socialist minister. And in Louis Blanc, here was a man who would be a dedicated socialist to his last days, and in 1848 he was the avowed representative of the revolutionary working class. It was an extraordinary triumph for a movement which had barely struggled into existence. Nothing like it had ever been seen.

There was widespread expectation, therefore, that the Provisional Government in France would do something for the workers. From our vantage point we are well used to the idea of governments promising heaven and the stars for ordinary people before dutifully bowing to the demands of market stability, hierarchy and the status quo. In February 1840, however, all seemed possible. It was this o'er-vaunting ambition which made the bourgeois majority of the French Provisional Government all the more anxious to reach settled waters.

In practical terms at least, something had to be done about unemployment. The number of businesses in Paris declined during the year of revolution by no less than 54 per cent. The rich were fleeing, and the luxury trade that was the mainstay of so many artisanal workshops was killed. By the spring of 1848, according to official figures, of 343,000 Parisian workers – men, women and children – 186,000 were out of work. Every day the unemployed would gather on the Champs-Élysées, set up makeshift stalls, and desperately attempt to sell or pawn their few remaining goods. 'Dentists' chairs, sideshows, and stalls where cutlets were fried filled the walks, also weighing machines – although,' it was reported, 'people did not like to get weighed because they were all thinner.'

Lamartine's government had to make some kind of concession to Louis Blanc and his followers. On 28 February, ministers established a 'Commission for the Workers' at the Luxembourg Palace, formerly the aristocratic upper house of parliament. Representatives from the workshops and left-wing intellectuals were invited to meet, mix and discuss, a permanent committee of the working classes, seeking to represent all trades. Louis Blanc was its undisputed leader as president, with Albert as his vice-deputy. The programme issued by this 'socialist parliament', calling for worker-run 'social workshops', clearly derived from Blanc's particular ideal, his 'organisation of labour'. One worker representative, Martin Nadaud, was a mason. That he ran his own collaborative team of building workers showed the potential for these social workshops. That he could only attend one meeting of the Commission, because otherwise his contractor boss would bring in a new team, showed the difficulties of realising the dream. Still, there was clearly enthusiasm. In Paris alone, 300 cooperative associations involving 120 trades and 50,000 members were set up during the four years of the second French Republic.

Separately from this, National Workshops were set up by the anti-socialist minister Pierre Marie. They were not the cooperative workshops envisaged by Blanc. He had wanted the organisation of individual trades, but the National Workshops admitted anyone and set tasks unrelated to the workers' skills.

Blanc later complained that they 'humiliated the working man, who was reduced to *accept* the bread which he desired to *earn*'. These were essentially traditional public work programmes and were modelled by the government to serve as a drilled army against the socialists. In his memoirs, Lamartine recalled how Marie organised them as 'a praetorian army in waiting, controlled and directed by leaders privy to the secret plans of the anti-socialist part of the government'. In the eyes of most people, however, the National Workshops subsidised idleness and incubated disorder. They did much to de-legitimise the socialist left – being a caricature of their ideals – while at the same time building up an army which could be used against it.

The National Workshops were particularly unpopular in the countryside, where peasants felt that money was being wasted on the upkeep of the dregs of Paris. Blanqui was to call the heavy tax imposed on the peasants 'the death sentence of the Republic'. It certainly did little to generate support for republicans in the coming elections for a Constituent Assembly. Aware that the French nation was by no means republican, Ledru-Rollin dispatched commissioners as 'republican missionaries' across the country, including former secret society activists such as Félix Pyat sent to Allier and Charles Delescluze to Lille. In the short time they had before elections were held, they made little headway. The peasantry never had much love for emissaries from the city. The new language of the Republic cut little ice with rural folk. They scratched their heads, turned away, and went to the local priest for advice.

Lamartine wanted the elections to be held as quickly as possible, to validate the revolution, while Louis Blanc vociferously argued that they should be put off for as long as possible to give time for republican ideas to filter out across the countryside. This was not an entirely fanciful conceit. In 1851 it would be the peasants of the South of France who were to put up most vigorous resistance to Louis Napoleon Bonaparte's *coup d'état* against the Republic. But in 1848, things were quite different. Time was not on the republicans' side.

Defeated in cabinet debate, Blanc attempted to mobilise the crowd to put pressure on his fellow ministers. A large deputation, led by delegates of the workers' Luxembourg Commission, set out to the government palace on 16 April, demanding that elections be delayed. The marchers called for the organisation of labour and shouted for the 'abolition of the proletariat', so that workers might instead become independent co-owners of their cooperative enterprises. They surged forward, proudly dressed in baggy workmen's blouses and loose-fitting trousers, in bright if dusty colours. Many brought with them the tools of their trade. Ledru-Rollin equivocated, but then authorised force to be used against the demonstrators. They were met by National Guards – one detachment, ironically, led by Blanqui's estranged comrade, Barbès – and soldiers were brought into Paris for the first time since the fall of the monarchy. The National Guards were resplendent in tight blue uniforms with red piping and shoulder tassels. Their headwear looked like a top hat – comfortingly bourgeois – with an embossed plate on the front depicting a rooster clutching Jupiter above clasped hands. A red pom-pom set it off. With their crimson trousers, soldiers of the line were an even more impressive sight. Behind them, workers ferried from the National Workshops to support the troops shouted, 'Down with the communists!' Blanc's demonstration was swiftly broken up, and when Ledru-Rollin met with its leaders, he rebuked them. Elections were adjourned only for a short time, to 23 April, with the right-wing 'Party of Order', led by Adolphe Thiers and strong in the provinces, winning a handsome victory.

The elections only served to stir the pot. On 4 May, *Le Représentant du Peuple* warned that they had done nothing to calm class conflict:

The bourgeoisie is determined to finish with the proletarian, who in turn is determined to finish with the bourgeois, the worker wants to finish with the capitalist, the employee with the contractor, the departments with Paris, peasants with the workers. In all hearts anger and hatred, threats in every mouth. What is the cause of this discord? The elections! Universal suffrage has lied to the people.

An unarmed workers' uprising in Rouen, in protest against the election results, was bloodily suppressed by the National Guard, leaving fifty-nine dead and several hundred wounded. The Rouen Court of Appeals characterised the socialist municipal workshops there as 'a vast hotbed of insurrection' where 'workers were incessantly incited against the employers, where the most perverse doctrines were taught, which can be summarised in the following words: hatred and death to the rich, to all those who own, to all friends of order and of true liberty'. The National Workshops in Paris were as yet nothing like as political, but despite Pierre Marie's best efforts there is no doubt that they left plenty of time for underemployed workers to mutter, grumble, and increasingly to vent their bitterness. 'Communists' might be the target for their resentment today, but tomorrow it could just as easily be the ministers of the government.

The new government, formed after the elections and excluding the *démoc-socs*, wished to suppress centres of sedition in Paris itself. They moved first to close down Louis Blanc's Luxembourg Commission. On 13 May, it held its last official session. The government did not even deign to discuss its report.

On 15 May, the streets of Paris were filled with a huge unarmed crowd of working-class men and women. They were allowed by the National Guard to penetrate into the Constituent Assembly. Surprised, the mob's leaders had no concrete request other than that the government undertake war on Russia to restore Polish sovereignty. The cause of Poland was always close to democratic hearts in nineteenth-century Europe. But such a quixotic and cataclysmic demand was indicative of little more than confusion on the part of the insurgents. To restore some focus, Blanqui made a dramatic appearance, addressing the Assembly in his dry, caustic voice. He only briefly referred to Poland, before attacking the class oppression of the masses and demanding revenge for the massacre at Rouen. Alexis de Tocqueville, a conservative liberal, was filled with horror. He was viscerally disgusted by Blanqui's prison pallor, his 'sunken, withered cheeks, white lips, and a sickly, malign, dirty look like a pallid, mouldy corpse .... He looked as if he had lived in a sewer and only just come out.'

Barbès attempted to persuade the crowd to retire, but another leader, Huber, thought by some to be a police agent, cried out, 'The Assembly is dissolved!' The crowd carried Barbès to the Hôtel de Ville, where he felt obliged to proclaim a revolutionary government and issued a few futile decrees. These favoured dictatorship of the working class, with the bourgeois National Guard replaced by a 'Workers Guard'. The National Guard had little difficulty in breaking up this *émeute* and arresting Barbès and other conspirators within the hour. After a few days on the run, Blanqui was also picked up and returned to prison, there to further develop the sickly complexion that so disgusted de Tocqueville.

The radical clubs had been defeated. And with that came the rapid demise of the National Workshops. On 21 June, an edict was issued ordering all their beneficiaries between the ages of seventeen and twenty-five to enlist in the army. Others without work were to be deported to the countryside. The novelist Gustave Flaubert described the reaction of the unemployed workers:

Many of them were, in fact, skilled craftsmen who regarded farming as degrading; in a word, it was a trap, an insult and a categorical denial of earlier promises. But if they resisted, force would be used, of that they were certain, and they were taking steps to forestall it.

There were now some 100,000 men and their families dependent on the National Workshops, far more than the drilled anti-socialist brigades of April. And they were no longer an army of reaction, but an inchoate mass increasingly influenced by socialistic ideas. A large procession took their rather incoherent demands to Luxembourg Palace, where formerly worker representatives had sat in assembly. When these met with no satisfaction, the petitioners scattered back into their quartiers with fury in their hearts.

As clouds gathered in the thundery sky, crowds massed on the Right Bank of the Seine.

At about 9 o'clock the crowds gathered at the Bastille and the Châtelet [in Les Halles] surged up on to the boulevard. From the Porte Saint-Denis to the Porte-Saint-Martin there was nothing but a swarming mass, dark blue, almost black, in colour, amongst which you could glimpse men with burning eyes and pale faces drawn with hunger and fired by injustice.

At ten o'clock on the night of 22 June, as rain fell from the black sky, insurrection broke out. A barricade was erected near the Porte St-Denis and on it was raised a flag inscribed 'Du Pain ou la Morte' (Bread or Death). Two women climbed up beside it and cried out to the people, calling on them to revolt. One of them was a well-known character in the Quartier St Denis. She stood in the wind and the rain, a strikingly beautiful figure with long black hair, wearing a light blue silk dress, and with head and arms uncovered. The soldiers were maddened by these viragos, as they saw them, stirring up bloodshed. Both women were shot down.

On the Left Bank, families receiving relief through the National Workshops had been used to gathering at the Place du Panthéon to receive their meagre stipend. Now 10,000 men, women and children stood there silently in the dark. An anonymous man was hoisted up on to the shoulders of others, and he addressed the workers, calling on them to rise in rebellion. Suddenly the crowd broke up. One strong column headed across the Seine to the Faubourg Saint-Antoine. Another descended the rue Saint-Jacques – 'preceded by a hundred children carrying candles' – making for the Hôtel de Ville.

The insurrection flared. Within a couple of days more than 1,000 barricades were erected, some tottering and slipshod but many formidably engineered constructions. More than half the city, including strategic points in the centre, was under rebel control. Lacking leadership and direction they failed to seize the Hôtel de Ville, however. It was a doomed rising from the start. The insurgents had just short of 50,000 fighters, out of a working-class population of 300,000 of both sexes. There were probably just as many in the National and Mobile Guards, who with the regular army made up the 80,000 troops mobilised to crush the insurrection. Even Caussidière's security police took sides against the rebellion.

The insurgents had no prominent political leaders. Neither Louis Blanc nor even Auguste Blanqui thought that a rising was wise – and from abroad Karl Marx also thought it untimely. This was a spontaneous rebellion of despair, but we should not forget that it was roughly bound together by the basic socialist demands of the right to work and the organisation of labour. One captured rebel interrogated by an army officer gave 'as the reason for the revolt the desire for a democratic and social republic ... the right of workers to form associations and to take part, according to their ability, in public and private enterprises'. This, in fact, was not a bad summation of social republicanism as it was then understood. Modern historians, jealous of their hard-won and expensive education, are far too inclined to assume that the untutored masses have no idea about politics. Actually, if people only fought in response to deprivation and desperation, they would hardly ever cease fighting.

The Constituent Assembly declared itself to be in 'permanent session', the old formula from the French Revolution signalling a suspension of the constitution, and granted dictatorial powers to suppress the rising to General Louis-Eugène Cavaignac, himself a republican, son of a Jacobin and brother of a famously principled anti-monarchist politician who had died in 1845. Perhaps only a military leader with such an unimpeachable political pedigree could deploy full force against a popular rebellion challenging the actually existing Republic.

Cavaignac waited for the rebels to build up steam and prepared to lay siege against the rebel-held streets. The army's artillery was to be deployed without remorse. They would sweep the streets clean with grapeshot. The regular army was supported by the largely middle-class National Guard and the Garde Mobile drawn from working-class slums. This collision of government and rebels might have been a 'servile war' between the classes, but it was also to a considerable extent a civil war within the working masses. Emmanuel Barthélemy had no role to play in the outbreak of the insurrection – he was not even in Paris at the time. But he would not stand aside. As soon as he learnt of this titanic duel between the workers and the government he felt compelled to join it.

Barthélemy would later write an account of his participation in the 'June Days' while in exile. As one might expect, it was an efficient dispatch without histrionics. He finished it on 26 December 1849, and it was subsequently published, though it was quite heavily redacted to pass the censor. It is the longest piece of prose we have from him and, in it, we hear his voice, and we look through his eyes at a turning point in history.

The piece was introduced by Barthélemy as an eyewitness account, not explicitly political in form but political in intent: 'The insurrection of June 1848, despite the stories that have been published, is not yet sufficiently known. It is the duty of every democrat to bring their share of materials on the history of this great struggle. I shall discharge this duty by telling the events of which I have been an actor or witness.' As the only rebel barricade commander of the June Days to leave a narrative, he had a dramatic tale to tell.

On the first day of the insurrection, the government was not too concerned. A strong force protected the Hôtel de Ville, and two insurgent barricades nearby, in the rue Blanche-Mibray, were easily taken by the National Guard. Rain fell in torrents, and it was hoped that the ardour of the rebels would be dampened. In reality, the rebellion was consolidating itself in the working-class districts. Its focus and citadel was the Faubourg Saint-Antoine, one of the oldest districts of Paris on the Right Bank of the Seine. Across the river, insurgents also held the Latin Quarter around the Panthéon. If they were to descend from the Right Bank down the rue St Denis and from the Left Bank along the rue St Jacques, they would meet on the bridge, Pont Notre-Dame, just above the Hôtel de Ville. General Cavaignac ordered his men to prevent the insurgents meeting up, and a sharp battle was fought at the Pont St Michel to block the approach from the Left Bank. It was a macabre place for a clash of arms, for it took place beside the morgue, or 'Dead House', where anonymous bodies retrieved from the Seine were exposed on tables so they might be identified by friends or relatives. By nightfall the barricade on the bridge that had been erected was taken by cannon, and there was a new set of corpses to add to the half-decomposed cadavers dragged from the river.

General Lamoricière, meanwhile, cleared the barricades in the Faubourgs Saint-Martin, Saint-Denis and Poissonnière on the Right Bank. Despite the assistance of Cavaignac, however, he was unable to overrun the Faubourg du Temple. As darkness fell, fighting died down, and throughout the night artillery trundled towards Paris.

Barthélemy had expected an insurrection for some time. He had little confidence in the government, and so far as he was concerned, the rebellion had erupted because the workers had foolishly abandoned their barricades after February and allowed the government to break its promises. The timing of the outbreak took him by surprise. He was with his family at Vitry-sur-Seine, about four miles from the city centre, when, on 23 June, the beating of drums in the town to call up reservists alerted him to the fact that 'Paris was in full insurrection'. Barthélemy mobilised for the insurgents. 'At this unexpected news, I left immediately, despite the rain, and arrived in Paris by the barrière de Fontainebleau, which I found highly barricaded and guarded by a fairly large number of men, only some of whom were armed with rifles, mostly unloaded for lack of ammunition.' Everywhere he went he found 'improvised fortresses but poorly armed and almost completely devoid of ammunition'. At this point, on Friday, 23 June, at five o'clock, it seemed to him that the government could easily have put down the rising with 2,000 men. Yet Cavaignac, Barthélemy believed, wished for a formidable rising so that it could be fully smashed.

As Barthélemy journeyed across Paris, he came across National Guards swearing their determination to do away with the revolutionaries who had imposed themselves upon the Republic. Those on the barricades, in contrast, were thinking only in defensive terms. A captured rebel was to tell his court-martial that he and his comrades had built their defences 'because they [the Government] wanted to send the workers away from Paris. We did not mean any harm. We thought it was just like it had been in February.' But it was not to be. The government was determined to destroy the insurgency, not to reach a deal with it.

After unsuccessfully trying to reach the Faubourg Saint-Marceau, Barthélemy crossed through the Paris Louvre, the Palais National and the Porte Saint-Martin, finally arriving at the Faubourg du Temple, where he met friends. This district, in the north-east of the city, flanked the Faubourg du Saint-Antoine, the epicentre of the revolt. The two districts were connected by the rue St Maur.

A British journalist and artist for the *Illustrated London News* saw the great barricade closing off the Faubourg du Saint-Antoine. 'Here,' he wrote:

I inspected the famous barricade: it was as high as the first floor and more than ten feet deep; the top was covered with double rows of well-armed men. A small passage near the corners was left, through which I passed. When inside this barricade, I was compelled to work like everybody else at removing the pavement, only to show that I sympathise with the insurgents. After this display of *bon volonté*, I was at liberty, and went up the faubourg to the fifth barricade, showing my dirty palms and muddy coat every time when called upon to assist, to prove that I had contributed my share. The aspect of the faubourg was formidable: one universal feeling pervading all the population; women, old men, children, and entire families were in the street, not at their doors, but in the very middle next with the workmen.

The barricades bristled with armed men and planted flags, and the windows and house-tops were crowded with people. Like Barthélemy, many of the insurgents had originally come from outside Paris itself. It was estimated that only one seventh had been born in the city. There were jubilant shouts and worried murmurings, the clatter of barriers being reinforced under the direction of older men, and the crack of firearms being set off. The smell of cordite hung in the air.

In the Temple district itself the atmosphere was much more sober. Here rebellion was being treated as a deadly serious business. Many of the locals worked in small metal shops in the decorative trade – *sertisseurs*, as Barthélemy had been. They were the elite of the June 1848 insurrection, using their technical skills to improvise bullets – moulded in sewing thimbles – and even to construct a cannon by boring through a length of requisitioned cast iron.

The central barricade of the Temple district was notable for its formidable solidity. It was virtually a fortress, spotted with small gaps through which weapons could be fired. Victor Hugo, who observed it from behind government lines, was awestruck. In an excursus on the June Days, which he included in *Les Misérables*, he set down his indelible memories of the scene:

> ... you could see in the distance, beyond the canal, at the very top of the street that climbs the slopes of Belleville, a strange wall ... built of cobblestones. It was plumb-straight, perfectly aligned, precise, perpendicular, squared, level .... Discernible at intervals in its grey surface were almost invisible loopholes, like black threads. These loop-holes were equally spaced .... Rising at the end of the street, this barrier created a dead end. A wall, still and qui-et. No one to be seen, nothing to be heard. Not a cry, not a sound, not a breath. A sepulchre. This terrible thing was bathed in the dazzling June sunlight. It was the Faubourg du Temple barricade.

On the remaining cobbles before the barricade lay a few corpses in pools of blood. 'I remember a white butterfly coming and going in the street,' wrote Hugo.

François Lecuyer, a captain in the National Guard and supporter of Ledru-Rollin, was nominally in charge of the rebel barricades at the Faubourg du Temple. In his subsequent trial, Lecuyer was to claim that he had been coerced into taking command by the local workers of the National Workshops, against his protestations. 'They would not listen to me. I had no strength and I was overwhelmed. I resigned myself to dying as a martyr.' Barthélemy vehemently denied that Lecuyer had done anything but take the command voluntarily. Lecuyer's role, moreover, was purely moral. The actual direction of the struggle was organised by veteran republicans belonging to the radical clubs. Barthélemy was, of course, a Blanquist, and he was quickly operating as a de facto officer.

On Saturday morning, the second day of the insurrection, the National Assembly issued a decree: 'Paris is in a state of siege. All powers are concentrated in the hands of General Cavaignac.' Proclamations were posted announcing a curfew. The National Guard patrolled the streets, stopping men, searching women, and arresting street-sellers suspected of ferrying aid to the insurgents. Barked orders told residents to move back from their windows. It was an oppressive and overcast weekend. Troops, artillery and munition carts clattered through the streets. Across the city rolled the dull heavy sound of cannon firing, buildings collapsing and barricades falling in.

Military operations opened with an attack on the Panthéon on the Left Bank – a grand mausoleum for heroes of the nation – occupied by 1,500 insurgents. The area was soon a storm of musketry and cannon fire. At length, the soldiers forced their way through the Panthéon's brass gates. Outgunned, its defenders retreated, but when they came up against a force of

Garde Mobile in their rear, they laid down their arms. The great fortress of the insurrection on the Left Bank had fallen.

On the Right Bank, meanwhile, General Lamoricière, short of troops, had been unable to consolidate his victories of the previous day, and new barricades had risen in Rochechouart, St Denis and Poissonnière. These were clustered around a half-mile stretch of the old city wall, and enclosed a patch of wasteland – surrounded by commanding buildings and scattered with blocks of stone for a large hospital under construction – called the Clos St Lazare. It presented a formidable defensive stronghold for the insurgents, protecting the flank of the Faubourg Saint-Antoine. Fighting raged here all day. There were now two main outposts shielding the rebel heartland of the Faubourg Saint-Antoine from attack: the Clos St Lazare and the Saint-Martin Canal.

Paris was now fully at war, a fratricidal struggle between republican brothers. A pro-government contemporary bemoaned the scene.

> The streets of Paris have a sinister and desert aspect like that of a dead city. All men are in combat, all women at the windows or on the doors, seeking news. At the sound of the grapeshot, which, from minute to minute, tears the air, the whole population trembles; every woman asks herself if this is the blow which has taken from her a husband, a son, a friend. On the different sides of the struggle ... what a strange and terrible spectacle, these thousands of citizens joining in the same cry of love: Fraternity! the same cry of war: Liberty! the same rallying cry: Long live the Republic!

One insurgent took aim from a window at an approaching National Guard, only to recognise him at the last minute as his own son.

From Friday to Saturday night, Barthélemy took command of the rue Grange-aux-Belles, 'a long, straggling, miserable street' boasting the largest number of barricades on the Right Bank. His anchor point was the locks of the Canal Saint-Martin. This was the barrier dividing the Faubourg du Temple from the Faubourg Saint-Antoine, and the last line of defence before the citadel of the insurrection could be penetrated by government troops. Crossing the canal, which ran through the Faubourg du Temple, was a double-level bridge; one was for carriages – and could be raised for passing boats – another was for pedestrians. Houses formed a semicircle on each side of the lock, from which streets radiated. Barthélemy ordered these approaches to be barricaded, and when the defences were ready he went scouting to check on enemy troop movements. He planned to go all the way to the Hôtel de Ville but was intercepted by National Guards at the entrance of rue Saint-Martin. His companion was captured, but Barthélemy 'miraculously escaped arrest', and he returned to his post and resumed command. Despite all his efforts to organise a solid resistance, Barthélemy was aware that their position was intrinsically weak. The defenders' gunpowder, which they were making themselves from scavenged chemicals, was of low quality and could barely serve. That his fellow insurgents could hold their positions at all, Barthélemy contended, was entirely due to the vigour of their fight.

On Saturday morning, Barthélemy had the barricades reinforced, and then he organised the disarming of people in the area who were not participating in the barricade fighting: 'no violence took place, properties and people were respected'. Food supplies for the barricade defenders were either given voluntarily or paid for with signed vouchers. Though Lecuyer would take credit for this orderly behaviour during his trial, Barthélemy denied that he was at all responsible: 'he himself said that his influence was zero outside the action of combat. If order had prevailed, it is only by the natural and spontaneous impulse of honour and probity' that characterised the masses.

Barthélemy rejected accusations that his men had domineered and terrorised the local population. Specifically, he refuted the allegation of a retired officer, Adjutant-Major Stack, that he had been threatened with death. Barthélemy had arrested Stack and questioned him politely about his identity and profession and his reasons for being in the area. 'He replied by giving me a false name and a false profession and by indicating intentions that were certainly not true. This gentleman was very pale, he was very scared and it is probably the troubled imagination that created in his mind the chimerical dangers to which he now believes himself to have been exposed.' Though closely questioned and guarded, all prisoners were 'treated fraternally'. Their wounds were bandaged and they were well fed, despite the general shortage of supplies.

On the Saturday night, Barthélemy's barricades on the Grange-aux-Belles were quiet, but a concentrated attack, led personally by General Cavaignac, fell on the barricade at St Maur, connecting the Temple and Saint-Antoine faubourgs. For three hours the defenders withstood fire from four or five pieces of cannon and hundreds of muskets. Two generals and about 400 soldiers were killed or wounded in the engagement. The assault was repulsed and the local barracks of the Garde Mobile were captured by an insurgent bayonet charge. Barthélemy denied allegations that the premises were wantonly looted. Nothing was taken except arms, ammunition and food, he said.

Barthélemy and his comrades were jubilant. Though lacking ammunition they were 'determined to be bombarded rather than let our adversaries pass through our area'. They believed that the enemy was weakening. But they had little idea of what was happening in the rest of the city. British reporters, enjoying relative freedom of movement, were in a better situation to see the grim reality:

The line [regular army], the National Guard, and the [Garde] Mobile marched up with cannon to each barricade, and once its strength loosened, charged at the bayonet, killing all whom they found either in arms, or with faces blackened with [gun] powder. Few prisoners were made in this quarter, which was the scene of many a horrid and cold-blooded massacre. When the insurgents, having thrown down their arms and demanded a quarter, found they were about to be slaughtered, they would kneel down, receive the shots coolly, and die, crying Vive la Republique! ... At one barricade, in the Rue Planche Mibray, forty prisoners were made. Every one was put up against the barricade and shot, amid the savage and exulting shouts of the soldiery, [Garde] Mobile and the bourgeoisie, always rabid in the hour of victory.

The vice was closing.

By Sunday morning, the third day of the insurrection, General Cavaignac had a clear plan of campaign. Two columns, one attacking through the Clos St Lazare in the north-west and the other from the Hôtel de Ville in the south, would meet in the Place de la Bastille and so cut off the Faubourg Saint-Antoine. After difficult fighting, inch by inch, the Clos Saint-Lazare fell to government troops, and the Faubourg du Temple was left exposed to attack. From the centre of the city, meanwhile, sappers and miners were being employed to tunnel under barricades. The winding streets made it near impossible to bring cannon to bear, and the insurgents had knocked through interior walls so they could pass to and fro under cover. 'The whole neighbourhood was in fact one immense fortress, which it was necessary to demolish stone by stone. The besiegers paid a heavy price in blood for their victory.' A British journalist witnessed 'heroism on both sides ... the burning houses, the rumbling work of the miners, the steady platoon fire of the insurgents, the charges, the retreats, the ambuscades and feints ... [an] awful and terrible struggle'.

One by one they fell and the insurgents, beaten from one stronghold, retreated to another.

The two columns met at the Place de la Bastille, with only the canal blocking their entry into the Faubourg Saint-Antoine. Paris held its breath. The anarchist thinker, Pierre-Joseph Proudhon – who thought the insurrection inopportune but in a just cause – perched in a house opposite the Canal Saint-Martin to admire the 'sublime horror' of the cannonade to come.

Around 9 a.m., Barthélemy was interrupted while he was interrogating a sergeant taken prisoner overnight. He was told that an attack force had presented itself with artillery on the Grange-aux-Belles street on the Right Bank of the Saint-Martin Canal. 'I immediately headed there, and after dodging a couple of gunshots from the front line, I opened fire.'

A battle lasting about six hours ensued. Artillery fire rained down on their barricade, but 'there were no casualties thanks to the poor aim of the artillery that was vomiting upon us a rain of useless bullets and projectiles'. The commander leading the enemy attack column attempted a flanking action, bypassing the greatest strength of barricade defenders, by over-running the barricade at the locks on the canal. Here Barthélemy's men lacked ammunition, and in much confusion, the fighters defending the barricade retired to the rue St Maur. 'This was a terrible moment,' remembered Barthélemy. Only five men remained, including Barthélemy, to fend off the combined efforts of the regular soldiers, the Garde Mobile and the National Guard.

Red-hot balls whistled all around. Within a quarter of an hour, one of the defending fighters had been hit in his upper chest, another square in the forehead, and a third had his right arm broken near the shoulder. Still the attackers did not dare launch a bayonet charge to seize the barricade. They assumed that the paucity of fire from the other side was due to 'calculated prudence' rather than a lack of fighters. Barthélemy and the one other fighter still standing continued to hold back for more than two hours the hundreds of men and horses facing them, until they had used up all their own ammunition and that of their fallen comrades. Only then did they retire, carrying back the wounded and leaving the dead on the battlefield. The onslaught had been intense. Three houses were nearly entirely destroyed and the bridge across the canal was 'liberally festooned' with bullets and cannonballs. Arriving back 'in the middle of those who had abandoned us,' recalled Barthélemy, 'we saw that indeed they completely lacked ammunition, and if they had tried to stay with us they would have been exposed to withering fire without the ability to retaliate'.

Barthélemy approached Lecuyer, the nominal commander, to angrily ask why the cartridges he had requested during the fight at the Grange-aux-Belles barricades had not arrived. Lecuyer protested that he lacked ammunition himself. The command was, in Barthélemy's opinion, 'in an indescribable state of disorder'. Men had been demoralised by the arrival of a mysterious letter from the centre of Paris carrying news of retreats and massacres. 'Lecuyer was prepared to enjoy the benefits of victory,' wrote Barthélemy scornfully, 'but not to suffer the consequences of the defeat that was becoming increasingly inevitable.' Lecuyer's men, suspecting him of wishing to desert, were maintaining an active surveillance on him. 'I heard on that occasion a worker say: "It is you who made me build the barricades and provoke the *Mobiles*. Now we are nearing defeat, you will share the common fate because if you try to abandon us the last ball [bullet] will be for you."' Barthélemy commented: 'It was probably this threat, well deserved by Lecuyer, which made him say that he had been forced to take part in the insurrection. He should have remembered that it was made on Sunday evening, when there was no longer any possible doubt on the outcome of events.'

The insurgents no longer had sufficient ammunition with which to fend off the well-provisioned army of General Lamoricière. Lecuyer was in full nervous collapse, so Barthélemy 'resolved to use every honourable means to save the men who had taken part in the action on the left bank of the canal'. Barthélemy left Lecuyer and returned to the barricade at the Grange-aux-Belles. In his absence, however, it had been abandoned by its worker defenders and had been overrun. While he and the insurgents had protected local property, Barthélemy observed, the National Guard had ransacked neighbouring houses. Barthélemy searched out and located some loaded guns and powder in a nearby house, and with these staged a counter-attack on the Grange-aux-Belles barricade. Knowing the area well, he led a team, dodging through houses and knocking through walls, to appear suddenly behind the enemy. The National Guard retreated in disorder, with only a few wounded on both sides. At this point, Barthélemy claimed, he was in a position to cut off and kill a National Guard detachment, but he exercised mercy and allowed them to retreat unmolested.

The suddenness of the surprise counter-attack convinced the government forces that the insurgents under Barthélemy's command had more ammunition than they actually held. Some of them decided to negotiate an honourable surrender for the rebels, if they could. After about an hour, five National Guardsmen, commanded by Lieutenant Boucher, approached in order to demand arrangements to end the fighting.

The parley between both parties was cordial, and Barthélemy and two comrades returned with Boucher to meet with the colonel commanding the line infantry, a man called Blanchard. The regular soldiers, stationed on the right bank of the canal with their cannons pointing towards the bridge, had not changed their position since the beginning of the battle. They were greatly agitated to see three armed insurgents approach and their first instinct was to fire on them, but Captain Ribot, Lieutenant Boucher and several other officers dampened their fury. 'I knew from that moment,' wrote Barthélemy, 'that Lieutenant Boucher, animated by the desire to end the civil war, had opened negotiations without consulting anything but his generous sentiments.'

Having exchanged a few words with Colonel Blanchard, Barthélemy was introduced to General Lamoricière, who had established his headquarters at the Café Amand. As Barthélemy recalled: 'The general received us politely and asked me what it was I wanted from him. I replied that I wanted to know the government's intentions with regard to citizens who had taken up arms to defend the Faubourg du Temple. Lamoricière told me that if we wanted to continue the resistance, it would be ruthlessly crushed, and if instead we wanted to surrender, he would intervene for us with the head of the Executive Power [Cavaignac].'

Barthélemy did not consider this to be the guarantee he required – that it would protect the lives and liberty of his men and perhaps thousands of civilians. He refused the conditions offered. An argument ensued, in which Lamoricière warned Barthélemy that the Garde Mobile had the rifles, powder and bullets to force an unconditional surrender. Barthélemy responded with a bluff: 'We too have weapons and I hope that they will be strong enough to confront the dangers that threaten us.' Barthélemy and his party left the general carrying with them a proclamation from General Cavaignac. This acknowledged that the rebels believed themselves to be 'fighting for the welfare of the working classes' and called on them to return 'to the arms of their country'. The aftermath of the June days, Barthélemy would remark bitterly, showed the true value of Cavaignac's embrace.

Back at the barricades at the Grange-aux-Belles and the canal locks, Barthélemy formed his men into a circle, and in their midst read out Cavaignac's offer. He told his attentive audience that he doubted the merciful intentions of the government, and that personally he would not surrender. It was said that the rebel band cheered his defiance. 'Those who were about to die saluted him,' a radical journalist would later write. Barthélemy resigned his post, allowing his men to shift as best they could, but determined to fire the few cartridges he had left as a simple combatant.

The men dispersed, each attempting to find their own escape. As Monday morning dawned, government troops broke into houses and swarmed over the barricades from the upper floors, to find the defences all but abandoned. Only a few stubborn fighters remained. The Garde Mobile commander, in his subsequent report, boasted of inflicting 'cruel losses' and capturing armed insurgents 'whom we shot immediately and without stopping'. As they advanced, firing wildly, the local population, of both sexes and all ages, fled in terror. One man, La Villette, was shot down merely because he was wearing a red blouse, the normal garb for his profession as sailor. Barthélemy blamed the massacre on the virulence of newspaper articles written during the battle:

All these stories of men sawn in two by the insurgents, d'eau-de-vie [brandy] and poisonous bullets, fists and feet cut off, heads still wearing their hats planted on stakes, or transformed into lamps, around which cannibals danced the 'saraband'; this deluge of accusations of looting, rape, and murder ... at the height of the struggle, whipped the victors onto bloody revenge against the vanquished. The wretches who wrote these articles must have on their conscience a heavy weight.

The Temple district was the second-last insurgent stronghold to fall. Its conquerer, General Lamoricière, moved on to the rue de la Roquette, penetrating like a dagger into the Faubourg Saint-Antoine. Resistance finally collapsed. At half-past-one on Monday afternoon, General Cavaignac announced that the rising had been suppressed. Antoine Sénard, president of the National Assembly, announced the news: 'It is all over, gentlemen, thank God!'

Barthélemy, having stashed his weapon, tried to return to the centre of Paris via the Faubourg Saint-Martin. There he was spotted by Captain Ribot of the National Guard, with whom he had amicably parleyed when attempting to negotiate a surrender. 'Unhappily, I called to him,' remembered Ribot. 'What are you doing here? I am compelled to arrest you.' Barthélemy was taken into custody and led away to the Town Hall in the 5th arrondissement. Yet Ribot had remembered his chivalrous behaviour which had saved the lives of the outmanoeuvred National Guard detachment at the Grange-aux-Belles barricade. This, Barthélemy believed, saved his own life. Other prisoners were being simply shot out of hand, if for no other reason than to make room for more prisoners who were being crowded into the cellars of the Tuileries or the military forts.

There were martyrs on both sides. Officers had led government forces from the front and suffered accordingly. 'Never had the battles of the empire been so murderous,' wrote an eyewitness: 'fifteen years of war in Algeria had scarcely cost as many generals and superior officers as those four days of civil war.' General Brea, a hero of the Napoleonic wars, had been captured by insurgents, abused, and was about to be released when approaching National Guards panicked his captors and they buried his own sword into his belly. Archbishop Affre, attempting to mediate, was killed by a random shot. Violent suppression of suspects after the rising further embittered feeling: 'From that day forward a river of blood separated the socialist workers from the republican bourgeoisie.'

Alexander Herzen, an aristocratic Russian exiled from his country for his revolutionary beliefs and resident in Paris in 1848, had seen the 'gloomy faces of the men dragging stones' to make the barricades, the 'women and children ... helping them'. Herzen kept away from the fighting, but he wrote of what he witnessed in Paris in the aftermath:

> After the slaughter which lasted for days, silence descended, the calm of the siege .... The bourgeoisie was triumphant. And the houses in the Faubourg Saint-Antoine were still smoking ... the interiors of rooms laid bare gaped like stone wounds .... But where are the owners, the tenants, where are they? No one gave them a thought. Here and there were men scattering sand in the streets, but the blood nevertheless kept oozing through ...

Herzen tasted the bitter cud of righteous fury. 'Moments like these make one hate for a whole decade, seek revenge all one's life. *Woe to those who forgive such moments!*' But how was one to bear the blasting of hope? Did one retreat into fanaticism or shed youthful illusions?

> Which is better? It is hard to tell.
> One leads to the bliss of lunacy.
> The other to the unhappiness of knowledge.

Herzen, as we shall see, came to know Barthélemy well. It is certain that Barthélemy did not forgive. Whether he lived in the bliss of lunacy or the unhappiness of knowledge is not so easy to say.

8

ESCAPE INTO A STORM

The June Days had been 'by far the bloodiest insurrection that Paris had yet experienced'. The city had endured a blizzard of lead. During the four days of fighting, 7 million cartridges had been distributed to government forces. All in all, 400 to 500 rebels had been killed on the June Days barricades. But more than 3,000 had been massacred in the aftermath by the soldiers of the Garde Mobile and the regular army. A total of 11,642 people were arrested, 80 per cent of them manual workers, including artisans and small employers. Barthélemy was one of those facing a heavy sentence. Lucky to be alive, he was held in custody until he could be court-martialled before a specially constituted 'Council of War'.

Initially Barthélemy was returned to the prison at Brest where he had served out his first sentence, but from there he was soon moved to the new military prison on the rue du Cherche-Midi in central Paris. Construction had begun in 1847, on the site of the old Good Shepherd Abbey. It combined the new cellular system – to maximise control of prisoners – with closely guarded dormitories. Large exterior walls of rough unshapen flint formed a rectangle three storeys high. Within this imposing structure were ponderous doors and heavy bolts, stone passages and broad corridors, solid staircases and deeply sunken windows, all oppressing the inmates with their gravity and power.

It was here that Barthélemy fell in with a leading revolutionary he had not seen since April 1848: Dr Cyrille Lacambre, a medical doctor, vice-president of the Central Republican Society and a close aide to Auguste Blanqui. His first cell was 'a kennel with oozing walls, the floor covered with semi-liquid filth ... [his bed] swarming with lice'. However, the authorities were not in complete control of the prison population, and well-organised revolutionary prisoners pressured and intimidated the warders. Lacambre managed to get himself moved from an isolation cell to one on the third floor. During the hours when he was allowed to mix with the general prison population, he was able to collect accounts from prisoners who had fought in the June Days. He was keen to escape the prison in order to bring their stories to public notice. A dedicated and methodical Blanquist, Lacambre was determined that the lessons of the failed rising be known and understood, so that the next insurrection would succeed.

Lacambre and Barthélemy made plans for escape. But they could not do so immediately as Barthélemy was in weak health, having fallen seriously ill in Brest, probably with smallpox. He recovered, but they decided not to make their break until Barthélemy had appeared in front of the court-martial, in the hope that he could seize the opportunity to secure and smuggle back into prison items that might be of use: a screwdriver, a small hacksaw, pliers, an iron 'rat-de-cave' candlestick, and some matches.

Barthélemy was still only aged twenty-six when, on 8 January 1849, he went up before the Council of War, established just across the street from the prison to try the June insurgents. This was a military court presided over by Colonel Cornemuse of the 17th Light Infantry Regiment. Himself a republican,

he was not unsympathetic to the defendant. The trial opened
at 10 a.m. with evidence demonstrating that Barthélemy had
acted as a barricade commander. Barthélemy handled himself
with characteristic coolness and acuity. 'His face had a noble
and energetic expression, his manners were fine, his words
carefully chosen.' When, in reference to his conviction in 1839,
Barthélemy was called an assassin, he protested vigorously
and refused to be silenced. 'I should remain silent when my
honour has been attacked? No, I must, I will reply ... Do you
think to terrorise me with your threats? I've already seen that
in the barricades, and here is no different – I have no fear of
you.' Barthélemy was applauded and Cornemuse had to clear
the public gallery.

Barthélemy continued to protest. He had been imprisoned
because, when 'given the choice either to denounce my former
comrades, or to go to the galleys', he had 'preferred the latter.
This is the truth, my word of honour!' Colonel Cornemuse
objected that a jury of his peers – men of his class – had
been lenient with him because of his youth. Barthélemy shot
back:

> Forgive me, you speak of men of my class. But is it not a
> joke to call a jury of the bourgeoisie, 'men of my class'? I
> would admit this designation if you were to speak to me
> of a jury sitting in judgement composed of craftsmen, as
> I am one. But did those who condemned me at that time
> have the same interests as me? Was I their equal? You can-
> not claim that.

Barthélemy objected to being treated as a common criminal.
In fighting on the barricades he had done nothing more than
the street fighters of February 1848, lionised as heroes by the
Republic. 'In 1839, instead of being condemned as a criminal,
I was condemned as a political enemy,' Barthélemy said. 'We

cannot recognise this distinction,' retorted the Prosecutor, 'in our eyes you are only a galley convict.' Barthélemy replied scornfully: 'And if the February heroes were defeated, would they now be galley convicts?'

When Colonel Cornemuse pointed out that the court represented the French Republic, Barthélemy retorted that it was nothing more than a political trial: 'I beg of you, do not conclude from my words that I traduce your character. No citizen, certainly not! But if I am to do you all justice, I cannot recognise in you any right to sit in judgement; I see in you only my political enemies before me.'

The President of the court proceeded to examine Barthélemy directly:

- You have been seen on the barricades of the street Grange-aux-belles; you are accused of having commanded on one of them. Was it you?
- *Yes!*
- In short, you admit to having participated in the insurrection.
- *Yes!*

Witnesses were then called. Rebillot, a wine merchant, told how Barthélemy sold his own watch for five francs to secure food for the insurgents, and how he had treated a captured officer of the National Guard artillery 'with all due respect, even courtesy'. When asked why, then, he had abandoned his house, Rebillot explained that the 'National Guard were so furious that I was afraid of their ill-treatment. When they overran the barricade, I fled to my neighbour.'

Testimony given by Ribot, himself an officer of the National Guards, was of no more use to the prosecution:

It is my duty to say all that I know, whether it be for the benefit or for the disadvantage of the defendant. Well! I must declare that he generously saved a great number of National Guards. As a result of a false surrender, the insurgents seized a barricade of which we were masters; we found ourselves then in the middle of the street, and exposed to their fire without being able to answer. As soon as Barthélemy saw this, he stopped the shooting and saved our lives.

This act of chivalry, as we have seen, saved Barthélemy's skin: 'I owe my life to the National Guard and Ribot who accompanied me, for instead of leading me to the barracks of rue Saint-Martin, they took me to the Mairie [Town Hall] in the 5th arrondissement, because the guards were shooting prisoners in the barracks.'

Here the President of the court interjected. 'It is well known to us that those guards frequently fired gunshots.' 'I know it well,' replied Barthélemy. 'I could tell you of deeds of unprecedented cruelty which would give you the proof that those insurgents, described as barbarians, were treated with the most profound brutality.' Colonel Cornemuse asked him to elaborate.

Barthélemy explained that he had been moved to a holding pen at the École Militaire. Even here, however, conditions were atrocious. Barthélemy was thrown into a cellar stuffed full of prisoners, with only a grating at pavement level to let in air. The heat was 'suffocating ... since we were very numerous'. Deprived of bread and water, the prisoners soon became desperate, crying out to be fed.

An officer walking up and down in front of the grating heard us:
   'Who complains?' he said.
   'We are hungry, give us bread.'
   'Wait ...!'

He snatched a gun from a guard and fired on us through
  the window. One of us fell.
'Who is still hungry?' he said, chuckling. 'I'll serve him
  next.'

Barthélemy went on to describe how guards had fired into a
cell full of prisoners where one insurgent had lost his reason
and started screaming. When he was brought to the police
prefecture on 3 July, he had seen at least thirty insurgent corpses,
executed while held prisoner. He told the tale of how, when 'a
wounded man fell into the hands of the National Guard, he
was shot and then, as if that was not enough to satisfy their
rage, they took straw, covering him with it, set fire to it, and
roasted him like a pig'.

Only now did the President of the court intervene. 'I cannot
allow you to continue in this way; such stories can only arouse
hate. By the way, crimes have been committed on both sides;
fortunately the rumours spread about it are exaggerated.' This
was true, no doubt, but there had been horrors enough.

As Barthélemy's friend, the Russian intellectual Alexander
Herzen, was later to write, Barthélemy had successfully 'turned
the prisoner's dock into a platform from which to attack the
National Guard'. Nonetheless, he was found guilty of 'having
taken part in an armed struggle aimed at overthrowing the
Government, exciting civil war and bringing looting, killing and
devastation upon the capital, and of having exercised a command
in the insurgency'. He was sentenced, once more, to life in the
galleys. Barthélemy crossed his arms, bent his head, and
muttered, 'For a republican, what an abomination!' Then he
stood and looked at the court President straight in the eye: 'I
hope that this condemnation may never cause you remorse; the
future belongs to me. Long live the democratic social Republic!'

Barthélemy's dramatic testimony certainly resonated with
a growing public scorn for the French bourgeois Republic. But

for many ordinary people in France, parliamentary politics itself had been discredited. Louis Napoleon, who had fought with Italian revolutionaries in 1830, and twice attempted to raise insurrection against the old monarchical regime in France, had been elected to the National Assembly, but refused to play the parliamentary game. He rarely spoke in the Assembly, instead promising in his own person an alternative both to bourgeois politicians and the *démoc-socs*. He was able to attract support from all classes, particularly the peasantry. The conservative 'Party of Order' hankered for a popular authoritarianism to smash the left, and its leader Thiers convinced himself that Louis Napoleon, 'the cretin', would be their docile instrument. After his overwhelming victory in the presidential election of December 1848, held while Barthélemy was still in prison awaiting trial, Louis Napoleon refused to attach himself to any political party or principle: 'I follow only the promptings of my mind and heart .... I shall march straight forward with no moral scruples in the path of honour, with conscience my only guide.' This was a promise of personal dictatorship. While Barthélemy looked forward to a democratic social Republic, the existing democratic Republic lay in peril.

Barthélemy's bravura defence had not been calculated to avoid the inevitable decision of the court martial. Once more he was facing hard labour for life, and was returned to the military prison across the street. Meanwhile, Lacambre, with the careful diligence of his medical profession, had been making further preparations for their escape. He had found in his cell a hatch that allowed workmen access to the roof of the prison. At considerable cost to his fingers, he managed to tear a nail from the oak table in his cell and used it to pick the padlock on the hatch. It opened into the roof space and from here he was able to peer through cracks into the cell block below. Creeping around the roof space every night for a week, Lacambre worked out the routine of the guards. A scheme formed in his mind.

The very laxness of the prison, however, nearly scuppered his plans. Lacambre had smuggled out a letter complaining about his conditions of incarceration, written with a sliver of wood for a pen and watered-down coal dust for ink. When this was published in the national press the embarrassed prison authorities came to him to offer better accommodation on the second floor. But his essential access to the roof would be lost. Thinking quickly, he feigned irrational anger. It is never pleasant to be confronted with fury in response to an offer kindly meant. Throwing up their hands, the prison governors left him where he was.

Lacambre's escape plan was 'simple but risky'. He and Barthélemy would break through the skylight of the 'new' cell block in which they were imprisoned. From here they would climb on to the roof of the taller adjoining 'old' cell block, the first to be completed when the prison was built, which over-looked the garden of a neighbouring building. Atop their roost, the plan was that Lacambre and Barthélemy would tear at the roof slates to reach a joist. Meanwhile, three confederates would be waiting in the rue d'Assas on the other side of the walled garden. Lacambre would throw down a line weighted with lead to the men below, to which they would tie a stout rope. Lacambre would then pull it up, attaching it to the exposed joist. Using this 'air bridge', they hoped to escape by descending hand over hand.

Again, however, circumstances intervened. The plan broke down when it became clear that most prisoners in Cherche-Midi, including Lacambre and Barthélemy, were about to be moved to holding centres in preparation for transportation to penal colonies overseas. The break-out would have to be brought forward, and there was no time to organise the confederates. The two still planned to get on to the roof of the old building, but thereafter they would have to improvise. The escape was set for the night of 10 January, only one day after Barthélemy's trial.

While Lacambre had his own cell on the third floor, however, Barthélemy was still detained in the large dormitory room on the second. Here he was able to use his authority as a barricade commander to mobilise help from his fellow prisoners. A rope had to be fashioned for the escape and one prisoner volunteered his bedding to be torn into strips and woven together. Sacrificing his blankets was to cost him dear. Unprotected from the damp and the chill, he fell ill, the sickness spiralled, and ultimately he lost an eye.

Once material for the rope was secured, the next hurdle was to get Barthélemy from the second floor to the third. Here again, comrades came to his aid as Barthélemy sneaked up there under the cover of disorder generated by a prison riot. He wore a large coat beneath which he hid a change of clothes, the bedding strips and the tools he had smuggled back after his trial. Lacambre, waiting at the barred door to the third floor, managed to persuade the guard holding the key to let Barthélemy through by flattering the guard's enthusiasm for the new president, Louis Napoleon. Once in Lacambre's cell, Barthélemy hid under the bed. When the 6 p.m. roll call was taken, another prisoner on the second floor answered for him.

While waiting for lights-out, Lacambre tried to persuade two other prisoners on the third floor, Schaller and Garnier, to join the escape. Schaller agreed when he saw that Barthélemy was coming. Garnier decided it was too risky, but helped with last-minute preparations.

When the coast was clear, the four men braided the strips of bedding into a rope about seven feet long. Suddenly they were interrupted. The alarm bell sounded and guards rushed up to the third floor. Barthélemy ducked under a mattress. When no guards appeared he gingerly peered out of the cell door.

From this vantage point he saw what had actually transpired and returned to his comrades wearing a wide grin. It turned out that a conscript guard had rung the bell only because he needed the toilet and was looking for someone to relieve his post. His commander was not impressed: 'Vile creature! You need someone to hold your gun. Must they also hold your dick?' The prisoners laughed uproariously, if rather hysterically.

They packaged up into bales a change of clothes for each of the escapees, to be exchanged for their convict uniforms once they were out of the prison, along with the tools and makeshift rope. These bales proved awkward to carry and Barthélemy, being much the strongest, took the largest. Lacambre, somewhat older, carried a smaller one, while Schaller, the slightest of the three, carried nothing at all. They wore thick heavy socks, to minimise any clattering on the roof. Their shoes they carried separately.

At 8 p.m., the escape attempt began. The three men squeezed through the hatch into the roof space. The prisoner left behind, Garnier, sang loudly in the hope of distracting unwonted attention. This might not have been necessary as a violent storm was raging around the prison; what sounded like a hurricane howled at the windows and 'smacked the slates like castanets'. The escapees emerged through a skylight on to the roof of their cell block. It was a stormy night of lashing icy rain, 'as black as the back of an oven', as Barthélemy put it. The roof slates were covered with ice, and the convicts had to be exceptionally careful not to slide to their deaths.

Barthélemy and Lacambre had tied the bales to their waists, leaving their hands free, and allowing Barthélemy to help the struggling Schaller. The three men crawled awkwardly on all fours along the gutter. Lacambre led the way, with Schaller in the middle and Barthélemy bringing up the rear. Eventually they reached the adjoining, taller wing of the prison. On a platform one storey below them they could see a sentry 'wrapped in his winter coat, walking uneasily, in the flickering light of a lantern tormented by storm'. Barthélemy dragged himself on to the higher roof. He drew breath as his comrades huddled in the 'hurricane whirling in fury, chasing us with rain and sleet in our faces. Our socks turned into ice boots.' Barthélemy braced himself and pulled them up. Precariously perched, they needed a platform to work from. Boosted by Lacambre, Barthélemy hoisted himself on to the flat top of a dormer window. From this vantage point, he began tearing up slates to create hand- and foot-holes leading to the chimney stacks at the side of the building.

As Barthélemy inched his way across the roof, pulling up slates as he went, his place on the skylight was taken by Lacambre, who reached over for the slates as Barthélemy removed them. Lacambre's intention was to pass them back to Schaller, who would deposit them in the gutter. But Schaller was so terrified that he could not bring himself to stand up to receive the broken slates from Lacambre's hands. Lacambre was forced to let them fall more than three storeys to the ground below. Despite the noise of the storm, the sentry on the floor below seemed to hear something. He emerged from his box to peer into the night. The prisoners froze. The sentry glanced around and returned to shelter.

By this time Schaller had had enough. He returned to the first skylight, dropped into the roof space again and made his way back to his cell. Unfortunately, he took with him many of the escape tools; in the adrenalin rush of the escape, all three men had forgotten that they had been stuffed into Schaller's shoes. Lacambre felt a pang of despair, but was emboldened by his partner's determination:

Barthélemy continued his tireless work and, from hole to hole, gained ground towards the [chimney stacks]. I would also leave our platform and follow my companion step by step, to collect debris from his hands which I returned to lay atop the skylight. Our progress was slow, the work hard and the cold a cruel aggravation. Though painful we had to insert fingers under each slate to break them off, a very rough operation in its first part. Our hands were mechanically set to the task, and our eyes to the sentry, our nightmare.

The sentry on the ground now heard something and came out to see what it might be. Lacambre threw a slate down at him and, believing that it was the storm ripping tiles off the roof, the guard quickly retreated to the safety of his box.

Barthélemy now realised that the easiest way of dealing with the broken slates was to slide them under those still attached to the roof. Using this method, he was able to move more quickly and reach the balustrade next to the chimney stacks. Forgetting caution, Lacambre clambered towards his comrade, only to find himself running out of hand-holds. Before he knew it he was spreadeagled on the roof, hanging on for dear life. Barthélemy grabbed his heavy bale from him, but Lacambre felt himself slipping:

'I can do no more ...! I'm going to drop ...!' At this cry, Bartholomew shudders. He had not suspected till then. His concentration was elsewhere. A glance reveals it all. 'Not here,' answered his calm voice. 'If you fall, you will make noise and everything will be discovered.' At the same time, with rapid movements, he grabs a rope from the bale, and fashions it into a loop which he floats below me. My foot meets it and is supported .... I breathe.

Barthélemy pulled Lacambre to relative safety.

By this time Barthélemy had already tied the makeshift rope to the chimney stack and dangled it over the north gable wall into the darkness. This was as far as they had been able to see from the first skylight. Would they find that their rope now hung uselessly in the air? Barthélemy stretched out over the edge of the roof, barely holding on. But when he turned back, Lacambre could see that his face was 'full of joy'. He had spotted below them a lead-covered roof overlooking the garden of the building next door. 'We threw ourselves, not on our knees, as any good novel requires, but into each other's arms.'

Having lowered themselves on to the terrace, the pair were not sure what to do next. The escape had taken three hours so far and they were exhausted. The temptation to look for an easy way out was powerful. There was a hatch leading into the next-door building but, without the tools left in Schaller's shoes, they could not prise it open. Below them stretched the garden. But how to get there? They were within view of the pavement outside, but there was no apparent point of attachment on the terrace for their rope, and they feared that if they tried to climb down it their feet would bang on the window below alerting the building's occupants. Their initial plan had been to stretch a line and abseil across to the garden, but they now rejected this as crazy.

After discussion, they decided that Barthélemy should climb from the terrace up on to the roof of the next-door building in the hope of finding a way in. He was gone for half an hour, those long minutes being, for Lacambre, 'the most cruel of the trip'. By now the rain and the sleet had stopped, but ice covered the terrace platform, and a keen wind penetrated Lacambre to the bone. 'On his return, Barthélemy found me nailed to the ground like a statue, shivering, almost frozen.'

Barthélemy brought back some bad news. Not the slightest opening could be found. Now it was Lacambre's turn to investigate. He too found that 'those damned roofs were closed like tombs'. Eventually, however, they spied an opening into the attic covered by a lattice grill. This likely led into the meanest garret room of the building, usually inhabited by servants or care-takers. Lacambre was jubilant. 'This is the way to freedom! ... We are in front of the humble home of a proletarian who will receive us with open arms. Ah! It is in the attics that we find our brothers.' Barthélemy carefully raised the grille and spoke reassuringly at the glass beneath: 'We are not criminals,' he whispered. 'Listen, do not worry ...' No response. Barthélemy raised his voice to demand entry. Lacambre joined in the harangue. But still no reply.

Although they had lost their tools, Barthélemy still had a small pocket knife and with this he worked to gently remove a pane of glass. But the glass slipped from his hand and fell into a 'thousand pieces on the floor, with a frightful din that multi-plies in the silence of the night'.

> We are devastated. It seems as if the house is collapsing and the whole neighbourhood will take up arms. We jump and freeze, silent and still, waiting in shock the results of the disaster. Four or five hours of perils and stress had so ter-ribly irritated our nerves that we had entirely lost our sense of proportion. We had lost touch with the real world .... But the minutes passed and the world is still in place.

Finally it dawned on them that the quiet attic room must be empty, or that the window looked down into a corridor. Barthélemy reached his hand through the broken glass, and, making sure it was out of the wind, he struck a match. What he saw was not a proletarian's garret, but a study or store room scattered with books and papers. They descended through the window, and crept through the attics, anxious not to awake any inhabitants. But there was no one there. Relaxing slightly, the pair washed themselves and put on their civilian outfits. Lacambre realised that he had forgotten to bring a hat, without which he would strike an incongruous figure in the streets of Paris. He decided to steal one, leaving an apologetic note:

> Citizen, I have been forced by necessity to take your hat, please do not be concerned. It shall be returned to you. Meanwhile, accept this five-franc piece for its hire and for the broken window.
> Salut et Fraternité
> Lacambre, D. M. P.
> 11 January 1849.

Revolutionaries were not low burglars.

Creeping downstairs, it was only when they saw some class-rooms, and dormitories full of sleeping figures, that they realised where they were: a boarding school. Barthélemy became concerned that they would not be able to walk out of the front door and on to the street without the concierge noticing (given his own father's occupation was the same, he no doubt had a respectful appreciation of their adherence to duty). So they returned to the attic room to recover their rope, and with this in hand they made their way to the back garden. The garden wall was towering and unbroken, but they found a bench which they could upend as a makeshift ladder. Lacambre clambered on to the top of the wall, then used the rope to lower himself to the other side. Though bigger, younger and more robust, Barthélemy was by now exhausted by his exertions. Four or five times he tried to climb the wall, but each time he fell back helplessly into the garden. On the other side, Lacambre was becoming increasingly agitated. A passing patrol of National Guardsmen could appear at any moment. Barthélemy told him not to wait but to run. Suddenly they heard footsteps approaching. Lacambre threw the rope back over the wall and, with one last frantic effort, Barthélemy scrambled over. He tumbled on to Lacambre, who cushioned his fall. They stole off into the night just as the soldiers closed in.

A brisk two-minute walk brought them to the river Seine as the clock struck 2 a.m., six hours after they had begun their escape.

> On the same thought, we stopped in the middle of the Pont des Arts, our lungs breathing in the fresh air of freedom. Our eyes could not get enough of the magical picture of the Seine at night: the dark waters of the river shimmered, lit here and there with bright streaks from the double line of flaming obelisks on the banks, and glittering with the reflections of long lines of lanterns on the docks. The bridge appeared to float like a gantry over fire, and in the distance the black towers of the [Notre-Dame] cathedral stood as silhouettes in the dark.

Dodging police patrols with baying bloodhounds, they made their way to a house where a fellow revolutionary worked as a concierge. He hid the fugitives in the little box room where he and his wife lived. A neighbour reported their arrival, but Barthélemy and Lacambre left early the following morning before the police swooped. Lacambre went to a barber's shop where he had his hair cut short and his beard shaved off. At which point the two men separated: a pair of escaped prisoners would have a greater chance of being spotted. After lying low for two weeks, Barthélemy slipped across the border into Belgium disguised as a priest. He made such a convincing cleric that he was saluted by unwitting fellow clergy and gendarmes as he made his way through northern France.

The escape had been reported widely, not just in France but across the Continent and in Britain. Even though it was Lacambre who had come up with the plan, it was Barthélemy, the dauntless barricade commander, who led the news. According to the press, he had been 'joined' in his adventure by the quiet conspirator Lacambre. A man of letters, Lacambre planned the escape so he could publish the truth of government repression. But long before he could set pen to paper, Barthélemy's story spread far and wide: how he had courageously accused his accusers at trial before promptly eluding their clutches. Radicals across Europe were delighted. Amidst the gathering gloom of counter-revolution, their hearts lifted when they read of Barthélemy's flight, accomplished with such 'admirable adroitness and daring'. The prisoners left behind in Cherche-Midi were punished by embarrassed and vengeful prison authorities. But even they were 'jubilant' about the escape: a 'real tour de force and master stroke'. The dashing young revolutionary had become a celebrity. For one provincial lady writer, Sophie Leroyer, Barthélemy's exploits were proof positive that the virtues of 'nobility, courage and intelligence' had passed from the decadent aristocracy and bourgeoisie to the 'race of proletarians'.

Barthélemy remained in Belgium for a few months, where he collaborated with other socialists, including Eugène Sue, on a short-lived journal, the *Veillées du peuple*, in whose pages he spoke up for his leader. Blanqui, he wrote, demonstrated 'the superiority of this elite man who has with good reason been called the most energetic figure of the revolution of February 1848'. But while Barthélemy promoted a cult of personality, he himself grew in reputation as a proletarian hero. His lawyer received numerous letters from 'beautiful ladies, young and wealthy, who declared themselves eagerly enamoured of his intrepid client, and willing to share with him their life and fortunes'.

It was perhaps one such admirer who paid Barthélemy's passage from Belgium to London in the autumn of 1849, most likely taking the steam packet from Brussels directly to the

London docks – it was cheaper than the boat to Dover. This was a first encounter liable to stun any European. As Frederick Engels wrote:

> I know nothing more imposing than the view which the Thames offers during the ascent from the sea to London Bridge. The masses of buildings, the wharves on both sides, especially from Woolwich upwards, the countless ships along both shores, crowding ever closer and closer together, until, at last, only a narrow passage remains in the middle of the river, a passage through which hundreds of steamers shoot by one another; all this is so vast, so impressive, that a man cannot collect himself, but is lost in the marvel of England's greatness before he sets foot upon English soil.

But Barthélemy had not left the revolution behind him. He immediately joined a socialist society based in St George's Tavern on Wardour Street, Soho. Life in London was not all politics for Barthélemy, however. Parisian police spies reported that he had struck up a relationship with a Madame Besson, and moved in with her in nearby Maddox Street, off Bond Street. She may well have been a French police spy herself: in later life she married a French intelligence officer. Barthélemy might have escaped the clutches of the French state, but, as he started his new life in London, he remained a watched man.

9

A MANUAL FOR REVOLUTION

Barthélemy arrived in London just as the smog was closing in, as it did every November. In the dim light he would have heard the sudden eerie screech of the newly invented 'fog screamer' from passing carriages. One thousand horse-drawn omnibuses ferried passengers around the city. Policemen, known as 'Peelers', paced the pavements at the regulation two-and-a-half miles an hour, dressed in swallowtail coats and top hats of varnished leather. While their Continental counterparts carried guns, the English bobby needed only a truncheon, lamp and rattle.

The streets heaved with people. In 1854 it was estimated that 200,000 commuters walked into central London every day. They were coming in from the rapidly expanding suburbs, where, as Charles Dickens disapprovingly noted, 'a disorderly crop of ... mean houses' were 'rising out of the rubbish, as if they had been unskilfully sown there'. Ladies swept about in long trailing dresses, shawls and poke bonnets. Mud on the ground meant that they wore boots nearly as large as those of men. In the late 1840s, many of the streets were being dug up to instal sewers and re-pave the roads with wooden blocks, which would eventually make the city a much more pleasant place in which to live. In the short run, however, it meant that the state of many of the capital's roads was deplorable. The King's Road was a particularly 'chaotic highway' with 'carriages floundering through pools of slush and over mounds of earth, and horses plunging amid rubbish heaps sticking in the mud'.

The river Thames stank – though the steamboats that ferried passengers across the river were nonetheless popular – and the open flame of coal gas-lamps, lighting streets and bridges, gave off a sickening smell. Few foreign visitors commented on the stench – cities such as Paris were at least as pungent – and they appreciated more the respite to be found in the many fine open spaces, particularly the elegant West End. Regent's Park, in the north-west, was larger than the Paris parks of the Jardin des Plantes and the Luxembourg put together. Though half hidden by smog, London was colourful. Every English householder, if they could manage it, had a little garden. Barthélemy walked these seemingly endless, poorly signposted streets in the greatest city in the world.

British public opinion generally regarded the Continent with benign indifference. But in the backwash of the June Days, it had been stirred into some mild interest regarding the phenomenon of 'Red Republicanism' apparently rampant in Europe. The *Spectator* magazine, in an article published on 20 July 1849, noted the prevalence of 'communism' as a descriptive label, and defined it as 'the antagonism of competition' and a general hatred of property. This communist principle had become the 'possession of immense numbers in France and Germany', a passion that the *Spectator* was concerned would explode if simply repressed:

Communism is in the position of an outlawed doctrine, and while it remains so it will continue to be destructive .... While we refuse to entertain the subject, we are refusing to understand the thing that moves these masses – we are refusing to understand the movements of Europe.

What the *Spectator* feared, Barthélemy desired. He devoutly hoped that the defeat of the June Days was only an episodic reverse in the ongoing advance of the communist ideal. Surely, he thought, 'the future belongs to me'.

Between 1838 and 1848, the mass Chartist movement had demanded democracy for all men – only one man out of six had the vote. Inspired by the French example, a small number of radicals had even planned barricade insurrection in London, a revolutionary legacy since 'erased from historical memory'. A large Chartist demonstration in 1848 left the government undisturbed – though the army had been put on standby in London and 85,000 men (including the exiled Louis Napoleon) enrolled as special constables to prevent an outbreak. It seemed that the old order was as secure as ever. 'The citadel of privilege in this country is so terribly strong,' complained Richard Cobden, a democratically minded liberal, in 1849. 'We are a servile, aristocracy-loving, lord-ridden people.'

It is perhaps only in retrospect that revolution in 1848 appears unlikely. The United Kingdom might have been the home of the Industrial Revolution, but it also contained the very darkest poverty of Europe. Out of a population of about 28 million in Great Britain and Ireland, there were 4 million 'potato eaters', mostly in the west and south of Ireland. One million at least had died in the terrible famine following on from the potato blight. Charles Greville, the political diarist, was sensitive to the irony, if less so to Ireland's national *amour propre*. 'Here is a country, part and parcel of England, a few hours removed from the richest and most civilised community in the world, in a state so savage, barbarous, and destitute, that we must go back to the Middle Ages or to the most inhospitable regions of the globe to look for parallel.' William Gladstone went so far as to argue that the famine had been sent by Providence as retribution for Britain's pride. Irish starvation, he believed, was God's rather indirect way of calling the English to atonement.

If so, it was no end of a lesson. Swarms of desperate Irish survivors crowded into English cities.

Barthélemy could certainly find sympathisers in the native population. London was a stronghold of Chartist opinion amongst the working class, both skilled and unskilled. A relatively moderate 'aristocracy of labour', politically distinct from the 'un-respectable' working class and hostile to revolutionary agitation, had yet to appear. But such radicalism was about to decline sharply.

By 1850, a period of economic growing pains was coming to an end. Textile production had been transformed by the factory system. Many of the old political vanguard of the working class – the hand-loom weavers – had descended from previous generations of refugees from persecution in France. It was still quite common for weavers to work in glazed attics, for better light, as was the practice across the English Channel. But they had been crushed by competition from the textile factories. By 1850, there were 331,000 factory workers and only 43,000 hand-loom weavers. A leading section of the working class had been more or less destroyed. Britain's main exports now were mass-produced: cotton, coal and pig iron. The railway system had expanded massively in the 1840s, to over 5,000 miles, and was now the largest single employer of labour. For most workers in Great Britain, other than the disappearing hand-loom weavers, it was not so much a question of absolute poverty as insecurity.

Factory conditions had been hideous, heavily based on extreme exploitation of child and female labour. By the middle of the nineteenth century, however, male factory workers were beginning to consolidate as a relative elite amongst the working class. Certainly their wages compared well to the fledging factory workforce of the Continent. According to the Factory Commissioner's Report, factory operatives in England worked an average sixty-nine hours a week for eleven shillings; in France, seventy-two to eighty-four hours for five shillings and sixpence; in Bonn, Germany, ninety-four hours for two shillings and sixpence.

As against this, British factory workers were seen as being particularly demoralised, drunken, even physically misshapen by their unhealthy working and living conditions in crowded, unsanitary towns and cities. For Engels, writing in 1843, workers who were 'treated as brutes, actually become such'. They could only 'maintain their consciousness of manhood ... by cherishing the most glowing hatred, the most unbroken inward rebellion against the bourgeoisie in power. They are men so long only as they burn with wrath against the reigning class. They become brutes the moment they bend in patience under the yoke, and merely strive to make life endurable while abandoning the effort to break the yoke.'

Certainly, a sense of pride in oneself is superior to servility. And indeed, according to Georg Weerth, a German poet and socialist who lived in England in the mid-1840s, British workers were notable for their proud class-consciousness. 'Compared to workers of other countries the English proletariat is clear-eyed in his attitude towards the bourgeoisie. They know that the gentlemen cannot do without the workers.' When a worker took his wages he felt no cringing gratitude. 'He counts the money bit by bit, checking that it is all there, weighs slowly and carefully in the hand, turns on his heel, without thanks, without greeting, and leaves the room just as stiff, as serious, as proud as how he entered.' Workers had come to see themselves not as wage slaves, but as sellers of their labour. This hard-headedness was, in fact, a positive force in British industrialisation. Employers were forced to grant improved wages and recoup their losses by investing in highly productive steam-driven technology. If 'wages had remained at a level, and workers' coalitions and strikes had remained unknown,' admitted the influential

Edinburgh Review in 1835, 'we can without exaggeration assert that ... industry would not have made half the progress.' A well-organised working class, ironically, is good for social progress under capitalism.

While Britain was known abroad for its large-scale industry, London, like Paris, was a city of distribution, manufacturing and small businesses. It was enormous, however – about thirty miles in circumference – and was in many respects an integrated economic organism. Its docks bristled with the masts of sailing boats and billowed with the smoke of steamships. Great warehouses clustered around the docks, from which raw materials and semi-finished goods were sent out to workshops for finishing. Twenty thousand smoking chimneys, rising from small factories, covered the city in a thick smog. Through it fluttered numerous carrier pigeons, much used for sending messages across the expansive capital.

At the bottom of the employment heap were the 'labouring poor', a mass of casual workers eking out a living often by the pettiest of trading. These 'street-folk', as the social investigator Henry Mayhew called them, came from all over the world: 'Among them were to be found the Irish fruitsellers; the Jew clothesmen; the Italian organ boys, French singing women, the German brass bands, the Dutch buy-a-broom girls, the Highland bagpipe players, and the Indian crossing-sweepers.' London was not the centre of luxury production that Paris was, but Barthélemy must have found it a less unfamiliar place than he might have expected.

Barthélemy's arrival coincided with a last spasm of the 'social question'. An outbreak of cholera in the summer of 1849, peaking in September that year, killed an estimated 13,000 people in the city within three months. A letter to *The Times* in 1849, accompanied by fifty-four signatures, voiced the desperation of the slum poor:

May we beg and beseech your proteckshion and power. We are, Sur, as it may be, living in a Wilderniss, so far as the rest of London knows anything of us, or as the rich and great people care about. We live in muck and filth. We aint got no privez [toilets], dust bins, no drains, no water splies [supplies], and no drain or suer [sewer] in the whole place .... The stenche of a gully-hole is disgustin. We al of us suffur, and numbers are ill, and if the colera comes Lord help us ....

This cry of fear and despair came from an area known as 'the Rookery', a notorious slum in St Giles described by a contemporary as a 'maze of narrow crooked paths', looking like a 'great block of stone eaten by slugs into innumerable small chambers and connecting passages'. It was a disgrace, and public conscience was stirred. Philanthropists proposed an Emigration Plan to help 'surplus labour' escape to the colonies. A small but energetic group of Christian Socialists argued in favour of the cooperative workshop on the French model. The intense class antagonism of the Chartist era, however, was fading fast. As English historian E. P. Thompson puts it, this was 'an effort at social reconciliation in the aftermath of Chartism and under the impulse of an acute, temporary, and almost hysterical wave of social conscience provoked by the plague'. It was not to last.

Within a year, falling prices were substantially advancing the real wages of most sections of the working class, except agricultural labourers. The cost of living figure for 1847 had been 116, based on an index figure of 100 for the year 1790; in 1850 it was only 83. Between 1850 and 1875 there was to be strong economic growth. The Victorian golden age was powering up.

*

Barthélemy reached London in 1849 as one of the first *procrists*, those 'proscribed' by the French government and so unable to return without facing imprisonment. He was a member of what was called 'the emigration', which over the next two years would grow rapidly in number. Barthélemy quickly established a Blanquist faction amongst the émigrés, vigorously defending the reputation of his imprisoned leader before all critics. Politically he identified with the socialist ideals of Louis Blanc, who had also fled France for London after the June Days. Still, Barthélemy by no means saw the diminutive Blanc, who had gone into exile with his comrade, the burly Marc Caussidière, as his 'revolutionary chief'. He told Blanqui, languishing in his cell, that 'the eager curiosity of the pretty women who wished to see the microscopic tribune accompanied by his mastodon' was 'more than was necessary to console them for having put and left the affairs of the people in perdition'.

Britain was an obvious destination for refugees, particularly given that 'the British government had absolutely no power to banish or exclude refugees or any aliens at all'. One can only imagine how the right-wing British press of the twenty-first century, normally so nostalgic for the Victorian age, would fulminate if ever Britain returned to this open-borders ideal. Dr Lacambre, who had escaped with Barthélemy, also came to London, but disliking 'the city of black mud and smoke' and the arrogance of the revolutionary leaders in exile there, he did not stay long, making his way to the sunnier climes of Valencia, Spain. A little later, in 1852, Alexander Herzen arrived, and was likewise initially put off by the loneliness of the big city and 'the sulphuric acid' in the 'thick, opaline fog'. Still, he was fascinated by the sheer size of the metropolis, 'street-lamps ... street-lamps without end in both directions', and he grew to love 'this dreadful antheap'.

Very many émigrés found it exceptionally difficult to find employment. According to the intelligence service of the

Parisian police, however, Barthélemy quickly secured a job with Mr Coptel in Berners Street, working for about twelve months as a 'mechanical steel staymaker', or corset-maker. The fashion for men in the 1850s was moving from colour – whites, greens, buffs and blues – to frock coats and waistcoats of sober black usually paired with checked or striped trousers held in tension by straps under the instep. Elegant women were wearing tight-laced corsets under panelled bodices, a short, tight jacket or shawl, and strikingly coloured skirts. It was observed that 'the gait of an Englishwoman is generally stiff and awkward, there being no bend or elasticity of the body on account of her stays'. Barthélemy was once again employed in the wealthy luxury market. At least in retrospect, his employer did not much like this new worker in the fashion industry, telling an investigator in 1855 that Barthélemy's 'countenance was very forbidding, his temper very violent, and his nature very revengeful'. (Some of the women obliged to wear his steel corsets no doubt felt much the same.)

While in England, Barthélemy would characteristically describe himself, on political proclamations and so on, as 'Citizen Barthélemy, *ouvrier mecanicien proscrit*'. *The Times* newspaper, noticing his presence, remarked sarcastically that in so doing he was presenting himself as rival, if not successor, 'of the celebrated Albert, *ouvrier*, who figured with so much éclat in the Government of the February Revolution'. It is certainly true that Barthélemy was keen to assert his proletarian authenticity amongst a gaggle of mostly middle-class socialist revolutionaries. Grumbling rivals would prefer to label him a 'galley convict'.

Barthélemy was certainly something of a celebrity in émigré circles. One who first met him in London was Wilhelm Liebknecht, a student who had participated in the 1848 revolutionary wave in Germany. After the fighting died down, Liebknecht found his way to England in May 1850. There he became close to Karl Marx and Frederick Engels, and he was to be a lifelong 'Marxist', and a crucial founding member of the German socialist party, the SPD, in the 1860s and 1870s. An amiable and conciliatory figure, he remembered the impact Barthélemy made:

> A short while after my arrival, a Parisian labourer came to London, in whom not only the French colony was deeply interested, but all of us fugitives as well, and most likely also our 'shadow': the international police. It was Barthélemy, about whose escape from the Conciergerie [sic], accomplished by him with admirable adroitness and daring, we had heard already through the papers. A little above medium height, powerful, muscular, coal-black curly hair, piercing black eyes, the image of determination – a splendid specimen of the type of Southern Frenchman. A wreath of legends surrounded his proudly erect head. He was a 'galerien' – a galley-convict – and had on his shoulder the indelible brand. When a seventeen-year-old 'gamin', he had killed a police sergeant during the Blanqui-Barbès revolt in 1838, and had been sentenced to the Bagno for it.

Naturally enough, Liebknecht's memory was uncertain. Barthélemy had actually arrived in London before Liebknecht. And there were other errors in his account. However, the impression that Barthélemy had made was evident enough. Amongst the émigrés in general he was considered 'one of the most eloquent orators of his party and enjoyed a great reputation for bravery'.

The remaining *démoc-socs* (democratic socialists) left in France gathered under the leadership of Ledru-Rollin. They were known as the 'Mountain', a name used to describe the Jacobins in the 1790s. They had to compete, however, with the growing appeal of Louis Napoleon, heir to the Napoleonic throne and legend, who presented himself as all things to all men, even as a 'working-class candidate' who supported his own concept of the 'organisation of labour'. Louis Napoleon Bonaparte was that new political phenomenon, since grown familiar, a scion of the elite who claimed to be the 'voice of the common people'. A somewhat unprepossessing man in the flesh, a poor speaker with a discernible German accent, long of torso and short of leg, with tobacco-stained teeth, he nonetheless had a crucial advantage: the press could not take their eyes off him. The people were hypnotised by his antics, and a growing constituency were prepared to invest their hopes in a man who offered neither consistent ideas nor policy, but soundbites and impalpable 'leadership'.

The new constitution drawn up for the Republic provided for a powerful president elected by universal male suffrage to counterbalance the parliamentary National Assembly. When presidential elections were held in December 1848, Louis Napoleon won an astonishing 5 million out of 7 million votes, handily defeating both Cavaignac and Lamartine. His studied ambiguity, combining radicalism and conservatism, appealed to the peasantry, 'whose hearts were on the left but whose pockets were on the right', as one historian has put it, but he also won significant support from the defeated urban working class.

In subsequent Assembly elections the 'party of order', now almost entirely monarchist, retained its majority. Ledru-Rollin's party, however, polled impressively amongst workers, soldiers and peasants. As discontent grew with the conservative National Assembly, prospects looked fair for Ledru-Rollin's supporters. He was never a nimble political operator, however, and he blew his opportunity. In June 1849, there was considerable republican discontent with a French expeditionary force sent to suppress the Republic of Rome and to restore the Pope to his earthly throne. Ledru-Rollin tried to turn the resulting protests into an insurrection. But in general, people are unwilling to die for even good causes in another country and the rising was a damp squib. When the army charged protesters at the rue de la Paix, Karl Blind, a German revolutionary close to Ledru-Rollin, recalled the dispiriting denouement: 'A few cries "To the barricades!" met with no response. In a moment the shutters of all houses were up –' doors locked – everyone in the streets helplessly at the mercy of the troops. I saw the whole to the last.' Order was smartly restored. Just as Ledru-Rollin had overestimated his support in the National Assembly in the first months after the February revolution, so now he had misjudged the willingness of the street to rise after the bloody Days of June.

Ledru-Rollin and his fellow *démoc-socs* were suppressed and forced into exile. Ledru-Rollin himself spent four years in Brompton in the west of London, before moving to St John's Wood in the north of the city in 1853. Like many refugees, he did not much love London. He was irritated by its lofty aristocracy and disgusted by the squalor of its slums. When in 1850 he published an intemperate attack upon his country of refuge, *De la décadence de l'Angleterre*, he alienated himself from the British and frustrated his fellow émigrés. Ingratitude is never a genial character trait, and people find frank speaking hardly more tolerable. Out of his element, Ledru-Rollin was an ineffective Tribune. The benefit of his martyrdom in France fell to Louis Napoleon, who in his absence was free to assert himself as the popular representative against the 'party of order'.

Despite his firm Blanquism, Barthélemy at first was able to work with those exiles who came from France in the train of Ledru-Rollin. Indeed, he would have known some of them from his secret society activities as far back as the 1830s. They included

François Pardigon, who had been editor of the *Vraie Republique* newspaper; Martin Bernard, a former member of the Society of Seasons; Etienne Arago, a National Guard commander; and J. N. L. Songeon, a lawyer in his early thirties. Barthélemy, it seems, was able to overlook the fact that these republicans had stood to one side in the June days, only rising against Louis Napoleon a year later. It had been the case, of course, that no socialist leader, Barthélemy included, had thought that the June insurrection had been timely or wise. Barthélemy had simply felt it his duty to lead the workers in their hopeless fight. His honour assured, he was able to countenance cooperation with those who had held aloof or had no military leadership to offer the rebels. Ledru-Rollin had no wish to be associated with the likes of Barthélemy, however. He compained bitterly when socially superior émigrés, such as himself, were treated 'as convicts of the galleys, as miserable bandits, as the filth of the sewers of Paris'. There is no doubt that he would cheerfully denounce Barthélemy in just these terms.

It may have helped that the English Fraternal Democrats, a radical group which had emerged from the mass Chartist movement, acted as a buffer. When the Fraternal Democrats welcomed the new exiles they pointedly remarked that their fate signalled 'another repetition of the lesson which Saint-Just was powerless to teach, but which the enemies of Democracy (thanks to be them!) are hourly teaching: that *"Those who make half-revolutions but dig graves for themselves!"*' Barthélemy, a latter-day Saint-Just, would certainly have agreed. At any rate, few could deny his credentials. On Christmas Eve 1849, he addressed a meeting of the Fraternal Democrats, organised to greet this wave of political outcasts, where he was introduced as the 'June insurgent and commander of the barricades in Faubourg du Temple'.

The new wave of exiles quickly took the leading role amongst the broader French emigration. A 'Society of the Revolution' was formed, led by Ledru-Rollin, Martin Bernard and Charles Delescluze. This was not explicitly socialist. Instead their emphasis was placed upon the unity of republicans of all shades, and the dependence of democratic revolution on the rebellion of nationalities against the great powers. They had expected the pan-European revolution of 1848 to unite the Germans, Italians and Polish, each in their own state, independent of foreign domination. But the empires of Russia and Austria had mobilised their armies to prevent revolutions of national unification and to maintain their domination. The British Empire had looked on with sympathy for nationalists, but offered little practical help. The exiles concluded that only the rising of oppressed peoples against the empires could break the logjam. Insurrection would lead to insurrection in a domino effect, they fondly hoped, and the spreading revolution itself would solve all problems. The notion that revolutionary turmoil spontaneously smooths over ideological divisions is an unconvincing thesis, to put it mildly, but it at least saved further thought.

With representatives of the exiles from Italy, Hungary, Germany and Poland, Ledru-Rollin formed a grandly named 'European Central Democratic Committee'. This blamed class struggle for derailing the revolution in Europe and favoured prioritising broad-brush republicanism and nationalism over socialism. Nothing should undermine the discipline of the revolutionary 'army', they insisted, and debates about the social Republic simply imperilled the unity of the revolutionaries' 'great church'.

Louis Blanc was irritated with this anti-intellectualism. It was not enough, he insisted, to simply call for the Republic: 'No, no: the Republican form of government is not the object; the object is to restore to the dignity of human nature those whom the excess of poverty degrades.' Blanc made a good point, but to many it sounded like a call for passive study rather than struggle. The English freethinker and cooperativist George Holyoake described Blanc as 'the greatest expositor of republicanism, democratic and social, of his day'. But he admitted that in the early years of his exile to London his authority was not great.

Barthélemy was very much of the Louis Blanc party politically, and from an early date was notorious for his hostility towards Ledru-Rollin. But he was not likely to be attracted to Blanc's call for patient study and meditation. Long years of prison life had given him enough of that. Barthélemy took the position of those who wished to combine republicanism and socialism with strict revolutionary unity, discipline and bold action.

At first Barthélemy found an outlet for his activity in helping other émigrés. To help provide for the many refugees who had wound up in London, radicals established the Société de Proscrits Democrats-Socialistes (SPDS). Even those refugees from comfortable backgrounds now had to deal with straitened circumstances. For working-class refugees, the situation was dire. 'It would be difficult to depict the destitution of the proletarian emigration,' wrote Barthélemy. Gustave Lefrançais, for example, did not have enough money to pay for lodgings and he was often forced to stay in pubs near the docks until they closed before trying to find somewhere to sleep outdoors. The *Illustrated London News* reported one particularly tragic case:

[Francis Goujon] was a poor, industrious mechanic, and was remarkable for his humanity and devotedness. In November last [1851], he rescued several persons from a dreadful conflagration at Dijon, and in this courageous act received many dreadful burns. Whilst suffering in bed from these injuries, the *coup d'état* of Louis Napoleon broke out; and Goujon, having belonged to certain political societies of that period, was compelled to quit France, which he did on foot, under great privations. He reached Brussels, but was compelled by the Belgian authorities to leave, and then fled to England; he was, however, in a wretched condition when he arrived in London; and he breathed his last in St Marylebone Hospital a fortnight since.

At his funeral in St John's Wood Cemetery, French republican dignitaries, including Louis Blanc and Ledru-Rollin, gave eulogies and a collection was made for Goujon's widow and five children, the receipt amounting to £6. 'This sum, although small in amount, is considerable in proportion to the means of the French refugees now in the metropolis, who are, for the most part, poor and destitute.'

The Société de Proscrits was 'essentially communist', with 'its most energetic section' being attached to the Blanqui party according to a London Blanquist, Jules Vidil, formerly a captain of the Hussars. Its directing committee of six included at least four Blanquists: Adam (a shoemaker), Barthélemy, Fanon, Edward Goûte (of Blois) and Jules Vidil. On 25 February 1850, the Société sponsored a banquet to celebrate the anniversary of the February revolution at Bayswater Tavern. Barthélemy was on the organising committee. An international gathering of some hundreds heard Frederick Engels offer a toast 'To the insurrection of June 1848!'

The Blanquists' leading role derived more from their organisation and dedication than any wide acceptance of their specific schemes for the revolution. Indeed, Barthélemy wrote to Blanqui admitting to him that the ideas put forward by the Blanquist Central Society in Paris were 'little esteemed' in London. Even the Blanquists were not solidly united.

One of their number, François Pardigon, was seeking to go beyond the tradition of the revolutionary secret society. It was true, he argued, that in the 1830s heroic conspirators, through propaganda and deeds, had played a noble role in spreading the revolutionary ideal. But the 'acorn had become an oak'. The workers and peasants had been politicised, and it was time for a new phase. 'Where is the revolution now? ... The revolution took refuge in the bosom of the masses; it ferments; it is reborn.' When Pardigon published these words in 1852, however, it was beginning to become obvious that the revolutionary upsurge of 1848 was spent. It had fermented and gone sour.

There were also refugees arriving from Germany. Karl Marx and his comrades, who had been based in Germany in 1848 and 1849, were forced into exile and re-established the Communist League in London. They uneasily linked up with August Willich, who arrived in London in 1850. Willich, of noble birth and from a long line of soldiers, was himself a Prussian military officer of the Seventh Regiment of Artillery. In the mid-1840s he began reading literature on the 'communist and socialist system' in which he found 'such beautiful things'. He concluded, however, that its victory 'could only be accomplished by the force of the masses driven by necessity to hatred'. In 1848 Willich organised revolutionaries into a military company and fought against the encroaching counter-revolution in Germany. Defeated by overwhelming odds he retreated into Switzerland and then fled, first to France and then to England. Before long he met with Barthélemy – Willich spoke fluent French – and they became fast friends. Barthélemy admired his bold confidence and thirst for armed struggle.

Willich joined the Communist League in London. In their immediate post-mortem on 1848, the League optimistically hoped that a new revolutionary wave was imminent, a conviction they shared with the Blanquists, including Barthélemy. There was, indeed, a marked convergence of strategic thinking between these two groups.

Marx and Engels, drawing upon the example of the French Revolution, were convinced that the armed demonstrations of the working class could hold a democratic revolutionary government up to the mark, and protect it against counter-revolution. This was 'an old revolutionary right of the people which could not be dispensed with in all stormy periods', they wrote. 'History owes to this right almost all the energetic steps taken by such assemblies' of the people. They favoured, therefore, a 'dictation' by the popular masses to the parliament and government. In March 1850, the Communist League issued a circular advocating a policy of 'permanent revolution', in which the armed and organised working class should apply pressure to drive a revolutionary government onwards without, in the first instance, seeking to seize power themselves.

The proletariat should not seek to take power prematurely, Marx stressed, writing, 'Louis Blanc offers the best example of how you fare when you come to power too early.'

Marx believed that the strategy he was promoting was not dissimilar to Blanqui's concept of an armed proletariat keeping the revolutionary government under pressure and intimidating the forces of reaction. When an official of the republican Provisional Government of France in 1848 had said to Blanqui, 'You wish to overthrow us?' he replied, 'No, to bar the road behind you.' This was a strategy Marx and Engels had much sympathy with.

However, Blanqui, in reality, was prepared to go further. He conceded that 'communism cannot be introduced by a decree; it can only be gradually realised by years of education and training'. Nonetheless, a *dictature parisienne* should assume direction of government until the country was right for democracy, the Republic and cooperative economy. The chief factor in a revolution is the seizure of political power.'

There was just enough ambiguity here for a political cooperation to be attempted between the Marx party and the Blanquists. What they had in common was a commitment to a 'dictatorship of the proletariat', a phrase evolved to bridge the gap. For the Blanquists, the dictatorship should be realised in full as soon as possible. For Marx and Engels, the proletariat should seek to 'dictate' conditions to a democratically elected parliament and government, and only after a drawn-out process of struggle would they assume power directly.

So long as the émigrés believed that a new outburst of revolution was imminent, they tried to smooth over their differences. In April 1850, Marx, Engels and August Willich, as representatives of the Communist League, met with Adam and Vidil, leaders of the London Blanquists, and with George Harney of the English Chartist left wing. They agreed to establish a new Société Universelle des Communistes Révolutionnaires (SUCR) on the basis of a six-point programme. This specifically mentioned the 'dictatorship of the proletarians' stretching unbroken to the culminating point of 'communism'. What exactly was meant by the 'dictatorship' was left undefined. This omission, clearly, was deliberate. It was a creative ambiguity that allowed some kind of dialogue between different revolutionary tendencies.

Barthélemy alluded to the functions of this new organisation in a letter he wrote on 4 July 1850 to the imprisoned Blanqui:

With the German Communists we have begun to draft a Revolutionary Manual containing, point by point, all the measures that the people will have to take immediately after the revolution to ensure its success and to avoid a repetition of what happened in February [1848]. Our intention is to reproduce the Manual in a little booklet that we can distribute among the workers so that everyone knows what he has to do to ensure the victory of the People. We will also have this manual printed in the form of proclamations to display in the streets of Paris. Please let us know if we can get our manuscripts to you without inconvenience so that you can put the finishing touches on it. On reading it you will see what our intentions are, and I do not doubt, on my part, that you will approve them.

These were to be printed in London and smuggled to workshops in Paris.

It was at this point that something like a friendship grew up between Marx and Barthélemy. As Wilhelm Liebknecht remembered, the scholarly Marx was willing to learn from the fighter Barthélemy. Marx's wife, Jenny, something of a snob but perhaps a better judge of character than her husband, was from the outset suspicious of the Frenchman. As Wilhelm Liebknecht wrote in his memoirs, '[Barthélemy] entered into closer relations with us and was frequently in Marx's house. Mrs. Marx did not like him – he was uncanny to her, his piercing eyes were repulsive to her.'

Despite this, Liebknecht and Karl Marx frequently sparred with Barthélemy – with swords, sabres and foils – at a 'fencing salon' in Rathbone Place on Oxford Street, then as now a bustling retail centre where the shops displayed their wares through large plate-glass windows. There is no doubt that at this stage they got on well. They were preparing for what they expected to be an imminent renewal of revolutionary warfare, and having fun besides.

Jenny was not the only one to be suspicious of Barthélemy. For Maurice Dommanget, the indefatigable historian of Blanqui and his movement, 'Barthélemy was an incessant cause of trouble and discord in the open as well as the covert struggle, and in both he turned as much on "comrades" as he did on the enemy.' So turbulently aggressive was Barthélemy, according to Charles Hugo, son of Victor Hugo, that his provocative extremism led to a 'vague distrust' and whisperings in the exile community of that 'terrible word – *Mouchard*' (informer). To be sure, Barthélemy was a strong and intimidating personality, normally self-controlled but with a fiery temper when provoked. It is unsurprising that he rubbed people up the wrong way in the claustrophobic émigré community.

By July 1850, the London Blanquists had fallen out. Some joined with Louis Blanc and Caussidière to establish a more moderate refugee organisation. Barthélemy wrote to Blanqui on 4 July 1850, that 'in so far as it was only a matter of aid questions [how to help impoverished refugees], everybody had been in agreement. But the discussions having been extended to first principles; a split took place; and we were immediately divided into two camps: that of rich founders, and that of the poor members.'

Barthélemy himself wanted to radicalise the Société de Proscrits in a left-wing, militantly pro-worker direction. With another Blanquist called Adam, a leather blocker who had also been associated with secret societies during the Orléanist regime, he joined a society 'composed of workers only, which had been formed in London after the February revolution' with the intention of using it to take over the Société de Proscrits. Against strong opposition, this group was admitted to the Société and, as Barthélemy was pleased to report, accentuated there the already visible dividing line between the society's 'rich founders' – who 'wished to protect the workers, but who did not wish to see equality with them' – and its 'poor members'. Barthélemy was self-consciously a representative of the proletariat amongst middle-class socialist leaders.

The Communist League was also splitting along class lines. August Willich, now a close friend to Barthélemy, wanted immediate action. His no-nonsense style clearly appealed to the German working-class members of the Communist League; certainly more than did the subtle dialectics of Marx and Engels. As a friend wrote to Marx, those who worked obsessively for the 'organisation of the revolution' 'honoured Willich as their

God-the-Father, or at least their Pope, and reviled you as their Anti-Christ or Anti-Pope'.

On 29 August 1850, at a meeting of the German Workers Educational Association, Marx attacked what they saw as Willich's reckless adventurism. Marx had concluded that socialist revolution was not an imminent possibility. As he explained it, 'communism could be introduced only after a number of years ... it had to go through several phases, and ... it could at any rate only be introduced through education and gradual development'. His opponents, he said, wanted communism 'to be introduced in the next revolution, even if only through the force of the guillotine'. He was not being slanderous. Willich himself frankly acknowledged his view that communism had to be introduced immediately in the next revolt, 'even if only through the power of the guillotine' and 'even against the will of Germany as a whole'.

Barthélemy clearly took the side of Willich in this dispute. When the 'revolutionary manual' was drawn up, being completed by 1 August, neither Marx nor Engels had a hand in it. It was, as Engels wrote sarcastically, 'brought forth of a gloomy evening in the inglenook [chimney-corner] by Mr Willich and Mr Barthélemy'. A version was seized by the French police when they raided a meeting of Willich's followers in Paris in September, and it was publicised in the French and German newspapers.

Willich and Barthélemy's 'Demands of the People – Instructions for the League Before, During and After the Revolution' discussed a revolution of the 'fourth estate', undertaken not just by the urban working class but also the rural peasantry. 'At the moment of the revolution,' the manual stated, 'all existing governmental authorities cease to exist.' The powers of the army, police and judiciary would be taken over by revolutionary committees and a working-class army. 'The People must never be disarmed again.' A revolutionary Central

Committee, established in the capital city, would exercise dictatorial control to violently suppress counter-revolution and the 'reactionary bourgeoisie'. 'Enemies of the nation' would be arrested: 'open-hearted traitors' submitted to immediate revolutionary justice – presumably execution – and doubtful cases put on trial before revolutionary tribunals. It was a frightful vision.

The Central Committee would take over the mines, the means of communication – railways and steamships – and all factories and workshops not kept in full activity by their owners. Employees in these nationalised enterprises would be loyal 'state workers ... their existence ... inextricably united with that of the new state'. Though state-owned these workplaces would be, ideally at least, self-governing. 'Where the workers are revolutionary, they are left to choose their managers themselves; where they are not, the Commissioner [appointed by the Central Committee] decides.'

This nationalised section of the economy, backed up by armed power, would enable the state – as the finance-providing 'collective capitalist' – gradually 'to overcome private capital through its competition'. As they enlarged and consolidated, they would become the electoral basis for a Central Government Committee, replacing the dictatorial Central Committee. Eventually, universal suffrage would come into operation. The principle of the resulting federal state would be, on the one hand, 'centralisation of all the economic means of production and political power' and, on the other hand, 'free self-administration, by which this centralisation will be required to operate'.

When he read about the Manual in the Continental newspapers, Engels recognised the concepts developed by himself and Marx, but 'converted into pompous nonsense'. Its core ideas, he implied, came from Barthélemy, Willich only adding an 'accretion of un-derived craziness', such as a plan to invade Germany with a revolutionary army of 5,000 hand-picked men. Marx was dismissive: 'This business of the Paris document is quite stupid.'

The Société Universelle des Communistes Révolutionnaires had effectively turned into a compact between Barthélemy and Willich, entirely excluding Marx and Engels. Barthélemy identified with a man of ruthless action more than the professorial intellectuals. As Liebknecht recalled, he 'drifted into the company of Willich and there contracted a spite against Marx. Marx was a "traitor", because he would not conspire and disturb the peace – we heard such phrases often enough later on – and the "traitors must be killed". I tried to reason with him – but in vain.' When Barthélemy made his mind up about a man, he rarely changed it.

Barthélemy was a dangerous enemy to make. In 1844 Marx had criticised a literary revolutionary, Rodolphe de Gérolstein, created as a popular hero by the left-wing author Eugène Sue in his bestselling novel, *The Mysteries of Paris*. Sue's readers had been invited to identify with Gérolstein as a hero. But, as Marx strenuously objected, Gérolstein's 'feverishly burning lust for revenge, his bloodthirstiness' and 'his calm and considered rage' were precisely 'passions for *evil*'. Always quicker off the mark in correctly evaluating writings than men, Marx may have finally come to realise that in befriending Barthélemy he had inadvertently invited a real-life Gérolstein into his circle.

10

'SNAKES WITH HUMAN FACES'

There was much about the British that Continental Europeans found odd. They were curiously reserved – 'the workman does not sing' – and dedicated to their jobs. London never seemed to sleep and its workshops bustled almost all hours. Shopkeepers were deemed honest, did not hassle customers, and declined to haggle: most unlike Paris. Streets seethed with traffic, and entire populations, it seemed, floated on the Thames. Eighty thousand private carriages trundled the streets of the capital. Horse-riding was the most popular genteel pastime.

Art and history were little regarded – the English had a mania for spurious restoration disfiguring their oldest monumental buildings – and there were only two abiding interests. The first was politics, but only if it related to matters practical and concrete. An Englishman would say, 'Principles! What are principles? Assuredly, one must be a Frenchman to fall into this unmeaning jargon!' The second was commerce. 'The business man's point of view is always the one forward in this country ... trade is the motive power of all social organisation.'

The English, nicknamed *Rosbifs* by the French, loved to gorge themselves with food, particularly fish and roasted meat. Nathaniel Hawthorne, from the United States, was typical of foreigners in observing that 'there is hardly a less beautiful object than the elderly John Bull, with his large body, protruding paunch, short legs and mottled, double chinned irregular aspect'. But they were not slobs: English cleanliness astonished visitors from overseas. In middle-class homes water was pumped to at least the second and sometimes the third floor. Despite the smoggy air, a great deal of white and light colours were worn. Women, trees and horses were 'marvellously beautiful'. Though London was three times the size of Paris, everyone seemed to wish to escape to the country, and amateur gardeners were numerous. The English loved animals: 'A legal action can be brought against those who ill-treat animals,' the Frenchman Francis Wey remarked wryly, 'and it is a much more costly pastime to beat one's dog than one's wife.'

Everyone wore a hat, even the most destitute; and the level of destitution in England's capital shocked visitors: 'Unless you have seen rags in London you can have no conception of the meaning of the word.' Even the poorest men eschewed beards, spending 1d twice a week on a shave. It was the long moustachioes on Julius von Haynau – the Austrian general who had brutally repressed the 1848 revolutions in Italy and Hungary – that allowed the drayman workers at Barclay and Perkins Brewery to identify and beat him up when he went on a London sightseeing tour in 1850.

The laws were generally fair and the public well informed. English liberty was no myth, and Britain was easily the freest country in Europe. Its citizens loved to read newspapers, usually in taverns and coffee shops, because the tax on the press meant that few people could afford to buy their own. Public opinion was despotic. Louis Blanc knew a Frenchman living in London who found wearing a hat uncomfortable. 'Well! He has never chanced to go up the street, hat in hand, without immediately becoming the jest of passers-by.' Perhaps the poor man thought he heard the laughing Londoners exclaim *God-damn!* as he passed – the French were convinced that the English were given to strong language, though the English indignantly denied this, at least for gentlemen.

One difference between British and Continental culture that was just coming into focus at the end of the 1840s was the rapid decline of the duel in Britain and its continuing popularity across the Channel. We have seen that Barthélemy had a penchant for resolving political differences through violence, and in the autumn of 1850 he arranged a duel with one of Ledru-Rollin's allies, J. N. L. Songeon. Then, there was a violent argument between Marx and Willich at a session of the Communist League's central committee on 1 September. Marx spurned Willich's challenge to a duel, but Conrad Schramm, a supporter of the Marx faction, insulted Willich, provoking a further challenge. Schramm, who had no experience of firearms, faced the prospect of duelling with the experienced soldier, Willich.

And so, since Barthélemy and Songeon were already due to fight, it was determined that all the participants would pool their efforts. In a duel, each combatant had to have two seconds to ensure fair play. It was arranged that Willich and Jules Vidil, a French Blanquist, would act as seconds for Barthélemy in his duel with Songeon. With his duel with Songeon concluded, Barthélemy would then stand for Willich in his duel with Schramm. That Barthélemy was to act as a second after his own duel perhaps suggests it was not intended to be a fight to the death.

The duels were to take place away from the long arm of English law. The two parties took the night boat to Ostend, in Belgium, and made their way to a lonely beach just outside Antwerp, ideal location for a duel – 'flat, open, relatively unpopulated and yet accessible'. The otherwise appealing grassy commons of England had become less attractive since the Earl of Cardigan endured the humiliation of a citizen's arrest at the hands of a miller following his participation in a duel on Wimbledon Heath in 1840. As it happened, Songeon did not turn up for his fight with Barthélemy – he would live to become a French senator – but the contest between Willich and Schramm was set to go ahead. Yet as Schramm and his second, a Polish officer named Henryk Ludvic Miskowshy, reached the appointed place at the appointed time, it became apparent that his opponent had taken advantage of the unanticipated lull in proceedings:

> Willich and his companions [including Barthélemy] were already at the scene of the duel when we arrived, and ... they had marked out the duelling ground, on which Willich took up a position that placed him in the shade. I pointed this out to Schramm, who said: let it be.

Willich was in an advantageous position. Being in the shade he was a less distinct target, while his opponent ran the risk of having the sun in his eyes. The two took their positions, while some peasants making hay looked on quizzically. Schramm was to shoot first. He raised his pistol, pulled the trigger and fired. The shot went wide. Willich, the experienced soldier, now took aim. The shot rang out and Schramm fell to the ground, bleeding heavily from his head. Barthélemy and Willich did not linger, immediately leaving for Ostend where they narrowly caught the steamer for England.

It fell to Barthélemy, as Willich's second, to tell the Marx party what had transpired. Marx was absent when Barthélemy called at his house at 28 Dean Street – a shabby three-room apartment in one of the cheapest quarters of London – but his wife Jenny was waiting. Barthélemy 'bowed stiffly and in answer to the anxious request for news announced in a sepulchral tone: "What news?" "*Schramm a une balle dans la tête*" – Schramm has a bullet in the head! Then he bowed stiffly again, wheeled round and went out.' Mrs Marx nearly fainted away: loyal Schramm was dead. The next day, however, Schramm appeared at the house, bandaged and laughing. Willich's bullet had knocked him unconscious, but he had survived.

Marx and his group deeply resented what they took to be Barthélemy's cold-heartedness and duplicity. More likely, he simply did not know whether Schramm was alive or dead. Still, he might have expressed himself more fully and sympathetically towards Jenny. It was clear that Barthélemy had lost any residual fondness for the Marx family, and they him. Although technically the political lash-up between Marx's Communist League, the left faction of the Chartists and Barthélemy's Blanquists was still in existence it was hardly likely to survive an episode such as this. Marx and Engels, moreover, had wearied of émigré politics and despaired of imminent revolution. They now rejected the adventurism, scheming and militarism – as they saw it – of the émigré revolutionaries, including Barthélemy. 'The leaders of the groups attacked one another most viciously,' recalled Jenny Marx wearily, 'and a band … eager for "deeds" and action" pushed to the fore.' They were hostile towards those who had come to accept that revolution was not imminent, and 'Karl above all was persecuted beyond measure, calumniated and defamed.'

On 7 October 1850, Barthélemy – who now seemed to be taking the lead in the Blanquist group – Adam and Jules Vidil sent a letter to 'Citizens Marx and Engels'. It was as coldly formal as Barthélemy's delivery of tidings to Mrs Marx.

We have the honour to inform you that we must have a meeting in the course of this week in order to take up the affairs of the Association we have formed. We have already informed Citizen Willich. We await your letting us know the place and the day you choose, these points being of no importance to us.

Indeed, it reads like a note from a second arranging a duel – 'Name the time and place, Messieurs!' On 9 October, Marx, Engels and Harney sent a flippant letter in reply:

Messieurs Adam, Barthélemy and Vidil

Gentlemen,

We have the honour of informing you that we have, long since, considered the association you speak of as dissolved by fact. The only thing remaining to be done would be the destruction of the fundamental contract. Perhaps Mr Adam or Mr Vidil will have the kindness to call, on Sunday next October 13 at noon, on Mr Engels at nr. 6, Macclesfield Street, Soho, in order to witness the burning of the same.

We have the honour to be, gentlemen, your most obedient servants, Engels, Marx, Harney.

In the initial draft of the letter, Barthélemy and co. had been addressed with the comradely term 'citizens'. This had been crossed out in Engels' hand and replaced with the distant 'gentlemen'. It is notable that the letter invited Adam or Vidil to the ritual burning of documents, but not Barthélemy. The authors, perhaps, knew to distinguish discretion from rash valour.

The Communist League itself was soon in free fall. On 11 November 1850, the London branch led by Marx proposed to the Cologne-based central committee of the organisation that the Willich-Schapper group be formally expelled since they had set up a parallel organisation. To make the situation worse, there was now pressure coming from outside. King Frederick William IV of Prussia had sent a secret memo to his prime minister proposing a plan to invent a 'communist plot' to discredit and roll up the League. This scheme was taken up and resulted in heightened secret agent activity against the communists in London and the wholesale arrest of their comrades in Cologne.

Marx and his band were isolated and increasingly inclined to shake the dust of the emigration from the soles of their feet. Marx himself retreated into private life while casting aspersions on his rivals. As the British philosopher Bertrand Russell surmised, he had 'a love of domination associated with the feeling of inferiority' (which Russell associated with Marx's troubled relationship with his Jewish ancestry), and this made him 'prickly with social superiors, ruthless with rivals, and kind to children'. If he could not be centre stage, he would prefer to be at home with his family.

Many of those in the socialist emigration, however, were prepared to cooperate across factional lines to oppose the increasingly centrist rather than left-wing Ledru-Rollin. In November 1850, Barthélemy's Blanquists were able to come to an agreement with most of the other refugee factions. Ledru-Rollin had reached an alliance with the Italian nationalist republican, Giuseppe Mazzini, a stern critic of what he saw as the divisiveness of class struggle. Ledru-Rollin and Mazzini issued a manifesto from the Central European Democratic Committee, signed also by representatives of German and Polish refugee groups, addressed to the peoples of Europe. The peoples of Europe did not pay much attention, but it was dynamite in the emigration.

The manifesto of Ledru-Rollin and co. was vaguely socialistic in that it promoted 'association' and 'credit' to support labour, ideas generally associated with worker cooperatives. But this was stated with deliberate ambiguity, and it was the oppressed nationalities – such as those Italians, Germans and Poles divided up for the convenience of empires – rather than the working classes who were expected to be the agents of liberation, with a self-sacrificing intellectual elite providing the leadership. The whole was overlaid with a heavy moralism. As they summarised it, 'We believe ... in a social state having God and his law at the summit; the people ... at its base; progress as a rule, association as a means, devotion for baptism, genius and virtue for lights upon the way.' This was a comprehensive mechanism for revolution in the imagination; but it had no place for gritty class struggle.

In November 1850, the French Société de Proscrits, dominated by Barthélemy's Blanquists, joined with Willich's splinter group and revolutionary organisations from Poland and Hungary to issue a manifesto 'To the Democrats of all Nations'. As a counter to what they saw as Ledru-Rollin and Mazzini's windy moralism, Willich and Barthélemy framed their manifesto in exaggeratedly 'hard-headed' and militaristic terms. In it they asserted that the armies of the great powers were about to descend upon France, 'the volcano of the Universal Revolution', and in particular that European civilisation was threatened, 'as of yore' by the 'hordes of barbarians' massed in Russia. In light of this, it was not 'moral law' that should be motivating revolutionaries but an urgent awareness of the impending threat of bloody conquest from the barbaric East. With pedantic precision they itemised the military forces available to the European monarchies. Republicans must prepare for the extremities of cataclysmic war, implying revolutionary terror against all enemies and the ruthless suppression of treachery: 'Enlightened by the examples of the past, we must provide against the betrayals of the future.'

In reading this, Frederick Engels recognised the characteristic voice of Barthélemy – unsentimental, militaristic and ruthless. He 'has at last given the world an example of "what blunt speaking is"', he wrote wryly to Marx. Counting soldiers and exhorting discipline seemed more practical than airy disquisitions on social classes and interests. Just at this time, Marx was in the midst of writing his series of articles on *The Class Struggles in France*, a complex study of multiple classes and parties jostling for advantage and only limited opportunities for the working class. It included his deflating if sober verdict on the June Days: 'The Paris proletariat was *forced* into the June insurrection by the bourgeoisie. This sufficed to mark its doom. Its immediate, avowed needs did not drive it to engage in a fight for the forcible overthrow of the bourgeoisie, nor was it equal to this task.' This was in sharp contrast to Barthélemy's battle cry.

For his part, Willich hoped to revolutionise the military garrisons of Germany. Such a strategy appealed to his army mentality and enthusiasm for conspiracy. And there seemed to be some sense in it. German soldiers, after all, were not known for their love of Russia. But clearly, his schemes ran toward the fantastic. H. Hermann Becker, a communist in Cologne, in January 1851 wrote a letter to Marx sarcastically commenting on Willich's strategising: 'Willich writes me the funniest letters; I do not reply, but this does not prevent him from describing his latest plans for a revolution. He has appointed me to revolutionise the Cologne garrison!!! The other day we laughed till the tears came. His idiocy will spell disaster for countless people yet; for a single letter would suffice to guarantee the salaries of a hundred Demagogue judges for three years. As soon as I have completed the revolution in Cologne he would *have no objection* to assuming the leadership for all subsequent operations. Very kind of him!' This was an unflattering but hardly unfair depiction of Willich irresponsibly manoeuvring imaginary regiments with himself as the generalissimo of revolution.

Individuals could snipe and laugh, but it's clear that Barthélemy and Willich were at the centre of the radical left wing of the emigration in London. The Marx group was increasingly isolated. By 1851, the Communist League rump led by Marx was little more than an intellectual discussion group (nicknamed by rivals 'the Synagogue'). It managed to hold weekly meetings of varying regularity, with only a handful of attendees. They had no newspaper. Engels had now moved to Manchester to work in management at his father's mill, leaving a gap which Marx was unable to fill, as Engels explained to a colleague: because 'Marx speaks little English, our connection with Harney and the Chartists was making little or no headway'. Engels had to admit that the leadership of the radical emigration now lay with Schapper and Willich for the Germans, and with Louis Blanc and Emmanuel Barthélemy for the French. Barthélemy was in the front rank of émigré radicalism in London, while Marx seemed destined for that most uninspiring of fates – bookish obscurity.

Barthélemy had status among his peers, but he was not content to be a big fish in the small pool of revolutionaries in London. He was impatient to resume the struggle directly with the government of France. His first priority was to liberate his old leader, Auguste Blanqui, and by early 1851, he was making plans for a descent on the rugged prison island of Belle-Île, nine miles off the coast of Brittany, to spring Blanqui from his penitentiary there. From the maps brought to him by Blanqui's mother, Sophie, he learnt by heart the details of the coastline. As Blanqui's biographer, Samuel Bernstein, puts it, 'he was just the right man for such a project':

> He was young, fearless and self-assured .... He was more to be feared than a swashbuckler. He moved silently and acted deliberately. He could calmly approach a foe, unload his pistol without blinking and just as calmly walk off as if he had performed an innocent and honourable deed. Such was the manner of the man who had set his mind on liberating Blanqui.

We can only agree that Barthélemy was a man of parts. What he needed for the enterprise, however, was money.

Barthélemy's dramatic revolutionary career, and particularly his escape from military prison, had given him a reputation which could be turned to good advantage. He had, moreover, a surprisingly felicitous way with words for a man of limited education. At one point, for example, he wrote to Blanqui reporting 'the most miserable palinodes' of faint-hearted émigrés. Derived from verse, this unfamiliar term – 'palinode'– means a withdrawal, retraction or recantation of statement. It was, to be sure, a word more commonly used then than now. But still it was a term of legal art, perhaps learnt in the galleys, deftly employed for the purpose of political gossip. Despite his hard schooling, Barthélemy could hold his own when conversing with those who made a living through their pen.

Barthélemy certainly had self-confidence. In December 1850 he braved a covert return to France, risking capture and transportation. We have no details on how he made the journey, but the refugee underground was clearly adept at manufacturing counterfeit passports and providing safe houses. From London he made his way to Paris, where he surreptitiously met with well-known radical intellectuals such as Pierre Leroux, Alphonse Esquiros and Pierre Lachambeaudie. One day he visited the house of Victor Schoelcher, a deputy in the National Assembly renowned for issuing the decree by which the Provisional Government abolished slavery in the French colonies. Barthélemy arrived hunched and dressed in shabby working men's clothes, quite unlike his usual neat attire. He was keeping a low profile. Schoelcher was very busy, but his visitor would not leave, and ultimately he agreed to receive him. Barthélemy silently handed over a triangle of paper with letters on it, as if ripped from the corner of a page. Schoelcher was confused: 'What is that? What does it mean?' Barthélemy simply turned to leave, saying, 'It's useless, I'll come back.' Schoelcher, who did not recognise Barthélemy, had been troubled by his grim visage and abrupt speech. He thought he was a crazy man.

The following day, Schoelcher was sorting through his newly delivered letters when he found one from Louis Blanc in London. It was missing a corner. In it, Blanc assured him that the man who brought the missing corner could be entirely relied upon. Almost immediately, Barthélemy reappeared. He drew his little horn of paper from his pocket as he had the first time, and presented it without saying a word. Schoelcher took it, also without speaking. He brought it close to the letter, saw that the two sections fitted together, and said:

'That's fine. What's this about?'

'Citizen,' said Barthélemy, 'I need six thousand francs; you are rich; you must give it to me.'

'I will give them,' said Schoelcher, 'if the use you make of them seems to me useful to the cause I serve.'

'That's fair,' replied Barthélemy. 'The republican party, very weak since the Days of June, needs six men to raise it up again. These six men are prisoners. To give them freedom, I need six thousand francs.'

'Who are these men? Where are they? And what are your means of escape?'

'These six men are at Belle-Île, and are called Barbès, Blanqui ...'

Schoelcher interrupted him. 'I do not want Blanqui.'

Barthélemy quickly reassured him. 'I will replace him with —' and he gave another name.

'As for the means of escape,' he went on, 'I will tell you: the gaoler, for five hundred francs per prisoner, undertakes to get all six of them out of the prison enclosure and to lead them to a boat on the shore. This will be manned by a crew paid the same amount as that given to the gaoler for each of the prisoners. Once the six fugitives are on board, she will set off and take them to England.'

'But I cannot see how the gaoler will be able to arrange the flight of so many prisoners,' objected Schoelcher.

'Oh!' said Barthélemy. 'That will be easily done. The gaoler will shackle them two-by-two, as if they are mutineers or witnesses called to the examining magistrate. This will allow him to march them across the courtyards without arousing the suspicion of the guards. Once outside, they are blessed!'

'It is doubtful,' said Schoelcher, 'that six prisoners may be taken out so easily. But,' he mused, 'perhaps it is possible that the sentries on the perimeter wall will not recognise the flight of these six prisoners and will not fire on them.'

'It is probable,' said Barthélemy, 'and anyway, you must risk something.'

'As for me,' said Schoelcher, 'I will not cooperate with this plan of escape until I have the certainty that the six prisoners are willing to risk it.'

'That's fair enough,' replied Barthélemy. 'I will go to Belle-Île, I will see them, and I will give you their answer.'

Disguising himself once again as an *abbé* (priest), with a breviary in his hand, Barthélemy visited the prisoners in Belle-Île. It seems that Barbès and his friends refused to cooperate if Blanqui was to be amongst the escapees: they could not abide his remorseless criticism. Despite the insincere hint he had given Schoelcher, Barthélemy had clearly no intention of leaving Blanqui behind. Nonetheless, he pressed ahead with this escapade that perhaps explains Marx's quip to Engels regarding 'Père [Father] Barthélemy, born for the galleys'. With his mind full of plans, he returned to England.

Though Louis Blanc had withdrawn from the Blanquist society of refugees, he remained on good terms with Barthélemy. As the third anniversary of the February revolution in France approached, he endorsed a project to hold a commemorative 'Banquet of Equals'. Organisers included Blanc, Willich and

Schapper, and for the Blanquists, Vidil and Barthélemy. They were able to agree a joint programme. This proposed 'democratic power' founded on universal male suffrage and guided by the formula: '*from* each according to his powers, – *to* each according to his wants'. The progress achieved by the French Revolution of the eighteenth century would be completed by 'striking down' the nineteenth-century 'aristocracy of money and intellect'. Capitalism must be abolished, but also 'the tyranny of intellect' which was 'fully as unjust as the tyranny of force, and far more criminal in its nature'.

Marx and Engels poked fun at this last injunction in favour of equality of income regardless of talent or intelligence. It was, however, an ideal favoured by Marx and Engels themselves. It is certainly true that the tyranny of the self-assured intellectual is extremely trying; perhaps only the rule of the bumptious ignoramus is worse.

Marx and Engels' sniping was understandable. Marx was frustrated to high dudgeon, even beyond his usual grumpy standards, by Barthélemy and Willich's success in having 'at long last succeeded in bamboozling Louis Blanc to such an extent that he has combined with this "scum" to arrange a banquet ... along with a kind of manifesto'. Marx felt betrayed because, since 1843, he and his party had 'maintained a kind of lukewarm alliance' with Blanc. Marx tried to persuade those left-wing English Chartists he was still in touch with to have nothing to do with the commemoration, but with little success.

The banquet went ahead at the Highbury Barn Tavern, with about 1,000 supporters in attendance, despite a rival meeting the same evening organised by Ledru-Rollin. Willich was in the chair and Louis Blanc gave the main address. Barthélemy, for his part, delivered 'an extremely grandiose eulogy of Blanqui', according to Marx, who was relying upon second-hand report.

Barthélemy's talk was more interesting than that, though certainly it followed Blanqui's line.

Barthélemy began his speech by firmly committing himself to 'the only doctrine that we recognize as the truth, communist doctrine, intended to bring in the near future the reign of Equality'. Rather than stick to platitudes, however, he took the opportunity to expressly criticise various formulations held by others who, like him, supported 'the definitive triumph of the true sovereignty of the people'. It was important, he said, not to flatter the people, but to serve them. He agreed with the previous platform speaker that the position of a president, in France or elsewhere, was to be opposed. It was anti-republican, and nothing but the last breath of royalty in a nascent republic. (Naturally Barthélemy was thinking about President Louis Napoleon, but we would do well to bear his general warning in mind.)

But Barthélemy certainly did not think that democracy could be installed on day one of the revolution. At first the people would not be in a position to exercise power. 'Indeed, what great peril confronts the fate of the revolution from the crowd of citizens whose political and especially republican education is still imperfect?' The working class, wearied by labour, were too often indifferent even to those politicians who had their interests at heart. One easily found the 'prejudices of some and the inexperience of others working to the ruin of civil liberties'. Without revolutionary representatives of the people able to resist passing moods of demoralisation, the republic would be thrown into chaos and the road opened to the return of monarchy.

Barthélemy went on to quote extensively and learnedly from Robespierre's polemics of the 1790s, and turned them against those 'Girondins of today' – he clearly meant Ledru-Rollin and his supporters – who, though they were republicans, objectively served the interests of reaction. They had slaughtered republicans in the June Days and 'with poisonous venom' slandered

Blanqui. True republicans must learn that half-hearted measures only succeeded in obstructing the path of revolution.

Barthélemy drew the conclusion that revolutionaries must drive quickly to introduce radical reform. As revolution would mean war with the reactionary powers of Europe, there could be no space for the idle chatter of parliamentarianism. A republican revolution in France would inevitably spark a war of peoples against foreign kings, as it had done in the 1790s. When this happened, the workers would fly to the colours. On the home front, the rich, the cowards and the weak, those natural friends of aristocracy, would come to dominate any elected assembly. It would be wrong to allow the leisured classes, those who live off the labour of others, to fill the elected assemblies, 'while the workers would be bound, by their need to live, to the fields or the workshops'. Were elections to be held prematurely, 'all the talkative and clever lawyers' would abuse 'the ignorance of simple souls, easy to deceive, by appealing to all their prejudices, and especially the narrow-minded ideology of property still so deeply imprinted in our peasants'. The message was clear. Revolution might clear the way to democracy, but it should not itself be a democratic process. Successful revolution, in the first instance, required war and dictatorship.

Barthélemy concluded with this thoughtful peroration: 'Well good citizens, we think just like Robespierre; we want the direct government of the people by the people, but we want it to be possible and real.' The implication was clear, and eminently Blanquist: a revolutionary elite would have to exercise power on the morrow of the revolution to fend against the counter-revolutionary threat. Only this would lead to the ultimate 'triumph of socialism, the true sovereignty of the people!' This is the clearest explanation of Barthélemy's credo that we have. It showed him as ruthless, thoughtful, and something more than a revolutionary adventurer. It is perhaps unsurprising that he enjoyed such authority, and inspired much fear, amongst the revolutionary exile community.

The banquet was by all accounts a considerable success, but it did not go all the way the organisers would have hoped. When two of Marx's supporters, Conrad Schramm and Wilhelm Pieper, entered the hall, there was a small riot. They were barracked, had their hats torn off, were manhandled, ejected and beaten up. Barthélemy ran up to Schramm, shouting, '*C'est un infâme! Il faut l'écraser.*' 'He is infamous! He must be crushed!' Schramm bit back, '*Vous êtes un forçat libéré!*' 'You're an ex-convict!'

Such scuffles were hardly unusual in political meetings. Just three months previously a mild-mannered Christian Socialist, Lloyd James, had been 'collared, and cuffed, and shouted at' by 'clergymen and gentlemen' at an anti-Catholic public meeting. But it was an unedifying fracas nonetheless. Two days later, Marx and Engels sent a letter to George Harney of the Fraternal Democrats sharply condemning him for his participation in the banquet and his new political alliance. Harney was unmoved, smelling sour grapes. All Marx and Engels could do was fume. They were to have their revenge in a most unexpected way, however, when they found an unwitting ally in Auguste Blanqui, who despite Barthélemy's efforts remained imprisoned in the French island-fortress of Belle-Île.

The organisers of the banquet had sent for messages of support from overseas revolutionaries, and naturally they deputed Barthélemy to secure one from his great hero. There was nothing in the programme underpinning the banquet which Blanqui would have objected to. But he was much opposed to any connection with Louis Blanc, the companion of his old enemy, Barbès. Blanqui was dismayed, then incensed, when Barthélemy wrote to him asking if he would provide a toast to be read at the banquet and cautiously defending Blanc, whose 'intentions had been far better than his deeds'. Blanqui at this time was being cold-shouldered by the partisans of Barbès, with whom he shared the prison of Belle-Île, and from outside Blanc had taken the side of his rival. He was in little mood for generosity.

In a cold fury, Blanqui sent to Barthélemy, as a memorandum, a 'Warning to the People' he had already written 'in a fit of disgust'. Here he bitterly attacked the Provisional Government of 1848 in France, and the role of Louis Blanc. The memorandum opened, 'What menaces the revolution of tomorrow?' He answered, 'The deplorable popularity of bourgeois disguised as tribunes of the people.' Such had been Lamartine, Ledru-Rollin, Louis Blanc, even Albert. They were 'Sinister names, written in letters of blood on the paving stones of democratic Europe.' To him, these Provisional Government ministers had been responsible for killing the 1848 revolution in France. They were traitors who had betrayed the people, and on their hands was the blood of thousands of victims.

On the outbreak of revolution, Blanqui went on, the first measure should have been 'the disarming of the National Guards, the arming of the workers and their organisation as a national militia'. This was a priority before anything else. 'Not a gun must remain in the hands of the bourgeoisie.' Armed action, therefore, trumped any social policy.

Arms and organisation, these are the decisive elements of progress, the earnest way of putting an end to misery. He who has lead, has bread .... France, bristling with the bayonets of armed workers, that means the advent of socialism. Obstacles, oppositions, impossibilities, everything disappears before the armed proletarians. But should they let themselves be beguiled by absurd parades, tree plantings and loud, lawyers' phrases, they will first get holy water, then insults, finally grapeshot, and all will be wretchedness. The choice is up to the people.

For Blanqui, any revolutionary who failed to establish the armed authority of the working classes to intimidate counter-revolution was in effect a traitor. There was nothing new in what he said, but the sharpness of his anger was unpleasantly coruscating.

Barthélemy had loyally put this statement before the banquet committee, but a motion that it be read out to guests on the evening was rejected by one vote. It was not mentioned at all at the commemoration meeting, though its substance was clearly evident in Barthélemy's speech. Nonetheless, and against the wishes of Blanqui, the 'toast' became public. A delicious scandal erupted.

The Blanquist party in London was split on this inflammatory message from their imprisoned leader. After all, it vehemently attacked the principal speaker, Louis Blanc. Barthélemy, in an unprecedented act of defiance to his chief, led the faction that took exception to Blanqui's undiplomatic philippic. In a letter to Belle-Île, Barthélemy frankly criticised the 'Warning to the People' as unrealistically purist and unfair in accusing Blanc of treachery: 'For my part, citizen, I do not hesitate to tell you that I do not see the similarity that can justly be established between Louis Blanc, loyally followed by Albert in all his acts, and the monsters who have confessed to having shot the people during the sinister days of June 1848.' Blanc, after all, had been forced to flee France after the June Days, having been accused of moral responsibility for the insurrection. Ledru-Rollin and the rest had supported its suppression. Barthélemy complained that Blanqui's message had alienated allies in the movement, though his objection was not itself a model of toleration:

Undoubtedly, we must threaten with popular justice all those who have made themselves the voluntary accomplices of the counter-revolution. But at the same time we must have some indulgence for those who have not been weak or unintelligent. The people, always too indulgent themselves, will not allow permit anything else; and the triumph of the cause we defend, and for which you suffer at this moment, comes at this price.

Scenting an opportunity, another Blanquist faction in London, led by Jules Vidil and Eduard Goûte, had openly approved of Blanqui's message. Barthélemy was scathing of 'this flock of imbeciles'. By defending the 'Warning to the People' they had alienated financial contributors and in so doing, Barthélemy pointed out to Blanqui, 'ruined all the steps [he] had taken' to spring him from his prison-island:

I had already half realised the amount I needed, and two days later I should have the other half. The boat and the men who were to make the expedition with me were already found. And all this was lost thanks to the stupidity and the jealous perfidy of these republicans whose character resides only in their beards.

Disillusioned with his comrades in London, but loyal still to his master in Belle-Île, Barthélemy announced his intention to form an independent Blanquist organisation in London.

Blanqui was only able to reply a year later. He was placatory, appreciating Barthélemy as an 'energetic revolutionary'. He explained that he had written the 'Warning' six weeks before he ever heard of the 'Banquet of Equals' and had never expected it to be delivered as a toast. When it was leaked, he was at first surprised and irritated. But over time he came to believe that it was salutary:

Yes, this unexpected publication irritated me, but I was wrong, for it did no harm; on the contrary. It may have put some democrats in a mood, but it was well received by the masses and it produced good results. This advice therein might not be yours, and it has not always been mine. It is, however, the truth. I am more sure of that every day. The alarm-bell rang in the ears of the people who reflected on the warning and it was profitable. This profit will be there for us one day.

But Blanqui did not wish to dwell: 'Let us leave it there. Much water has since passed under the bridge.' Marx and Engels, in contrast, delighted in stirring troubled waters when the controversy went public. The banquet's organising committee, including Barthélemy, sent a letter to the Parisian press declaring that Blanqui had not submitted any toast to any member of the committee. This was truthful, but evasive. However, when the *Patrie* newspaper made enquiries it discovered that Blanqui's brother-in-law had dispatched the message, it having arrived first with Blanqui's sister, to Barthélemy, who had acknowledged receipt of the same. Blanqui had complete confidence that Barthélemy would keep the incendiary missive to himself, but had not reckoned on his brother-in-law leaking it. Its scoop by a right-wing French newspaper was highly embarrassing for the banquet's organisers. 'You can imagine the lamentations in that camp!' wrote Marx delightedly.

Defending as best they could, Louis Blanc in *The Times* and the entire banquet committee including Barthélemy in *Patrie* denied knowledge of the toast. But their embarrassment scaled new peaks when Vidil admitted that Blanqui's message had been suppressed by the organising committee on a formal vote, seven votes to six. Vidil claimed to be motivated only by 'his sense of honour and feeling of truth' but no doubt he saw an opportunity to outflank Barthélemy as leader of the Blanquist true-believers.

Barthélemy then dug himself in even further. He was not aware of Vidil's confession and a few days later, in a desperate but noble attempt to save the reputation of his allies by taking the blame on himself, he sent a statement to *Patrie* saying that he had received the toast but had not informed the others. Beneath this letter, the *Patrie* appended a contemptuous note that must have cut proud Barthélemy to the quick:

> We have often asked ourselves, and it is a difficult question to answer, whether the demagogues are notable more for their boastfulness or their stupidity .... the following letter from 'citizen' Barthélemy ... [is] the last proof of the authenticity of Blanqui's famous toast whose existence they first all denied and now fight among themselves for the right to acknowledge.

'Is that not SUPERB?' Marx crowed with spiteful glee. In order to capitalise on their rivals' embarrassment, and at what must have been considerable financial and organisational cost to themselves, Marx and Engels in March 1851 produced 30,000 copies of the Blanqui toast and distributed them internationally.

It had been a miserable affair. Barthélemy and Willich continued to conspire, whispering to one another in fireplace inglenooks, but the broader alliance had been dealt a considerable blow. The scandal of the banquet meant that Barthélemy's attempts to raise money to spring Blanqui from prison were badly hampered. A year later he wrote to Sophie Blanqui, 'most venerable mother of the only republican whom I admire and whom I love without restriction', blaming the affair of the toast and 'the petty jealous passions ... fatal to our cause' for his failure to execute his plans. 'Beware of snakes with a human face,' he warned her. He must certainly have been deeply embittered towards Marx and Engels.

Barthélemy had shown he was his own man, standing up to Blanqui and taking upon himself the burden of leadership in London, but he remained loyal to his old master. But Blanqui's toast had embarrassed the party and Barthélemy's reputation had suffered badly. His desire to escape the narrow back-biting of émigré politics in London and return to revolutionary action in France had only been sharpened.

11

PLOTTING, TRAGEDY, FARCE

In France, political developments were hurtling toward a historic denouement. Since the expulsion of Ledru-Rollin and his party of *démoc-socs* from France in June 1849, the conservatives of the Constitutional and then the National Assembly had had it all their own way. The 'party of order' pushed on with piously religious and repressive legislation. They forced through a limitation of the suffrage so that most workers were disenfranchised and unable to vote. President Louis Napoleon adroitly positioned himself as a defender of the lost democratic rights. His intention was not, however, to restore a constitutional democracy but to angle for supreme power. He was his uncle's nephew, and had never hidden his desire to restore the Napoleonic Empire.

As president, Louis Napoleon was head of the armed forces, and there was many a soldier who identified his lustrous family name with military pride and glory. The Assembly, shot through with contempt for the masses, was in no strong position to oppose the ambitions of a democratically elected head of state and president who retained considerable support amongst the people. Admittedly, republican opposition was rising, but Louis Napoleon had his strong-arm supporters, the '10 December

Society', to thrash with sticks any who dared oppose him too loudly. Most of all, Louis Napoleon's propaganda emphasised the ruinous political and class divisions within France, suggesting that only he could preserve the country from civil war.

On 21 September 1851, Barthélemy was deputed to welcome to England Louis Kossuth, hero of Hungary's defeated revolution against Austrian rule, on behalf of the émigré 'Republicans, Revolutionists, Socialists'. Kossuth's reply to Barthélemy's address was affable, but mentioned in passing the conflict of opinions dividing the people of France. The implication was clear: French democracy was not yet capable of sustaining itself. Barthélemy could not forbear from retorting:

> You have spoken of the divisions which agitate France. These divisions are not so numerous as you seem to think and as the journals of the government represent. There have been in France, as throughout the world, but two parties, the one of men who produce without possessing, and the other of men who possess without producing. There is in this unquestionable fact an attack upon natural justice; and the socialists are the republicans who combat this iniquity – their adversaries are those who defend it.

This was a rather undiplomatic rebuttal to a stalwart republican, and Barthélemy softened it: 'The present is neither the time nor the place to discuss socialism, and I comprehend that your mission may not be to apply the principles of your own country, where all that is practicable is, as you have said, the Republic based upon universal suffrage, with the solidarity of peoples.' But if Hungary was not ready for socialist class struggle, in Barthélemy's view France certainly was.

Shortly after this, Barthélemy again smuggled himself back into France. It is quite likely that he went in the company of his Blanquist comrade, Vidil. Barthélemy managed to keep his movements secret, however, while Vidil's were quickly exposed. Early in November 1851, Vidil arrived in Paris 'with the design of organising an insurrection, and executing a project still less avowable', as the government let it be known, presumably the assassination of Louis Napoleon. Vidil and another Blanquist, Goute, formerly a master tanner at Blois, were arrested on 7 November at the lodgings of Vidil's mistress. Papers were discovered, including three passports under false names. Other papers led to a search of the lodgings of a mechanic called Guerin, at Montmartre, where a large quantity of firearms were found along with bomb-making materials and an 'infernal machine', 'capable of discharging fifteen projectiles at the same time'.

Following the passport trail, police tracked down another man called Dupostel to a wine shop in the Faubourg du Temple. Ammunition and a number of letters of compromising character were seized. Police also descended upon Madame Antoine, Blanqui's sister, who tried to burn incriminating letters and papers before they could be seized. She was prevented, and amongst them was found a copy of Blanqui's 'famous' message, the 'Warning to the People'. In the aftermath, the police descended upon a secret organisation, the Jeune Montagne, associated with the Vidil plot. Firearms were seized, along with ammunition, badges and 'an enormous quantity of socialist writings of the worst kind'. Those arrested were chiefly of the working class. Their aim had been to recruit supporters in the army, the strategy favoured by Barthélemy's German comrade, August Willich.

On 2 December 1851, Louis Napoleon unleashed his forces against the fragile Republic. Under the pretext of the presence of dangerous refugees from London being found in Paris, the capital was flooded with soldiers. At five in the morning, officers were informed that they were to close down the National Assembly. This was a violation of the constitution, but not one officer demurred. Generals loyal to the Republic – including Cavaignac and Lamoricière, who had led the repression of the June Days – were put under arrest. Two battalions disarmed the guard at the National Assembly and occupied the building. Opposition politicians were roused from their beds and marched into custody. Seventy-eight civilians, 'known for the energy of their Republican convictions, and feared as "Chiefs of barricades"', were scooped up. By 7 a.m., the initial operation was virtually complete, and proclamations announcing a new regime were being posted around Paris. This was the classical *coup d'état* of the nineteenth century: the state apparatus had broken the constitution that restrained it.

Louis Napoleon's move did provoke some physical opposition: barricades were built in Paris and there were serious outbreaks of violence in the provinces. The surviving Jeune Montagne gave leadership to peasant resistance in the south of France. Twenty-six thousand *démoc-socs* were detained and martial law was put in place in thirty-two departments until the end of March 1852. Military force and the President's promise to restore universal male suffrage at length proved sufficient to suppress resistance. People could vote, but only for those prepared to support the new regime, and the government would be a creature of Napoleon, not of the elected representatives. The police repressed political opposition. Napoleon was able to secure 7,439,216 votes in a plebiscite to legitimise the new regime, as against 640,737 cast against. In November 1852, following another referendum, Louis Napoleon was declared Napoleon III, 'hereditary Emperor of the French'.

As Louis Napoleon carried out his seizure of power and his soldiers cleared the streets, a group of republican 'Representatives' of the National Assembly, along with workers and journalists, met at the home of Frédéric Cournet on the rue de Popincourt: a two-storey building, still under construction, arranged round a little square courtyard. They assembled on the first floor, sitting on stools cushioned with straw in a large room with low ceiling and whitewashed walls. Victor Hugo, positioned between fireplace and stairway, presided. Reports were given on the popular mood. The news was not good. A workman, leaning against the mantelpiece, muttered in a low voice to one of his comrades: there was no counting upon the people. If they tried to fight, it would 'be doing a crazy thing'. 'One after another, our hopes were extinguished,' recalled Hugo. 'But, as I thought, this was all the more reason why we should astonish and arouse Paris by some extraordinary spectacle ... by the audacity of an immense devotion.' He proposed that they gather the following morning at the Café-Roysin in the nearby Faubourg Saint-Antoine, once the shops had opened: 'There must be people in the streets, that they may see us, that they may know who we are, that the glory of our example may meet every eye and thrill every heart.' The next morning the politicians gathered uncertainly on the street for an act of heroic demonstration.

They erected a barricade on the rue Sainte Marguerite. Frédéric Cournet, a naval hero turned republican activist, took charge of its construction. But it was an unimpressive sight, a meagre jumble of stones and carts clearly intended to be little more than symbolic. The pavements were left unblocked. One of the insurgent leaders, Charles Baudin, stood atop the barricade. He was barracked by a gaggle of Bonapartist workers, who shouted their scorn at these politicians only concerned for their daily stipend as members of the National Assembly. 'Down with the twenty-five francs!' they jeered. Baudin turned to stare at them: 'You will see how one can die for twenty-five francs.'

A small battalion of the 19th Regiment of the line was sent to disperse the protest. It was evident, as soon as they turned up, that the insurrectionists did not wish to fight. Their leaders, including the burly Cournet towering above the rest, drew themselves up in front of the barricade, all wearing their official insignia as elected members of the Assembly. They did not take cover, and Cournet ordered their followers to lower and conceal their muskets. There followed a tense stand-off.

With a copy of the constitution in his hand, one of the National Assembly representatives, Victor Schoelcher, began to speak to the soldiers. He appealed to their sense of duty, telling them that they were not mere mercenaries; their first loyalty was to the law and the constitution, not to the commander-in-chief. Schoelcher was interrupted by a shot from the barricade, wounding a soldier. The regiment's commanding officer lost his patience and ordered his soldiers to fire a volley. There was a crash of gunfire, and Baudin fell with two bullets in his head. One other insurgent, a workman, was also killed, and others were wounded by the hail of lead.

This was now a fight in earnest. The insurgents dashed behind the barricade and began to return fire, killing a soldier and the officer who had ordered the fusillade. Meanwhile, a macabre scene played out around the mortally wounded figure of Baudin. An officer of the line and Frédéric Cournet grappled in an attempt to pull him over to their respective sides. Backed by the bayonets of his men, the officer won this grisly tug-of-war, and four soldiers carried Baudin away. Rioting escalated until suppressed on 4 December.

It was a half-hearted struggle, even now, and nothing like as substantial as the June Days insurrection. Louis Napoleon's hope for a near bloodless coup, however, was dashed on 4 December. As workers were being repressed in the east of Paris, a column of soldiers under the command of Canrobert lost discipline and opened fire in the bourgeois boulevards. Bullets poured forth for ten minutes and well over one hundred were killed in the fire zone. In a ferocious polemic against Louis Napoleon, Victor Hugo wrote bitterly of 'the inoffensive inhabitants of Paris, the citizens who are not in any way mixed up with the fighting' being 'shot down without warning and massacred merely for the sake of intimidation'. This slaughter would not be forgiven.

Louis Napoleon, who more than anything wished to be loved by the people, was bitterly disappointed. Future dictators would revel in such brutality as expressions of iron will. But for the second Napoleonic Empire, it was an indelible stain.

Not uncommonly, historical turning points only fix their meaning when they are fictionalised. Imaginative treatment gives emotional charge and dramatic narrative to the hurly-burly of events. It was the great novelist Victor Hugo, a blockbusting writer for all classes, who wove together the street battles of this period. In so doing he transfigured Barthélemy into the very personification of the unyielding revolutionary. In his famous novel, *Les Misérables*, Hugo compared the ferocious resistance of the June Days to the much less impressive rebellion of December 1851 – and he had witnessed both. In so doing, he made the names of both Emmanuel Barthélemy and Frédéric Cournet legends and archetypes: Barthélemy's plebeian seriousness and action as against Cournet's rhetorical defiance and windy playacting:

> That barricade at the Faubourg du Temple [of June 1848], defended by 80 men against 10,000, held out for three days .... Not one of the 80 'cowards' attempted to escape. All were killed except their leader, Barthélemy, of whom we shall have more to say.
>
> The Saint-Antoine barricade [of December 1851] was a place of thunderous defiance, the one at the Temples a place of silence. The difference between these two strongholds was the difference between the savage and the sinister, the one a roaring open mouth, the other a mask. The huge, mysterious insurrection of June '48 was at once an outburst of fury and an enigma: in the first of these barricades the Dragon was discernible; in the second, the Sphinx.

These two strongholds were the work of two men, Cournet and Barthélemy, and each bore the image of the man responsible. Cournet of Saint-Antoine was a burly broad-shouldered man, red-faced, heavy-fisted, daring, and loyal, his gaze candid but awe-inspiring. He was intrepid, energetic, irascible and temperamental, the warmest of friends and the most formidable of enemies. War and conflict, the melee, were the air he breathed, they put him in high spirits. He had been a naval officer, and his voice and bearing had the flavour of sea and tempest – he brought the gale with him into battle. Except for genius there was in Cournet something of Danton, just as, except for divinity, there was in Danton something of Hercules.

Barthélemy, of the Temple, was thin and puny, sallow-faced and taciturn, a sort of tragic outcast who, having been beaten by a police officer, waited for the chance and killed him. He was sent to the galleys at the age of 17, and when he came out he built this barricade .... Barthélemy at all times flew one flag only, and it was black.

Hugo's striking diptych, first published in 1862, immediately entered into historical consciousness as a true description of the June Days. It had its errors. Few described Barthélemy as puny, and of course he had not killed the policeman in 1839. The 'black flag' had been unfurled by the canuts rebels of Lyon in 1832 and 1834. It was a symbol of proletarian anguish and desperate revolt. Hugo wished to identify Barthélemy with the people of the abyss, not ideologues but workers driven by ferocious instinct. This certainly underestimated Barthélemy's political consciousness.

But these caveats did not matter. Hugo's depiction was soon taken as the ultimate representation of the June Days. It was forgotten by many that the Saint-Antoine barricade battles actually referred to a later time, after the June insurgents had been extirpated, killed, repressed or dispersed.

In 1879, the republican newspaper *Mot d'Ordre* recalled that when the fighting of June 1848 was over, and the heroic proletariat ridden down by the forces of the bourgeoisie, the red flag which had been hoisted on the formidable barricade defended by Cournet, and the black standard which had floated over Barthélemy's redoubt in the Faubourg du Temple, were picked up from among the corpses and carried to the Constitutive Assembly, where the representatives greeted them with jeering applause. For years they had been left forgotten in the garret of the palace, a heap of old, faded and blackened rags covered in dried blood wound over half-broken flagstaffs still pitted with bullet holes. In 1879 they were recovered as a revered memorial for the new Republic. Of course, the two men had not actually fought in the same insurrection. But Barthélemy's fortitude and Cournet's braggadocio had entered into the historical record more powerfully than mere fact.

Radicals had seen in the proletariat an unbending defiance. The failure of the workers of Paris to effectively resist the coup, however, dealt a heavy and demoralising blow to this mythology. Another novelist inspired by 1848, but turned by it in the direction of cynical intelligence rather than grand psychodrama, was Gustave Flaubert. In his 1869 novel, *L'Éducation sentimentale*, Flaubert put into the mouth of one of his characters, Charles Deslauriers, a typically middle-class exasperation with the fickle working class. 'Oh, I've had my belly full of that bunch, kowtowing to Robespierre's guillotine, Napoleon's jackboot, Louis Philippe's umbrella, a rabble who'll swear undying allegiance to anyone who'll toss them a crust of bread to fill their guts.' The novel's protagonist, Frédéric Moreau, defends the workers, but weakly. 'As for the workers, they have got a right to complain because ... the only thing you ever gave them was words, words and still more words! ... In fact, the Republic seems to me to have run out of steam. Who knows, perhaps progress can only be achieved by an aristocracy – or by one man? Initiative always comes from above! The masses aren't yet grown-up, whatever people claim.' Here Flaubert captured the thinking of those who unwillingly agreed with Louis Napoleon when he wrote that 'the nature of [modern] democracy is to personify itself in one man.'

We can see here an ever-present danger to representative democracy. Political parties, it is commonly felt, represent their own particular class factions and interest groups, as well as those oddities who find a career in politics to be satisfying. But they do not represent, either singly or together, the 'national will'. Normal politicians are rarely taken, at their own estimation, as being entirely committed to the national collective good, as evidenced by their overcompensating and wearisome patriotic flag-waving. Who has not heard, in the pub or the office, the complaint that 'politicians are all in it for themselves'? 'Not in our name,' is the cry of the street demonstration. No doubt political parties, or at least their leadership groups, are mortal, and often need a good shove to be moved on to the political graveyard (or corporate lecture circuit). But there is always a risk that suspicion of politicians can curdle, and there emerges a leader claiming to represent not so much a party as a national 'movement'. Such a leader eschews the politics of policy-formulation, which implies balancing between interest groups, and instead relies upon charisma and leadership.

It is all too easy for such movements to represent themselves as being above mere sectional parties, and to ventriloquise the voice of the people. Not for nothing do they have a fondness for the referendum and the plebiscite. They will emphasise that which brings the nation together, and that which excludes those unfortunates who are seen as outsiders, interlopers or subverters of the nation. They offer an enticing vision of unity and inclusiveness, all the more attractive to societies deeply divided by class, ethnicity or religion. In the mid-nineteenth century, revolutionary democrats were obsessed by Napoleon III and what he represented. Usually they would diminish and deprecate him. Victor Hugo called him 'Napoleon the Little'. Marx dismissed him as a ridiculous caricature of his illustrious uncle. In reality, they were afraid. They perceived, if dimly, a popular Bonapartism that would darken into twentieth-century fascism. Authoritarian populism is hardly absent in our own time.

In France, the Solidarité républicaine organisation, a coalition of socialists and radical republicans, with the Blanquist Martin Bernard as president and the neo-Jacobin Charles Delescluze as secretary, had been confident that they could win the next scheduled elections in 1852. The *coup d'état* shattered their hopes. From his prison cell, Blanqui was distraught at the failure of the masses to oppose Napoleon's destruction of the revolution. Characteristically, he pinned the blame on the lack of a determined insurrectionary leadership. As he wrote to Barthélemy, 'To say that no one was to be found anywhere to rally this mob. What a depressing experience!' He was particularly pessimistic because he saw France as the very fount of revolution in Europe. If reaction was triumphant in France, revolution had no chance anywhere else. 'When France falls back, Europe becomes lax.' Barthélemy blamed the poor showing of republicans against Napoleon's coup on the imprisonment of Blanqui. 'I don't doubt that had Blanqui been able to join the organisation we have formed in London,' he wrote to Willich, 'the events of second December would have found a republican organisation ready to resist.' He said the same to Blanqui's mother:

If I had been able to execute the project I intended to execute myself at Belle-Île, your son, when he came to London, might have completed the already powerful organiza-

tion which I had begun, and which … I am sure, would
have averted the shame of recent events. If we had Blanqui
in our midst, his presence would have eliminated petty rivalries and retied the bonds of union between men whom
envy had divided. The party would have prepared itself for
the struggle which everyone had foreseen, and Bonaparte
would have found not a crowd but an army on the battlefield of 4th of December.

For Barthélemy, the presence of a determined, ruthlessly realistic
organisation of revolutionaries, based upon charismatic unity,
was ultimately crucial to preserve the gains of revolution.

Frederick Engels looked upon the failure of the French proletariat to effectively resist the destruction of the Republic with
frustration but also a wry amusement. Absurdity had finally
replaced serious revolutionism. In a letter to Marx, written
from Manchester, he sarcastically compared Louis Napoleon's
seizure of power to the analogous coup of his great-uncle,
Napoleon Bonaparte, on the '18th Brumaire', as the revolutionary calendar of the 1790s had dated it.

The history of France has entered a stage of utmost comi-
cality. Can one imagine anything funnier than this travesty
of the 18th Brumaire, effected in peacetime with the help
of discontented soldiers by the most insignificant man in
the world without, so far as it has hitherto been possible to
judge, any opposition whatsoever? … It's enough to make
one despair. And now there's no longer even a National
Assembly to foil the great schemes of this unappreciated
man … Appalling, a prospect devoid of conflict!

In this private letter, Engels let rip his disgust at the failure of
the French masses to effectively resist the coup. They had been
fooled by Napoleon's promise to restore universal male suffrage,

even though this would mean empty votes with no direct influence on government. Engels had grown tired of those who would celebrate 'the people'. And those who would seek to lead them were but pale shadows of the great leaders of the French Revolution.

> 'But the people, the people!' The people don't care a damn about this whole business. [They] are happy as children over the franchise accorded to them and which, indeed, they will probably make use of like children … after what we saw yesterday, there can be no counting on the *peuple*, and it really seems as though old Hegel, in the guise of the World Spirit, were directing history from the grave and, with the greatest conscientiousness, causing everything to be re-enacted twice over, once as grand tragedy and the second time as rotten farce, Caussidière for Danton, L. Blanc for Robespierre, Barthélemy for Saint-Just, Flocon for Carnot, and the moon-calf [Louis Napoleon] together with the first available dozen debt-encumbered lieutenants for the little corporal [Napoleon Bonaparte].

Characteristically, the one comfort for Engels was the demoralising effect he expected the coup to have on their rivals in the emigration: 'The news from France must have had a jolly effect on the European émigré rabble. I'd like to have witnessed it.' We all of us take comfort where we may, and in extremis *Schadenfreude* is not to be sniffed at.

Engels here had compared Barthélemy to Saint-Just, the youthful, plebeian, idealistic but unrelentingly stern Jacobin revolutionary of the French Revolution. Saint-Just had famously defined 'revolutionary government' as a regime of force and domestic terror to bend all the forces of the nation against the threat of counter-revolution, both internal and external. But, in the view of Engels, Barthélemy was little more than a pale shadow cast by the reputation of Saint-Just.

Marx was evidently struck by what he read in Engels' letter. Never one to let a good idea go to waste, he repurposed the comparison, and in his 1852 publication *The Eighteenth Brumaire of Louis Napoleon* he casually attributed it to the better-known German philosopher, Georg Hegel, as mentioned by Engels. In so doing, he created one of his most famous phrases, which has resonated ever since, but left Barthélemy as a silent and overlooked presence:

> Hegel remarks somewhere that all great world-historic facts and personages appear, so to speak, twice. He forgot to add: the first time as tragedy, the second time as farce. Caussidière for Danton, Louis Blanc for Robespierre, the Montagne of 1848 to 1851 for the Montagne of 1793 to 1795, the nephew for the uncle.

For Marx, the pathetic outcome of the 1848 revolution was evidence enough that revolutionaries of the nineteenth century should finally leave the great French Revolution behind them. Jacobin politics was exhausted. No doubt Marx did not consider Barthélemy well enough known to include him in this work for public consumption. But perhaps, also, he did not think it entirely right to number Barthélemy amongst the figures of casual comedy. For Barthélemy had not been sitting on the sidelines when Louis Napoleon launched his coup.

When fighting in Paris broke out to resist Louis Napoleon's soldiers, Barthélemy was in the thick of it. We have no detailed account of his participation, but most likely he had returned to his old stamping ground of the Marais and Temple district. On Wednesday, 3 December, barricades went up and soldiers

were pelted with paving stones. General Magnan, Commander
of the Troops of Paris, 'resolved to leave the insurrection to
itself for some time, to allow it an opportunity to take up its
ground, to establish itself upon it, and finally to form a
compact mass which I would come up and fight with'. The
troops were ordered to return to the barracks and wait. By
the following day, large bodies of rioters were on the streets
in the districts of Saint-Antoine, Saint-Denis and Saint-
Martin: the core of the revolt was the Temple district. By
noon, about a hundred barricades had been erected, but the
workers had few weapons, having been disarmed after the
June Days. Magnan then launched his 30,000 troops in a
three-pronged assault:

> The barricades, attacked with cannon in the first place,
> were carried at the bayonet. All that part of the city lying
> between the Faubourgs Saint-Antoine and Saint-Martin,
> Pont Saint-Eustache and the Hôtel de Ville, was ploughed
> in all directions by our columns of infantry; the barricades
> were carried and destroyed; the insurgents dispersed and
> slain .... Assailed at once on every side ... hemmed in, as
> in a network of iron ... [the] insurrection had been sub-
> dued on the ground chosen by itself.

Most of the fighting was over within two hours, though there
were mopping-up operations to intimidate diehards and the
populace in general.

As the resistance fell apart, Vassel, an ex-officer of the 9th
Hussars, since won to the Republic, sought Barthélemy out as
an experienced street fighter. Vassel had changed into the civilian
clothes of a bourgeois after fighting against the coup, but the
authorities were closing in. 'I need to hide, save me!'

'Willingly,' replied Barthélemy. 'Come to one of my friends,
Besançon. He will hide you at his home.'

Barthélemy and Vassel went to Besançon's house, where they found him with a young woman named Mademoiselle Goldsmith. Besançon received the two arrivals gladly. With a cheerful demeanour he turned to Vassel: 'I leave you with Mademoiselle, who will keep you company; I have an extremely urgent affair outside; I am leaving.'

Two hours later, when the treacherous Besançon returned in the company of police, it became clear that a trap had been set. Barthélemy and Vassel were arrested. According to Charles Hugo, both men somehow escaped, though he gives no more details. Vassel must have been recaptured, for he was in fact transported to an overseas penal colony, amnestied years later, and in 1862 was still active as a secret society revolutionist. Barthélemy, however, apparently made good his getaway, smuggling himself from France to Germany and, ultimately, Switzerland. His having so narrowly eluded the authorities, while others were snatched, must surely have created suspicions in the minds of Barthélemy's revolutionary comrades. Was he allowed to go free in return for passing information to the police? But in the confusion of the *coup d'état*, it seems just as likely that Barthélemy had enough experience, skill and – most importantly – luck to avoid the dragnet.

Switzerland was a centre for many Italian and French refugees, including Félix Pyat, a radical republican journalist, who went about Geneva disguised as a Moor. He would later become notorious for writing a pamphlet calling for the assassination of the Emperor Napoleon III. The mood of émigrés here was one of preparation for armed struggle. While in the country, Barthélemy devoted himself to the military arts. Beside his bed he kept a copper plate, and every morning he would practise firing at it with a pistol. He studied weapons manufacture, his remarkable mechanical aptitude and sharp intelligence put to work in the invention of a specialised gun, which automatically loaded as it was fired, enabling a succession of bullets to be rattled off at a single target. It was with such a weapon that he dreamt of assassinating Napoleon III.

Cold-blooded certainly, but Barthélemy's projected terrorism was not the slaughter of innocents as indulged in by the death-cult Islamist fanatics in our own time. Rather, it followed the logic of Saint-Just's icy rationalism: a monarch or pretender to the throne, and his satraps, were at war with society, and must take the consequences. Such a conclusion was quite unjustifiable, but it had a certain perverse logic. The enemy was not to be allowed any repose. As Barthélemy wrote to Willich after the coup, he 'found himself unable to resign himself to allowing Louis Napoleon to enjoy his triumph in peace'. In early July 1852 a number of French and German newspapers reported the arrest of conspirators in Paris. They were mainly workers, some of whom who had participated in the June uprising. They had been planning to assassinate the Emperor. Engels was not alone in suspecting the involvement of 'sinister Barthélemy'. His priority remained, however, springing Blanqui from prison. His inability thus far to pull off this daring escapade was deeply frustrating. 'You cannot believe what sorrow I feel,' he wrote to Blanqui's mother. 'I always roll this project in my head, without being able to find the way to overcome the obstacle, always the same, which has already failed me once: lack of money.' He decided, therefore, to return to the recently expanded exile community in London. 'The events of December,' he wrote hopefully, 'have had to modify a little the antipathies of certain men whom I shall see again in the company of new men, *proscrits* of the 2nd of December [*coup d'état*]. I'll try again.'

It was not all work and worry for Barthélemy while he sojourned in Switzerland, however. He met and had an affair with an Italian actress, his 'beloved Maria', and for a time they lived together. This led to tittle-tattle on the international grapevine: revolutionaries are no more immune to gossip than anyone else. Barthélemy's friends in London wrote to him of the chatter about his lover being passed around by Frédéric Cournet, the leader of the insurrection against Napoleon's coup in 1851, and now an exile. 'What a pity,' Cournet is supposed to have said, 'that this most socialist of socialists should have let an actress keep him!' It did not help that some believed Barthélemy's mistress to be an agent of the French police. Barthélemy was enraged at these ungracious imputations, and it was with a vengeful heart that he made his way back to England from the Continent in October 1852.

12

BARTHÉLEMY AND COURNET

On his return to London, Barthélemy made the acquaintance of the Russian, Alexander Herzen. This must have been a welcome opportunity for him. England was a peculiarly hidebound society in many ways. The genteel classes were unfailingly polite, but the rules of etiquette were 'so rigid and intolerant as to be inconceivable'. The French were surprised to see people meet and depart without even an affectionate hug. 'I knew English men were averse to kissing,' wrote Wey, 'but I did not know it amounted to positive revulsion!' A rather austere religion permeated all classes, and overt atheism could hardly be found. Visitors were depressed to see every attraction and retail outlet shut up on Sunday, though it did allow a welcome sight of blue sky in the industrial cities. Arriving in Leith on a Sunday in December 1850, the German émigré Carl Schurz had to 'saunter around for seven continuous hours' before finding an inn that would agree to serve him. Britain could feel like rather a dour country, particularly for the French. When Barthélemy became friends with an elegant, rich, free-thinking and warm socialist in Herzen – aristocratic though he was – he was charmed.

For the biographer, and this book's reader, it is a particularly fortunate happenstance that Herzen found him. Or rather, not such a stroke of unlikely good fortune. For Barthélemy was a magnetic personality and Herzen an acute observer with an unquenchable fascination for the revolutionary demi-monde on the fringes of society. So it was that Barthélemy found a place in Herzen's memoirs, one of the literary masterpieces of the nineteenth century.

Herzen was a wealthy, sophisticated and observant man, possessed of considerable psychological acuity. After his expulsion from Russia in 1847 he found himself in France in time to witness the revolution. All his sympathies were with the socialists and worker movement. Herzen was no straightforward progressive, however. The experience of the French Second Republic disillusioned him with parliamentary democracy. Though critical of the tsarist regime in Russia, he thought he saw in the Russian village, organised collectively between its inhabitants, a superior basis for civilisation compared to anything to be found in the West. The foundation of Russia, he wrote, 'is a communistic peasantry still slumbering, with a surface scum of cultivated people'. For Herzen, only a more primitive society could provide a basis for an egalitarian society where everyone, without exception, had a place at the table.

Marx and Engels, who despised tsarism and disdained the peasantry, refused to have anything to do with Herzen. For these two Westerners, the road to socialism must go through capitalist development and the modern proletariat. Herzen, despite his own university education and subtle mind, saw in the primitive instincts of the untutored masses a simple goodness, so long as he did not have to live amongst them. When in London, he lived a life of elegance far above that of most émigrés. But into his company he was pleased to welcome Emmanuel Barthélemy – as an intriguing specimen, but also, it must be said, as a true friend.

Herzen arrived in London in 1852, and was immediately welcomed by the revolutionary emigration, not least because of his largesse. 'Herzen kept open house, and any exile down on his luck knew that he could come, any evening, to drink his wine, to smoke his tobacco, and to talk, gaily or gravely as the mood served, till any hour of the night.' August Willich introduced Barthélemy at one of these soirées. Herzen was immediately impressed by the 'great sympathy and confidence' Barthélemy showed him. Barthélemy, it seems, avoided the faux pas made by Wilhelm Weitling when he met the poet Heine, behaving amiably to this potential benefactor for the cause.

Herzen in his memoirs left a vivid description of Barthélemy as a physically impressive man, compact and lithe: 'He was a young man, short, but of a muscularly powerful build; his pitch-back curly hair gave him a Southern look; his face, slightly marked with smallpox, was clear-cut and handsome.' More striking, however, was the psychology of this true-born proletarian revolutionary:

> Continual conflict had aroused in him an inflexible will and the power of directing it. Barthélemy was one of the most single-minded natures which it has been my lot to meet. Of bookish school education he had none except in his own line: he was an excellent mechanic .... The thought of his life, the passion of his whole existence was an unflagging thirst like that of Spartacus for the revolt of the working people against the middle classes. This idea was in him inseparable from a savage desire to massacre the bourgeois.

Spartacus had been the legendary slave general who had led a heroic and doomed rebellion against the Roman Republic of Caesar's time. He was a name to conjure with in revolutionary circles. Marx selected him as his favourite personality from antiquity. German revolutionaries, led by Rosa Luxemburg and Karl Liebknecht, son of Wilhelm, were to name their organisation after him during the First World War. No figure better represented the heroism and combativity of the risen oppressed.

Barthélemy also reminded Herzen of those sans-culottes radicals who had turned their fury against traitors to the revolution during the violent days of the 1790s. He saw in him a ferocious will born of the most rigid fortitude. Barthélemy had that hatred which drives 'the parties nearest of kin' to destroy one another. 'In him I saw face-to-face how a man can combine a thirst for blood with humanity in other relations, even with tenderness, and how a man may be at peace with his own conscience while like Saint-Just sending dozens of men to the guillotine.' Engels, of course, had made the same comparison.

Herzen was impressed with the clarity of Barthélemy's spoken thought. 'He talked in a masterly fashion, a talent that is growing more and more rare.' Barthélemy was not an empty orator, he did not preach, but he could 'talk for the benefit of a room'. He spoke with remorseless conviction. 'Barthélemy's one-sided logic, continually turned in one direction, acted like the flame of a blowpipe. He spoke smoothly without raising his voice or gesticulating; his choice of words, his sentences were correct, pure, and completely free from the three curses of modern French: revolutionary jargon, legal expressions and the easy familiarity of shop boys.' Herzen was astonished that a workman, 'brought up in the stifling foundries where iron was forged and wrought for machines, in stifling Parisian alleys, between the pot house and the forge, in prison and in penal servitude' had acquired a 'true conception of beauty and proportion, of tact and grace'. For Herzen, Barthélemy was a kind of noble savage.

In their conversations together, Barthélemy spoke of how the revolution was to be protected against the weakness or treachery of its own partisans. 'That the revolution may not be for the tenth time stolen out of our hands,' Barthélemy would say, 'we must crush our worst foe at home, in our own family. At the counter, in the office, we always find him – it's in our own camp that we ought to destroy him!' These 'enemies within' included nearly all the prominent refugees: Victor Hugo, Mazzini and Kossuth among them. He had a special animosity for Ledru-Rollin, 'the peculiar object of his most genuine hatred'. Only Ledru-Rollin could make him lose his cool. 'The keen, passionate but extremely composed face of Barthélemy would twitch convulsively when he spoke of "the dictator of the bourgeoisie".' One of the very few excused from Barthélemy's scorn was Louis Blanc.

Herzen introduced Barthélemy to the former governess of his children, Malwida von Meysenbug. Von Meysenbug, aged thirty-six, was a German of French Protestant descent. Two of her brothers made prominent political careers in the service of German and Austrian monarchy, but she split from her family due to her republican and social democratic beliefs. Later in life, despite poor health, she would become a close friend to avant-garde intellectuals, notably Richard Wagner and Friedrich Nietzsche. When Herzen promised to introduce her to Barthélemy – 'a very odd person' – she was eager but nervous: he had a reputation as a stone-cold killer. Any anxiety was dissipated by his 'deep, melodic and irresistibly soothing voice'. Barthélemy was 'reserved, modest, even shy' and reassuringly gentle with von Meysenbug. But 'his dark eye, which glowed in a melancholic face under a thoughtful brow' would sometimes 'flash like the distant lightning flashes of a threatening storm'.

She agreed with Herzen's conviction that Barthélemy was hypnotically direct and precise in his speech, a sharp contrast to the sentimental rhetoric of the middle-class French émigrés:

He never became animated in a discussion, never yelled like the other French, never recited like they, didn't speak rhetorically, in fact, didn't speak much at all. But when he

spoke, all drew silent, one after the other. His deep, soothing voice sounded clear and determined above the echoing
chaos and uttered opinions seemingly cut from stone, they
seemed so unshakeable.

She was fascinated by those flashes of his daemon held under
restraint: 'Only seldom was a note of passion mixed in his
voice, which revealed that not only could his opinion lead to a
deed, but that it could be such a rash deed that he himself
might later regret it.'

Von Meysenbug was clearly quite besotted with Barthélemy.
She found in him an exceptional product of the heroic yet
terrifying proletariat:

> I was so taken by my acquaintance with this man that Her-
> zen laughed about my enthusiasm, even though he him-
> self found him very important and magnetic. In Germany,
> I had been accustomed to dealing with educated workers
> who discussed social issues earnestly and thoughtfully; but
> I had never encountered such a harmonious and thorough-
> ly educated man as Barthélemy or such a complete devia-
> tion from social class manifested through his decency and
> behaviour. He gave me new-found respect for the French
> working-class which justified me in assuming that the sal-
> vation and future of that country lies in this class alone.

Barthélemy, it seemed to these observers, both transcended his
own class and represented its best potential.

It was around this time that Carl Schurz met Barthélemy in
the drawing room of the Baroness von Brüning, a Russian of
Germanic background from the Baltic. Her St John's Wood
salon was a regular gathering place for refugees. Schurz had
dramatically escaped from the prison fortress of Rastatt in 1849.
Like August Willich, he would go on to fight with high rank

and distinction in the Union army during the American Civil War. Unlike him, he would subsequently rise to high political rank. The description Schurz gives of Barthélemy matches that of Alexander Herzen and Malwida von Meysenbug, but he found in him a far more chilling character.

Schurz described Barthélemy as 'a man of a little more than thirty years, of sturdy figure, a face of dusky paleness with black moustache and goatee, the dark eyes glowing with piercing fire'. He was struck, once more, by Barthélemy's diction and unsentimental focus: 'He spoke in a deep, sonorous voice, slowly and measuredly with dogmatic assurance, waving off contrary opinions with a word of compassionate disdain.'

For Barthélemy, nothing could be allowed to get in the way of the revolution. He was a man who had killed, and without compunction would kill again:

With the greatest coolness he explained to us his own theory of the revolution, which simply provided that the contrary minded without much ado be exterminated. The man expressed himself with great clearness, like one who had thought much and deliberately upon his subject and had drawn his conclusions by means of the severest logic.

Schurz recognised in Barthélemy not just an individual but a type:

We saw before us, therefore, one of those fanatics that are not seldom produced in revolutionary times — men perhaps of considerable ability, whose understanding of the moral order of the universe has been thoroughly confused by his constant staring at one point; who has lost every conception of abstract right; to whom any crime appears permissible, nay, as a virtuous act, if it serves as a means to his end; who regards everybody standing in the way as outside of the protection of the law; who consequently is ever ready to kill anybody and to sacrifice also his own life for his nebulous objects. Such fanatics are capable of becoming as cruel as wild beasts and also of dying like heroes. It was quite natural that several of those who listened to Barthélemi in the Brüning salon felt uneasy in his company. Never was Barthélemi seen there again.

This was a hostile pen portrait, and Barthélemy would certainly have had little time for Schurz's non-socialist and moderate republicanism. But one can hardly deny that Schurz had accurately identified a chilling ruthlessness in Barthélemy's devotion to revolution.

There is much romanticism, both positive and negative, in these accounts of Barthélemy, but they also give us unsurpassed psychological insight, if only through the eyes of others. Barthélemy saw himself as a professional revolutionary. Just as his employment in fine metalworking and engineering called for organisation, a steady hand, a clear head and a firm strike, so the job of revolution required preparation, planning, measure and resolution. Personal sentiment could not be allowed to intrude, and individuals were as of nothing compared to the great cause. Enemies and inconstant friends must be swept away. The workbench of revolution was an ordered place, kept clean of waste and with tools regularly sharpened.

Barthélemy was not a creature of instinct, however, but a man who had educated himself and was possessed of a tremendous sense of personal dignity. He was no ruffian. Willich, the braggadocio soldier, would find himself turned out of Brüning's salon because he could not keep his hands to himself: his reputation ruined by sexually assaulting the hostess. Barthélemy never behaved in such an uncouth fashion. He was aware of himself as a representative of his class, and in preserving his honour he preserved the honour of all those who had to work for wages. Barthélemy would not allow himself to be intimidated by the rich and the educated. Privilege, he knew, did not affix itself to intrinsic merit. Nor, however, would he throw snippy proletarian contempt in their face. As he wrote in his last letter to Malwida von Meysenbug, it was because she was 'above all the petty considerations which motivate the people who take social prejudice for virtue' that he called her his friend. Barthélemy judged men and women by their usefulness to the cause, no doubt, but also by their respect for themselves, for him, for those dear to him, and for the much maligned class he represented. Barthélemy lacked spite, but he would not stand for humiliation. Those who would betray the movement for working-class liberation could expect his professional enmity. Those who would seek to abase him could expect his fury.

A very different man from Barthélemy was Frédéric Cournet, the rumbustious, tempestuous and larger-than-life figure described by Victor Hugo in his account of the building of the Faubourg Saint-Antoine barricade. Where Barthélemy was focused and sharp, Cournet was expansive and wild. That the two men would collide seemed fated.

Frédéric Cournet, eight years older than Barthélemy, came from an old Brittany family. After leaving college he joined the French navy where he earned a reputation for courage and intrepidity. In 1826, when aged only eighteen years, Cournet and six other men in a small boat captured a Spanish frigate under English command in an action on the Tagus river, on Spain's frontier with Portugal. For this he was awarded the prestigious *Légion d'honneur*. Before he had attained his twenty-first year he was made a lieutenant in the navy. Cournet was held in high favour and he was included as part of the French naval deputation at Queen Victoria's coronation in June 1838. He looked well set for a splendid military career.

Cournet developed republican convictions, however, and they put paid to any hope of further naval promotion. When the February revolution broke out in 1848, he resigned his commission and threw himself into politics. Cournet was nominated commissaire of the Provisional Government in the Department of Morbihan as one of Ledru-Rollin's trusted agents. He identified himself with the *démoc-soc* wing of the revolution. On 11 March 1848, Cournet was tried by the Tribunal of Correctional Police, with twenty other persons, on the charge of having formed part of an unauthorised political association called the Comité central des républicains socialistes. Ledru-Rollin managed to have the case thrown out. Cournet brought into his politics the rough-housing characteristic of military life. He was involved in a political disturbance at a banquet that May and given ten days' imprisonment. This did not prevent him from continuing to advance politically, and it was while serving as president of the Parisian Comité démocrate socialiste, that Cournet was elected to the National Assembly for the Saône-et-Loire department in 1850.

On 21 March 1850 he was condemned to a year's imprisonment for having facilitated the escape from prison of two men: Monsieur Emery and Eugène Pottier. (Pottier, condemned to ten years' imprisonment for his participation in the June days, would later write the Internationale, the famous anthem of international socialism.) After release from prison, Cournet, along with the republican journalist Félix Pyat, in May 1851 sent a challenge to Monsieur Lapierre, one of the editors of the royalist pro-Bourbon periodical, *Mode*. They had been offended by an insulting editorial article making fun of a letter addressed by Pyat to the Count de Chambord – the putative Bourbon heir to the throne. As a consequence, Cournet and Lapierre fought a duel, in which Lapierre received two sword thrusts and Cournet a small wound near the eye. The two combatants were tried by the Tribunal of Correctional Police on 20 May 1851, for 'inflicting voluntary wounds'. Lapierre was sentenced to six days and Cournet to a month's imprisonment.

In the autumn of 1851, Cournet visited England to see the Great Exhibition, a magnificent showcase of commercial and industrial technology, splendidly housed in the Crystal Palace at Hyde Park, which attracted visitors from across Europe. It was opened publicly by Queen Victoria despite concerns that the refugees crowding London might include anti-royalist fanatics with assassination on their minds. Prince Albert, the Queen's German consort and a moving force behind the exhibition, had been mildly concerned. 'The strangers, they say, are certain to begin a revolution here and to murder Victoria and myself.' As it turned out, most refugees were content to gape at the industrial wonders on display. 'I was struck by the number of foreigners in the streets,' the historian Lord Macaulay wrote in his diary on the first day of the exhibition. 'All, however, were respectable and decent people. I saw none of the men of action with whom the Socialists were threatening us.'

While in London, Cournet planned to make contact with his republican friends forced into exile. Before leaving Paris, he had been entrusted with a parcel, containing letters and engravings – perhaps plans of Blanqui's prison island – which was to be delivered to Emmanuel Barthélemy. Cournet, who did not personally know the addressee, asked one of his friends in London about him. This friend, unfortunately, was a political adversary of Barthélemy and he told Cournet that 'Barthélemy was a disreputable character, and that he ought to avoid him'. Specifically, he accused him of pimping his lover. Believing the stories, Cournet decided to post the parcel through the mail rather than hand-deliver. He sent with the package a cold letter.

Arthur Reeves, an Irishman with a degree from Trinity College Dublin, who had lived for twenty-two years in France, knew the French émigré community in London well. He dined almost every day at their regular meeting place, 26 Grafton

Street in Soho. Reeves had an insight on the affair. Cournet, he reported, had 'unfortunately listened to what the French call *cancans*, i.e. backbitings, in the *School for Scandal* style' and 'yielded to their malevolent influence'. To make matters worse, Cournet wrote back to friends in Paris, spreading the slanderous rumours concerning Barthélemy. Barthélemy had not received Cournet's parcel and letter, as he was in France, but Cournet's slanders spread from one gossiping revolutionary to another until they reached his ears. When Barthélemy heard, he was gripped by hatred and a '*rancune* grudge'. 'And hence,' as Reeves summed it up, 'what the French call a *brouille*, which in plain English signifies a "blow up".'

Upon his return to Paris, Cournet continued to speak ill of Barthélemy and he received a letter from the man himself demanding explanations. Cournet consented to give them, but in his reply haughtily responded that he was unaware of Barthélemy's political significance. In a cold fury, Barthélemy issued a challenge, which was accepted. The affair was inter-rupted by Napoleon's *coup d'état*, however: Cournet achieved his place in history and Barthélemy went on the run.

Cournet was arrested on 5 December 1851, three days after Napoleon's coup, and faced possible summary execution. His mode of escape, as described by Charles Hugo, was testament to his great strength – Cournet stood nearly six foot tall, weighing between thirteen and fourteen stone – and steely ferociousness. As an important prisoner he was placed in a cab under the guard of a government agent tasked with transporting him to the Police Prefecture. What happened next, according to repute, was rather extraordinary and chilling.

As the cab went into a small deserted street Cournet, hith-erto motionless, sprang like a tiger, and two giant hands descended upon the officer and took him by the throat. The man could not scream. No noise betrayed the fearsome drama of silent struggle. The great vice of steel muscles that gripped the agent slowly closed on his neck. He went livid, his arms and legs twitched convulsively, and when Cournet let go, he was dead.

Cournet jumped out and fled from the cab, the other passengers understandably frozen with shock. The next day Cournet was in Brussels and two days after that he arrived back in England, leaving behind his wife and one son in Paris. Now an exile, he found a place to live at number 41 Lisle Street, off Leicester Square.

At first Cournet was still in receipt of £80 per annum in naval pension from the French government, but otherwise he had no employment. When his pension was cut off, Cournet fell on hard times. A government propaganda sheet reported after his death that Cournet 'was in an estate nearly approaching indigence, and had scarcely a friend on account of his violent and quarrelsome disposition'.

In London Cournet was close to Ledru-Rollin, and a friend of his party. Otherwise, he was not particularly active in the politics of the emigration. He did, however, join the 'Fraternal Society', the mutual support organisation for exiles which tried to stay above the political quarrels of the community. Before long, however, he had deeply divided its membership. As Gustave Lefrançais remembered, Cournet was a 'quarrelsome character' with 'brutal manners'. A close friend, Edmond Allain, called him 'a killer, tall, strong, solid, defying everybody, and ultimately inspiring real terror'. Rumours spread that he was a Bonapartist spy. Barthélemy, who was still in Switzerland, took no part in this malignant gossip, but later on he was to repeat the allegation.

A secret letter itemising the case against Cournet was circulated among the exile community by one Monsieur H. Perrie. Cournet tried to have a 'Tribunal of Honour' convened by the Fraternal Society, but as he had stormed out of the organisation, he was refused. As was his character, he turned to violent threats against his rivals. Arthur Reeves remarked that Cournet habitually 'acted savagely with almost everyone', relying upon his reputation as a duellist to intimidate. Gustave Naquet, Cournet's friend, admitted the truth of this. 'He called out two or three of his defamers, who all refused his challenge. He then threatened them to "pull their ears", and actually did so on several occasions, without knowing whether any of them had previously had his arm broken or not.' This last was an oblique reference to an egregious assault that caused particular upset. The physically powerful Cournet had struck a blow at another émigré, Couturat, who was unable to defend himself because he carried an injured arm.

Cournet was intimidating not only for his size, military training and bellicosity, but because he was notorious for his readiness to challenge. He had fought and survived no fewer than fifteen duels, sustaining a serious injury only once. But it is clear that his reputation was in freefall. Aware that he was quick to anger, particularly when drunk, he was said to have abandoned the use of wine and come to live abstemiously. Still, he cut a rather bombastic figure which Herzen wrote up in his memoirs as an unflattering pen-portrait of the 'duellist, rake and scapegrace':

> Cournet was one of that special class ... like a fish in water, but a fish with polished, varnished scales. These men are brave, reckless to the point of insolence and senselessness, and very dull-witted. They live all their lives on the memory of two or three incidents in which they have passed through fire and water, have sliced off somebody's ears, have stood under a shower of bullets .... They are dimly conscious that their recklessness is their strength ... and they have a mortal passion for boasting.

For Herzen, Cournet's type was quite common in France, but barely to be found in England at all. That he had fought so many duels at all was proof enough that 'he could not be considered a rational man'. While Barthélemy was politically committed, Herzen suggested, Cournet was a braggart whose politics were rather accidental. This seems unfair to a man who had given up a career and a family for the republican cause. But there is no doubt that Cournet was a bully, with all that bullying belligerence masking an inner uncertainty.

The French émigrés were in the habit of visiting a restaurant and coffee house at number 53 Old Compton Street in Soho, run from his home by a Frenchman called Guisland Patrice Denis. He certainly had a market in the refugees. Alexis Soyer, a French chef heroically attempting to educate English tastes in this period, wrote despairingly that 'it is a very remarkable fact that but few persons in England know how to make good coffee'. Food was also an issue. In England the well-off ate gargantuan meals: a simple breakfast might consist of tea, coffee, chocolate, cold meats, game, broiled fish, sausages, eggs, kidneys, bacon, toast, muffins, butter, marmalade and, mostly for decoration, fruit on the table and sideboard. When the rich dined out, it was in the exclusive clubs of London: Boodle's, Brooks's or the Athenaeum, for example. Common folk would dine on bread, butter, cheese, potatoes, fish and – by no means standard on the Continent – butcher's meat. Very many would buy quick meals from street sellers: oysters, whelks, shrimps and watercress – fresh because still alive when sold. Taverns would provide a good meat pie, and supper was most popularly eaten by working people about midnight.

Restaurants and even cafés, in the French style, were virtually unknown, and French cuisine generally mocked. The French loved potatoes – generally looked down upon as a food of the poor in England – bread, milk products, meats and, of course, garlic, escargot and *cuisses de grenouille* – frogs' legs. More than this, the restaurant had become part of French national

culture since the Revolution. It was a social experience, where
food mixed with drink, smoking and talk. The English cult of
domesticity, and a wave of anti-smoking sentiment in the 1850s,
meant that French exiles preferred their own eating houses. In
time, of course, the *restaurant* would be absorbed into Britain's
native culture. In 1890, Guisland Denis's establishment would
be remodelled into the Swiss hotel. It retained a whiff of the
counter-culture, and in the 1940s it was cautioned by the police
for 'harbouring sodomites'. In the 1980s it became Compton's,
a jewel in the crown of London's gay nightlife.

In 1854, Cournet was in the habit of taking meals at Denis's
establishment in the company of Etienne Barronet, Charles
Delescluze and Monsieur Recherolles. It was from Denis that
Barthélemy learnt, on 4 October 1852, that Cournet was now
also living in London. Barthélemy asked for pen and paper and
immediately began writing a further letter to Cournet, once
more demanding a retraction and apology for the slanders he
had spread. Denis knew well Cournet's reputation for duelling,
and warned Barthélemy that Cournet 'was a very fine man, and
a strong man – a strong and robust man'. In response,
Barthélemy held up his hand, 'as if in the act of firing off a
pistol, towards a looking glass, and said, "At this, I don't fear
the first comer."'

The letter was delivered to Cournet by two of Barthélemy's
friends, a Frenchman and his Prussian comrade, August Willich.
At first, all seemed well. Cournet at once stated to his visitors
that he had forgotten the name of his original informant –
perhaps he did not wish to acknowledge a disreputable colleague
– and was therefore happy to retract the expressions he had
used. This was considered satisfactory. But when he read
Barthélemy's note again, Cournet decided that he detected a
'menace' in its tone, and he immediately wrote to Barthélemy
refusing an apology. 'This in the eyes of French men rendered
a hostile meeting inevitable.'

Herzen was told of the encounter by Willich. According to him, Cournet admitted that he had merely repeated a rumour, and that he regretted it.

'That,' said Willich, 'is quite enough. Write what you have said on paper, give it to me, and I shall go home truly delighted.'

'If you like,' said Cournet, and took up his pen.

At this point, one of Cournet's friends, who had just entered the room, interrupted.

'So you are going to apologise to a fellow like Barthélemy.

Cournet stopped short.

'Apologise? Why, do you take this for an apology?'

'For the act of an honest man,' interrupted Willich, 'who having repeated a slander regrets it.'

'No,' said Cournet, flinging down the pen, 'that I cannot do.'

'Didn't you say so just now?'

'No, no, pardon me, but I cannot. Tell Barthélemy that "I said that because I chose to say it."'

'Bravissimo!' cried Cournet's friend.

Willich looked at him accusingly.

'On you, *monsieur*, rests the responsibility for the misfortunes that will follow.'

He left the room.

The French refugees, Arthur Reeves reported, were 'most sensitive upon the point of honour, but so guarded are they against the boiling nature of their blood, that they have instituted here, in London, a "Tribunal of Honour", which decides upon every case of discussion, disagreement, or quarrel'. Cournet claimed to have informal evidence of Barthélemy's perfidious behaviour, but he refused to cooperate with the Tribunal of the Fraternal Society given his previous dealings with the group. It seems clear that most saw Cournet as the unreasonable party, in neither withdrawing nor substantiating his allegations. The challenge must certainly have come from Barthélemy, however. It was no doubt delivered with icy politeness – 'avoiding all strong language' – as this was the correct form and it suited Barthélemy's austere ideal. But all those who saw him in the days following recognised a dangerous anger in his manner. Turning a grim face against fear and a sense of proportion, he muttered through gritted teeth that he would burst Cournet's belly. The emigration was disturbed. The fact that Barthélemy had to find new seconds – or witnesses, for Willich would not act for him – suggests that even his close friends thought that he was being irreconcilable.

There was a fixed procedure in French duelling tradition, which was always committed to writing. The principals always had two 'seconds' each. Among gentlemen the privileged weapons were pistols and swords, though seldom both in the same fight, and – when both parties agreed – it was a duel to the death. Normally, however, the principals would fire no more than twice and if swords were used the duel would end when first blood was drawn. It was quite rare for a duel to end in loss of life. An authority calculated that of two hundred duels in Britain, only one in fourteen ended in fatality. The offended party had the choice of arms, but this often led to disputes over who had first provoked. If agreement could not be reached a coin was tossed to determine weapons and who should fire first. If pistols were the weapons of choice, they were brought to the scene of the duel, examined, and then the duellists drew lots to determine their weapon before they were loaded. Gallery pistols were the most dangerous as they required no wadding between the ball and the powder. The seconds displayed the gunpowder and held up the ball to the seconds on the other side. Each second then loaded the pistol of his principal. When one of the parties was considered to be a better shot than the other the distance between the duellists was increased in order to place them on an equal footing. Usually the distance chosen was forty yards. Each duellist walked up to a certain point, turned and, upon signal, opened fire.

There was an initial arrangement for Cournet and Barthélemy to fight the duel on Thursday, 14 October, at Richmond Park in the London Borough of Richmond upon Thames, where a quiet spot might be found away from prying eyes. They met, but disagreed about the choice of weapons. Barthélemy preferred swords while Cournet insisted upon pistols. Being unable to agree, the two parties separated. Cournet complained 'in an exasperated tone' that Barthélemy had kept him waiting for an hour and a half, had raised objections over weapons, and finally refused to fight. Barthélemy said angrily, 'The coward would not accept me today.' The duel was rearranged.

A specific protocol was now agreed. The two men would be placed at forty paces' distance, each duellist to have the option of advancing ten paces before discharging his pistol. Each party was to have two shots: once the signal was given, either could shoot at any time, but after their first shot they must wait to receive return fire. In the event of none of the four shots taking effect, the duel was then to be continued with swords. If any of the pistols misfired that was not to be considered a shot.

On 16 October, Cournet met with a friend, Louis Joseph Soulli, another inveterate duellist who had fought nine encounters, during one of which he had received a sword wound to his leg, leading to an amputation. The crippled Soulli was now a corpulent man with a wooden prosthetic, but no less enthusiastic for the honourable pursuit of duelling. Cournet told Soulli that he had a desire to avoid the duel, but such was the nature of the offence that he could not. He felt that he could neither withdraw nor offer any explanation, and the insult from Barthélemy was in the nature of a menace. Cournet then met with an old comrade, Gustave Naquet, on the next day – a Sunday – and they dined late into the evening. Cournet told his friend that the duel was to take place in three days' time.

At this point, the mysterious Mademoiselle Goldsmith, who had betrayed the insurgents of December 1851 into the hands of the police, once more appeared on the scene. She turned up at the door of Giuseppe Mazzini, demanding an audience and bearing shocking allegations. They talked.

'You are the friend of Ledru-Rollin. You know that Cournet, who is also Ledru-Rollin's friend, is going to fight with Barthélemy.'

'Yes,' said Mazzini.

'Well,' said Mlle Goldsmith, 'this Barthélemy is attached to the police.'

'They say that,' said Mazzini, 'but I do not think so.'

'I'm sure,' said Mlle Goldsmith.

'What proof do you have?'

'The proof,' said Mlle Goldsmith, 'is first of all that I myself am with the police, and then that my close friend Besançon is also a police officer, and he is the intimate of Barthélemy, who is himself also with the police.'

'Come,' said Mazzini, 'there must be other proofs than that to prevent the duel from taking place.'

'It will take three days to produce certain proof,' Mlle Goldsmith admitted.

'We do not have those three days,' Mazzini replied. 'All the same, we shall go to Ledru-Rollin's house at 3 p.m on Monday and notify him.'

When they met with him, however, Ledru-Rollin thought that there was nothing to be done; they could not wait for any evidence. 'Cournet would look as if he were putting off the duel,' said Ledru-Rollin, 'and Cournet cannot look like a coward.'

It is difficult to know what to make of this episode. Its source was Edmond Allain, a close friend to Cournet and his second in the duel. It was on Allain's evidence that Charles Hugo wrote his published account of the duel. Nonetheless, despite his clear hostility to Barthélemy, Hugo declined to mention the Goldsmith affair. And whilst he referred to the rumours that Barthélemy was a police informant, he gave them no credence. Barthélemy was 'sinister, but a man of conviction'.

We enter here the murky world of police informers. Their use was already a commonplace in French crime detection, though in England it was a despised practice thought only appropriate when it came to the Irish. A hundred years later, Jean Belin, commissioner of the French security police, explained the difference in attitudes:

> In France we first look for material clues, and afterwards check up on their significance through contacts with our informers, whom we use freely to obtain corroborative evidence or even straight tips. Scotland Yard [the metropolitan police headquarters in England] does not encourage the employment of informers, and is reluctant to do so, I believe, on ethical grounds .... The science of British detection is based on deduction, the close following up of small clues, and the full exertion of the reasoning faculties. It suits the English temperament, but, to my mind, this method takes up too much valuable time. Whether I am right or wrong in this contention, one thing is certain – the British method is invaluable to writers of crime novels, for it is founded on the assumption that a case is a puzzle which has to be solved. If a link is missing in a chain of evidence that has to be built up you must come to a full stop.

Informers, however, can very easily turn into agents provocateurs used to poison the well of political opposition. Émigré politics, under the gaze of governmental agents from abroad, was rife with such skulduggery. Following the clues, and avoiding any full stop, we may come to a reasonable conclusion. Mlle Goldsmith had appeared once in Paris in a sting operation to trap insurgents during Louis Napoleon's *coup d'état*, casting suspicions on Barthélemy's role (particularly given his escape from police custody), and then almost a year later in London, to dramatically reveal herself and Barthélemy as informers. It seems rather too convenient. Mazzini was avoided by many leftists because he was 'so completely surrounded by spies, who completely befooled him', as one put it. Was this episode an example of the French secret police stirring the troubled waters of émigré republican politics? This is the most likely conclusion.

Mlle Goldsmith's intervention failed. There was no going back.

The duel was fixed for Tuesday, 19 October 1852.

13

THE LAST DUEL

It is rather difficult for us now to understand the mentality of duelling. But in the much less developed and more personalised economy of the early modern era, a person's credit depended upon their honour. Add those other determinants of masculine pride, sex and courage, and you have a noxious brew. For centuries gentlemen regarded the right to bear arms and to use them in defence of their honour as a very badge of status and caste.

In the nineteenth century, developing capitalism was changing all of this. Personal honour was becoming a less fragile entity, for which we should be grateful. In the 1840s Thomas Carlyle famously coined the term 'cash-nexus' to describe the social bonds that were replacing personal reputation. Marx in 1844 remarked sardonically on the power of money in such a society. 'Money is the supreme good, therefore its possessor is good.' Nonetheless, obsession with honour dragged on well into the century, with the duel regarded as the ultimate protector of reputation. Though duelling had clearly begun to fade in Britain by the late eighteenth century, it had held on in the military. In the first half of the nineteenth century, refusing to accept a challenge could result in an officer being court-martialled and cashiered for failure to uphold the honour of the regiment. It was not until 1844 that duelling was effectively banned in the army, hastening its demise throughout the kingdom. 'To prove the absurdity of the duel is not worth while,' wrote Herzen. 'In theory no one justifies it except a few bullies and fencing masters, but in practice everyone gives in to it in order to prove – the devil knows to whom – his courage.' It was a diminishing but still potent social institution.

Cournet chose as his two seconds Edmond Allain, a thirty-six-year-old captain in the French army and now a wine merchant, and Etienne Barronet, a forty-six-year-old notary. Both men had held high positions in France, being engaged in lucrative merchant activities. Barronet was 'a short, stout, gentleman-like person, with full features, rather of the Napoleon cast, his hair cropped short, and wearing a moustache but no beard or whiskers'. Allain was 'tall and thin' with a thick black beard. Barthélemy's seconds were of more plebeian stock: Philippe Eugene de Morney, a labourer – 'a tall, close-shaved man, without anything very remarkable in his expression' – and one other called Brisson, who was described as looking like a hotel porter or waiter. Barthélemy himself was described by *The Times* as 'of the middle height, wears his hair turned back off his face, the lines of which are irregular and full of passion, but not repulsive'. Cournet's party was evidently a higher class than Barthélemy's. Though a duel amongst revolutionists, it was heavily overlaid by class tension.

François Pardigon, a former republican journalist who now lived as an exile in London at 78 Wardour Street, working as a bootmaker, knew Barthélemy very well. Pardigon had made his name in France on the radical newspaper, the *Voix du Peuple*, and had fought in the June Days. After his capture he had been flung into the crowded cellars of the Tuileries, among thousands of others, including the cholera-stricken, the wounded and the dying. When Pardigon had craned his head to the window, gasping for fresh air, he had been ordered back by a National Guardsman, who shot him in the face when he failed to retract quickly enough, gouging a wound in his lower jaw and cheek. Though mutilated, Pardigon had survived and escaped into exile where he was a comrade to Barthélemy in the Blanquist party.

Pardigon had been told by both Cournet and Barthélemy of the approaching duel. On Monday, the day before the two men were due to meet, Pardigon was asked by Allain and Barronet, seconds for Cournet, and Brisson, one of Barthélemy's, to accompany them to act as an interpreter in their task of securing the two pistols required. After failing to find pistols ready for hire 'for practice' at two gunsmiths, the four of them entered the Shooting Gallery, Leicester Square, at about 7.30 p.m. Here they found what they needed, having turned down the first set with which they had been presented. They left a deposit of £8 and were supplied with a brace of pistols. They were rifled and thus very accurate by the standards of the day. These relatively new 'percussion guns' were more advanced than the old flintlock, the standard weapon in the French barricade fighting of 1848. They had just been used in the gallery, and so were known to work perfectly. They were not loaded. At about 8.30 p.m., Allain, Cournet's second, returned seeking more balls for the gun.

The party returned to Pardigon's room. One of the men put his finger in the barrels of the pistols, which emerged blackened showing that they had been recently fired. As the pistols had been cleaned that morning, before they had been fired at the range, it was determined that a quick rub to dry them out would be sufficient. Allain and Brisson were given the task. As they had no ramrod to hand something had to be improvised. Pardigon cut notches in a large pencil and tied it to the end of a German silver-and-whalebone ferrule, the reinforced end of a walking stick. Pardigon then took pieces of linen, which he kept in his house for cleaning the boots he manufactured, and tore them into rags the size of a handkerchief. Each of the parties took a pistol and, wrapping the rag around the makeshift ramrod, cleaned the inside of the barrels. When the job was finished, the rags were thrown into the fireplace. 'They blew down the muzzles of the pistols …. They found the wind came out, and said, "It is well." (*c'est bien*); we must now seal up the pistols.' The pistols had thus been cleaned with rag rather than with tow, which was normally used as it was much less likely to shred and cause blockage. The pistols were wrapped in brown paper and string, and closed up with thirteen red wax seals each. They wrote on the paper, 'Allain, 13 seals – Brisson, 13 seals.' The weapons were ready.

The night before the duel, Barthélemy stayed at Guisland Denis's open house in Soho. He came in a little before midnight and went to bed immediately. He left again at 6.15 in the morning to meet with the other participants, and six persons went out from London to Windsor by the 8 a.m. South Western train. They were seen off at Waterloo station by a large gathering of émigrés. Supporters of both parties were present. A voluble group of Frenchmen always caught attention, with their beards and moustaches – most Englishmen went clean-shaven, though mutton chops were coming into fashion – and their habit of gesticulating in a way that London natives found slightly alarming. Waterloo, the terminus of the London and South Western Railway, was only four years old, having been opened in 1848. There was little grandeur about it, being still not much more than a muddle of miscellaneous wooden sheds and platforms: 'a strange mass of ugliness in its present form', wrote an unimpressed guide. Nonetheless, there was an irony that these French fighters were leaving from a station named after a famous French defeat, and as the train came in, there was the usual rush. As Herzen observed, the Londoner 'never in any case knows how to form a queue'.

The two parties climbed aboard a single train but took separate carriages. Jane Pettingal, a commuter who happened to share a carriage with one trio, heard Barthélemy and de Morney speak together in French. They were not to know that she understood their language. 'I heard one of the gentlemen say he would kick him and cane him to death' – presumably a warning of Cournet's well-known physical brutality – 'and I saw Barthélemy take his right hand out of his pocket and look at it and say *"je ne suis pas agité"* ("I am not worried").' In the other carriage, Cournet's seconds *were* worried, but Cournet himself was cheerful. After all, he had emerged victorious in numerous duels: 'That scoundrel Barthélemy, I'll do him in. How can I suppose that this vile *canaille* alone can reach me?'

The two parties arrived at the Berkshire village of Datchet, then the terminus of the South Western railway, at about 9.10 a.m., a little late. In the station they were approached by Francis Farquharson, a local who made a living by seeking out strangers and offering to act as a guide to nearby Windsor. He reported, 'Six foreigners were on the platform, in two parties of three each. I asked them if they wanted a carriage to go to Virginia Water [the largest artificial lake in Great Britain]. They said "no, no," and walked up the street.' Farquharson followed them, and saw one party go into the Grapes public house, and the other into Mr Wicksey's cook-shop. After about a quarter of an hour, they came out and asked him the way to Windsor Royal Park. He directed them, and they walked on. In retrospect Farquharson was unperturbed that he had inadvertently guided a man to his death, though he was indignant that they paid him no money for his services.

The parties set off quickly through Old Windsor and up the Long Walk through the Great Park. This was a renowned beauty spot. The Long Walk had been constructed for the pleasure of Queen Anne in the early eighteenth century. It was a carriageway lined by a double row of elms, running for almost three miles from Windsor Castle – Queen Victoria's preferred residence when she was England – to the top of Snow Hill, where stood the 'Copper Horse', an equestrian statue of George III. This was royal territory, an incongruous locale for a republican duel. It was said locally that there were three attempts made to stage the duel in the park, but each time preparations were interrupted by passers-by. Finally they exited by Bishop's Gate, which led out into Englefield Green, a picturesque common surrounded by detached villas and gardens. Here lived the aristocracy of Egham. The men climbed a steep heath leading up to Priest Hill, the east of which was broken up into small pastures divided by hedges ten feet tall. The parties went through a gate on the road leading on to Crown Farm, about halfway between Windsor and Chertsey. Across a field they found a hollow behind a hazel hedge. On the other side of the hedge was Sir John Cathcart's farm on Cooper's Hill. Rising above the Vale of the Thames, this was a famous viewpoint from which could be seen Windsor Castle, the surrounding Chilterns countryside and London itself. The duellists were concealed from the road, but they were within sight of some builders and gardeners on the farm. Herzen thought this a peculiar place for a duel, which would normally be held near a frontier, where ships, boats and horses could spirit away the participants. But with the field shrouded in fog, it seemed to be a fairly secluded spot. The scene was set.

It was a duel fought *à la barrière*. Lines were marked on the ground twenty paces apart; neither principal could move closer to the other than this. They pulled back a further ten paces, and when the signal was given, either man could advance up as far as the barrier and fire at will. Once a shot was given, the principal had to stop and receive any return fire. It was as though the two men were fighting over an invisible barricade. In Paris, it had been all clamours, gunsmoke and the waving of flags. At Egham, it was a misty silence and strained nerves. Once Barthélemy and Cournet had fought on the same side, 'like brother linked to brother', sharing the same dangers, 'but now ... hereditary foes they seem, and as in some appalling dream each coldly plans the other's slaughter'.

The duel took place at about 1 p.m. The choice of position, pistols, and the right to give the signal for fire were all tossed for in succession and all were won by the friends of Cournet. The seconds – turning their backs on each other – loaded the pistols. The principals took their positions a total of forty paces from each other. Cournet advanced his ten paces forward by military sidestep – *un, deux, trois* ... Barthélemy, however, stood still. Cournet was surprised. 'Well, sir, do you intend to remain yonder?' 'I will do what I think proper,' replied Barthélemy. 'If such be the case,' said Cournet, 'we may long stay here.' Barthélemy replied, 'As long as you please.' He would not budge. 'Well,' exclaimed Cournet, 'I am to fire.'

Both men stood sideways to each other, to minimise their profile. Cournet withdrew the pistol from the perpendicular position in which he had been holding it by the side of his head, took aim as he lowered his weapon, and discharged at Barthélemy. His shot missed. Barthélemy, who had reserved his fire, now addressed Cournet: 'There is still time, Monsieur, for you to retract. Do so, and all will be well. I have sustained your fire. Now do your duty.' Cournet replied, 'No, no. It is not in the presence of your pistol that I shall retract. It would be cowardice. I will not; no, I will not. We shall see afterwards.'

Barthélemy only now advanced his ten paces. Baronnet, second to Cournet, professed to be shocked: 'You call yourself a gentleman when you dare to fire at a distance of twenty paces at a man who fired at you at a distance of thirty?' 'You have no right to interfere,' said Barthélemy. 'It is not only my right but also my duty to do so,' replied Barronet.

Having reached his firing position, closer to Cournet, Barthélemy 'addressed him in the true style of French rodomontade,' reminding him that his life was now at his mercy, but that he would waive his right to fire if Cournet would consent to continue the duel with swords. Rapiers had been brought for this eventuality – light cut-and-thrust weapons. Cournet refused and reminded his antagonist that he still had the right of another shot if he should miss.

Barthélemy raised his pistol, drew the trigger, exploded the percussion cap, but failed to discharge the contents. The pistol had misfired. A new cap was inserted, and a second attempt was made, but with the same result. Barthélemy again appealed to Cournet to have the duel decided by swords. Cournet refused indignantly – '*Sacrebleu*! Sir, you laugh at me?' – and threw his firearm at Barthélemy's head. Barthélemy at first refused to use it, being unwilling to fire at an unarmed opponent. Cournet insisted, however, and the pistol was loaded by Barronet, while Cournet and Barthélemy paced around their positions. This took about ten minutes, and the break gave Barthélemy time to recover from the shock of having been fired at. The weapon was handed to Barthélemy. Slowly he took aim and pulled the trigger.

It went off. Cournet fell, raised himself, tried to take a few steps, and then collapsed. Barronet, seeing that his friend had been seriously wounded, shouted furiously at Barthélemy, 'Away with you, wretch! And remember you have shot my friend at a distance of twenty paces, when he fired at you at thirty. His blood will be an eternal stain to you.'

The sun suddenly broke through the mist, and the duelling parties became aware that they were near a settlement of houses around the Barley Mow Inn. After the fatal shot, Barthélemy and his seconds, de Morney and Brisson, left the field together. On Priest Hill Road, they stopped a passing grocer, Charles James, and asked where they might find a cab or conveyance. Pointing back to the field they said that there had been an accident. Mr Hayward, the local surgeon, was passing by and he saw Barthélemy, de Morney and Brisson leaving the field by a gate. 'One of them asked me for the road to Windsor. He put the question in broken English.'

Other passers-by, meanwhile, were getting involved. Captain Enery heard Barthélemy's pistol misfiring at 1.15, as he passed down Priest Hill. He saw Allain and Barronet, mistaking them at first for land surveyors. William Herbert, a labourer, heard shouting: 'I heard a man halloo, and soon after I heard him halloo from a different place, as if he had run away.' William Overton saw Barronet running from the field, crying to him, 'Come, come! A pistol, a pistol!' Not wishing to get involved, Overton pointed out the passing doctor. Barronet told Dr Haywood that his friend had been wounded by a pistol, and asked him to accompany him to the spot. Here the surgeon found the stricken Cournet whispering to Allain, who seemed 'very sorrowful, and to be in great distress of mind at what had occurred'. When addressed, all Allain could do was to point at Cournet and say 'my friend'.

Hayward asked William Herbert, the farmhand, to take care of his horse as he attended. 'I found a person lying on the ground, close under the hedge ... lying on his back, with a wound in his right side, which passed through the body and out on the left side .... There was a man by his side endeavouring to staunch the wound.' Hayward directed some other labourers who had arrived at the scene to get some brandy from Sir John Cathcart's farm. This was given to Cournet as a crude painkiller. Hayward, believing Cournet to be insensible with pain, spoke to Allain in French:

- *Votre ami est perdu.* ('Your friend is lost.')
- *Oh, mon dieu! Monsieur*, said Cournet, 'I heard you quite perfectly saying: '*Votre ami est perdu*'; only in French we say, '*Votre ami est fout* ...' ('Your friend is fuck'd.')

A rough-hewn sailor to the last.

Barronet, increasingly anxious, insisted to Allain that he must rush to London and alert a French doctor – Louis Veron, an exile, music critic and himself a duellist – who had been put on standby. 'You're a coward,' spat Allain contemptuously. Both men thought that Cournet, crumpled on the ground, was at last unconscious, but their argument was suddenly interrupted by his groaning voice. '*Mon dieu, Monsieur Barronet*, I have been hearing you for a quarter of an hour. You want to go, then go!'

Cournet having rallied a little, Hayward directed his removal to the Barley Mow Inn, about half a mile distant. He was carried on a door resting on hurdles and bedded with straw supplied by the farmhands. Cournet said nothing of the duel, but 'complained of cold and slight pain'. Hayward remained with him until five o'clock that evening. 'He was sensible at the time I left him. He made no statement to me whatever, except that he was in pain.' Veron, the French doctor, arrived at the Barley Mow Inn to attend on Cournet.

Barthélemy, de Morney and Brisson, meanwhile, had returned to Windsor on foot. Here they were spotted again, at about 1.30, by the Windsor guide, Francis Farquharson. 'Their trousers were covered with dirt, as if they had been in wet grass and then covered with dust from the road. They asked me when the next train would start. I showed them from the timetable that they would have some time to wait, and we went into the Royal Oak and had some ale together, and bread and cheese .... One of them had a blue cloak on in the morning; in the afternoon he had it rolled up under his arm like an umbrella, and two white handles were sticking out of it.' These were the rapiers.

At about 2.30, the three men went to Datchet to catch their train, and were noted there by the station manager, John Madigan, from the booking office. 'I observed them, because one carried a cloak under his arm as a soldier would carry his sword, and the other from his peculiar beard and forbidding cast of countenance.' This latter was probably Barthélemy. They took their places on the train, due to arrive in London at 3.30. After they had boarded, Barronet arrived at Datchet Station from the duelling field, looking to catch the same rail service. He paced along the platform, peering through the windows of the carriages, and spotted Barthélemy's party. Barronet turned and went to the ticket office to change his ticket to first class. He would not travel in the same carriage as Barthélemy and his comrades.

Back at the Barley Mow Inn, Cournet refused to make a dying declaration, *in articulo mortia*. In his last extremities of pain, however, his restraint slipped, and he bitterly lamented his life's sacrifices: he was leaving a widow and son of twenty years. He finally slipped away at 6 p.m., aged forty-three years.

Superintendent Biddlecombe of the Surrey police arrived at the Barley Mow at 6.15, and was ushered into a bedroom where lay the body of Frédéric Cournet. After taking Allain into custody, he had the cadaver stripped and identified a bullet hole in the breast of the coat, waistcoat and shirt. He ascertained, as the doctor had before him, that the bullet had entered the right side of the body and come out on the left. In Cournet's pocket he found some money and change, keys, gloves, and a passport in the name of Francis Bonquet issued by the British Embassy in Paris and dated 18 May. Hayward conducted the post-mortem, and found that the bullet had fractured the eighth rib, gone through the liver, grazed the stomach, passed through the diaphragm, torn a wound in the left lung, and passed out at the upper part of the eighth rib on the left side. The bullet was later found amongst the sheets of Cournet's deathbed by Mary Day who had been engaged to lay out the body. Well into the twentieth century it was kept on display in the inn as a memorial, along with a 'strangely shaped clasp knife' that belonged to Cournet.

The news of the duel had travelled the road from Cooper's Hill to Windsor almost as fast as Barthélemy and his seconds. That afternoon, Mr Heywood, landlord of the Bells public house, had ridden at full gallop into town to alert the police. He was on his way to the electric telegraph station. Since 1837, when the first commercial line had been laid between Euston and Camden Town in London, the telegraph had tended to follow rail routes. The spread of this technology, wrote the Austrian Stefan Zweig in 1940, was a psychological revolution, making 'isolated human experiences simultaneous for the first time'. A telegraphic message to the London police was transmitted from Windsor along the Great Western line more quickly than Barthélemy and his comrades could reach the city. The policeman on duty at Waterloo station, John Underwood, took delivery. 'I received intelligence from the electric telegraph that a duel had been fought near Windsor; that three foreigners were expected to arrive from Windsor at Waterloo station at thirty-five minutes after three.' No other identification was given other than that they were travelling together in the second-class carriage.

Underwood took a squad and dutifully watched for three foreign men disembarking from the train. He was only able to identify two foreigners, recognisable by their style of beards and gesticulations, and he closed in on them. Barronet, Cournet's second who had been travelling first-class, saw Barthélemy and de Morney being apprehended. He considered it dishonourable to allow them to be captured while he escaped, so he joined them as they were being walked out of the station. Thinking that they had now all three of the men mentioned in the telegraph, the police took them into custody and called off the hunt. Brisson, who had been second for Barthélemy, was able to slip away.

Constable Underwood reported that as he emerged from Waterloo station with his captives, 'several foreigners come up, and one of them came up to me and said, "I'll give you a sovereign to let him (pointing to one of them) go."' Quite possibly, Underwood fell to temptation, for it seems that Barronet was briefly allowed to escape, and was only later again taken into custody from his rooms. De Morney also tried to pass the weapons hidden amongst the cloak held under his arm to one of the party of Frenchmen. Underwood prevented this: 'No, leave that alone.'

The émigrés, mostly but not entirely French, had been milling around the station waiting to hear the outcome of the duel. Alexander Herzen, walking along Pall Mall, bumped into Willich looking pale and agitated and striding rapidly away from the scene. He recalled the conversation:

'What is it?'

'Killed outright.'

'Who?'

'Cournet. I am running to Louis Blanc for advice what to do.'

'Where is Barthélemy?'

'He and a second and Cournet's seconds are in prison. Only one of the seconds was not arrested; by English law Barthélemy may be hanged.'

Whereupon Willich jumped on to an omnibus, leaving Herzen to ponder.

Underwood took the suspects to the station at Tower Street, and telegraphed back to Windsor that he had got the wanted men in custody. On examining the cloak, he found three rapier swords tied together by a pocket handkerchief. He afterwards handed the suspects over to John Smith, a Windsor policeman who had come up to take the prisoners into his charge. They were transported back to Chertsey, near Windsor, where Barthélemy, de Morney, Barronet and Allain were all lodged in Horsemonger Lane Gaol. Here the suspects were searched. On Barronet was found a knife stained with blood, which had been used to cut open Cournet's shirt for investigating the wound, and on de Morney a passport. On Barthélemy's person police found two right-handed gloves slashed across the palm. These were clearly duelling gloves designed to absorb sweat whilst retaining responsiveness.

Herzen attributed the duellists' blunders, which led them so easily into police custody, to their 'absolute ignorance of England and English law'. They had underestimated the ability of the police to respond quickly, imagining that 'they could go home, change their clothes and be in Belgium when the next morning the disconcerted constable would come to fetch them, and that he would infallibly be armed with a staff (as described in French novels), and would say on finding they were gone, "Goddam!" All this in spite of the fact that constables do not carry staffs nor English men say "Goddam!"'

Only Brisson, of Barthélemy's party, had escaped, and at 5 p.m. that evening he was able to take the pistols back to the Shooting Gallery and recover £6 15s of the deposit, just over £1 deducted for the time and the powder flask which had not been returned. One of the pistols was still loaded. Upon testing it, Henry Hand, the secretary to the proprietor of the Shooting Gallery, found that the undischarged pistol was misfiring. He drew the charge and spotted a rag jamming up the chamber. 'The rag rendered it next to an impossibility that the powder should explode. The rag was where the gunpowder should have been.' Hand was of the opinion that the manner in which the rag was folded and twisted in the barrel meant that it could not have been left there accidentally in cleaning. Brisson had by this time left and, having completed his duty, made his escape to Belgium.

Even though it soon got round the gossip mill that Barthélemy had been a principal in the duel, the English police refused to state this as fact without hard proof. Louis Blanc had secured good lawyers for Barthélemy and de Morney, and they were advised to keep concealed who had been duelling and who had simply acted as seconds. By English law, all those involved were equally guilty of murder if a death ensued from a duel, but it was hoped that the court would not press the case to this extremity if a principal could not be identified. It was necessary, however, for all the defendants, of both parties, to agree a common line. Herzen was the intermediary who passed this strategy on to Cournet's supporters via Giuseppe Mazzini, the Italian nationalist revolutionary. Mazzini was not particularly sympathetic to Barthélemy and unwilling to trifle with English law. (He was accompanied, during his audience with Herzen, by a belligerent comrade: 'a young English radical with his hair done à la Jesus', who approved of Mazzini's resentful attitude by gestures and 'indistinct polyphones in which two or three vowels flattened together made up a single sound'.) Nonetheless, Cournet's friends had independently decided to adopt the same tactics. Mazzini and Ledru-Rollin paid for Allain and Barronet's trial defence.

The inquest on Cournet was conducted by Mr West, coroner for West Surrey, at the Barley Mow Inn, where the body still lay. There were fourteen jury men, all of whom, it seems, were impressively girthed. The local newspaper remarked with satisfaction that they must have averaged thirteen stone each, ample proof that since the arrival of the railway Egham was enjoying prosperity. The railway also meant that curious visitors could come from far and near. The coroner himself showed ample evidence of material prosperity, and was much annoyed by the flippant attitude of the irrepressible local guide, Francis Farquharson, who enjoyed no such good living. When asked as a witness to give a description, he described one of the duelling party as a fine stout man – 'almost as fine and stout as you are, Mr Chairman'.

There was considerable excitement in the little village and the gentry attended to watch from across the neighbourhood.

The local press was particularly enthused by one visiting couple. 'As a striking proof of the all-pervading interest created by the sad event, we may mention that her Majesty the Queen and His Royal Highness Prince Albert, in one of their recent drives, proceeded to Priest Hill, and stopped for some time, in their carriage, when the spot where Cournet fell was pointed out to them by their attendants.' Perhaps they remembered that he had attended Queen Victoria's coronation.

Mr Ashurst, a lawyer who worked in the 'Old Jewry', was paid by Louis Blanc to represent Barthélemy and de Morney. Gustave Naquet, Cournet's close friend, came forward to let it be properly understood that this had been a political dispute. He wished to scotch the rumour that the quarrel had been about a lady, 'a report which, besides being untrue, could only serve to embitter the feelings of the deceased gentleman's relatives in France, where he had left a wife and children'. Naquet was overcome with emotion as he gave evidence. He refused to reveal that Barthélemy had been the man who shot Cournet: 'A thing I cannot state. I have a character .... I cannot tell you, sir, under any penalty.' Under pressure to reveal more information, he asked the permission of the court to consult with his friends held in custody. This was declined, and he was released.

Barthélemy and de Morney declined to speak at all, but Barronet and Allain submitted a statement. This read as follows:

Whatever may be the consequences of the severity of the English law against duelling, of which I was ignorant, I declare that I was the second of Mons. Cournet, on the 19 October; that the obligations and sincere friendship I entertained for him would not allow of my refusing to accompany him in this fatal rencontre. He was my best friend, and I have found so many noble qualities in him, that I did all I could to avoid this rencontre, but I had to obey the laws of honour, friendship, and the customs of French duelling. Were I to pass the remainder of my life in prison, I would never disclose the name of the person who was the adversary of M. Cournet, now I know the English law. Honour forbids my mentioning the name of an antagonist, if he will not, or cannot do so. I am a prisoner, but will never quit a prison by a declaration which is repugnant to my character and my habits.

(Signed) Barronet.

I adhere to this declaration; it is quite in conformity with my sentiments.

(Signed) Allain.

This was, in the eyes of English law, in effect an admission to murder, for the seconds of the principal in a duel were equally liable. It is little wonder that their lawyers and even the magistrate had warned against their making any kind of declaration.

Friends of Cournet also passed a note to the reporters of the *Morning Post*:

It is truly to be regretted that a certain class of exalted and misguided men, who have found a safe and hospitable asylum in England, should abuse the hospitality granted to them, and take upon themselves the right of avenging their political squabbles by pistols or swords. The unfortunate deceased [Cournet] was an intimate friend from the Republic 'Ledru Rollin', an honour also claimed by two of the partisans now in custody, – Etienne Barronet and Edmund Allain. The other two parties in custody, – Philippe Eugene de Morney and Emmanuel Barthélemy, – claim to be the friends of Louis Blanc. We do not know if these two republican chiefs are or are not the friends of the unfortunate men who infringe the laws of the country that found them a shelter.

Irritated by this attempt to continue a political feud, the coroner made clear that 'in the eyes of the law all were equally guilty' and he announced a jury verdict of 'wilful murder' against the four prisoners in custody, and against a fifth person, unknown. They would be facing a murder trial in a criminal court.

Upon being returned to Chertsey gaol, Barthélemy and de Morney were visited by Louis Blanc, and Barronet and Allain by Ledru-Rollin. Both sides discussed how to expose their rivals without condemning themselves to murder convictions. At this time in England, accused persons were not allowed to enter the witness box to give evidence on their own behalf. The law was changed in this respect only by the Criminal Evidence Act of 1898. There would be no heroic sparring with the judge as had characterised Barthélemy's previous judicial encounters in France. If the feud was to be continued, it would have to be through witnesses and press alone.

14

A BITTER MASQUERADE

Funerals can provide great opportunities for political demonstrations. We may think of Émile Zola, the novelist and defender of the persecuted Jewish officer Alfred Dreyfus, laid to rest in 1902, or Bobby Sands, the Irish republican hunger striker, buried in 1981. Tens of thousands gather to stand with bowed heads, and know that they are marking history. But while most demonstrations seek to project out, the funeral folds in. They are intense, communal affairs in which the mourners reflect on the cause for which a life has been given, and imagine their own eulogy. The emotional charge is tremendous.

Cournet's funeral was organised by the Council of the French Refugees, based in London's Soho, a district of narrow byways. It was a secular affair. Most French radicals felt that the priests had turned on them in the days following Louis-Napoleon's coup, and the funerals of exiles in the 1850s were increasingly 'civic' rather than religious. Cournet was interred on a Sunday afternoon, 24 October 1852, in Egham parish churchyard, near the scene of his death. This was a great event for the émigré community. They descended in traps, carriages and conveyances of nearly every description. There they milled about, 'in all sorts of costume and every variety of beard, many having pipes in their mouths'. Large numbers arrived by the 11.33 train at Staines station, on to which additional carriages had to be attached, from where they proceeded to Egham and took refreshment at the King's Head and the Catherine Wheel inns. From here they walked to Barley Mow at Englefield Green where Cournet lay in his coffin, carried down from the top floor where he had died. In the years after the duel, guests at the Inn reported hearing the ghostly sound of Cournet's body being dropped into his coffin and carried down the stairs from the garret room.

Soon after 1 p.m., the funeral procession started. Present were many former deputies of the French National Assembly. Rather incongruously, a royal coach was numbered in the funeral train, a compliment returned because of Cournet's position as a representative of the French navy at Queen Victoria's coronation. A red flag was placed longitudinally over the roof of one of the carriages, and another draped over Cournet's large coffin, borne on the shoulders of six countrymen over a distance of more than a mile and a half. Five different parties relieved each other along the way. At the head of this procession of about 150 Frenchmen was carried a large red flag, hung with black crêpe, and bearing the inscription, '*Republique Democratique et Sociale*'.

Between two and three thousand people lined the route, with many well-dressed women who appeared to be much affected. Ledru-Rollin and Félix Pyat followed the coffin. The churchyard itself was crowded with spectators, including much of the local gentry. No funeral service was read, but after the coffin had been lowered into the grave, Charles Delescluze, a close friend of Cournet and later military commander of the 1871 Paris Commune, read a eulogy in French:

Citizens ... Cournet was a great and courageous citizen, and the name which he leaves to his son as his only fortune is one of those which will remain as the symbol of political honesty and an unlimited devotion to the cause of the people. On his deathbed one thought alone occupied Cournet – the

Republic and the revolution. Let us give him, then, the only farewell worthy of him by repeating the last words that fell from his lips – *Vive la république, democratique et sociale.*

The crowd cheered, cried *Vive la république!* and the red standard was unfurled. The French émigrés marched under their flying flag to the King's Head and Catherine Wheel, heard speeches for two hours, and then returned to London. Yet also mingling with the crowd – and listening to its chatter – were reporters looking to ascertain exactly who had killed Cournet. There was only one name on the lips of the gathering: Barthélemy.

From that time to this, Cournet has lain in a neglected part of Egham churchyard, about forty paces to the south-east of the church door, under a fir tree. His grave is covered by a flat grey stone on which is inscribed:

La Démocratie Française
À
Frédéric Cournet,
Proscrit,
Né à Lorient le 21 Fevrier, 1808,
Mort le 19 Octobre, 1852

A corner of an English field that is for ever French.

The funeral was clearly a demonstration by the Ledru-Rollin party. Cournet's close friend Gustave Naquet wrote a letter to the *Windsor and Eton Express* to give his side of the duel. His conclusion was bitter, directed not just or even primarily against Barthélemy, but even more so against the entire emigration who had distrusted and condemned Cournet as a rogue and possible spy:

I will add only a few words. Cournet is dead without having been able to revenge himself of the cowards who poisoned his last days by their base calumnies. In the week before his death he said to some friends of his, with a bitter expression, 'What endeavours they have made to put me down!' Down he is, in fact, but we will not allow his vile defamers to pursue against our late friend the same slanderous system they so wilfully organised against him when alive; and we shall defend his memory against his secret or open enemies by every means in our power.

The contest of honour had not ended with Cournet's death. It is not surprising, therefore, that the two parties barely cooperated as the legal process unfolded.

After the coroner's verdict, the four prisoners were brought before the Surrey magistrates at Chertsey on 27 October. A great many Frenchmen were present in court, including Louis Blanc. Blanc was rather embarrassed by the attention, and wrote a note to *The Times*: 'It is true that some of the persons are personal friends of mine, but this has nothing to do with the melancholy occurrences alluded to; and I leave to the English public to judge for what purposes my name has been implicated by your correspondence in an affair to the motives and fatal result of which I am an utter stranger.' It is fair to record that there is no evidence that Blanc was ever party to the dispute. But he did not abandon Barthélemy.

Mr Parry, engaged at considerable expense by Ledru-Rollin, appeared on behalf of Barronet and Allain. The *Windsor and Eton Express* reported 'that Mr Parry ... distinctly named Barthélemy as the surviving principal of the duel'. This was in violation of the understanding that the principals would not be named before the court. The *Express* saw Barthélemy start.

Barthélemy, who speaks English very well, immediately saw the force of the admission, and cast an indignant glance at Barronet. When Mr Parry again mentioned Barthélemy as one of the principals, the same look was reported with additional force, which seemed to say to Barronet 'Have you turned approver [informer]? Did you instruct him to denounce me?'

Parry requested that Barronet and Allain be granted bail as respectable businessmen. He also cited, as a precedent advantageous for his clients, the recent legal proceedings surrounding the Sixmilebridge killings in Ireland. Forgotten now, something of a novelty for an Irish massacre, this episode requires some explanation.

The 'Sixmilebridge affray', as it was delicately known, referred to a mass shooting that took place on Thursday, 22 July 1852, during the general election campaign, in County Clare in the west of Ireland. Sixmilebridge was a relatively prosperous market town of about 850 people, which boasted one of the few woollen factories in the southern half of Ireland. County Clare, however, was particularly devastated by the Great Famine of 1845 to 1850. Captain Edmond Wynne, stationed in the district, wrote of what he saw in the bleak winter of 1846:

I ventured through ... this day, to ascertain the condition of the inhabitants, and although I am not easily moved, I confess myself unmanned by the extent and intensity of the suffering witnessed, more especially amongst the women and little children, crowds of whom were seen to be scattered over the turnip field, like a flock of famished crows, devouring the raw turnips, mothers half naked, shivering in the snow and sleet, uttering exclamations of despair, whilst their children were screaming with hunger; I am a match for anything else I might meet here, but this I cannot stand.

'Black '47' was the worst year for deaths in Ireland, but in County Clare the agony dragged on into 1851. The last starvation victim of the Great Famine that can be ascertained was a nameless stranger who, in April of that year, stumbled into the town of Ennis, about twenty miles from Sixmilebridge, and expired in a cellar.

In Ireland, the voting franchise extended only to a very small percentage of the population. Polling was public and open, under the eyes of landlords, priests and people. Rallied by the priests, the local peasantry had gathered around the polling station at Sixmilebridge to oppose the landlord candidate, Colonel Vandeleur. The crowd had surrendered their sticks to a Protestant gentleman, Mr Wilson of Belvoir, before entering the town. They were enraged, however, when they saw eighteen voters being escorted to the poll under military 'protection'. It appeared to them that these voters were being coerced into voting for the landlord. The priests, it was reported, urged the crowd to 'rescue' them from their military escort. A bayonet charge drove the crowd back, but stone-throwing continued. The front rank of the soldiers found themselves confined in a lane confronted by a crowd. One shot was heard, then another, followed by a fusillade. The soldiers had opened fire. No order to shoot had been given, and the Riot Act had not been read as warning. When the firing ceased, six local men lay dead.

A coroner's court was convened, after an unusual delay of two weeks, to hold an inquest into the death of the first of the victims, Jeremiah Frawley. The majority of the jury, defying the lengthy and forceful direction of the presiding coroner, brought in a verdict of 'Wilful Murder' against the magistrate, John C. Delmege, and eight soldiers. Five jurors dissented, though they still thought the soldiers culpable and very reasonably recommended a verdict of manslaughter. The prisoners were lodged in Ennis gaol, held on remand until their criminal trial. At this point, the Irish Attorney General appointed from London intervened to secure their release on bail. His action was contrary to the standard practice that bail was not given for those indicted on serious offences such as homicide. This was not the least of it. He then quashed the Coroners' Court conviction as 'radically and thoroughly bad'. The County Clare Grand Jury the following year threw the bills for murder out. Instead, Fathers Burke and McClune were put on trial for instigating a 'seditious' riot, and the election of the Liberal candidates for the county was declared void due to priestly intimidation.

This massacre in Ireland has been lost to historical memory. This is probably because it involved no obvious nationalist principle. The victims were a 'mob' led by priests, in support of a Liberal candidate from the very party that would ultimately be swept away by nationalists in the 1870s. It is a good thing, however, that Sixmilebridge and its attendant legal chicanery should now be remembered. At the time, the affair caused some turmoil, less because of the peasant Irish dead (hardly an unfamiliarity in the years after the Great Famine), more because of the flagrant obstruction of legal procedure. The English government in Ireland had rather obviously interfered with the normal course of law to protect the soldiers. This upset the precedent that suspects facing *prima facie* evidence of a serious offence such as murder should be held on remand.

Lawyers are practical souls, and if they earn their stipend at all they will turn any precedent to the advantage of their clients. Mr Parry, representing the French duellists, wished to use the Crown's innovation against the prosecution. Barronet and Allain had admitted to acting as seconds in a duel, which was, indeed, an admission to murder, but their moral stature, Parry argued, had not been impugned, and they were not going to flee the jurisdiction. The Irish case, Parry went on, had established the principle that suspects could only be remanded in prison if they were believed to be a flight risk. (In the Irish case, it had been stated that soldiers of the Crown would never seek to escape justice. Generously this had been ascribed to their high moral standards, rather than a justified faith that the government would get them off the hook.)

The court turned down Parry's application for bail, and the prisoners were remanded in custody. Nonetheless, the government's actions in Ireland had created a tricky precedent, and the trial judge asked for judgment from the Court for Crown Cases Reserved, a court established in 1848 to consider points of law regarding criminal cases. This met on 3 November 1852. As a higher court, it was a suitably grand affair, and either for effect or in a confusion of memory, Herzen in his memoirs mixed it up with the final assize trial of the defendants. He was part astonished, part impressed, and part amused by the flummery of English court ritual.

About 10 o'clock the first masqueraders, heralds with two trumpeters, appeared before the hotel in which Lord Campbell was staying, announcing that Lord Campbell would judge such and such a case in the open court at 10 o'clock. We rushed to the doors of the court, which was a few steps away; meanwhile, in a gilt carriage, Lord Campbell moved across the square, wearing a wig which was only surpassed in size and beauty by the wig of his coachman, upon which was perched a minute three-cornered hat. Behind his carriage walked some twenty attorneys and solicitors, picking up their gowns and wearing no hats, but instead woollen wigs made intentionally as little like human hair as possible .... There is a knocking on the door. A gentleman, also in masquerade attire, shouts, 'Who is there?' 'The judge,' is answered on the other side; the doors are flung open, and Campbell enters, wearing a fur coat and something like a lady's dressing gown; he bowed to all four quarters of the compass and announced that the Assizes [sic] were open.

Such archaic grandeur was appropriate for throwing fairy dust over the shambolic legal makeshift produced by the government's violation of justice in Ireland.

Lord Campbell sat with three other judges: Coleridge, Wightman and Erle. Mr Chambers QC opened his case on behalf of the defence by pointing out that duelling had for centuries been tolerated in England.

> The law, no doubt, was that duelling was a crime, and that killing an adversary in a duel was murder. The Court could not alter the law, but, where the letter of the law was strict and severe, the Judges, in administering it, would temper its severity in accordance with the state of feeling, and even the prejudices and infirmities of society.

He gave examples of well-known duels: between the Duke of York and Colonel Lennox, between Lord Norfolk and Lord Maldon, between the politicians Mr Adam and Mr Fox, between Lord Lonsdale and Captain Duff, between Mr Tierney and the Prime Minister Mr Pitt, and between two senior lawyers, Mr Adolphus and Mr Alley. None of these men had been remanded in custody or heavily sentenced. Society, Chambers argued, had long indulged duelling for the upper classes 'where the rank of the parties led to the impression that they had acted, however wrongly, in accordance with the feelings of the class of society to which they belonged'. In such cases, it was rare to keep the suspects in prison before trial, and rarer still, unless there had been unfairness in the duel, that the sentence according to law was carried into effect.

This was an appeal to class justice, with the hope that it would be applied to Cournet's seconds, both respectable gentlemen.

Chambers passed over the complication that their opponents, Barthélemy and his second de Morney, were working men from the Continent, very far from the traditional duelling classes of England. Chambers' application was rejected. The defendants would have to throw themselves on the mercy of the court.

The court then dealt with the case of Barthélemy and de Morney. They had not admitted to any offence, so should they be allowed bail? Their lawyer, Mr Huddleston – no expensive Queen's Counsel for Barthélemy and de Morney – argued the case. Again, it was rejected. Lord Campbell gave a ringing judgment:

> There is, in this instance, no distinction between the case where murder takes place in a duel and in any other trans-action, and it would be inexpedient that there should be. Time was when public opinion was contrary to the law of the land, but it has now taken a turn, and it is more in ac-cordance with it, and I trust that the time will soon arrive when duelling will be considered not only as illegal, but as absurd.

Campbell refused Barthélemy and de Morney bail, but he was very far from condemnatory of the prisoners. He abstained from giving any opinion that the evidence was conclusive and wished for the prisoners in the dock that 'God grant them a good deliverance!' The defendants were perhaps lucky that the Lord Chief Justice was presiding. Campbell had been censured for playing down the gravity of the offence when prosecuting Lord Cardigan for duelling in 1841. 'I confess I do not see how such a man in going into the field of honour violates the law of God more than by firing against a public enemy on the field of battle,' he wrote in his autobiography.

Nonetheless, an age-old ambiguity over duelling had been over-turned. No doubt, Campbell was right: public opinion had turned against the practice. But the massacre at Sixmilebridge, the Crown's legal shenanigans to protect its perpetrators from justice, and the fact that, almost without precedent, a commoner had been considered fit for duelling by his social superior – Cournet's last act of commitment to social republicanism – had all come together to dramatically undermine the concept of duelling as an honourable preserve of the aristocracy, gentry and professional classes. Lord Campbell had overturned the precedent that extended bail to murder suspects whose alleged crimes had arisen from duelling. This did not quite put it yet on a level with other homicides, but the end of an era was clear. Barthélemy and Cournet's meeting was to be the last fatal duel ever fought in Britain.

Thus was the suppression of duelling in Britain linked not just to French revolutionary politics but to the double standard applied to the Irish portion of the United Kingdom. Sir John F. Fitzgerald, a Queen's Counsel and MP for Ennis, was scathing: in Ireland, a coroner's jury enters a verdict of wilful murder against a magistrate and eight soldiers, and the magistrate and soldiers are liberated. In England, four foreigners are imprisoned for being implicated in a fatal duel and the Chief Justice of England sententiously delivers himself of the opinion that 'if a person of the highest eminence was found guilty of murder by a jury, no tribunal of the country would liberate him without trial'. A line was quickly drawn under the Irish massacre. 'It is, Sir, a common saying, that it is a long lane which has no turning,' quipped Home Secretary Lord Palmerston in Parliament. 'Even the longest lane has a turning; and I think that the longest bridge, even the Sixmilebridge, ought to have an end.' It was not forgotten in the west of Ireland, however. For decades after, British soldiers were referred to by locals as the 'Sixmilebridge assassins'.

As he awaited trial, Barthélemy campaigned as best he could to blacken the name of his rival and vindicate his own. He sent numerous letters seeking information on the past life of Cournet, both 'private and political'. His prize acquisition was a letter from Charles Baudin, an admiral of the French Navy. In a letter from Paris, dated 6 January 1853, Baudin wrote of his frustration at the extent of 'public credulity' concerning Cournet's reputation for 'courage and patriotism.'

> As a sailor, he did not want of a certain degree of resolution and audacity, but these qualities were tarnished by the absence of all principle and of all moral feeling. Multiplied acts of sharping [cheating], several of which came to my personal knowledge, while he was serving under my orders in the Mediterranean in 1847, caused me to take severe but futile measures.

A month later, Barthélemy had a notice placed in *Reynolds's Newspaper* stating that this letter – though hardly a warrant for homicide – could be 'seen by those who feel interested in the matter, by visiting M. Barthélemy in Horsemonger-Lane gaol'.

Barthélemy looked forward to another opportunity for self-justification in court. Along with de Morney, Barronet and Allain he went on trial for murder on 22 March 1853, before Mr Justice Coleridge at Kingston. The defendants stood in the dock while a jury of twelve men looked on. Dressed in gowns and horsehair wigs, the barristers prepared to argue their case before the judge. The public benches bobbed with curious onlookers, including many of the French refugees. Louis Blanc, sympathetic to both parties, was present. Even more had hoped to get in. The police had to form a human chain to hold back the crowd. Reporters scribbled notes knowing that this was a story that had grabbed the attention of the country.

Until 1870, foreign defendants could elect to be tried before a jury *de medietate linguae*, meaning it was split between native-born subjects and their own co-nationals. The jury here, therefore, was half composed of Frenchmen, and an interpreter was available to explain the evidence.

It was clear from the outset that Mr Locke, the learned counsel for the prosecution, was not inclined to be hard-line. He told the jury 'not to shrink from returning a verdict of guilty' but reassured them that 'the punishment that would follow such a verdict would, of course, be left to other hands and, no doubt, the clemency of the Crown would be extended to the utmost in such a case'. Locke did, however, assert that the rag found in the misfiring pistol indicated that it had been deliberately sabotaged. He let the implication hang in the air that Barthélemy, or one of his seconds, had been responsible for jamming up the weapon.

Mr Chambers for the defence naturally urged clemency:

The law of England ... was merciful, and made great allowances for the infirmities of human nature, and did not require from mankind more than mankind was capable of performing. The law of England also mercifully considered that foreigners might be ignorant of the customs on the laws of this country and therefore gives them greater privileges than were conferred upon Englishmen, upon that supposition. What, then, were the circumstances of the present case? Here were four unhappy exiles from their own country – a portion of a vast number of others similarly situated – who had been obliged to seek shelter and asylum in England, charged with an offence of the most serious character .... They were called upon to brand as murderers men who had only done what had been done on many other occasions by persons infinitely above them in station and rank.

Chambers attempted to name some such men, but he was interrupted by Mr Justice Coleridge. Chambers concluded by arguing

that 'killing in a duel had never been looked upon as an ordinary murder, and the reason was, it could not be so'. The
defence dismissed the argument that the pistol had been deliberately interfered with. It was, they argued, 'perfectly clear from
all the circumstances that [the] piece of rag must have remained
in the pistol by accident at the time it was cleaned, and that if
blame was to be attached to anyone, the seconds of the deceased
alone were responsible, as it was their duty to have seen that
the weapon was properly loaded; and if there had really been
anything wrong they must be supposed to have sacrificed their
own friend.'

According to Herzen, both parties had hoped to blackguard
the other, and to turn the trial into a political reckoning between
the Ledru-Rollin party and the Blanc-Blanqui party. They were
stymied, however, by the court's lack of interest in pursuing
the case to its bottom.

> The opinion of Barthélemy's case formed by the judge ...
> was clear from beginning to end, and he retained it in spite
> of all the efforts of the French to turn it aside and change
> it for the worse. There had been a duel. One man had been
> killed. Both were French men, refugees having different
> ideas of honour from ours; it was difficult to make out
> which of them was in the right, which in the wrong. One
> had fought in the barricades, the other was a notorious
> duellist. We could not leave this crime unpunished, but we
> ought not to use the whole force of the English law to crush
> foreigners, especially as they were all straightforward peo-
> ple, and had behaved honourably though stupidly. There-
> fore we shall not enquire who is the murderer ... Let them
> go wherever they choose.

The court responded indifferently to the political passions of
the witnesses and cut across their attempts to make speeches.

Herzen thought that the grave old judge was silently laughing at the French witnesses.

In his summing-up, Mr Justice Coleridge rebuked the defence for asserting, against clear English law, that the honour code of duelling was any defence to murder.

> The law was this: – If one or more persons went out together, armed with deadly weapons, for the purpose of committing an unlawful act, which fighting a duel undoubtedly was, and the death of one of the parties ensued, it was, in the eyes of the law, murder by every person connected with the transaction, and this applied equally to the seconds of the deceased as to those of the survivor.

This was clear enough. How could the verdict be anything but guilty of murder?

Nonetheless, the jury, which retired at 6.45 p.m. and returned in about an hour, came back with a verdict of 'guilty of manslaughter'. This was something like jury nullification, but the judge did not seem too concerned. Coleridge sentenced the prisoners to only two further months of imprisonment on top of the time already served. The defendants were astonished, having expected three or four years at a minimum.

Their joy was tightly constrained, however. Barthélemy and his friends were certain that Pardigon, who had organised the cleaning of the guns with rag, had somehow sabotaged his weapon. They pointed out that the rag in the pistol was not wrinkled and torn, as one would expect had it sheared off by accident, but was of a regular oval shape. They knew, however, that public opinion suspected Barthélemy. After all, he had been the one who survived the duel. When Herzen spoke to the condemned men at the end of the trial, Barthélemy's bitterness was palpable: 'I went up to Barthélemy,' Herzen recalled, 'he pressed my hand gloomily and said: "That Pardigon has got off clear, and Baronée [Etienne Barronet] ...” he shrugged his shoulders.’ Barronet was no less furious with Barthélemy: ‘I would rather have been sent to prison for a year than mixed up with that scoundrel Barthélemy.’ What was the pleasure of escaping long years in prison if the other side escaped also? Each defendant was bitterly regretful that English justice had not cut off their nose to spite the other’s face.

The point of a duel was to vindicate honour. Which this fatal *rencontre* between Barthélemy and Cournet had signally failed to do. There hung over it more than a whiff of foul play. Once the trial was safely out of the way, Barthélemy had his defence lawyers write a letter to the press to assert in the strongest possible terms that the gun had not been tampered with on his behalf. After all, the pistol in which the piece of rag was found had never been in Barthélemy’s hands before the duel. The operative weapon had in fact been allocated to Cournet, and Barthélemy had only fired it with fatal effect after his own weapon – the one with the rag in it – had failed to go off twice, and Cournet had tossed him his working gun. ‘There was no ground for supposing,’ the letter concluded, ‘but that the duel was conducted in good faith and in all honour.’ But it was so supposed. It was the common coin of gossip wherever the adherents of the Ledru-Rollin party gathered and found a ready ear.

In prison, Barthélemy fumed. Karl Marx was shocked to hear that Barthélemy had a message smuggled out and sent to Ledru-Rollin warning that as soon as he got out he would ‘shoot him down like a dog’. As Marx reported it, ‘Ledru replied that he would not exchange shots with such a scoundrel. Barthélemy retorted that he would resort to boxing Ledru’s ears in the open street, spit in his face and other such tested methods until he provoked a challenge. Ledru-Rollin was contemptuous: in that case he would regale Barthélemy with a stick and acquaint them with an English magistrate.’ From this account, it was clear that Marx sympathised with Ledru-Rollin rather than Barthélemy, his former comrade-in-arms. We cannot imagine that he was alone. Barthélemy's hot-blooded rage was alienating those who otherwise might have sympathised.

It seems most likely that the pistol had indeed been sabotaged: certainly Henry Hand, the man who had provided the weapons from his shooting gallery, was convinced that the cloth could not have found its way into the pistol mechanism by accident. But who was responsible? When, after his release, Allain visited the family of Victor Hugo to tell the story of the duel from his vantage point as Cournet's second, it is significant that he did not seek to implicate Barthélemy or his party in the malfunctioning of the pistol. Instead, he emphasised – and certainly exaggerated – Barthélemy's daily routine of target practice while in Switzerland, allegedly in preparation for the duel. In examining Allain's account we might ask why he refused to allow that a revolutionary fighter and putative assassin might have other reasons to develop his skills with firearms. And if Barthélemy considered himself to be such a dead-eye with the pistol, why then did he repeatedly offer to fight the duel with swords?

When Cournet himself proposed that the duel be fought with pistols, Allain and Barronet had been deeply worried. 'You are making a mistake,' they said. 'Barthélemy is of an extraordinary strength on the pistol, and does not know how to fight with the sword. You, on the contrary, are of only an ordinary force with the pistol, and you will completely skewer Barthélemy if you fight with the sword.'

Cournet replied, 'Do you think a miserable man like Barthélemy can kill me? Do you think it's possible? So, let me fight with a pistol!'

Allain stressed to Hugo that Cournet's friends remained very deeply concerned at his unwavering bravado. They believed that

Cournet underestimated his opponent, and put himself at a disadvantage. He was a much larger man than Barthélemy, and made a better target.

In his account, Allain implicitly made the case that he was justified in sabotaging Barthélemy's pistol. It was close to an overt confession. Perhaps the weapon had been tampered with in collusion with Pardigon, though we have no evidence for this. Perhaps Allain had brought the pistols with him when he returned by himself to the Shooting Gallery, the night before the duel, to pick up ammunition. This would certainly have given him a chance to insert the cloth. He could not anticipate which man would use the pistol, unless he actually sabotaged it on the field, but he must have expected that Cournet, the experienced duellist, would get his shot in first, as indeed he did, and would either hit Barthélemy or misfire. If the gun failed to go off, he must have hoped that the duellists would switch to the rapiers. The advantage would then definitely have lain with Cournet. He was not to know that Cournet would refuse to fight with swords when Barthélemy's weapon jammed and instead proffer his own. Cournet was a victim of his own contempt for the low-born Barthélemy, and of his pride.

It seems that most of London's radical community accepted that Barthélemy had not sabotaged the gun to his own advantage. Nonetheless, many still held that he had behaved immorally. For George Holyoake, the English radical, Barthélemy had violated the rules of honour by taking a third shot after having had two opportunities to take aim, making his own shot virtually certain. 'The seconds ought to have forbidden such murder. Now the object of the duel is not murder. Its purpose is to vindicate courage. Death is an accident, not its purpose. The duellist is not a murderer in intent. In this case Barthélemy made death his object.' Herzen was unusual in wholly taking Barthélemy's side. He was delighted that the 'stern tranquillity' of English law had remained unmoved by the plotting and scheming of Ledru-Rollin's party.

Very clearly, the trial had healed no wounds. Nonetheless, the refugees on both sides of the dispute were generally happy that the sentences had been so light, and the stigma of murder had been averted. A terrible blow had been parried. On the train ride home from the trial, the French émigrés broke into a rendition of the '*Marseillaise*', the French revolutionary anthem, to celebrate the triumph. Herzen, ever ironical, reminded them that the defendants had managed to escape only because of the fairness of English law and persuaded them to add a chorus of 'Rule Britannia'. The Irish victims of the 'Sixmilebridge Affray' might not have appreciated the gesture.

15

THE ROAD TO
WARREN STREET

Cournet's controversial death completed the rift that had been growing between the different factions of England's French exiles. The scandal so sullied the reputation of these refugees that sixty of them, including doctors, artists and craftsmen, concluded that they could no longer hope to find work in the country. They petitioned the British government to help them start a new life in America. Lord Granville, the Foreign Secretary, was so happy to get rid of these troublesome foreigners that he had their passages paid for and instructed the British ambassador in the United States to grant them $100 each on arrival. By departing across the Atlantic they definitively left behind them the revolution in France. Those who remained in England were cast into despondent demoralisation.

In 1852, a group emerged calling itself Commune Révolutionnaire. It was comprised of about sixty to eighty persons dedicated to the grim goal of assassinating Napoleon III. Its moving force, now living in exile in London, was Félix Pyat. Pyat, not quite a socialist, was a republican to the bone, and full of hatred for the petty Napoleonic regime in France. He would become infamous for his open support for tyranni-cide. From 1853, he was plotting in earnest, seeking to send assassins against the Emperor who had usurped the Republic and slaughtered its defenders. 'When a man raises himself above public justice, he ought to fall under the hand of an individual,' he declared. 'When, then, shall an heroic hand settle the account of blood?'

When the revolutionary émigrés buried a young veteran of 1848, Henri Beaugrand, in January 1853, the great leaders – Louis Blanc, Martin Bernard and Ledru-Rollin – were absent. They had heard rumours that unacceptable speeches, implying support for a policy of murder, would be made over the coffin and they feared a new nihilism. The funeral procession included Félix Pyat and François Pardigon carrying the 'Revolution' flag of Commune Révolutionnaire. It started off from Gray's Inn Lane in the pouring rain. The streets were muddy and potholed, and the mourners slogged through the mire. The English passers-by recognised the French and their red flag, and the mourners heard them 'laugh, hiss [and] boo'.

It only got worse as the procession moved into proletarian quarters, as one participant, Philippe Faure, recorded:

> The more we advance into the poor neighbourhoods – with their grimy houses, their pallid population, dull, haggard, thin-blooded, faces distorted by suffering – hostile feelings manifest themselves outrageously. It is for them, for all the workers, we are proscrits ... and they insult us!

Intended as a demonstration as much as a cortège, the march to the graveside was uncommonly long. After two hours, Beaugrand's last resting place was reached and speeches were declaimed without much passion. Worn out by exile, painfully aware that the revolutionary energy of 1848 had disappeared, and embarrassed by the Barthélemy-Cournet duel, the French exiles seemed to be burying their cause as much as their comrade. Soaked by the continuous downpour of soot-darkened rain, the marchers prepared to retreat to the comfort of a local hostelry. But suddenly Pardigon grabbed the 'Revolution' flag, roused twenty-five or so uncertain disciples, and began haranguing the astonished crowd. 'He speaks warmly, and while our feet are icy on the wet grass, our hearts are stirred.'

These were the diehards of the Commune Révolutionnaire. Cut off, as it seemed, from the tides of history, they were determined to defy their fate. On 5 July 1853, the group demonstrated that it was in deadly earnest when it made a serious if unsuccessful attempt to assassinate the Emperor in Paris. A gang were captured outside a new opera house, the Opera Comique, on its opening night as they waited to burst in and kill the imperial family. Within days, more than 200 people were arrested. A trial held in camera exposed the machinations of the refugee leaders and sentenced them – rather mildly – in their absence.

The survivors of the duel, meanwhile, were duly liberated on Monday, 2 May 1853. Upon his release, Barthélemy moved into an apartment with Tony Petitjean, a fellow republican exile, at Upper John Street, off Tottenham Court Road, near Fitzroy Square. The rent was a substantial one guinea a week, but included a workshop. There they were joined by Jean Pierre Bourquin and the three set up as craftsmen. To finance their operations, Barthélemy took out a loan of £15 from Herzen, which he paid back promptly. Together they invented a new process for colouring glass. Hydrofluoric acid was used to create the impression of decoration painted by the brush of an artist. It was an ingenious innovation, and very much of its time in this age of technical advance. The patent was granted on 25 November 1853, costing £60. They went on to sell it for £250.

No doubt Petitjean was the primary intelligence behind this creative workshop. The following year he pioneered a method of silvering mirrors without the use of mercury which poisoned, crippled and killed scores of workers every year. This new technique even came to the attention of Michael Faraday of the Royal Society. Barthélemy's mechanical talent and organisational acumen had clearly been valuable to Petitjean's project. He was a man of no mean abilities. It is rather tragic to consider what might have been had he decided to continue cooperating with Petitjean.

Parting ways, Barthélemy moved into number 10 Gerrard Street, off Soho Square, a fine-looking brick house on the outside, formerly a gambling den, but now kept for French refugees. There he had a small apartment and a workshop. Barthélemy remained industrious, though now, we can surmise, he was constructing instruments of assassination. His neighbour complained to the local police station that Barthélemy, working late into the night, was preventing him from sleeping.

Barthélemy was not done with politics. In November 1853, alongside Louis Blanc and Édouard Vaillant, he spoke before 2,000 mourners at the funeral of another French émigré, James Folssy, a member of Commune Révolutionnaire. Barthélemy carried a black flag on which were painted key dates from the 1848 revolution:

16 April 1848
[Louis Blanc's demonstration in favour of delaying elections, dispersed by troops]
Massacres of Rouen, 15 May 1848
Massacres of June 1848
Massacres of December 1851

Félix Pyat listed 'the crimes of our enemies ... massacres, imprisonments, dispersions of families' and promised vengeance. There would be no pardon or clemency, only stern justice. By lumping together the 1848 Provisional Government, the executive government of General Cavaignac, and the Napoleonic dictatorship, Commune Révolutionnaire branded most of the French refugee *proscrits* as little different from the current imperial government in France. Devoted republicans were being lumped in with Bonapartists as enemies of the people. For the more moderate emigration, the 'black flag' of vengeance seemed to have been raised against their own red flag.

It's likely that Barthélemy was not formally a member of Commune Révolutionnaire. Politically, he remained an adherent of Louis Blanc and strategically a follower of Auguste Blanqui. Pyat's close relationship with François Pardigon, who Barthélemy blamed for double-dealing in the duel, must have put him off. Barthélemy was increasingly a lone wolf, nonetheless his 'ruling idea, his passion, his monomania', as Herzen put it, was the assassination of Napoleon III. Moving on again, he took lodgings with Thomas Coddery, of 42 Upper John Street. Coddery was foreman to Mr George Moore, and he secured employment for Barthélemy at Moore's factory, carrying out repairs on his machines for making ginger beer and soda water. It may have been working with the sulphur compounds used in making the fizzy drinks that led Barthélemy to his scheme for assassination. According to Wilhelm Liebknecht, Barthélemy planned to soak deer-shot with which to shoot Napoleon in sulphur, a corrosive agent. Should that miscarry, he would stab him.

Barthélemy's new employer, by all accounts, was a genial and quite innocent man. George Moore was aged about sixty years and married, though living separately from his wife. He dwelt at 73 Warren Street, 'an avenue of respectable houses' off Fitzroy Square, that was the location of both his home and his soda-water factory in the same building. Moore had risen to moderate social status. As an Upper Warden of the Wheelwrights Company, he was only one year away from being made a Master of this guild.

Moore was not a native Londoner. His father had come from Sandhurst and George was educated at the Crypt Grammar School in Gloucester. There he was known still as a writer 'in a small way' and he composed poetry, some of which had been set to music. After his death, a local newspaper reprinted one of his verses, about a visit from London back to Gloucester, which began by making light-hearted fun of his own weight and that of his brother:

Two gentlemen of London, no common cockney 'Gents',
But men of weight and substance, (that's true at all events),
Set out upon a journey to visit country friends,
And for the cares of business, to gather brief amends.
They got a peep at Maidenhead, then rattled on to
    Reading,
And read in that red prison there how crime is always
    spreading;
Then on, on, on, they rushed along, o'er many miles of
    down,
With now and then a house or two, but scarce another
    town;
O'er doubtless many a lovely spot, but thro' the mist they
    miss'd 'em,
For mist and rain first dimmed the scene, and night came
    on to assist 'em.
They tunnelled through the Cotswold chain, but when they
    hardly knew,
As wrapt in noise and darkness, their illumined carriage
    flew –
Till at last a city reached, which should be bright and
    glowing,
'Tis Gloucester named, to its old walls the modest Severn
    flowing,
. . .

Now Thursday comes, and London homes demand our
   travellers' cares;
Though scant and hearty are their thanks, yet fervent are
   their prayers,
That each kind friend may live to enjoy from many ere
   coming year
Good health, good spirits, good report, and Gloucestershire
   good cheer.

For George Moore, London meant money and modernity; but
his heart, it seems, was still in Gloucester.

Moore does not seem to have been particularly political.
Rather, he was a true-blood Englishman, typical of his age and
background. He had favoured the ultimately successful campaign
for the repeal of the protectionist Corn Laws, which were seen
as overt class legislation in favour of the landed gentry. John
Manners, the 7th Earl of Rutland, and a leading light in the
Tory 'Young England' movement, had written a provocative
poem in 1841, a line of which ran, 'Let wealth and commerce,
laws and learning die, But leave us still our old Nobility!' This
clearly irritated Moore, who had responded with his own verse:

To which, I answer if thus our 'old nobility' can feel,
The sooner they all 'die', the better weal;
For of all the worthless things upon the earth,
Mere 'old nobility' is least in worth.

There is no particular reason to think that Moore would have
had much in common with Barthélemy politically. He was,
however, opposed to arrant privilege and likely shared the
common English hostility to the authoritarian Napoleonic
regime in France. Moore was an unlikely target for Barthélemy's
frustrated rage.

*

Sometime in November 1854, Barthélemy, in the company of a woman, arranged to look at a house in Millman Row, Chelsea, about a mile from Sloane Square and the King's Road. The house was in good condition, and Barthélemy agreed to rent it. In making his arrangement with the landlord, Barthélemy explained that he wanted it for a French family of high respectability who were coming to spend a few months in England, from around Christmas, and whose business called them to that particular part of West London. Barthélemy moved in with his woman companion, the very same who would be with him on the night he killed George Moore. He was, according to Carl Schurz, 'passionately attached' to her.

This was almost certainly Sarah Lowndes, a young woman who for some time had worked as a servant in Windsor. Though aged only about twenty-five, Sarah was already widowed and without means when she met Barthélemy. She was smart, though. Later, when in desperate straits, she stole goods by pretending to be a servant picking up provisions for wealthy Windsor families. The magistrate in the subsequent court trial concluded from 'the adroit mode in which she had gone to work' that she was 'a proficient, if not a professional thief'. We know that Sarah met Barthélemy around the time of the duel, presumably while he was being held in gaol, though the exact circumstances are murky. Clearly, they had fallen in love, and they were often seen together after his release. We need not assume that Barthélemy initiated the affair. In London, there were 200,000 more females than males, and women of marriageable age won independence from their parents by finding a partner. This meant, a London friend told Francis Wey, that there 'are no more relentless flirts in the world than English girls'. Or, as we might say, there is every reason to believe, given what we know of Sarah Lowndes' resourcefulness, that she saw in Barthélemy a man she desired, and she won his heart.

Soon after moving to Chelsea, Barthélemy bid farewell to his intimate associates, informing them of his decision to settle in Germany. But this was a cover. His real intention was to travel as far as Holland, pass through Belgium via secret revolutionary safe houses, and make his way back to France. His true destination was Paris, where he would seek out and kill the Emperor. As Wilhelm Liebknecht recalled, Barthélemy 'had obtained an admission card for the next ball at the Tuileries which Napoleon would be sure to visit. Money and everything else he had, but after the French fashion, also a "lady friend" whom he wished to take with him.' He had set out for the boat to the Continent on the morning of 8 December, but missed his train. He still carried on him a pair of pistols, with barrels about six inches long; twenty-four cartridges; percussion caps; and a dagger with a nine-inch blade.

That same day, Barthélemy and his female companion met up and made their way to Warren Street. It was a Friday evening. Quietly they moved down two of the long rows of uniform houses, 'with little windows like guillotines ... enclosed by black railings'. It brought to mind tombs in parallel between which phantoms walked. Half an hour later, George Moore was dead, Charles Collard fatally injured, and Barthélemy in police custody. The woman, however, had disappeared like a spirit in the night.

16

'DOUBLY HORRIBLE AND HORRIBLY DOUBLE'

In custody after the killings at Warren Street, Barthélemy retained his composure and refused to speak, not even divulging his address. Anxious that his mysterious partner escape, he denied that any woman had been with him. If one was seen, he surmised unconvincingly, she must have simply happened to enter the house at the same time. Naturally his interrogators did not take this seriously. The police initially suspected that Barthélemy had been accompanied by a man dressed in female attire but his companion most certainly did exist, and had rushed back to their shared lodgings at Millman's Row in Chelsea. A neighbour saw a woman go 'over the railings' and later hurry off, leaving 'the street door wide open'. When the police came to check, they found an apartment devoid of furnishings, excepting only a pickaxe, a saw, a mattress, a bedspread, and her discarded disguise of cloak and hat.

Barthélemy had no money for a lawyer, being able to offer only a credit of £21 owed to him. Nonetheless, lawyer himself presented himself: Mr John Sloman Herring. Herring once had chambers at 17 Stafford Street in Middlesex, but this seems to have been a hole-in-the-wall operation and he had gone bankrupt. As recently as May 1854, he had been lodged in the Gaol of

St Thomas the Apostle as an insolvent debtor. Herring was a lawyer of the 'Better Call Saul' type: an ambulance-chaser with an eye for the main chance. He saw in Barthélemy's case a good opportunity to advertise his flailing business. His new client made it clear to Herring, however, that he had no wish to be saved.

Why had the crime been committed at all? There was little evidence as to motive. Moore had an iron safe where he kept his money and valuables in the front parlour which he used as his business office. The key to the safe was discovered after the murder in the back parlour, the other keys belonging to Moore being found upon his person. There was no evidence, however, that the safe had been interfered with.

Without the knowledge of his landlord, Barthélemy had lifted the flooring of the back kitchen of his lodgings in Chelsea and dug a hole, measuring four foot six inches by four foot eight inches and about the same in depth. After Barthélemy was arrested for killing Moore, the police searched the building and found the hiding place. At first the police suspected that Barthélemy was attempting a scheme similar to that which had recently shaken the capital in 1849: 'The Bermondsey Horror'. This outrage had been committed by husband and wife team the Mannings, who had lured and murdered a victim, Patrick O'Connor, and then buried him under the flagstones of their kitchen floor. (The couple had blamed one another for the crime. Maria Manning, born Marie Roux in Switzerland, cried out in court, 'There is no justice and no right for a foreign subject in this country. There is no law for me.' Both were hanged.) The police speculated that Barthélemy at first had intended to invite George Moore to his house in Millman's Row, kill him, and bury him in the ready-made 'grave'. Only when he failed to entice Moore did he proceed to Warren Street and attack him there. This theory seems to have been dropped quite quickly, and there is no evidence for it. Most likely, the hole was for secreting away revolutionary documentation to keep it safe from prying eyes. It may also have been an escape route, as it seems that the hole led out to the large water drains towards the river Thames.

Another theory was presented by the downmarket *Sunday Times*. The paper alleged that previous to the duel at Egham taking place, Barthélemy had married a daughter of George Moore. When Barthélemy was sent to prison, the paper reported, his wife almost lost her reason and Mr Moore took his daughter away, so that Barthélemy would not be able to find her. Upon release, Barthélemy made enquiries after his wife, but when these were of no avail he gave up the search and settled down as a single man. Nonetheless, the *Sunday Times* claimed, he was known on several occasions to have made violent declarations about Moore. Other than this, things went on quietly until Barthélemy solicited Moore to give him a character reference for new employers. Moore was believed to have refused, and ordered him to quit the house. A struggle resulted. According to the paper, it appeared from various circumstances that Barthélemy had a 'firm and deadly hatred' towards George Moore, and his attack on him might well have been long premeditated.

There was little to support this speculation, nor was it accepted by any other newspaper. George Moore's son, at the subsequent trial, 'asked ... to be allowed publicly to deny that the prisoner was connected with his deceased father by marriage. There was not the slightest foundation for the assertion.' Mr Herring, Barthélemy's solicitor, added that the prisoner admitted to him that he had seen Mr Moore only three times in his life.

The inquest met on 12 December 1854, at the Goat and Compass Tavern in the New Road. Barthélemy was absent. Mr Herring made it clear that his client wished to be present to hear the evidence against him. The coroner also desired that Barthélemy be brought before the inquiry. When the jury eagerly concurred, it was resolved that they should send a deputation to Lord Palmerston, the Home Secretary, to request that the prisoner be produced. The inquest was adjourned to the following Thursday.

On the Wednesday morning, a deputation from the jury waited upon Mr Waddington of the Home Office. First, Palmerston said he would attend within the hour, but later called off the meeting because of pressing business. The delegation spoke with his subordinates. They were told that Palmerston declined to interfere, as he doubted his power to compel the magistrates to produce the prisoner for such a purpose. They were offered, however, a letter indicating that Palmerston had no objection to Barthélemy being present at the inquest. This was declined, as it would have no legal standing and would be ignored by the governor of the House of Detention holding Barthélemy. When the inquest resumed, the coroner complained that the law was deficient in preventing a person from being present to hear the very evidence given against him. From this episode it seems that rumours had started amongst the emigration: Palmerston did not wish for too much scrutiny of Moore's death.

Nonetheless, Barthélemy was indeed allowed to attend the inquest. At ten a.m. on 14 December, a horse-drawn cab drove Barthélemy to the Police Court on Great Marlborough Street. It was followed by an immense and excited crowd, fascinated by what they had read in the papers. They were yelling as they ran beside the vehicle, and as it stopped there was a strenuous attempt by the jostling swell to get a glimpse of the prisoner. Several constables were required to restore order. The curiosity of the crowd was disappointed, however, as Barthélemy was hustled in by the back entrance, handcuffed and guarded by two officers and a gaoler. He was described by one reporter as 'a man of very repulsive appearance, about 5'7" high, with very high cheekbones, sallow complexion, a great quantity of black bushy hair, and a scowling cast of features'. Another, however, described him as 'a remarkably fine looking young man, about the middle stature, and with the foreign expression of countenance'. A third account had Barthélemy as 'above the middle size, with a fine development of features, and a remarkably well formed head, and exhibiting in his countenance an amount of resolute calmness seldom witnessed, and particularly so under such appalling circumstances'. An eminent musical composer, present at the inquest, thought that Barthélemy's voice, 'ordinarily subdued and gentle ... was absolutely melodious'.

The room was crowded. 'There is a class of people who have a morbid predilection for attending coroners' inquest,' wrote George Augustus Sala, an English journalist, and they were out in force to hear all the bloody details. Charlotte Bennett, the servant at 73 Warren Street, gave evidence that she had seen Barthélemy at her master's house perhaps half a dozen times. By that time, Barthélemy had been working for George Moore for about three or four months. She had never heard the two men argue. Barthélemy was in the habit of coming in the daytime, and only ever went into the factory, where several persons were employed, to repair the machinery. Before the night of the murder, he had never been in George Moore's private residence. She had no evidence that the two men knew each other at all well.

George Moore Jnr, the son of the deceased, also testified. Mr Hardwicke, the magistrate, asked him, 'Do you happen to know whether your father was in the habit of going to Paris?' Moore's son replied, 'I never knew he went to Paris. I never knew my father to leave England to go to Paris.' The servant was recalled. She was also not aware that he had ever gone to France. Sometimes he would be gone for two or three days at a time, but she understood he had been in Brighton, where his brother ran a school of gymnastics.

The several witnesses examined agreed that Barthélemy had shot Collard – the ex-policeman who had attempted to prevent his flight from the scene of the crime – though one at least was of the opinion that the pistol had gone off by accident. Nonetheless, the jury lost no time in returning a verdict of 'wilful murder'.

In a letter to Engels, Marx reflected ironically on his former comrade's imminent fate, but worried that police might find incriminating papers connecting Marx's party to Barthélemy. No doubt he had in mind documentation relating to his 1850 collaboration with the accused, the Société Universelle des Communistes Révolutionnaires:

> Barthélemy's end is a GLORIOUS one. At yesterday's hearing (or rather CORONER'S INQUEST) it was said that important papers, though not relating to the [planned] assassination [of Napoleon], had been found on him. It would be annoying if these included papers from the old days, so that we seemed to be connected with a fellow who – or so the louts boasted – was 'saving up' a bullet for us in the event of our returning to Paris.

The old bitterness against Marx, it seems, had not waned.

Understandably, most of the French émigrés were anxiously distancing themselves from Barthélemy. Alexander Herzen was rather disgusted, and recorded a meeting with two refugees:

'We have come to you,' they said, 'to assure you that we have not the faintest share in Barthélemy's terrible crime; – we had work in common, one has to work with all sorts of men. Now it will be said ... it will be thought ....'

'But have you really come all the way from London to Twickenham to tell me that?' Herzen asked.

'Your opinion is of very great value to us.'

'Upon my word, gentlemen! Why, I was a friend of Barthélemy's myself – and worse than you, because I had no work with him; but I'm not denying him now. I know nothing about the case, the verdict and the sentence I leave to Lord Campbell, while I weep to think that powers so young and so rich, that a talent that has been so trained by the bitter conflict and hard environment in which he lived – that in the flower of his age he should lose his life at the hand of hangman.'

There seemed little doubt about Barthélemy's fate, and there could hardly be any political reason to diminish the horror of his crime.

By English law at this time, a suspect could only be tried for a single murder, no matter how many he might have committed. Barthélemy was indicted for the murder of Collard before the grand jury on New Year's Day 1855. The George Moore case was allowed to drop. There had been multiple witnesses to the shooting of Collard, but only Charlotte Bennett had witnessed the killing of Moore. Moreover, if a suspect killed a person attempting to prevent their flight from a felony crime, it automatically meant a conviction of murder. From the legal point of view, therefore, prosecuting the Collard case over the crime against Moore made solid sense.

But as well as police procedural reasons for focusing on Collard, there were likely also political reasons. The police were fully aware of Barthélemy's revolutionary activities and rumours could easily have got back to them that he planned to assassinate the French Emperor – and that his visit to Moore that fateful evening had something to do with these schemes. Since October 1853, Britain and France had been fighting as allies against Russia in the Crimean War. It was not a good time to be delving too deeply into Barthélemy's true intent. It was very much in the government's interest that this troublesome émigré be dealt with as quickly as possible, and as a common criminal.

The trial of Barthélemy for the murder of Collard took place on 3 January 1855, at the Central Criminal Court: the Old Bailey in London. This was, *par excellence*, the criminal court of the country: here judges, jury and barristers were better informed, more sophisticated, and perhaps less scrupulous than their country counterparts. The 'bench', on which the judge sat, directly faced the dock where stood the defendant. On the right of the bench were the jury box and the witness stand. On the left were seats reserved for privileged visitors and reporters. Within the square thus formed, barristers for prosecution and defence moved around: arranging papers, listening intently or lackadaisically – as the case may be – and preparing to speak. Over the dock was a public gallery, accommodating about thirty people. From this vantage point they could see nothing of the defendant except the top of his head, and could hear little of what was going on. 'Probably the first impression on the mind of a man who visits the Old Bailey for the first time,' wrote an irreverent and sensibly anonymous journalist, 'is that he never saw so many ugly people collected in any one place before.'

Barthélemy, marched over from the adjoining Newgate prison, was ushered in before Lord Chief Justice Campbell and Mr Justice Crowder. Mr Bodkin and Mr Clarke appeared for the prosecution. Mr Collier, QC, defended the prisoner. In a strong clear voice, Barthélemy pleaded 'not guilty', and claimed his right to be tried by a jury partly composed of foreigners. A mixed jury, only half of whom were Englishmen, was accordingly sworn. Through his interpreter, Barthélemy successfully objected to some of the French candidates suggested. Even now, he suspected the perfidious machinations of the Ledru-Rollin party.

The trial lasted for nearly eight hours and for its entirety Barthélemy was required to remain standing erect at the bar. Throughout the proceedings, as we have come to expect, he showed no flagging and no emotion. Though the evidence against him was overwhelming, the defence complained that the prosecution had been brought for the death of Collard rather than the first and primary charge of killing Moore. Mr Collier, the defence lawyer, 'said that if that had been gone into [Moore's death] he felt some confidence that he should have been able to satisfy the jury that in that case he had not committed the crime of wilful and deliberate murder, and that at most he was only amenable to a charge of manslaughter'. He proposed that had Barthélemy gone to Moore's house with a premeditated intention to kill, it was most unlikely that he would have brought a female with him. Instead, some dispute had suddenly arisen, and under the impulse of passion Barthélemy had committed the dreadful act of killing Mr Moore.

There was nothing to show, Collier argued, that Barthélemy had deliberately fired at Collard. Having fallen from six-foot-high railings, his client had been immediately laid hold of by three or four men, and nothing was more likely than the pistol going off by accident. It was true that Barthélemy had been carrying a considerable quantity of arms on his person, but 'it was the custom among foreigners to do so, and he observed that if the prisoner had really been actuated by the murderous intention imputed to him, the dagger that was found upon them was a much more ready and deadly weapon than even a pistol'. Not many foreigners, even Frenchmen, habitually carried around with them the weapons found on Barthélemy's person; but the point regarding the dagger was a compelling one.

In his summing-up, Lord Chief Justice Campbell made it clear that whether the killing of George Moore amounted to the crime of wilful murder or manslaughter, in either case it was a felony. By the law of England, it was the right and duty of any of the Queen's subjects to assist in the apprehension of a felon, and if he was killed by the felon's resistance, that act in itself amounted to the crime of murder. There could be no doubt whatever upon the point. It was a clear direction to the jury to convict.

The jury retired at 5 p.m. and in about three quarters of an hour they filed back in. They had listened to the instructions delivered by the judge, but were still clearly unhappy with the logic of the prosecution case. They returned a verdict of guilty, but coupled it with a strong recommendation to mercy.

This recommendation provoked much disapproving comment, in the conservative press at least. *The Times* was particularly outraged. It was widely implied that the French jurors were unwilling to see one of their own sent to the gallows. One of the panel wrote a letter to *The Times* to explain the reasoning of the jurors and to defend them against the imputation that their conduct had been 'horrible in the extreme'. The jury was not concerned, he wrote, with any murders Barthélemy might have committed except for that of 'poor Charles Collard', the only one for which he was standing trial. In their view, Barthélemy's killing of Collard was not in itself murder, because it had been 'forced upon him, and by the first law of nature – self-preservation'. Killing in an attempt to escape was not the same as cold-blooded murder with malice aforethought. However, they all agreed that by English law the crime of murder had been committed; for, as the Lord Chief Justice has explained to them, if a fugitive from the scene of a crime kills a man who is lawfully seeking to apprehend him, no matter how inadvertently, then he must be found guilty of murder. The jury, therefore, were not divided on the question of Barthélemy's legal guilt. But a number of them argued strongly that Barthélemy should not hang. One in particular made an impression: '"Were we capable," said my brother juror,'

> ... were we capable of judging the hearts of our fellow creatures – were we capable of knowing the real truth of all things, without the chance of ever being in the wrong – were we possessed of one of the glorious attributes of

God, that of omniscience – then, if death punishment was right, we could not err in carrying it out.

But can we, poor ill-judging mortals as we are, decide, without the possibility of being in the wrong? No! It is presumption for any man to say to the contrary. The best and the wisest men living are not always capable of judging right.

It was as Christians, the juror wrote, that they recommended mercy. It was well known that men had been sent to their deaths on false evidence. The death penalty was irreversible. In a world of imperfect knowledge, therefore, it was morally impermissible. The juror concluded his letter: 'I would rather that ten thousand guilty persons should escape with impunity from the legal effects of the crimes, than that one innocent individual should suffer.'

The emphasis here was upon the illegitimacy of the death penalty, a quite just and convincing argument. Karl Marx, no Christian himself, had written in 1853 that 'it would be very difficult, if not altogether impossible, to establish any principle upon which the justice or expediency of capital punishment could be founded, in a society glorying in its civilisation'. But there's little doubt that the jurors felt there was more to the Moore killing that met the eye, and they were annoyed at being kept in the dark. They positively wished to find mitigation in Barthélemy's case.

Upon receiving the verdict of the jury, however, Lord Campbell did not hesitate. The learned judges donned their black caps, as was the practice when penalty of death was about to be handed down, and Lord Campbell, from his eminence fixing the prisoner with a solemn gaze, addressed him as follows:

Emmanuel Barthélemy, the jury, after careful deliberation, have returned a verdict, in your case, in writing, which now lies before me, in these words, 'We find the prisoner Guilty, but strongly recommend him to the merciful consideration of the Court and Her Most Gracious Majesty the Queen.'

That is a verdict of guilty, and in that verdict I entirely concur, and I think that no twelve honest men of any country in the world could have given any other.

The evidence was most clear. Knowing that you had committed a felonious act, you were trying to escape from justice, and when Collard, the unfortunate deceased man, attempted to apprehend you, you deliberately and designedly put him to death. That, by the law of this country, is murder; and by the law of every civilised country such an act should be punished with death ...

Campbell made abundantly clear that he disapproved of the jury's recommendation of mercy.

I will lay before Her Majesty and Her advisers the recommendation of the jury, but ... I do not know upon what ground the recommendation is given. I look upon your crime as one of great atrocity and without any mitigation.

In his mind the jury had spoken quite inappropriately, and he had no intention of supporting it. Without judicial approval, ministers of the Crown were hardly likely to listen.

Barthélemy had been on trial only for the murder of Charles Collard. But Campbell in his summing-up, and again in passing sentence, let it be known that he considered George Moore's killing to have been murder in itself.

It is quite clear that on that evening you committed two crimes of great magnitude; and I must say, that upon the evidence relating to your attack upon Mr Moore, I cannot see any circumstances that would reduce that crime below wilful murder.

Campbell urged Barthélemy to let go of this life and to make peace with his God. 'I implore you ... to repent. You will have the assistance of a clergyman of your own religious persuasion, whatever that may be, in so doing; and I entreat you to take advantage of it.'

He finished with the standard sentence of death:

Emmanuel Barthélemy, you are sentenced to be taken hence to the prison in which you were last confined and from there to a place of execution where you will be hanged by the neck until dead and thereafter your body buried within the precincts of the prison and may the Lord have mercy upon your soul.

The French press reported, perhaps with some licence, that Campbell wept as he delivered sentence, and the audience in the court were deeply moved. 'As for Barthélemy, he was impassive; however, it was obvious that he was making strenuous efforts on himself not to share in the general emotion.' Most English reporters saw no sign of any reaction at all from Barthélemy during Campbell's sentencing. He was aware, however, that his political nemesis, Ledru-Rollin, was in the court. 'Ah!' he sighed later. 'No doubt he was glad to hear the sentence of death passed on me.' With the judgment concluded, Barthélemy quietly spoke to one of his guards, and then walked deliberately down the stairs leading from the dock. He was taken back to Newgate prison. The newspapers were impressed by his conduct. 'Every great criminal presents some pre-eminent characteristic,' wrote the reporter for the *Daily News*; 'that of Barthélemy seems to have been remarkable impenetrability to common emotions.'

*

As he was being taken down, Barthélemy whispered to one of his friends – an exile who had spent years in Belle-Île and was now struggling with hunger on the streets of London – that if he had to die he preferred to go out quietly, without witnesses, rather than be strangled by the hangman. His friend understood his meaning.

Poisons were not difficult to lay hands upon in Victorian London, though there was often a problem with the quality in this most unregulated of markets. A few days later, his friend was able to smuggle a quantity of strychnine to Barthélemy in Newgate prison. Nonetheless, he harboured doubts about its potency and upon returning home, he tried it out on his dog. The unfortunate beast did not die, only writhed about in horrible pain. Clearly it was insufficiently pure to kill a man. On 19 January, according to Malwida von Meysenbug – who had been so taken with Barthélemy when she made his acquaintance through Alexander Herzen – his friend broke the news and 'in this way, he prepared the unfortunate man for the gruesome torture of not knowing whether his means of liberating himself from his disgraceful death would actually work or whether it would merely rob him of the strength to suffer the unavoidable with dignity'. If Barthélemy was to die, he wished to die in full control of himself.

Alexander Herzen gave another account of the story of how the news of the poison's inefficacy was revealed by the friend:

Panic stricken, he rushed off to Newgate, obtained an interview with Barthélemy through a grating and, seizing a favourable moment, whispered to him, 'Have you got it?'

'Yes, yes.'

'Well, you see, I have great doubts. You had better not take it. I have tried it on my dog, it had no effect!'

Barthélemy's head sank – then, raising it with his eyes full of tears, he said: 'What are you doing to me!'

'We'll get something else.'

'No need,' answered Barthélemy. 'If it is inevitable, so be it.'

And from that moment he was prepared for death.

Von Meysenbug, characteristically, saw the episode as another example of Barthélemy's male fortitude. He would rather go to the gallows than have himself break down in agony. 'His proud soul shunned this prospect of perhaps condemning himself to unmasculine weakness, and he decided not to use it.'

Barthélemy certainly kept his composure before his gaolers at Newgate. He amused himself by taking up the chair in his cell and walking around with it balanced on his fingers, 'preserving the equilibrium of the chair with the dexterity of an accomplished tumbler'. The turnkey posted to prevent any suicide attempt was astonished, and he suspected Barthélemy of watching for an opportunity to dash the chair on the guard's head, grab his keys, and make another famous escape. Newgate's governor intervened to warn the prisoner that he must desist from his unusual pastime and observe the rules of the institution. Barthélemy agreed without argument, and passed the time by amiably conversing with prison officials, and writing a memoir of his life for posthumous publication.

The conservative press, meanwhile, was fuming about the jury's recommendation for mercy. 'There was not a single mitigating circumstance in the case,' The Times thundered, 'and if ever a man was justifiably hung, it will be Emmanuel Barthélemy, the slayer of Cournet, at Egham, and now Mr Moore and poor Collard. How any English man, even an advocate for the abolition of capital punishments, can have joined in such a recommendation we cannot conceive – all who did so ought never to sit on a jury again.'

This bloodthirsty outrage was hardly surprising in *The Times*, but it was given added force by another crime within days of Barthélemy's arrest. London was shocked by a second act of violence involving a foreigner. This was the case of Luigi Baranelli, an Italian tailor and formerly a gentleman's butler and valet.

At about 9.30 in the morning of 7 January 1855, the residents of Foley Place were alarmed by the sounds of gunshots and piercing screams coming from number 5. A woman burst out of the house shrieking that her master had been murdered. The police were alerted and rushed to the scene. On entering a bedroom at the back of the ground floor, they found Mr Lambert, resident of the house, lying dead on his bed with a bullet through his head. He had been shot while sleeping. By his side was his wife, gravely injured in the arm and the neck. It turned out that the perpetrator was still in the house. Luigi Baranelli had locked himself into a room on the first floor. As the police attempted to force the door, they heard the report of a pistol from within. When they broke in they saw through gunsmoke Baranelli lying on the floor, bleeding from a self-inflicted wound to the face. He was gasping to himself, 'I am a murderer! I am an assassin!'

It turned out that 'Mr Lambert', the victim, was really Joseph Latham, a former clerk at the Greenwich hospital. Latham had assumed a false name when he had left his wife to take up with the wife of a friend. Though they had been living together now for fourteen years, they remained outcasts and associated 'with persons of a low character'. When living in Newman Street, the Lamberts had let rooms to lodgers, including Jane Williamson, a dressmaker, and Luigi Baranelli. Their lodgers had gone with them when they moved to Foley Place. Jane Williamson had become pregnant by Baranelli, but she had tired of his obsessive jealousy and at her request the Lamberts had sent him away. In an emotional state Baranelli arrived at 9 Foley Place, shot Mr Lambert dead, struggled with and shot Mrs Lambert, and made his way up to Jane Williamson's room. When she would not admit him, he locked himself into the other room and shot himself in an unsuccessful suicide bid. As Baranelli lay gravely ill in hospital, Jane Williamson was frequently admitted to his bedside, and treated him with the greatest affection. When Baranelli's condition was stabilised, he was put on trial at the Central Criminal Court on 12 April. His insanity plea was rejected, and he was sentenced to death. Baranelli died a penitent in the faith of his fathers, though he refused the pressure of the priest to have his yet unborn baby brought up a Roman Catholic. He would not go against the wishes of the Protestant woman he saw as his wife. He was executed on 30 April 1855.

The coincidence of murders committed by two hot-blooded Continentals within days of each other aroused intense interest, distracting even from the ongoing Crimean War, and generating much self-righteous and anti-foreigner opinion. A fine example was to be found in the *Durham County Advertiser*:

> With the dreadful head-roll still ringing in our ears of thousands of brave men slaughtered before Sebastopol, and the dreadful statement still staring us in the face of thousands more groaning in hospitals and Balaclava and Scutari; – we can still muster a fair amount of interest for two domestic horrors – murders of the most atrocious nature.

Having soothed the conscience of readers for having turned so quickly from dreary pages on grinding war to a juicy crime story, the *Advertiser* then reached for a brace of reliable hand-me-downs in nineteenth-century English journalism: crime as an illness in the body politic, and the transcendental wisdom of Shakespeare:

> Certainly, crime, like disease, is epidemic. A single atrocity is very singular. They hunt in couples. Let one man – native or foreigner – commit some deed of almost unparalleled wickedness, and immediately another man, a native or foreigner (just according to the previous case), parallels it with great felicity. This contagious or sympathetic blood shedding was, as Hamlet says, 'sometime a paradox; but now the time gives it proof'.

The paper took delight in the exotically named killers, so redolent of cheap theatre melodrama:

> Here, within a very brief period of each other, are two dreadful murders – both double murders – committed by two men, both foreigners – Emmanuel Barthélemy and Luigi Baranelli – both names excellent for the nomenclature of minor theatre, 'dramas of thrilling interest,' and both persons admirably fitted to 'take their leave of the public stage' at Newgate.

That public hanging was an entertainment was rarely made so clear. Winding up the article, the worthy correspondent shook his head dolefully over the soft-headedness of a half-foreign jury, and reposed faith in the splendid wisdom of the British constitution:

> What a fit of romantic pitifulness or sentimental foolery induced the jury who found Monsieur Barthélemy guilty to 'recommend him to mercy,' is to us absolutely incomprehensible. His crime was doubly horrible and horribly

double. It was 'gross, open, palpable', – and for the ends of Justice and Humanity we trust our great mistress [Queen Victoria] and her advisers will allow the law in this case to 'take its course'.

This homily obscured the fact that Barthélemy's conviction of murder for killing Collard, rather than manslaughter, rested on rather dubious legal grounds.

The prosecution had not attempted to demonstrate the intent normally required for murder, and the defence had been able to point out that in the struggle with Collard it was quite likely that Barthélemy's pistol had fired accidentally. Lord Campbell, however, had directed the jury that any fatal injury inflicted on a person attempting to capture a criminal fleeing a felony was itself sufficient to bring in the conviction of murder. Campbell in his sentencing had remarked that whether Barthélemy's killing of George Moore amounted to murder or to manslaughter, it had certainly been a felonious crime. There was a missing link in this chain of reasoning, however.

A concerned correspondent from Oxford made points adverting to this problem in a letter to the editor of *The Times*. The killing of Collard, he wrote, had been an act of 'self defence' and as such lacked 'the two great elements of a crime – malice and deliberation'. Barthélemy was morally guilty only of manslaughter. The law which made this murder was, the writer argued, unjust and inefficacious. Would a fugitive fearing the death penalty, or even lengthy incarceration, really be deterred from violently resisting apprehension by the mere addition of a further capital charge to their rap sheet? The letter finished with a line certain to raise the hackles of any patriotic Englishman: 'It is, perhaps, not unworthy of consideration just now that Barthélemy is a French man, and that he could not be legally put to death in France under such a verdict.'

The Times responded to this 'Oxford casuist' with an irritable and patriotic repudiation of his arguments: 'The custom of England is that murderers must die on the scaffold.'

Such complacent national chauvinism did not cut ice with all the newspaper's readers, and a more exacting argument, from the legal point of view, was published just over a week later. This correspondent, a lawyer, had 'no sympathy with the murderer, either sentimental or prosaic, domestic or foreign' and was 'rather disposed to think that few culprits have so thoroughly deserved to be hanged as the convict Barthélemy'. He was, however, 'a great respecter of English law' and feared that in this case it was being perverted or misunderstood. 'I cannot help feeling that there has been some error in the conviction of Barthélemy.'

Barthélemy, he explained, had been found guilty of murder in killing Charles Collard, the essence of the offence being that Barthélemy had been running away, having just committed a felony. Had he not committed a felony immediately previous to his encounter with Collard, the offence would have been manslaughter, and he would not hang. Now, it was entirely reasonable to suppose that Barthélemy had indeed committed a felony in killing George Moore. The problem was, he had not been found guilty of so doing by a jury of his peers. And, by any legal standard, 'we have no right to declare Barthélemy guilty of that offence until he has been tried for it, and found guilty of it by a jury'. After all, a fundamental maxim of the law was that every man is presumed innocent until a jury shall have pronounced him guilty.

It was true that Lord Campbell had declared Barthélemy's killing of George Moore to have been felonious: most likely a murder, certainly no less than manslaughter. But a judge had no right to find a man guilty of felony 'by a sort of *obiter dictum*' without the accused having the right to defend himself against the charge. The conclusion of this well-argued letter was ringing:

> It may often be necessary to hang a man on presumptive evidence; but in this case we seem to be preparing to hang a man on a presumptive verdict, for the offence he committed in killing Moore is a question that has never been submitted to jury. The conductors of the prosecution have been praised, and, at first sight, with apparent reason, for taking the clear case of Collard, instead of the doubtful case of Moore, but a moment's consideration shows us that, if the case of Moore is doubtful, it was more necessary to submit it to a jury, instead of deciding upon it in the course of a judicial summing up.

This was a damning critique, which received no reply. Barthélemy's conviction for murder, a capital crime, had been bootstrapped by an unproven assertion that he had illegally killed George Moore. That Lord Campbell, in his summing-up, had adverted to Moore's killing as an undoubted felony suggested nothing more than a troubled legal conscience. Barthélemy's sentence may not have been a miscarriage of justice, but it does appear to have been a miscarriage of law.

17

'NOW I SHALL KNOW THE SECRET'

In January 1855, the war in Crimea was going disastrously for the British Army. In that month over 23,000 soldiers were treated at the Barrack Hospital of Scutari, just outside Constantinople and 300 miles from the front lines at Sebastopol. Most were suffering from acute infectious disease rather than battle wounds. This was the worst month in the war for mortality at the hospital – 1,473 died. Provision for the ill was desperately inadequate. A campaign by *The Times* raised money for clothes and blankets to be sent over from Britain, but these had yet to be distributed. Florence Nightingale was horrified by what she saw as she nursed the stricken soldiers. They lay 'without other covering than a dirty blanket and a pair of old regimental trousers ... living skeletons, devoured with vermin, ulcerated, hopeless and helpless [they] die without ever lifting up their heads'.

William Howard Russell sent back damning reports from the war via electric telegraph and the editor of *The Times*, John Thadeus Delane, published them. Scandal was growing at home. One particularly outraged pamphleteer asked, '*Whom Shall We Hang?*' At the end of the month Lord Aberdeen was forced to resign as Prime Minister – ending his political career – and a new government was formed led by Lord Palmerston. The reputation of the aristocratic governing class never quite recovered from the horrors of the hospital at Scutari.

Barthélemy, in contrast, had a relatively comfortable if austere situation at Newgate. Once notorious for its overcrowding, the number of inmates in the 700-year-old prison had dipped sharply from 1850. It now held only those awaiting trial at the Old Bailey, or those sentenced to hang. Barthélemy expected to go to the gallows almost immediately after conviction – as was the standard practice in France – but in England there was a two-week pause to accommodate appeals for clemency. This gave time for a renewed battle to burst out over this most notorious of men.

Malwida von Meysenbug, herself deeply attached to Barthélemy, found the Ledru-Rollin Party 'almost glad' that he faced the rope. Those French émigrés who rallied to defend Barthélemy's reputation were led by Joseph Domengé, a French refugee personally very close to Alexander Herzen. He was a tutor to Herzen's children. Domengé and his comrades publicly vindicated Barthélemy's reputation against a campaign of character assassination prosecuted by political rivals. This was the old struggle between the parties of Ledru-Rollin and Blanc-Blanqui rolling on.

An account of Barthélemy's life was anonymously planted in *The Times*, but we can be sure that it came from the Ledru-Rollin party. It was reproduced widely across the press. From early youth, it said, Barthélemy had been 'conspicuous in the French capital by the turbulence and levity of his character'. After deliberately shooting a policeman he had been incarcerated in the *bagnes*. 'In these receptacles of crime evil tendencies of his nature were, of course, aggravated by contact with the worst criminals in France' and 'his moral perversion' was there completed. Barthélemy was particularly condemned for his presumed disloyalty to Ledru-Rollin who, as Minister of the

Interior in the revolutionary Provisional Government of 1848, had been ultimately responsible for his release from the galleys. 'It is a curious illustration of the old adage, "Serve a bad man and he'll never forgive you," that Barthélemy has ever since been the mortal enemy of his benefactor, and that he has repeatedly declared his determination to kill him on the first opportunity – a determination which, no doubt, he would have carried into effect had he not been cut short in his career of crime.'

The account mentioned Barthélemy's fighting in the June days of 1848, 'and the credit of undoubted bravery upon that occasion is not to be denied to him'. His political activities in England were not dwelt upon, his time in London being described simply as 'a very equivocal life'. After a period in Switzerland it was said that he returned with the express intention of killing Frédéric Cournet in a duel and suggested that in so doing he was in practice working for Napoleon III: 'This duel, it was believed at the time, was promoted by the French police, as a female agent of that body had lived with Barthélemy for some months previously as his mistress; at all events, it was a "God send" to them to get Cournet out of the way, he being a man of immense energy and strength, and an honest unswerving Republican officer in the French Navy.'

Barthélemy was effectively accused of fixing the duel with Cournet: 'That there was "foul play" in the case is pretty clear, and that the rag did not find its way into Cournet's [sic] pistol by accident before the charge few men will doubt.'

Morally, according to this – by now widely distributed – account of Barthélemy's life, the killing of Cournet had been murder.

Upon release, Barthélemy had apparently 'resumed his old habits of life'. The implication that he was in the pay of French intelligence was made clearly enough. How he made a living 'no one seemed to know ... but he was always well-dressed, always dwelt in apartments for which not less than a guinea a week was paid, had constantly on hand two or more sets of such apartments in different quarters of the town, uniformly consorted with loose women and disreputable men, and was never without plenty of money.' Credence was given to the story that the 'grave' found in Barthélemy's Millman Row lodgings was evidence that he had planned criminal dastardy on the level of the 'Bermondsey horrors'. No definitive reason was proffered as to why Barthélemy had shot George Moore – 'it is perhaps one of those things that will remain for ever in obscurity' – but the account speculated with some confidence that premeditated robbery and even killing had been intended. 'The probability is that, having worked for Moore, he was well aware that Moore made his weekly payments on a Saturday morning; and the wages of Moore's men were known by him therefore to be in the safe in the back parlour on the Friday night, the night of the murder. The supposition explains the ticket for Hamburg, heavy bludgeon, the poniard, and the loaded pistol.'

Barthélemy was to his last days bitter about the Ledru-Rollin party. Their calumnies against him filled his mind as he wrote his final letter to Malwida von Meysenbug, dated 8 January 1855 and delivered through intermediaries. 'The only thing that seemed to outrage him were the slanderings of his own countrymen,' she recalled. Barthélemy thanked von Meysenbug for thinking of him as more than just 'a miserable wretch', in contrast to his enemies amongst the émigrés.

> Nothing I have gone through amazes me; I know enough about these people to know what they're worth. If I were free, I would face my accusers and put them to shame, despite negative popular opinion. But what would be the point? I'm a dead man, and if it helps our cause for them to drag me through the mud, then let them do so. It's the only thing they're good at.

*

Perhaps, he mused, the reputation of the revolutionary party as a whole demanded that his own reputation be buried under a mountain of lies? This kind of reasoning – passively accepting moral abasement as 'a last service to the Party' – would be identified decades later by the ex-communist, Arthur Koestler, as the ultimate self-annihilation required by an inhuman revolutionary discipline. But if Barthélemy incubated the psychology of a party fanatic, there was as yet no Stalinist party with the monolithic control to crush out individuality. 'I wish that my fall could exalt them,' Barthélemy said of the émigré red republicans, 'but this will not be the case. They are destined for mediocrity.' Finally he turned again to Pardigon, the man he blamed for planting the misfiring pistol during the duel. 'I will die; but the proof of this fact remains and will come forth in its good time. Fare well!'

To the last, Barthélemy denied the easy correlation of character with success, privilege and wealth: he was attached to von Meysenbug because she did not confuse 'social prejudice for virtue', as he put it. As a committed revolutionary with likely a bad conscience, he desperately wished his death to be of some advantage to the cause. But he remembered his grudges to the end.

Barthélemy's friends, meanwhile, were desperately using the two weeks' grace period to petition the government for mercy. What slim chance they had diminished to almost nothing so long as his name was being traduced. They wished to save his honour. Alexander Herzen, who was a partisan of Barthélemy's party, denied that robbery could have been the motive for the mysterious fight in George Moore's house. For him, the evidence did not stack up: 'It is hard to suppose that any man, but utterly mad, would go to commit an act of open robbery in one of the most populous quarters of London, to a house where he was known, at ten o'clock in the evening, accompanied by a woman: and all that to steal a paltry hundred pounds.'

A letter of rebuttal published in *The Times*, systematically countering accusations made against Barthélemy, certainly had significant input from Herzen. Of its three signatories, at least two, Alfred Talaudin [Talandier] and Joseph Domengé, were his close friends. They clearly had put effort into gathering together 'unquestionable evidence' to counter 'imputations of an erroneous character' against Barthélemy.

Their letter took on the main allegations against him one by one. First, on the affair of Barthélemy's firing at a sergent de ville in Paris in 1839, they wrote:

Perhaps it is fair to observe first that the sergents de ville, essentially a political institution, are a very different set of men from your municipal constables, and at the time when the transaction took place – viz., in the middle of an insurrection – they were looked at by the party to which Barthélemy belonged, not as representatives of Law and Order, but as the satellites of a political opponent.

Then, to counter the idea that Barthélemy had been singularly ungrateful to Ledru-Rollin for securing his release from prison in 1848, they reproduced extracts from a letter from Monsieur Cremieux, Minister of Justice of the French Provisional Government at the time. This letter had clearly been solicited as a kind of affidavit – 'Given in Paris, as the expression of truth, which I attest before God and men, on 21 February, 1853' – and it showed that rather than Ledru-Rollin ordering the release as an act of mercy, met by ingratitude and bitter spite, Barthélemy had been legally amnestied upon the recommendation of Faustin Helie, the director of the Department of Crimes and Mercy, by the competent party, the Minister of Justice (Monsieur Cremieux). 'Thus falls to the ground all that we read about the supposed ingratitude of Barthélemy towards M. Ledru-Rollin, who was never his benefactor.' They dismissed allegations that he had repeatedly threatened to kill Ledru-Rollin as malicious tittle-tattle. (Though, there is ample evidence that this tittle-tattle was accurate – George Holyoake, the British secularist and radical newspaper editor, confirmed that Barthélemy's 'threat to take the life of Ledru Rollin rests upon clearer foundation than report. It was real, and the letter [in which he made the threat] was real.')

Regarding the duel, the authors accused Cournet of circulating false rumours about Barthélemy and denying him either an apology or a retraction. If he was to avoid accusations of cowardice, Barthélemy had no choice but to resort to the duel 'according to our French ideas on the matter'. The infamous rag in the pistol could not have been a devious ploy on the part of Barthélemy. It had been his gun that had been rendered inoperative 'and it so happened that Cournet was killed with his own pistol'.

The letter then turned to Barthélemy's private life in England. He was no bohemian degenerate, and had proven himself to be an honourable and industrious workman, even an inventor: was this a 'life of laziness and dissipation'? The letter then adverted to Barthélemy's heroism and mercy to enemies during the June days of 1848. Even his most implacable enemies had been admiring of his conduct. The authors offered no theory to explain the Warren Street crime, but ended by echoing the jury's recommendation of mercy:

We will not add a word about the Warren Street tragedy. The facts are lying before the public, and open to every interpretation. However, we perhaps shall be allowed to observe that twelve men of honour, in the best position to judge, have, by recommending him to the mercy of the

Crown, solemnly acknowledged that he had not altogether forfeited his claim to the interest of honest men.

Barthélemy still had his partisans. They could do little to save his life, but as their admiring account was elaborated in Herzen's beautifully written *Memoirs* he could hardly have hoped for a more elegant apologia.

As the end to life draws near, perspectives shift and contemplation comes as second nature. After his conviction and sentencing, Barthélemy's conduct changed. No longer tight-lipped, he was free in his conversation. Certainly he had a sympathetic if small audience. Barthélemy was treated well by the officers of Newgate prison. They not unkindly advised him against putting any hope in the jury's recommendation of mercy. Barthélemy thanked them for their solicitude, and assured them that he entertained no such illusion.

There is no evidence that the Lord Chief Justice put forward the jury's recommendation and Barthélemy does not appear to have pressed his solicitor, Mr Herring, to pursue the matter. At any rate, Lord Palmerston never formally received the jury's request. A petition to Palmerston from those sympathetic to Barthélemy, and a communication from the Catholic priest attending on him in his prison, were also ignored. After being told that his execution was fixed for Monday, 22 January 1855, Barthélemy remarked, 'Then I have only sixteen days to live. I hope the law will be executed upon me. If it be not, I shall execute it on myself, for I am tired of life.' To prevent any such attempt, two officers were placed in the cell and remained with him day and night.

Barthélemy's room in Newgate was comfortable, an apartment of some extent, complete with a fireplace. It was normally employed to accommodate a number of prisoners, but on occasion served for the detention of capital convicts. He was attended by several Roman Catholic priests, but Barthélemy wanted to be rid of them and said that if he were forced into receiving any religious consolation it would be from the Protestant prison chaplain, Mr Davis. However, he was no more willing to indulge the religiosity of Davis, who found him 'the hardest criminal with whom he ever had to deal'.

On the Saturday before his execution, Barthélemy's solicitor, Mr Herring, had an interview by appointment in the private rooms of the Court of Queen's Bench with Lord Campbell, who had presided at the trial. Mr Justice Erle and Mr Justice Crompton were also present. Herring took issue with the judge's summing-up of the case. Campbell had emphasised a deadly weapon with which Barthélemy was supposed to have assaulted Mr Moore when they were in the back parlour together. Campbell had implied that Barthélemy had brought this weapon with him and without provocation struck at Moore with it. Herring pointed out that this deadly weapon had not been taken to the house by Barthélemy. It had, in fact, been a kind of mallet for corking bottles that Moore used in his business and had been lying about in his parlour. The evidence strongly suggested that Barthélemy had picked it up during a struggle and swung it at Moore in the heat of the moment. As this appeared to show a lack of premeditation, Herring hoped that such evidence might lead to a stay of execution. Lord Campbell declined, however, to set the sentence aside.

Campbell then mentioned a letter he had received from a woman in France, which came with a request that it be given to the prisoner. He passed the letter to Herring, who went on to Newgate, where he disclosed the existence of the letter to the prison authorities. While they discussed what to do with it, the Catholic priest who had been in attendance on Barthélemy came in, and the letter was read to him. It had been sent from

Poitiers in France, and was signed 'Sophie'. It was written in French, and contained an earnest entreaty that Barthélemy devote the short portion of time left him to make his peace with God. It made no reference to any other matters.

The Catholic priest present at the reading of the letter urged that it be given to Barthélemy at the soonest opportunity. It might lead him into a pious frame of mind, which he did not appear hitherto to have much cultivated. No doubt, too, the priest hoped that it might elicit a confession. Herring duly handed the note to Barthélemy, who read it without any emotion. When it became apparent that Barthélemy was going to say nothing in response, Herring informed him that there was now no hope of reprieve and he asked him whether he wished to make a statement. Barthélemy simply asked for pen and paper to allow him to write to his father. Herzen later had the opportunity to read this letter, which he found altogether admirable: 'Not a high-flown sentence, the utmost simplicity; he tries gently to comfort the old man, as though he were not speaking of himself.'

Malwida von Meysenbug read Sophie's final correspondence with Barthélemy.

It was a brief, emotional letter with many spelling mistakes, signed by a woman. It contained nothing but the simple as-surance of a love greater than guilt or death. [Barthélemy] had been deeply moved by this letter. Perhaps it was an echo of his first love, from the time before wild passion and misdirected energy filled his soul with sinister guilt, which now could only be atoned for with his death ...

Meysenbug's supposition was that the letter came from an old sweetheart and not, as was universally assumed by the newspapers and the authorities, from the woman who had accompanied Barthélemy to George Moore's house. Everyone believed that she had fled to the Continent.

The national press and the memoir writers, however, missed one obscure and revealing case. Sarah Lowndes, aged twenty-seven, was arrested for petty theft in Windsor about a month after Barthélemy's arrest. She refused to say anything to the police, other than to give false information about where she had recently been living. Rather than submit to a full trial she pleaded guilty and the court sentenced her to one year of hard labour. Though Sarah wore a veil during the hearing and refused to speak more than a few words – perhaps to hide a French accent – she was quickly recognised by Windsor locals as Barthélemy's partner. The mantle she had worn while carrying out her theft matched the description of the eye-catching cloak worn by Barthélemy's companion at Warren Street: dark brown Merino cloth trimmed with satin. The Windsor police wrote twice to their colleagues in London to alert them that they had identified a likely suspect. But they were ignored. Sarah slipped quietly out of history.

Everyone wished to have some idea of why Barthélemy had attacked George Moore. It was a mystery. Herring disclosed that Barthélemy made a full statement to him, but he did not feel himself justified in divulging it. He did say, however, that up until a quarter of an hour before his visit to Moore's house, Barthélemy had no intention of going there. It had not been a premeditated robbery or murder.

In his conversations with prison officials, Barthélemy made only passing allusions to the 'affair', as he always described the fatal events at Moore's house. The prison chaplain, Mr Davis, however, was able to piece together and pass on Barthélemy's explanation. The woman who had accompanied him to Moore's house on the night of the shootings had an illegitimate child by a Catholic priest. For some unexplained reason, it was Moore's duty to help support her financially, whether from his own funds or by passing on money from the alleged priest. It was not, however, entirely a personal affair. 'Some political subjects connecting the French government to this money were also mentioned.'

On the night of the shootings, reported Davis from his discussions with Barthélemy, some debt was owing to the mysterious woman, and Barthélemy accompanied her to the house with the purpose of obtaining it. He had at this time no idea of committing any act of violence. George Moore refused to pay what was owed. The woman began reading out loud from a letter she had received from Paris. When she came to a particular passage, Moore became extremely agitated and attempted to snatch the letter from her hand. 'A scuffle ensued, during which, in order to protect the woman, [Barthélemy] struck Moore with the butt end of his pistol.' He admitted also that he took up the heavy leaden instrument, later found broken, and struck Moore with it. With the same instrument, and presumably now in a towering fury, he smashed a heavy mahogany chair. Barthélemy was emphatic that he had not brought the bludgeon with him to the house, but found it lying on the table between them. He likewise insisted that Charles Collard had been accidentally shot during the scuffle that took place between them.

Barthélemy was visited once again by a Catholic clergyman. He was now willing to talk, but on his own terms. 'I'm visited by a Roman Catholic priest,' he told the Protestant chaplain of the gaol, 'but he has the good taste not to speak to me on matters of religion.' The prisoner and the priest jousted: 'The priest tells me to think of my soul; I tell him to think of my body first, and then to think of my soul.' When asked to pray for forgiveness, Barthélemy responded that only man can forgive, and if they did so they would open the prison doors and break the rope. 'I want no forgiveness of God: I want the forgiveness of man, that I might walk out the door.' Did he believe there was a God? If there was he hoped that he could speak good French, otherwise God would be no good to him. Alluding to the trial, he declared that Lord Campbell had committed a greater crime in sentencing him to death than he had in killing Collard. (He seems, at any rate, to have seen Collard's death as an accidental tragedy.) These conversations were held in passably good English and with Barthélemy maintaining his customary poise.

Sheriff Crosley, one of the administrators of the prison, tried to convince Barthélemy to accept religious instruction.

'Now take my advice; you have but a short time to live, and while you have that time to live, try and make your peace with God.'

'I am no believer; I understand geometry and sciences, but I don't understand faith.'

'You are a scientific man, and know the meaning of experiments; now try this – pray to God, and see whether He will not give you that faith which you cannot say you will not have if you do not try for it.'

His logic was unavailing, Barthélemy simply protesting that there were a vast number of men as bad as he and their crimes went unpunished. Emperor Napoleon III, Barthélemy said, had committed more daring and more violent acts, and while the Emperor was now receiving the acclamations of Europe, he was sentenced to death on the gallows. 'What is the use of you talking to me of these things? You speak of the deluge to punish men for their sins – mankind is as wicked now as ever.'

All this time, Barthélemy kept calm. Only at one point did he show any strong emotion.

Sheriff Crosley asked, 'You have a father – a good man I understand; is he a disbeliever?'

'No, he is a believer.'

Crosley then asked, 'Why do you not follow his good example?'

Barthélemy shook his head – 'no' – but then strode over to the fire, stared into it intently, and burst into tears. He exclaimed passionately, 'I have committed no sin. I have done wrong perhaps, but no sin.'

Crossley asked Barthélemy if there was anything he could fetch for him, and Barthélemy asked for a copy of Jacques Delille's translation into French of John Milton's *Paradise Lost*. With some effort, a copy was secured. Barthélemy read it intently in the following days. Perhaps he identified with Satan, Milton's great anti-hero in combat with the imperious might of a monarchical God:

> His utmost power with adverse power oppós'd
> In dubious Battel on the Plains of Heav'n,
> And shook his throne. What though the field be lost?
> All is not lost; the unconquerable Will,
> And study of revenge, immortal hate,
> And the courage never to submit or yield:
> And what is else not to be overcome?
> That Glory never shall his wrath or might
> Extort from me.

Barthélemy had fought in dubious battle against the mortal gods of monarchy and class. He had never submitted, nor had he yielded. This in itself was a victory. Though the field had been lost, nothing would extort from Barthélemy any deference to the supposed glory of Emperor, Law or God.

Malwida von Meysenbug, meanwhile, was in a torment of emotional agony and searing pity for the man for whom she clearly felt something more than friendship: 'I suffered immensely during this time. My heart was filled with boundless compassion. I knew that I could not save him, but I desperately wanted to let the condemned know on his last journey that there were people who thought differently than his enemies and earthly justice.'

She was also outraged at what she saw as 'the English government's obsequiousness'. She was convinced that Barthélemy
was to be executed to satisfy the demands of the Napoleonic
government in France, which had much reason to wish
Barthélemy dead. This, she believed, was why the jury's clear
recommendation for mercy was being ignored.

Von Meysenbug was distraught at the thought of Barthélemy's
lonely trudge to the gallows, and imagined herself by his side
at the end: 'I suggested to Herzen and Domengé that we three
ask for permission to accompany the unfortunate man on his
last difficult journey. I sensed that I would be strong enough
to do so. I longed to do so, because I was convinced that
Barthélemy had paid for his blind act with deep pain and now
wanted to pay for the guilt with a silently and nobly suffered
death. To leave him alone during this exalted moment of
penance, surrounded by a repugnantly gawking mob, was
insulting to me.'

She wished to comfort Barthélemy in his final minutes, and
to forgive him his crime 'in the name of a future [and] more
just order of human society'. Herzen and Domengé were rather
bemused by von Meysenbug, but they dutifully made enquiries.
The prison authorities made it clear that in no circumstances
would permission be granted for Barthélemy's friends to accompany him to the drop, 'because such a thing would go against
all tradition and disturb the procedure's routine'. It was established practice that only a clergyman was allowed to accompany
the condemned in his last minutes, to provide spiritual consolation. Out of options, von Meysenbug swore to remain with
Barthélemy in spirit.

There was nothing more for me to do than to suffer with
him in my heart and to struggle through the solemn hours
thinking about him. I spent the Sunday which was to be
his last in a mood which I can only describe as a constant,

heated, and fervent prayer, and if there is such a thing as telepathy, Barthélemy surely must have felt that he was not alone during the hours of his difficult trial.

In her heart, von Meysenbug was comrade, confessor and perhaps lover to her heroic and tragically flawed proletarian.

Barthélemy did have friends visit him in his last days. Two Frenchmen, who went by the names Pirelli and Peyre, and with whom he had been acquainted for several years, called upon him at Newgate prison. But there was no display of feeling during the meeting. Was he relaying a last message for his leader Auguste Blanqui, still languishing on the prison island of Belle-Île?

The traditional day of execution at Newgate prison was a Monday. It was usual for prisoners under sentence of death to attend religious service in the prison chapel on the Sunday previous to their execution. Barthélemy declined to avail himself. On his last night, he went to sleep at ten o'clock. On the next morning, the day he was to be hanged, Barthélemy rose at four o'clock. A last prison meal was brought over from the coffee shop across the way and Barthélemy ate it with relish. Then he wrote several letters.

The execution party began arriving. Barthélemy was first visited by the Catholic priest, the Abbé Roux. At about 7.45 a.m. he was joined by the prison sheriffs and the prison chaplain, and as they entered Barthélemy – standing at the fire – bowed and smiled. Sheriff Muggeridge asked him whether he had anything he wished to say. He shook his head thoughtfully, 'No. I have written to my father and friends, and I have given the letters to the governor.' Muggeridge confirmed that they would be forwarded. He then asked, 'Have you made a confession or statement to anyone relative of this affair?'

Barthélemy – 'The last one who knows the secret can tell if they please.'

Under-Sheriff Farrar – 'Is this Mr Herring, the solicitor?'

Barthélemy seemed surprised. 'Oh, no,' he replied. 'No! No! It is very likely he may say that I have done so, but I have not.'

'I did not know Mr Herring, and I could have no confidence in him. He came to me when I was first brought before the magistrate at Marlborough Street, and he said "Mr Barthélemy, I have come to you by desire of Mr Cooper, who has no time to defend you himself." I did not know Mr Cooper, and I warned Mr Herring that I had nothing to give him on my behalf. I said – "There was £21 owing to me by one person, and if he could get that, he might have it."'

Barthélemy here, with the emphatic action characteristic of the French, laid his hand on his breast, quoting Mr Herring's words of reply: 'Money is no object!'

Barthélemy continued: 'Some time after, Mr Herring came to me again, when I was before the magistrate; and on this occasion he asked me if I had any objection to assigning him my clothes and my boots. I said I had not; and he produced a paper, which he asked me to sign, agreeing to give him these things.' Herring's payment, it seemed, was to be the costume of a hanged murderer.

Alexander Herzen had heard of this strange transaction and in his memoirs gave a report on the episode.

Herring did a great deal, wasted time, bustled about. When the day of execution was fixed, Herring came to the prison to say goodbye; Barthélemy was touched, he thanked him and among other things said to him: 'I have nothing, I cannot repay your trouble with anything but my gratitude. I should have liked to leave you something, at least for keepsake, but I have nothing I could offer you. Perhaps my overcoat?'

'I shall be grateful to you, I meant to ask you for it.'

'With the greatest pleasure,' said Barthélemy, 'but it is a wretched thing.'

'Oh, I am not going to wear it; I will tell you frankly, I have already disposed of it, and very well too.'

'Disposed of it?' repeated Barthélemy in astonishment.

'Yes, to Madame Tussaud for her special gallery.'

Barthélemy shuddered.

So, on his last morning, Barthélemy addressed the sheriffs: 'I pray you, Sir, I pray you, if you have the will, to ask Mr Herring for what purpose he does require my clothes; because, although I have no objection that he should have them, still, if it be for the purpose of exhibiting them at Madame Tussaud's, I think it would be very abominable, and I should be obliged if you would prevent it.'

Farrar replied, 'Your clothes will belong to the sheriffs who will not allow them to be given for any such purpose.'

Barthélemy was relieved: 'I thank you, sir.'

As the *Daily News* reported, 'This dialogue occupied only a very few moments, but the subject of it appeared to engage more deeply the mind of the prisoner than even the awful moment which was at hand to usher him into the unseen world.'

The executioner, William Calcraft, was then introduced. He was a short, thickset shabby man, with white hair and beard and a rather sinister face. Calcraft, now aged fifty-four, had first met John Foxton, his predecessor as public executioner, while hawking pies around hangings at Newgate. He had been taken on as apprentice in 1828, his first duty being to flog juveniles. Calcraft trained with enthusiasm, practising his art by hanging dogs. When Foxton died in 1829, Calcraft had taken over as public executioner. Though he loved his work, Calcraft was frequently drunk while on duty and notorious for his cack-handedness. Often he miscalculated the ratio of body weight to drop and the unfortunate felon would be throttled rather than have his neck cleanly snapped. Then Calcraft would grab the writhing man's legs and dangle until the death agonies ceased.

The condemned man's first encounter with Calcraft would often elicit a panic attack. Barthélemy, however, was not at all shaken. He sat down when asked and said, 'I suppose you want my hands,' holding them up so that they could be bound.

'I hope I shall prove a good example, and be the last,' said Barthélemy, with feeling.

Sheriff Crosley appeared deeply affected by this, saying, 'I hope, Barthélemy, that you have made your peace with God!'

Barthélemy replied, 'I do not believe in God. I make no resistance. Faith is out of the will more than the mind. I have no faith.'

'I am very sorry for it,' said Crosley.

'Yes,' said Barthélemy, 'and I am very sorry too; for if I believed in it, perhaps it would give me strength at this moment. The will of man is independent of an outward show of faith. I do not believe in a God, and, therefore, it is no use for me to ask Him for forgiveness. I shall soon know the secret whether there is one or not.'

The under-sheriff then asked, 'Have you anything more to say?'

Barthélemy replied, 'I wish to be permitted to hold this paper in my hand. After my death you may do what you please with it.' It was the letter from Sophie.

It was snowing heavily outside, and the time had come for Barthélemy to leave his cell for the gallows.

At five a.m., the scaffold had been drawn from the Press Yard and assembled in front of the black-painted Debtors Door, the place of execution. French exiles had already gathered before the drop. The church bell of St Sepulchre's began tolling at 7 a.m., and inside Newgate the procession was formed. The sheriff led the way, followed by the under-sheriff, the chaplain, and the

Abbé Roux. Barthélemy had his wrists pinioned by a broad leather strap and his shirt was opened at the neck. Behind him walked Calcraft. They wound their way out through a passage of the prison known as 'dead man's walk'. As Barthélemy passed by Mr Cope, the prison governor, he bade farewell with calm self-possession. Barthélemy then turned to Calcraft behind him: 'I have one thing to ask of you. Do it quick.' Finally, to himself, 'Now I shall know the secret.'

Barthélemy was hanged that Monday morning, 22 January, at eight o'clock. There had been rumours that an attempt would be made by some of Barthélemy's associates to shoot him upon the scaffold, to save him from the ignominy of a criminal's death. And indeed many French refugees took up a prominent position near the gibbet, placed under the close surveillance of police. A large audience turned up to watch the hanging – estimated variously between 4,000 and 10,000 – and barricades were erected to bear the extra weight of pressure. Despite extremely inclement weather – the air swirled with fog and snow – the whole area of the Old Bailey was densely packed, the windows of surrounding houses crammed with spectators. With the exception of some well-dressed foreigners, this was an entirely working-class crowd, 'in general, one of the very lowest ever congregated', sniffed one newspaper. But the press was equally fascinated. As the *Daily News* reported, 'The execution was ... one of the most remarkable in modern times; and the circumstances connected with it possess features of interest rarely exceeded.'

Barthélemy appeared before the audience looking little changed, except that his beard and moustache had been allowed to grow back. As soon as the people saw him a great shout went up. He strode to the gibbet with certain step and twice bowed deeply in acknowledgement. Then Calcraft strapped Barthélemy's legs together and pulled a hood down over his face. He stood calmly as the noose was looped around his head. The rope was adjusted through a chain and about his neck. The crowd fell silent. 'There was no ebullition of feeling, as on ordinary occasions, and, if any emotion could be traced, it appeared to be one of mistaken sympathy, arising, perhaps, from the mystery attending the crime of the assassin.' Perhaps the working-class crowd identified Barthélemy, though a foreigner, as one of their own. Barthélemy took his place under the beam. Calcraft turned, descended the steps, and pulled the bolt. The trapdoor fell wide and Barthélemy dropped. There was no struggle. He died instantly.

At nine o'clock Barthélemy's body was cut down. There was no sign of death agony on his face, and in his left hand was firmly clenched the letter from Sophie. A cast of his head was taken in stucco before his body was buried in one of the passages of the gaol. The cast was put on display in front of the prison as a warning to other malefactors. Wilhelm Liebknecht, gazing upon it, saw Barthélemy's expression as 'changed very little – the face still showed an iron determination'.

In the prison records, Barthélemy's death was neatly recorded, his age being given as thirty-two years, his profession listed as 'engineer'.

18

BARTHÉLEMY'S CONFESSION

Barthélemy's refusal to accept God, even at death's door, caused consternation and some horror in Victorian England. Perhaps unsurprisingly, one of the most vehement condemnations of him for his irreligion was to be found in a newspaper from the Protestant north of Ireland, the *Belfast Commercial Chronicle*: 'It belongs to the all-seeing and infinitely just God to discern ... the eternal destinies of men,' it began humbly. 'It is not, therefore, for us to dogmatise on the doom of Barthélemy.' Having got this disclaimer out of the way, the newspaper went on to dogmatise:

> ... if ever a human spirit departed this life, giving assurance that it was about to plunge into 'the blackness of darkness forever', it was the soul of Emmanuel Barthélemy. A more hardened sinner never passed under the hands of the hangman, and to the last he was an inveterate Atheist, and a daring blasphemer. He said that he hoped his end would be an example; and surely it will – a most appalling one – to show to the rising generation the evils of infidelity and the blessings of religious education. Like the fool, he said in his heart, 'There is no God' – no judgement – no sin – no responsibility – no future existence.

Such sanctimonious lessons thickly littered the press. A cheap broadsheet simply created its own truth by depicting Barthélemy's figure on the scaffold with hands clasped in prayer. A versifier imagined weepy last thoughts: 'O pity me, O God on high, and pardon me before I die.' This was produced for the execution itself and accuracy was not at a premium. But the newspapers had to acknowledge Barthélemy's defiance to the last.

The Abbé Roux, who had been on hand in Barthélemy's last days, was obviously unhappy at the wide reporting of Barthélemy's sarcasm about religion and rejection of last confession. He wrote a letter to *The Times* in which he explained that his position as a Roman Catholic priest meant that there was much he could not say about what had passed between himself and Barthélemy, but he wished to deny 'the imputation that has been adroitly placed in the mouth of the prisoner, "that I had too much good sense to trouble him on the subject of religion"'.

Now, Abbé Roux did admit that Barthélemy might well have actually uttered these words. Yet the newspapers were wrong, he said, to imply that this remained Barthélemy's position throughout. Certainly, he refused to talk about religion on the first three nights Roux had visited him, but Roux had deliberately avoided matters of faith, seeking instead to build some rapport. From his fourth visit, they spoke frankly together on the subject of God.

On the night before his death, Barthélemy had continued animatedly to refuse faith in Christianity. He had quoted Voltaire's searing lines on the supposed Mercy of God:

De Dieu qui sur nos jours versa tant de bienfaits
Quand ces jours sont finis nous tourments a jamais.

The God who bestowed so many gifts upon us,
When our days are done, torments us for eternity.

Despite this evident scepticism regarding the deity's loving nature, Roux implied that Barthélemy had begun to reach out to God in the quarter of an hour before he ascended the scaffold. He declined to quote their discussion as he had no guarantee other than his own testimony. He did, however, cite a letter written by Barthélemy on the day of his execution, at 6 a.m.:

Dear Monsieur L' Abbé, – Before ceasing to beat, my heart feels the necessity of showing you all its gratitude for the affectionate cares you have so evangelically bestowed on me during my last days. If my conversion had been possible, it would have been effected by you: I have told you; I believe nothing! Believe me, my incredulity is not the result of a proud resistance. I have sincerely done all I could, aided by your counsels; unhappily faith has not come to me, and the moment is near .... In two hours I shall know the secret of death. If I am mistaken, and if the future confirms your assertion, I do not doubt appearing before our God, who in His infinite mercy would willingly pardon me my sins in this world.

Yes, I wish I could share your belief, for I can understand that those who take refuge in religious faith find, in the hour of death, strength in the hope of another life; while I, who believe in nothing but eternal annihilation, I am obliged to lean at this awful moment on the reasonings, perhaps false, of philosophy, and on human courage.

Once more, thanks, and adieu!

E. Barthélemy.

Newgate, 22nd January, 1855, 6 o'clock in the morning.

Even Roux had to admit that this letter showed Barthélemy unreconciled to religion, which he endeavoured to pass off as 'a few phrases, the last concessions to human pride'.

Barthélemy told the priest that – finally – he pardoned all his enemies. Roux claimed that Barthélemy then asked him to stay by his side at the scaffold. This, however, was not possible as the authorities most unusually refused to grant permission for a clergyman to administer last-minute religious consolation. Roux did not give the reason for this denial; it might have been because there was fear of shots towards the scaffold emerging from the crowd, or perhaps it was thought that a priest would stir up the sectarianism of the London mob. At any rate, Roux remained on the last step of the scaffold.

> For the rest, I fulfilled religiously the last wishes of my un-happy countryman. He said to me, on leaving me, with an accent I shall never forget, 'Pray, pray, pray!' I prayed with fervour, and I trust that he, who declared that he was born a Catholic, and that he wished to die a catholic, felt at that awful moment one of those ineffable penitences that puri-fies the soul and opens the gates of eternal life.

We may admire the Abbé Roux's piety and understand that Barthélemy's convictions might have quavered as he faced the last seconds of this mortal life. Catholics take to heart the words of the sixteenth-century scholar and historian, William Camden: 'Betwixt the stirrup and the ground, mercy I asked, mercy I found.' But there is little doubt that for all human purposes Barthélemy died an atheist.

Von Meysenbug was much impressed with the Abbé Roux's letter, and wrote to the priest asking him to tell her of Barthélemy's state of mind before his death. Clearly she hoped for some evidence as to Barthélemy's motivation for his crime, and perhaps some kind words for herself. In his reply, the priest indicated that he knew more than he felt able to say, but he willingly agreed with von Meysenbug that 'Barthélemy possessed a brilliant mind, great character, and generous heart', but his passions had 'led to his disgraceful death'. The priest did not believe that Barthélemy was guilty of premeditated murder. While he deserved punishment, 'an impartial justice system would not have sentenced him to death'. Roux had done 'everything in my power to save his life' and indeed had received assurances that clemency would be forthcoming. He clung to these hopes until the Sunday evening, only hours before Barthélemy's execution the following morning. However, he wrote cryptically, 'Circumstances out of our control tipped the scales in favour of severity.'

The Abbé Roux admired and pitied Barthélemy:

> He died in a truly courageous manner, but he suffered greatly. He felt the need for the consolation of religion, but was ashamed to receive it in front of on-looking friends standing far below. His soul went through an enormous struggle which would have broken a less determined man; but I have reason to believe that my presence and my words made the cup less bitter which he was forced to drink to the last drop. I have to admit that I cried, for he had become like a friend to me. Who knows how things might have turned out if I had known him when you did? 'Your teachings are very beautiful,' he told me on one of his final days; 'if life permitted me, I should have spread them, without believing them myself, and perhaps I would have even learned to believe them myself.' He bequeathed me a little book [likely his copy of *Paradise Lost*], his only possession in the world.

Malwida was deeply moved and heartbroken at Barthélemy's death. He was 'one of the most nobly significant men I have ever known, a man of action, full of spirit, beauty, poetry and immense energy'.

Much mystery remained about Barthélemy's life and last crime. Herzen confirmed that Barthélemy 'wrote some memoir' while in prison, but this remains tantalisingly out of reach: it 'was not given after his death to the friend to whom he had bequeathed it'. Malwida von Meysenbug thought that the memoir had been spirited away: 'When his lawyer came after the execution to collect the letters and other papers written to Barthélemy during his imprisonment, he found nothing but a few insignificant papers and denial that any others had ever existed: it was clear that people still feared the dead man. The things had probably been immediately delivered to the proper authorities.' Any such writings have been lost.

Barthélemy did speak from beyond the grave, however. After his death, Barthélemy's solicitor, Mr Herring, released the confession Barthélemy had in fact given him, excluding only those parts which would lead to the identification of the female.

In this, Barthélemy said that he had no intention of visiting Moore's house until he met by chance with 'the female', who asked him to accompany her. Inside the house, the woman began speaking in French, which irritated Moore.

'Why don't you talk to me in English?'

Barthélemy interrupted: 'You know she cannot understand English, and you have talked to me in French.'

'It is no business of yours,' responded Moore.

This seems like an anomalous piece of detail. Was Barthélemy anxious to give the impression that his female companion, apparently monolingual, was unlikely now to be found in Britain? Moore's son and maid had sworn that Moore had never been to France, and there is certainly no evidence of French language competence in Moore's quite substantial 'commonplace book', still extant, which comprises his handwritten poems and mementos collected over a lifetime. Barthélemy, it seems likely, was going out of his way to misdirect about the identity of his female partner.

His account continued, describing how the woman at this point took a letter from her pocket and began to read; again, ostensibly, in French. As she had nearly reached the end of the first page, Moore rose from his chair in a passion, and endeavoured to snatch the letter out of her hand. According to Barthélemy, at this point he also stood and pushed Moore back. Moore recovered himself, picked up the mallet and himself smashed the chair – which seems most unlikely – before advancing upon his visitors. He continued hitting Barthélemy, 'although I was trying to get out as fast as I could'. As the servant was opening the door, 'I ... let the pistol off that shot Mr Moore, for which I am sorry – I having no ill will towards him.'

Unable to exit at the front, Barthélemy described how he went to the back of the house, lifting the distressed female over the wall, and then taking off in another direction. He was chased by a number of men and grabbed by one, 'and then the pistol went off and shot poor Collard, which I feel much at, for I had never seen or known him before'. He was finally caught. Barthélemy ended his confession by referring once more to the duel: 'I can assure you, Mr Herring, there was no foul play respecting the duel at Egham – the person I shot was a French spy.'

This was Barthélemy's confession as published in all the newspapers. We may read from it that he had deliberately fired at Moore – 'I let the pistol off' – but had not intended to fire at Collard – 'the pistol went off'. The question of motivation was hardly cleared up, however. One must bear in mind that Barthélemy had evinced on his last day of life little confidence in Mr Herring and implied that he had been forced upon him as his defence advocate. The mystery was not yet solved.

Carl Schurz, who as a German radical refugee had briefly met with Barthélemy in London and disliked him, wrote in his memoirs years later that he was not convinced that Barthélemy had cold-bloodedly killed at Warren Street, but believed that his political zealotry meant that he was very much capable of it. His execution was all to the good: 'Nothing could be more certain than that if a pardon had liberated him his insane fanaticism which made him speak of a murder as of a breakfast would have led him to other bloody deeds, and would finally again have placed him in the hands of the hangman.' Malwida von Meysenbug, of course, was more sympathetic. She accepted the rumours swirling amongst the refugees that Barthélemy had been seeking money from Moore to fund his assassination plans in Paris. Moore, it was said, had already promised money, but then changed his mind. As Barthélemy made ready to depart, 'an argument ... ensued which unnerved Barthélemy greatly and led him to commit the dastardly act'.

The mysterious woman, she learnt, was widely rumoured to be a French police spy, 'sent to ruin the energetic refugee. She had succeeded all too well.' She had, von Meysenbug believed, rushed back from the scene of the crime to their joint lodgings where she had seized Barthélemy's most important papers from the hiding-hole dug in the kitchen and delivered them to the authorities in France. When the police arrived, there were no papers to be found. Carl Schurz also heard that she was a spy of the French government, 'sent to London with instructions to watch Barthélemi and finally to betray him'.

Wilhelm Liebknecht, writing on the affair in his memoirs of Marx, thought that the woman was not a spy as such, but had relations with policemen, 'after the French fashion'. Though uninitiated in the plot, 'she had heard this and that and gave information to the police that led to the right trail'. Liebknecht believed that the argument between Barthélemy and Moore had been simply over money owed for work done, though Barthélemy himself had let it be known to Mr Davis, the Protestant clergyman at Newgate, that there had been a political dimension to the quarrel. As Liebknecht heard it, 'On the way to the boat

[Barthélemy] remembers that he ... has a debt outstanding with his last "patron" (boss) .... Barthélemy asks for his money, the proprietor directs him to his office, Barthélemy becomes violent, the proprietor threatens to throw him out, thereupon Barthélemy who feels that he is the weaker man sees "blood", draws his revolver, fires and kills.' But if this was simply a row about unpaid work, why would Sarah have read the letter?

The story that Barthélemy was seeking to extort funds from George Moore to carry out his plans to assassinate Napoleon III seems the most convincing. True, he already had a ticket for the boat to Hamburg and some little money for the onward journey. Having missed the train, however, his immediate plans had been set awry, and he was intensely frustrated. Rather than simply wait, he would make use of his last hours in London to add to his revolutionary kitty. There can be little doubt that the woman was part of the scheme. Sarah Lowndes had been attracted to Barthélemy as an imprisoned revolutionary. She had lived with him after his release and we can assume that she shared – or at least, went along with – his passionate ideals and ruthless convictions. In rushing back to their joint lodgings to clear away any incriminating conspiratorial documents before making her escape, she behaved as a self-conscious revolutionary operator.

We can surmise that the letter Sarah read to Moore was both a Blanquist screed condemning the tyranny of Emperor Napoleon – we know that revolutionaries like Barthélemy never wished to be seen as mere criminals – and a menace demanding funds in the great cause of liberating France. There was also in it a threat which roused Moore's anger. Barthélemy had told the prison chaplain at Newgate that his companion was the disowned daughter of a French Roman Catholic priest. Other rumours had it that she was the daughter of George Moore himself. We will never be sure. But all the evidence converges on a threat to implicate Moore in a sexual scandal involving Sarah's parentage. Little wonder that Moore reacted with such fury. But in grabbing at Sarah's letter and bellowing at both his visitors, Moore inadvertently broke through Barthélemy's customary but brittle self-control to unleash his instinct for flight or fight. There is little evidence that Barthélemy went to the house intending violence. As Herzen pointed out, if he had intended murder, the knife he carried would have been a silent and more efficient weapon than the pistol he in fact used. Liebknecht's final suggestion, that Barthélemy 'saw blood' when he thought that he and his female companion were being bullied, is consistent with what we know of Barthélemy's personality. George Moore had every right to be angry when faced with extortion and we can understand why he grabbed the letter from Sarah's hands. It was his misfortune that he triggered the tightly wound personality of a man who had killed before, and who was set on killing again.

EPILOGUE

Plots to assassinate Napoleon III continued. In 1856, an Italian nationalist, Felice Orsini, arrived in London where, with comrades, he fabricated bombs with which to kill the Emperor. He hoped to spark a French democratic revolution that would then engulf and unify a divided Italy. In 1858 he made his attempt, in Paris, killing eight people and blinding three in the carnage. Napoleon emerged with scratches. Orsini was guillotined.

The British government was deeply embarrassed that the plot had been hatched in their country. Then, to make things worse, Félix Pyat – Barthélemy's old comrade in Commune Révolutionnaire – wrote a pamphlet celebrating Orsini's intention to kill the Emperor. A criminal prosecution was launched against his publisher, but this outraged liberal opinion in Britain and the jury threw it out. The exiles exulted.

Marx, however, continued to remain quite aloof from the other refugees, and as he became increasingly settled in Britain he turned his eyes ever more to the society in which he lived. It is little remarked, because apparently pedestrian, that an 1858 dispute of carpenters, joiners, stonemasons and bricklayers with the master builders of London had a profound influence on Marx. By the system of 'strapping' and subcontracting, these labourers were worked to full capacity and complete exhaustion. 'We are used for all the world like cab or omnibus horses,' said one, 'tearing along from first thing in the morning to last at night' and 'ready to drop' at knocking-off time. 'As for Sunday, it is *literally* a day of rest with us, for the greater part of us lays a bed all day, and even that will hardly take the aches and pains out of our bones and muscles. When I'm done and flung by, of course I must starve.' In the 1858 dispute, the workers presented a 'memorial' to the employers in which they pointed out that such continuous ill-paid exertion progressively diminished their vitality until they were left as nothing but wasted husks, a burden on society. They wanted time and leisure to improve their intellect, 'so as to acquire the knowledge and skill requisite for the rapid progress of invention'. The request was denied, though it attracted considerable public sympathy, and a major lockout, in which the building masters refused to employ union members, took place in London in 1859–60. John Ruskin, England's leading art critic, likened the episode to an employee assaulting the master in his own drawing room – shades of the Warren Street murder – but on a social scale. He was driven to conclude that a socialistic 'organisation of labour' had become a necessity.

It was precisely at this time that Marx introduced into his theory a concept which he would come to see as his most distinct contribution to economic thought: the concept of 'labour power'. Previous to this, Marx, like all economists, thought that workers sold their *labour* to the capitalist. Now, he realised, workers were actually selling their *capacity* for labour, what he called 'labour power', their particular property. Capitalists bought 'labour power' for a set amount of time, paying for it with wages, and within the term of that contract they tried to extract as much from it as possible, even if this meant exhausting workers of their vitality. But the workers understood that their property required protection if it was to preserve its value. They favoured shorter hours, higher wages, anything that maintained or improved themselves as creative beings. This was the axis of class struggle.

In a crucial section of his 1867 master work, *Das Kapital*, Marx virtually paraphrased the labourers' memorial in a pivotal section imagining the worker in dialogue with the capitalist:

> You and I know on the market only one law, that of the exchange of commodities .... You preach to me constantly the gospel of 'saving' and 'abstinence'. Good! I will, like a sensible saving owner, husband my sole wealth, labour-power, and abstain from all foolish waste of it .... By an unlimited extension of the working-day, you may in one day use up a quantity of labour-power greater than I can restore in three. What you gain in labour I lose in substance .... You pay me for one day's labour-power, whilst you use that of three days. That is against our contract and the law of exchanges. I demand, therefore, a working-day of normal length ... I demand the normal working-day because I, like every other seller, demand the value of my commodity.

This was a key development in his system. Marx explicitly recommended *Das Kapital* to German readers as a weapon in their own struggle for a maximum working day protected by legislation.

Under the direct influence of the workers' struggle in Britain, therefore, Marx had carried out a radical reconceptualisation of the proletariat. This was the proletarian not as Barthélemy the desperate outcast, but rather as Barthélemy the creative and aspiring inventor. In this view, the proletariat was not merely a degraded, hopeless, propertyless class, driven to revolt by sheer misery, but wage-workers intent on self-improvement, as striving individuals with a property to protect. Workers, Marx intimated, could only defend their 'labour power' collectively.

He saw social legislation – Factory Acts and limitations on the working day – as the first victories of proletarian economy. As they won room for self-improvement, workers' horizons would be expanded. But all the time they would be struggling against the logic of the capitalist labour market. In Marx's view, the labour-power of workers could never be securely protected under capitalism. The remorseless class struggle, however, would ultimately serve to organise the working class until it was fit to assume power itself, and then would begin the construction of a socialist order.

Unsurprisingly, therefore, when Marx became the leading member of the International Workingmen's Association in 1864 – an organisation at first principally comprised of French and British supporters – he strongly emphasised working-class support and open organisation rather than any precise political programme or conspiratorial method. He was increasingly opposed in this by an emerging 'anarchist' tendency, led by Mikhail Bakunin, which put its faith in the cleansing violence of the 'great *rabble of the people*'. Like Blanqui, Bakunin was convinced that such a primal revolutionary force would require an elite of conspirators to direct their efforts from behind the scenes.

Napoleon III, meanwhile, finally fell from his throne in 1870, when his army was horrifically shattered by the Prussians at the battle of Sedan. Many of the French exiles took this opportunity to return home. Most found themselves the following year sucked into the Paris Commune, a kind of repeat of the 1848 June Days, but on a much larger scale. In a mostly spontaneous working-out of Marx and Blanqui's concept of an armed working class applying pressure on the vacillating republic – and Marx was indeed to call the Commune not socialist, but a working-class rule – Paris attempted to stiffen the national government from the left. When the government, refusing intimidation, unexpectedly withdrew from the city, left-wing enthusiasm filled the vacuum. This was very much in the mould of the cooperative socialism predominant in France since the 1830s. 'The day of justice approaches with great strides,' a speaker thundered to a meeting of women, 'the workshops in which you are packed will belong to you; the tools that are put into your hands will be yours; the gain resulting from your efforts, from your troubles, and from the loss of your health will be shared among you. Proletarians, you will be reborn.'

Paris elected a city government which held power in cooperation with the largely working-class National Guard. Nonetheless, the national government, led by Adolphe Thiers – who in 1830 had helped orchestrate the elevation of Louis Philippe – sent the army in and the Commune was crushed in blood. Perhaps 25,000 people were killed. Louis Blanc thought the Commune experiment was in flagrant opposition to the national will and publicly opposed it. His reputation never quite recovered. Karl Marx also thought that the Commune's defiance was unwise, but he saved his condemnation for its assassins. His *Address on the Civil War in France*, written on behalf of the International Workingmen's Association, was a masterpiece of excoriation.

At the graveside of Cournet, Charles Delescluze had predicted that the son would follow in the footsteps of the father. This prophecy came true. Cournet's son, also called Frédéric, became a commercial traveller, and went to sea for a short time, before returning to France and acting as a railway clerk. He was then employed as a master of ceremonies at the casino of Arachon. On ball nights, he would welcome the beauties of Bordeaux and introduce them to suitable partners. He also wrote radical journalism and incurred various sentences for offences against the Second Empire regime. At a state trial at Blois in 1870 he was charged with inciting people to murder the Emperor, but he protested indignantly, and was acquitted by the jury. During the Prussian siege of Paris, Frédéric became an officer in the National Guard, and was afterwards elected as a deputy from Paris. He resigned this position in order to follow the Commune, being appointed one of its delegates at the prefecture of police. Cournet Jnr was 'perhaps the most urbane, the most courteous of the Commune's members' but, thought an English witness, 'in spite of his polished manners [he] did not hesitate to carry out some of the Commune's most abominable decrees'. Though denounced as a suspect and with a warrant for his arrest, he managed to escape abroad.

Charles Delescluze, the police chief of the Commune, mounted a barricade as government forces slashed and battered their way into the insurgents' last redoubt. He was shot down and his body never found. There is no grave for Delescluze. He remains an individual symbol of the anonymous and heroic dead. Félix Pyat was a Commune leader and an enthusiast for destroying symbols of the old regime. When the fighting became fierce, he absconded from the city and survived. Ultimately he was elected to the French Chamber of Deputies in 1888, a year before his death.

Alexander Herzen never saw the Commune, having died at the beginning of 1870. Ledru-Rollin, who returned to France after twenty years' exile, held aloof from the new Republic with blood on its hands, before being persuaded to stand for the National Assembly in 1874. He died the same year. Louis Blanc was active in the National Assembly from 1871, sticking to his convictions, and when he died in 1882 he was awarded a state funeral. August Willich, who played a prominent and heroic role in the Union forces against slave power in the American Civil War, died in 1878. Auguste Blanqui was released from prison in 1859, but, as might be predicted, missed the Commune because he was once again incarcerated. He died in 1881 whilst delivering a speech to his revolutionary club. Marx passed away quietly, in his armchair, in 1883. There were few at his funeral in London, which was arranged as an intimate affair, but he had become a recognised sage of the international worker movement. Without his partner, Engels laboured to tie together a new Socialist International, formed in 1889 on the anniversary of the French Revolution. He died in 1895. Wilhelm Liebknecht, who had returned to Germany in 1862, died in 1900 as the revered elder statesman of the German Social Democratic Party, the most powerful socialist organisation in the world. Malwida von Meysenbug wrote a memoir which inspired generations of feminists. She was the first woman to be nominated for the Nobel Prize for Literature. She died, aged eighty-six, in 1903. She had never married.

There can be little doubt that, had he survived, Barthélemy would have been a commander in the Paris Commune. Instead, he lived on as a subject of fascination. The death masks of Emmanuel Barthélemy and Luigi Baranelli, both hanged for murder at Newgate, were acquired by James Stratton of Dundee, a proponent and practitioner of the pseudoscience of phrenology, which tried to link character traits to the size of various regions of the brain, read from the size and shape of the skull. It never commanded universal respect, and by the mid-1850s was increasingly seen as quackery. Nonetheless, it was a popular dilettante diversion, and Karl Marx himself, for example, liked to dabble, examining his comrades' heads. For our purposes it is of interest because Stratton and his colleague Dr Elliotson made efforts to investigate Barthélemy's life, mostly examining newspapers, but also talking to some who knew him, or at least employed him. Their analysis was in reality a psychological profile. Stratton found that in Self-esteem, Firmness, Destructiveness and Secretiveness Barthélemy was 'a very giant', while in Wonder, Ideality, Wit and Reflexion he was 'a tiny dwarf'. Barthélemy was, he concluded, proud and stubborn, cunning and conceited, cruel and coarse. He 'showed enormous resolution'.

These scientists were not the only ones to show an interest in Barthélemy's mind. His character, it was clearly felt, merited examination 'from a psychological point of view'. And if the psychology could be read from the physiognomy, Madame Tussaud's was there for an eager public to examine for themselves: only 6s entry plus another 6d for the 'Chamber of Horrors'.

Despite promises given by the prison authorities at Newgate, it seems that Herring did indeed get Barthélemy's clothes, and they were handed over to Madame Tussaud's waxworks museum on Baker Street. Barthélemy was exhibit number 290, described in the catalogue as follows: 'Executed for the murder of Mr. Moore and a policeman [sic]. Barthélemy was by business an engineer, but having joined the ranks of the Red Republicans, was exiled from France, his native country, and terminated his existence on the gallows at Newgate.'

The French émigrés were not too happy to see Barthélemy up there amongst 'robbers and murderers' in the Chamber of Horrors. But they did not go as far as Italian émigrés who threatened to beat up Tussaud's staff until they removed the sign reading 'the wicked murderer [Felice] Orsini, the monster of mankind' beside the model of the man who in 1858 attempted to assassinate Napoleon III. Ironically, Orsini's assassination attempt awakened in Napoleon a consciousness of the fervent nationalism of those Italian patriots who bitterly resented Austrian domination of their divided country. The following year, in alliance with the liberal monarchy of Piedmont in the north of Italy, Napoleon made war on Austria. This kicked off a process that would lead to the unification of Italy, which in turn would inspire the unification of Germany through three wars conducted by Bismarck's Prussia. The Times in 1855 had been more nearly right than they could have imagined: 'a

Barthélemy is not powerless. The hand of any ruffian who has been roused to madness … may change the destinies of Europe.'

Barthélemy, at least, held pride of place amongst the tableau of prisoners at Tussaud's, for he stood in the dock. A visitor in 1866 rightly said that his catalogue description was quite inadequate. It gave 'not the slightest notion of the real character and exploits of the man before the ill-fate that led him to visit this country'. He wondered whether the waxwork was really a good likeness: 'We should be inclined to say not, from what we have heard from a gentleman who acted as interpreter at the trial for shooting Cournet, in the duel at Windsor, and he described Barthélemy to us as being of the most lion-like appearance.'

Barthélemy was indeed both ferocious and majestic. Atrocities carried out over prolonged periods of time are born of contempt for the victim. In contrast, people who lash out in anger are responding to that perceived contempt, and perhaps to the demeaning thoughts they have about themselves. Barthélemy was a proud man with a strong sense of personal dignity. Those who treated him as a worthy interlocutor or adversary – Alexander Herzen or his National Guard opponents in the June Days fighting – he respected and behaved honourably towards. Those who would treat him as a 'wretch' or intimidate him – Frédéric Cournet or Ledru-Rollin and his party – earned his bitter enmity. 'Do not abase me!' the young Barthélemy had exclaimed when men laid hands upon him after he shot Zôphirin Beudet, the police officer who had dared to beat him like a dog. It was George Moore's cruel fate to provoke his savage instinctive reaction.

Barthélemy's rebellion against condescension, his insistence that he was as good as any other man, matched and prefigured the rise of a working-class democracy determined to challenge the hierarchies of birth, wealth and education that had reigned from time immemorial. Perhaps most grating to workers was the casual assumption of bourgeois sophistication and social grace that so easily shades into a sense of entitlement. '*Savoir-faire*, that sucking vampire, is the sovereign master of our cruel society,' wrote Blanqui fifteen years after Barthélemy's death. 'Woe to those who lack it!' It was this self-regarding privilege that Barthélemy wished to see overturned. He was painfully aware that the job was not near half done by the French Revolution, nor by the revolutions that followed. It is hardly half done yet.

In life, Barthélemy, the disciplined, inventive, sleepless revolutionary, rejected the casual injustices of a class-bound society. His failings were his bursts of seemingly uncontrollable brutality, but also the creeping, dehumanising cold-eyed ruthlessness that grew over him. As W. B. Yeats said of revolutionaries, 'Hearts with one purpose alone ... seem enchanted to a stone to trouble the living stream.' Certainly Barthélemy's heart was much hardened. But he also had in him a capacity for courage, dignity and loyalty that lasted to his death on the scaffold at Newgate.

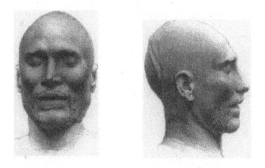

A drawing of Barthélemy in death, 'newly executed at Newgate', from *The Zoist*, July 1855.

ACKNOWLEDGEMENTS

I was first turned to the theme of this book by Raymond Postgate (1896–1971), whose classics of revolutionary history and crime writing moved me to attempt a history that combines them both.

The Bodleian Library at Oxford and the USA National Library of Medicine jointly procured for me a copy of Cyrille Lacambre's *Evasion Des Prisons Du Conseil de Guerre*. I acknowledge their great help.

Research and writing is a curiously verbal process, and I thank all those who bore with me, including Michael Fisher, Icarus Panchaud, Jessica Thomas, James Thompson, Barbara Warnock and Laura Warnock. Axel Thomas, new to the century, has been reliably inspiring.

My colleagues at work have been sources of profound understanding in every problem I have tackled. My thanks in particular to Amanda Power, Bill Booth and Cressida Chappell. Bart van Es, with whom I bounced ideas on registers of writing, as we both worked in forms novel to our experience, has immeasurably added to the sense of discovery that has made this project such a joy.

All members of my family were as supportive as one could possibly hope. My thanks to Kathleen, Ciaran, Padraig, Deidre, Niall (who closely read a draft), Ita, Áine and *Breandán*.

I am grateful to Pete Collin, who tracked down an acronym that confused me. Dan Rutherford, director of an award-winning short film depicting Barthélemy and Cournet's fatal encounter, *The Last Duel* (2010), generously provided sources. Jessica Goodman, Ultán Gillen and JC Smith saved me on finer points of French translation.

Dr Cecilia Biaggi did heroic and invaluable work in translating from Italian, transcribing from French, and helping to construct the notes. Her attention to detail and historical sense have made an enormous contribution to this book. I was lucky to have the aid of her great talent and skills.

Barrie and Ivy Lill read a draft of the manuscript and made very helpful comments. My mother, Ita, read the text with enormous care and provided invaluable feedback and information.

Sally Holloway at Felicity Bryan Associates and Sarah Rigby, Senior Editor at Hutchinson, have been stalwarts of support and sage advice. Much of merit in the book owes to them.

This true story is dedicated to my mother, Ita, and to the memory of my father, Dominic. Together they have been *an réalta thuaidh* of my life. My parents are exemplars of the dignity, heroism and love to be found in those who must work hard all their lives.

My partner, Victoria Lill, has inspired, cajoled, discussed and joked, always keeping my spirits high. She has shared with me the dream of restoring an extraordinary life and time to our troubled present. I cannot imagine a person with whom I would rather share a project – and a life.

Marc Mulholland
St Catherine's College & History Faculty, Oxford University

NOTES

These notes are arranged by page number and an indicative quotation or paraphrase drawn from the main text.

PREFACE

ix   'ONE CANNOT IMAGINE'. Francis Wey, *A Frenchman Sees the English in the 'Fifties*, ed. Valerie Pirie (London, 1935), p. 118.

ix   'A MERE MURMUR PUNCTUATED BY SOFT, HISSING SOUNDS'. Ibid., p. 5.

x   'HEADLONG INTO THE MIDST OF THE THRONG'. Charles Baudelaire, *The Painter of Modern Life and Other Essays*, trans. Jonathan Mayne (London, 1964), p. 7. Baudelaire, though a cynic in politics, took part in the barricade fighting of February and June 1848 and December 1851, just to feel the thrill of the masses in revolt. F. W. J. Hemmings, *Culture and Society in France, 1848–1898: Dissidents and Philistines* (London, 1971), pp. 36–41.

xi   IRISH ACTRESS, HARRIET SMITHSON. Linda Kelly, *The Young Romantics: Paris 1827–37* (London, 1976), pp. 11–13.

xi   VICTOR HUGO RETURNED TO HIS NOVEL. David Bellos, *The Novel of the Century: The Extraordinary Life of Les Misérables* (London, 2017), p. 113.

1 – 'THE MAN I NOW SEE IS THE MAN WHO SHOT ME'

1–2   'THE CAPITALIST' LENT THEM HOUSEKEEPING MONEY. George Augustus Sala, *Twice Round the Clock or Hours of the Day and Night in London* [1858] (New York, 1971), pp. 254, 266.

3   'IN THE DAYS OF ADAM'. Leading article in *The Economist*, 25 January 1851, in E. Royston Pike (ed.), *Human Documents of the Victorian Golden Age (1850–1875)* (London, 1967), p. 41.

4   'PURE UNDILUTED GENTILITY'. James Laver, *The Age of Optimism: Manners and Morals, 1848–1914* (London, 1966), p. 37.

5   HE HAD MADE A GOOD LIVING BY THE MANUFACTURE OF FIZZY DRINKS. Visitors to the Great Exhibition of 1851, where alcohol was banned, consumed more than a million

bottles of soft drinks. Elizabeth Burton, *The Early Victorians at Home* (London, 1972), p. 144.

5   'EVERYTHING WAS MADE TO LOOK AS HEAVY AS IT COULD'. Charles Dickens, *Our Mutual Friend* (two volumes: London, 1865), I, p. 99.

6   FROM HER ROOM DOWNSTAIRS. 'Horrible double murder', *Cheshire Observer and General Advertiser*, 16 December 1854.

6   'I DO NOT KNOW'. 'Old Bailey Online' Project, *Proceedings of the Central Criminal Court*, 1 January 1855, p. 33.

7   'A LARGE QUANTITY OF BLOOD'. 'The double murder in Warren Street', *Daily News*, 11 December 1854.

8   'I HAD NOT THE HEART TO DO SO'. 'Confession of the murderer Barthélemy', *Reynolds Newspaper*, 20 January 1855.

8   AT THE FRONT OF THE HOUSE. 'Old Bailey Online' Project, p. 36.

9   HE WAS FINALLY BROUGHT DOWN. 'The double murder in Warren Street, Fitzroy Square', *Morning Post*, 15 December 1854.

9   MADDEN WAS AFTERWARDS HAILED AS A HERO. 'The Warren Street Murder', *Morning Post*, 9 January 1855; 'The Warren Street Murders', *Morning Post*, 1 December 1856.

9–10   POLICE CONSTABLE JOHN MUNDY. 'Old Bailey Online' Project, p. 38.

10   'HE ASKED ME IF I WOULD LET HIM HAVE A CAB'. 'Old Bailey Online' Project, p. 38.

10   'MY GOOD MAN'. 'Old Bailey Online' Project, p. 36.

10   'OH, YOU CRUEL MAN!' 'The double murder at Warren Street', *Daily News*, 11 December 1854.

     I, CHARLES COLLARD'. 'The double murder in Warren Street', *Morning Post*, 11 December 1854.

11   BARTHÉLEMY, WHEN TOLD OF COLLARD'S DEATH. 'The late murder in Warren Street', *Daily News*, 16 December 1854.

2 – THE CRIME OF BEING A KING

12   A 'VERY HONEST, OBLIGING AND WORTHY MAN'. 'The Warren-Street murderer', *The Times*, 11 January 1855.

12   'A SIMPLE WORKER FROM HOT-BLOODED MARSEILLE'. Monte Gardiner, 'Malwida von Meysenbug's "Memoirs of an Idealist", translation of *Memoiren Einer Idealistin*', Thesis (MA), Brigham Young University, Dept of Germanic and Slavic Languages, 1999, p. 212.

12   ANTI-CLERICALISM STRONG. Roger Magraw, *France, 1815–1914: The Bourgeois Century* (Oxford, 1983), p. 115.

13   'THE PEOPLE WILL RISE UP'. Georges Guibal, *Le mouvement fédéraliste en Provence en 1793* (Paris, 1908), p. 11.

13   'I DIE FOR OUR COUNTRY'. Augustin Fabre, *Histoire de Marseille* (two volumes: Marseille and Paris, 1829), II, pp. 506–7;

Laurent Lautard, *Esquisses historiques: Marseille depuis 1789 jusqu'en 1815* (two volumes: Marseilles, 1844), II, pp. 224–5.

13   'STONY ABYSS'. Honoré de Balzac, *The Ball at Sceaux* [1830], trans. Clara Bell (Epub, 2014), p. 32.

13   'HOW UGLY PARIS SEEMS'. Quoted in Andrew Lees, *Cities Perceived: Urban Society in European and American Thought, 1820–1940* (Manchester, 1985), p. 73.

14   'IT IS TRUE, THAT THERE IS SOMETHING MOST EXCEEDINGLY EXHILARATING'. Frances Trollope, *Paris and the Parisians in 1835* (two volumes: London, 1836), I, p. 33.

14   THE 'DANGEROUS CLASSES' WERE 'SCATTERED MORE OR LESS IN EVERY QUARTER OF PARIS'. H. A. Frégier, *Des classes dangereuses de la population dans les grandes villes* [1840], excerpted in Irene Collins (ed.), *Documents of Modern History: Government and Society in France, 1814–1848* (London, 1970), p. 144.

14   IT REQUIRED 1,050 TO 1,300 FRANCS FOR A FAMILY TO LIVE DECENTLY. William L. Langer, *Political and Social Upheaval, 1832–1852* (New York, 1969), pp. 187–8.

15   'PARIS PORTERS HAVE A KNOWING EYE'. Honoré de Balzac, *Cousin Bette* [1846], trans. Sylvia Raphael (Oxford, 1992), p. 6.

15   THEY WERE CERTAINLY IDENTIFIED WITH SOCIALIST IDEAS. Desportes, 'Éducation' in Jean Aicard et al., *Un million de faits: aide-mémoire universel, des sciences, des arts et des lettres* (Paris, 1842), cc. 1374–5; Émile Varin, 'A Tous', *La Ruche populaire*, I (December 1839), excerpted in Paul E. Corcoran (ed.), *Before Marx: Socialism and Communism in France, 1830–48* (London and Basingstoke, 1983), p. 95. Britain was impressed and had some success with the similarly organised Monitorial System. The rector of the High School in Edinburgh in 1830 was able to report that amongst its agreeable results was the total abolition of corporal punishment. *Quarterly Review*, 1831, vol. xxxix, 'Book Review' in Lloyd Evans and Philip J. Pledger, *Contemporary Sources and Opinions in Modern British History* (two volumes, Melbourne, 1966), I, p. 109.

16   'MAN MAY BE TRAINED TO ACQUIRE ANY SENTIMENTS'. Robert Owen, *A New View of Society, or Essays on the Principle of the Formation of Human Character and the Application of the Principle to Practice* (London, 1814), p. 2.

16   THE DESIRE FOR LEARNING WAS STRONG IN FRANCE'S URBAN WORKING CLASS. Jules Michelet, *The People*, translation of *Le Peuple* (1846) by John P. McKay (Urbana, 1973), p. 59.

16   'BECAUSE I FOUND IT THE MORE CONVENIENT POSITION'. 'Tentative d'assassinat, par un coup de pistolet, sur un sergent de ville', *Journal des débats politiques et littéraires*, 21 December 1939. 'Affaire Barthélemy', *Gazette des tribunaux: journal de jurisprudence et de débats judiciaire*, 21 December 1839.

16   HIGHLY SKILLED CRAFTWORKERS GATHERED AT THE MARAIS. By the middle of the nineteenth century there were 2,017 jewellery workshops in the Marais employing 10,196 workers.

17   IT WAS BORDERED ON THE WEST BY LES HALLES. Comte d'Haussonville, *Misère et remèdes* (Paris, 1886), pp. 220–21. Killian Barthélémy, 'L'Histoire de l'orfèvrerie et de la joaillerie dans le Marais' (2015): http://www.parismarais.com/fr/arts-et-culture/l-histoire-de-l-orfevrerie-et-de-la-joaillerie.html.

17   'THE WORLD'S GREATEST MANUFACTURING CITY'. Mark Girouard, *Cities and People* (New York and New Haven, 1985), p. 286.

17   BY 1847, THERE WERE 330,000 INDUSTRIAL WORKERS IN PARIS. Philip Mansell, *Paris between Empires, 1814–1852* (London, 2001), p. 386.

17   'ENDOWED WITH A VERY REMARKABLE MECHANICAL GENIUS'. 'The Warren-Street murderer', *The Times*, 11 January 1855.

17–18   'NEVER TAUGHT ME TO LAY OUT OR ASSEMBLE'. Agricol Perdiguier, *Mémoires d'un Compagnon* [1854–55], excerpted in Jan Goldstein and John W. Boyer (eds), *Nineteenth-Century Europe: Liberalism and its Critics* (Chicago, 1988), p. 205.

18   PARIS TAILORS ON STRIKE IN 1833. Jacques Rancière, *The Nights of Labor: The Workers' Dream in Nineteenth-Century France*, trans. John Drury (Philiadelphia, 1989), p. 41.

18   'DERIVED DIRECTLY FROM THE ACTUAL EXPERIENCES OF MEN IN SMALL-SCALE GROUPS'. Keith Taylor, *The Political Ideas of the Utopian Socialists* (London, 1982), p. 9.

18   'YOU MAY FORM SMALL SOCIETIES OF SIX'. Issue of September 1840. Quoted in Georges Duveau, *1848: The Making of a Revolution*, trans. Anne Carter (London, 1967), p. 64.

18–19   'THE SOCIALISM WHICH WOULD MAKE THE STATE'. Quoted in Dorothy Thompson, *Queen Victoria: Gender and Power* (London, 1990), pp. 102–3.

20   'A CENTRAL FEATURE OF SANS-CULOTTES PSYCHOLOGY'. Gwyn A. Williams, *Artisans and Sans-Culottes: Popular Movements in Britain and France during the French Revolution*, 2nd edition. (London, 1989), p. 25.

20–1   THE WORKMEN OF THE FAUBOURGS – 'COVERED WITH RAGS'. Marchand de Breuil, *Journées mémorables de la Révolution française* (three volumes: Paris, 1827), III, p. 29.

21   'SHOW THEM THESE PIKES'. Paul H. Beik (ed.), *The French Revolution: Selected Documents* (New York, 1970), p. 262.

21–2   'LIKE EVERYBODY ELSE, I WAS SHAKING WITH TERROR'. Peter Vansittart, *Voices of the Revolution* (London, 1989), pp. 179–0.

22   BOTH MEN PRIDED THEMSELVES ON THEIR SPARTAN SIMPLICITY. Ibid., p. 318.

22   'REPUBICAN CHILDREN MUST BE STRICTLY TRAINED TO
        SPEAK LACONICALLY'. Ibid., p. 249.

22   HE CARRIED HIS HEAD LIKE A 'SACRED SACRAMENT'.
        Moshe Hazani, 'The Duel That Never Was', *Political Psychology*,
        Vol. 10, No. 1 (Mar., 1989), pp. 111–33, 120.

22–3   'AND I SAY THAT THE KING MUST BE JUDGED AS AN
        ENEMY'. Jean Jaurès, *A Socialist History of the French
        Revolution*, trans. Mitchell Abidor (London, 2015), p. 133.

23   THEY WANTED TO JUSTIFY THEMSELVES TO HISTORY.
        Simon Schama, *Citizens: A Chronicle of the French Revolution*
        (London, 1989), pp. 651–3.

24   'REVOLUTIONARY UNTIL THE PEACE'. Saint-Just, 'Pour un
        gouvernement révolutionnaire' in *Discours et rapports*, ed. Albert
        Soboul (Paris, 1988), pp. 116–31.

24   'THOSE WHO ONLY HALF MAKE REVOLUTIONS'. 'February
        26, March 3, 1794: Saint-Just on the Ventôse Decrees' in Paul H.
        Beik (ed.), *The French Revolution: Selected Documents* (New York,
        1970), p. 294.

25   'C'EST POURTANT MOI QUI AI FAIT CELA'. Karl Marx, 'The
        Holy Family' [1845] in *Marx–Engels Collected Works* (fifty
        volumes: London, 1975–2004) [Hereafter *MECW*], IV, p. 122.

25   'WE MUST BE GOVERNED BY THE BEST'. Quoted in Florence
        Gauthier, 'The French Revolution: Revolution of the Rights of
        Man and Citizen' in Mike Haynes and Jim Wolfreys (eds), *History
        and Revolution: Refuting Revisionism* (London, 2007), p. 90.

3 – THE REPUBLIC IN THE WORKSHOP

27   'THE LAST PROMENADE FOR THE *FLÂNEUR*'. Walter
        Benjamin, *The Arcades Project*, trans. Howard Eiland and Kevin
        McLoughlin (New York, 1999), p. 10.

28   'I WAS AT ONCE STRUCK WITH THE OBVIOUS
        SUPERIORITY OF THE WORKING PEOPLE'. Robert Lowery,
        Radical and Chartist [1853–57], ed. Brian Harrison and Patricia
        Hollis (London, 1979), p. 168.

28   'NOTHING STRUCK US ENGLISH MORE IN THE MANNERS
        OF THE FRENCH'. *The Autobiography and Memoirs of
        Benjamin Robert Haydon* [1853], ed. Malcolm Elwin (London,
        1950), p. 216.

28   COUNTLESS SMALL WINE SHOPS AND *CABARETS* 'MORE
        CHEERFUL'. Quoted in Roger Price, *People and Politics in France,
        1848–1870* (Cambridge, 2004), p. 360.

28   EMPLOYERS HUFFED AND PUFFED. W. Scott Haine, *The World
        of the Paris Café: Sociability among the French Working Class,
        1789–1914* (Baltimore, 1996), p. 60.

29   'THERE WAS SMOKING AND DRINKING'. Victor Hugo, *Les Misérables*, trans. Christine Donougher (London, 2013, 2016), p. 584.

29   PERHAPS THIS IS WHERE BARTHÉLEMY FIRST CAME INTO CONTACT WITH THE REVOLUTION. Frances Trollope, *Paris and the Parisians in 1835* (New York, 1836), pp. 174–6.

29   BARTHÉLEMY WAS 'CONCERNED ABOUT POLITICAL THINGS'. 'Tentative d'assassinat, par un coup de pistolet, sur un sergent de ville', *Journal des débats politiques et littéraires*, 21 December 1939.

29–30 A DAGGER WAS PLACED IN HIS HAND. 'Oath of Membership into the Société des Saisons', Paul E. Corcoran (ed.), *Before Marx: Socialism and Communism in France, 1830–48* (London and Basingstoke, 1983), pp. 34–5.

30   IT WOULD HAVE BEEN TRADITIONAL IN SUCH CIRCLES FOR THE LEADER. James H. Billington, *Fire in the Minds of Men: Origins of the Revolutionary Faith* (London, 1980), pp. 176–7.

30   BARTHÉLEMY WAS DEDICATED REVOLUTIONARY. 'Tentative d'assassinat, par un coup de pistolet, sur un sergent de ville'.

30   'I HAVE SERVED THE CAUSE'. 'Tentative d'assassinat, par un coup de pistolet, sur un sergent de ville'.

31   IN RETROSPECT, THE 'HEROIC' PERIOD OF JACOBIN DICTATORSHIP. See Étienne Cabet's *Histoire populaire de la révolution française de 1789 à 1830* (four volumes: Paris, 1839). An example of Cabet's analysis: '… the bourgeoisie deprived the aristocracy of everything it could take from them without injustice …. [But] the [1789] Revolution gave [the working-class] people nothing of these: neither political rights, nor property, nor safer and better paid work, not even daily bread; on the contrary … when the fear of starvation led to riots, they killed them with bullets to maintain public order.' Volume II, p. 102.

       BLANQUI WAS A DEDICATED REVOLUTIONARY. His eminent and talented brother, Jérôme-Adolphe, preferred the fanaticism of free-market political economy.

33–4   'WHO STOPS REVOLUTIONS IN MID-COURSE?'. Victor Hugo, *Les Misérables*, p. 745.

34   THE DEMOCRATIC SOCIALISTS 'LIKED TO IMAGINE'. Edward Berenson, *Populist Religion and Left-Wing Politics in France, 1830–1852* (Princeton, 1984), p. 102.

34   THE BOURGEOISIE A VERY DEFINITE CLASS WHO OWNED AND PROFITED FROM THE INSTRUMENTS OF PRODUCTION WORKERS NEEDED TO LIVE. Emile Barrault, and Prosper Enfantin, *The Doctrine of Saint-Simon: An Exposition; First Year, 1828–1829*, trans. Georg G. Iggers (Boston, 1958), pp. 83–4.

34   'THE REPULSIVE MASK OF PAUPERISM IN REVOLT'. Quoted in Louis Chevalier, *Labouring Classes and Dangerous Classes in*

Paris during the First Half of the Nineteenth Century, trans. Frank Jellinek (London, 1973), p. 79.

34   WAGE-EARNERS REJECTED THE TERM 'PROLETARIAN' AS OFFENSIVE. Dietrich Mühlberg, *Proletariat: Culture and Lifestyle in the 19th Century*, trans. Katherine Vanovitch (Liepzig, 1988), pp. 12–15.

34   'WE ARE ALL IN QUEST OF THE GOLDEN APPLE OF SECURITY'. Iorwerth Prothero, *Radical Artisans in England and France, 1830–1870* (Cambridge, 1997), p. 47, see also p. 139.

35   'AT LAST THE REGIMENT CAME OUT'. Stendhal, *Lucien Leuwen*, trans. H. L. R. Edwards (two volumes: London, 1951), I, pp. 237–8.

36   'THE HEADS OF THE WORKERS CAUGHT FIRE'. *Mémoires d'un touriste par de Stendhal* (Paris, 1891), p. 342.

36   'VIVRE EN TRAVAILLANT OU MOURIR EN COMBATTANT'. L. S., '*Aperçu sur la question du prolétariat*', in *La révolte de Lyon en 1834, ou la fille du Prolétaire* (Paris, 1835), pp. ii–iii, ix.

37   'A SHORT FAT MAN, THICKSET AND COMMON LOOKING'. *Flora Tristan's London Journal, 1841*, translation of Flora Tristan, *Promenades dans Londres* by Dennis Palmer and Giselle Pincetl (London, 1980), pp. 53–9, quotations pp. 54, 48.

37   'FOR THE POOR WORKER WHO POSSESSES NEITHER LAND NOR HOUSES'. Flora Tristan, *Union ouvrière* [1843], trans. Doris Beik and Paul Beik, *Flora Tristan, Utopian Feminist* (Bloomington, 1993), pp. 108–9; Flora Tristan, *The Workers Union*, trans. Beverly Livingstone (Urbana, 2007), pp. 48 [usefulness not poverty], 52–53 [the example of Ireland]. The significance of Tristan's insight for socialist theory has not been sufficiently appreciated. See, for example, the dismissive remarks of George Lichtheim, *The Origins of Socialism* (New York, 1969), p. 70. Workers claiming ownership of their own labour was in fact widespread amongst French wage-earners. As one worker put it, 'our industry … belongs to us alone': William H. Sewell, Jnr, *Work and Revolution in France: The Language of Labor from the Old Regime to 1848* (Cambridge, 1980), p. 200. Chartists had a similar view on 'strength in arms' as a form of property to be defended: 'Rethinking Chartism' in Gareth Stedman Jones, *Languages of Class: Studies in English Working Class History, 1832–1982* (Cambridge, 1982), pp. 108–9. Though Sewell and Stedman Jones prefer to distance discourse from social class, it seems evident that this conceptualisation of labour as subsistence property – rather than land, tools or market – was a reflex consciousness of workers as wage labourers rather than aspirant master artisans or peasant farmers.

38   'REPUBLICAN DEMOCRATS, ALREADY TAKING AS THEIR MOTTO THE ABOLITION OF THE PROLETARIAT'. Louis Blanc, *Histoire de dix ans: 1830–1840* (two volumes: Paris, 1842), II, p. 270.

38   MARTIN BERNARD ON 'INDUSTRIAL FEUDALISM'. J.
      Tchernoff, *Le parti républicain sous la monarchie de juillet; forma-
      tion et évolution de la doctrine républicaine* (Paris, 1905), p. 366.

38   THE MASSES WERE MOTIVATED NOT BY 'LOW MONETARY
      INTERESTS'. 'Discours prononcé à la séance du 2 février 1832 de
      la Société des Amis du Peuple' in V. P. Volguine (ed.), *Auguste
      Blanqui, textes choisis* (Paris, 1971), p. 76.

38   'THE POOR MAN DOES NOT KNOW THE SOURCE OF HIS
      ILLS'. 'Qui fait la soupe doit la manger' (1834) in V. P. Volguine
      (ed.), *Auguste Blanqui, textes choisis*, p. 81.

39   'BEYOND THIS THEY ARE MORE OR LESS RESIGNED TO
      THEIR DISCOMFORTS'. 'Police bulletin, Paris, 1 October 1817',
      Arch. Nat., in Irene Collins (ed.), *Documents of Modern History:
      Government and Society in France, 1814–1848* (London, 1970), p. 67.

39   'THE RECRUITMENT AMONG THE ILL CONDITIONED
      MEMBERS OF THE BOURGEOISIE'. A. J. Grant, Harold
      Temperley, *Europe in the 19th and 20th centuries (1789–1939)*
      (London, 1939), p. 582 [chapter by Raymond Postgate].

40   NO FEWER THAN 60,000 HAD DECLARED WAR ON
      SOCIETY. Jacques Droz, *Europe between Revolutions, 1815–1848*
      (London, 1967), p. 67.

4 – 'ANGER DOES NOT CALCULATE'

41   'AS FOR THE BEARDS, THERE IS NO END TO THEM'.
      William Makepeace Thackeray, *The Paris Sketch Book* [1840]
      (London, 1869), p. 38.

41   'THEY LAUGH AT RELIGION'. William Makepeace Thackeray,
      Contributions to Punch [1844] (New York and London, 1903),
      p. 151.

42   'A POLICEMAN ... GRABBED ME AND BEAT ME'. 'Tentative
      d'assassinat, par un coup de pistolet, sur un sergent de ville',
      Journal des débats politiques et littéraires, 21 December 1939.

42   YEARS LATER HE STILL BORE SCARS FROM THE ATTACK.
      'Ein Kriegsgericht in Paris', *Rheinisches Echo* (Cologne, 1849), p. 82.

42   BARTHÉLEMY ... GOT UP THE NEXT DAY TRANSFORMED.
      Alexander Herzen, *My Past and Thoughts*, trans. Constance
      Garnett (London, 1925, 2008), IV, p. 252.

43   THREE HUNDRED REBELS WERE PUT ON TRIAL. Pamela
      M. Pilbeam, *Republicanism in Nineteenth-Century France, 1815–
      1871* (London, 1995), p. 137.

44–5 BEUDET ... SAW A YOUNG MAN APPROACHING HIM WITH
      ... A FIREARM IN HIS HAND. 'Nouvelles et Faits Divers', *La
      Presse*, 6 December 1839. *Journal des débats politiques et littéraires*,
      7 December 1839. *La Presse*, 7 December 1839. 'Tentative
      d'assassinat, par un coup de pistolet, sur un sergent de ville'.

'Affaire Barthélemy', *Gazette des tribunaux: journal de jurisprudence et de débats judiciaire*, 21 December 1839.

45   YOUNG REPUBLICANS ... WERE VERY BADLY BEATEN. F. Rittiez, *Histoire du règne de Louis-Philippe 1er, 1830 à 1848* (three volumes: Paris, 1856), II, pp. 30–31.

45–6   POLICE FORCE WAS HEAVY-HANDED. Jill Harsin, *Barricades: The War of the Streets in Revolutionary Paris, 1830–1848* (New York, 2002), p. 74; Etienne Garnier-Pagès et al., *Dictionnaire politique: encyclopédie du langage et de la science politiques* (Paris, 1860), p. 118.

46   THE 'MASSACRE DE LA RUE TRANSNONAIN'. Colin Jones, *Paris: Biography of a City* (London, 2004), pp. 315–17.
    'WHEN THE HOUR OF TRIAL STRIKES'. Honoré de Balzac, *Scenes from a Courtesan's Life* [1838], trans. James Waring (London, 2014), p. 389; Alexandre Dumas, Le Chevalier de Maison Rouge [1845] (London, 1912), p. 227.

46–7   THE TRIAL ATTRACTED INTERNATIONAL ATTENTION. *Morning Post*, 23 December 1839.

47   THE DEFENDANT APPEARED WITH HIS HAIR CUT IN REPUBLICAN FASHION. 'Affaire Barthélemy', *Gazette des tribunaux: journal de jurisprudence et de débats judiciaire*, 21 December 1839.

50   EIGHTEEN PEOPLE WERE KILLED. Rayner Happenstall, *French Crime in the Romantic Age* (London, 1970), p. 153.

51–2   BARTHÉLEMY 'LISTENED TO THIS JUDGMENT'. 'Tentative d'assassinat, par un coup de pistolet, sur un sergent de ville'. 'Affaire Barthélemy', *Gazette des tribunaux*, 21 December 1839.

52   BARTHÉLEMY'S SENTENCE OF PUBLIC HUMILIATION WAS LIFTED. *Journal du droit criminel, ou Jurisprudence criminelle du Royaume* (Paris, 1840), p. 278; *Bulletin des arrêts de la Cour de cassation rendus en matière criminelle* (Paris, 1840), p. 20.

52   THE DESIGNATED ASSASSIN HAD BEEN CHOSEN BY LOT. 'Ein Kriegsgericht in Paris', *Rheinisches Echo* (Cologne, 1849), p. 83.

5 – GALLEY CONVICT

53–4   BARTHÉLEMY WAS TAKEN ... FOR TRANSPORTATION TO THE GALLEYS. In 1828, the novelist Victor Hugo witnessed the removal of convicted prisoners for their transport to the galleys. Exactly the same process would have taken place for Barthélemy. Victor Hugo, *The Last Day of a Condemned Man* [1829] (London, 1907), pp. 55–61.

55   IN THE EVENT OF 'TUMULT OR REBELLION'. J. Murray, *Hand-Book for Travellers in France* (London, 1843), pp. 123–4.

55   THE PRISONER'S GRIM LIFE: 'TO BE SHOWN NO RESPECT
          BY ANYONE'. Victor Hugo, *Les Misérables*, trans. Christine
          Donougher (London, 2013, 2016), p. 216.

55–6   'THE   RELATIVE   TRANQUILLITY'   OF   'HAPPY
          CRIMINALITY'. Michael A. Osborne, *The Emergence of Tropical
          Medicine in France* (Chicago, 2014), p. 38.

56   'THE RIOTOUS LIFE THEY LEAD'. Eugène Sue, *The Mysteries
          of Paris* (three volumes: London, 1846), III, p. 124.

56   BARTHÉLEMY'S TIME IN THE *BAGNE*. *Rapport De La
          Commission D'enquête Nsur L'insurrection Qui A Éclaté Dans
          La Journée Du 23 Juin Et Sur Les Évènements Du 15 Mai* (three
          volumes: Paris, 1848), II, p. 218.

56–7   'SINCE THE CONDEMNATION OF BARTHÉLEMY'. 'Ein
          Kriegsgericht in Paris', *Rheinisches Echo* (Cologne, 1849), pp. 85–6.

57   'THEIR COMMUNISM IS FROM THE HEART'. Wilhelm
          Weitling, *Garantien der Harmonie und Freiheit* (Hamburg, 1842),
          p. 180.

57–8   'WHAT PARTICULARLY OFFENDED MY PRIDE'. David
          Riazanov, *Karl Marx and Friedrich Engels: an Introduction to
          their Lives and Works*, trans. Joshua Kunitz (New York and
          London, 1973), p. 69.

58   'MODERN UNIVERSAL INTERCOURSE'. *The German Ideology*
          [1846] in David McLellan (ed.), *Karl Marx: Selected Writings*, 2nd
          edition (Oxford, 2000), p. 194.

60   'SOMEDAY, IF THE DEAREST HOPE OF OUR HEART IS NOT
          MISTAKEN'. M. Louis Blanc, *Organisation du travail* (Paris, 1839,
          1847), p. 20.

60   ONLY 'REVOLUTIONARY PRACTICE' WOULD DEVELOP
          WORKING-CLASS CAPACITIES. Marx, 'Theses On Feuerbach'
          [1845] in *Karl Marx: A Reader*, ed. Jon Elster (Cambridge, 1986),
          p. 21.

61   GERMAN REVOLUTIONARIES ... FORMALLY ABANDONED
          'HANKERING AFTER CONSPIRACY'. Frederick Engels, 'On
          the History of the Communist League' [1885] in Karl Marx, *The
          Cologne Communist Trial*, ed. Rodney Livingstone (London, 1971),
          p. 48.

62   MARX AND ENGELS ... ALLIED TO ... FRENCH SOCIAL
          DEMOCRATS. Karl Marx and Frederick Engels, *The Manifesto
          of the Communist Party* [1848] in *MECW*, Vol. 6, p. 518.

          6 – BARRICADES PILED LIKE MOUNTAINS

63–4   REPUBLICAN ACTIVISTS MOVED SILENTLY ... 'SOUNDING
          THE DISPOSITION OF THE PEOPLE'. Percy B. St. John, *The
          Three Days of February, 1848: With Sketches of Lamartine, Guizot,
          etc* (New York, 1848), p. 69.

64 'THEY HAVE BEEN STRUCK BY ASSASSINS!'. Walter Keating Kelly, *Narrative of the French Revolution of 1848* (London, 1848), p. 75.

65 'NEVER STEPPED FORTH SO SMALL A MAN'. Percy B. St. John, *The Three Days of February, 1848*, p. 190.

65 THE AILING POLITICAL POET, HEINRICH HEINE. Heine quoted by Leslie Bodi, 'Heinrich Heine: The Poet as *frondeur*' in Eugene Kamenka and F. B. Smith (eds), *Intellectuals and Revolution: Socialism and the Experience of 1848* (London, 1979), p. 45.

66 'ON EVERY STREET, ALMOST EVERYWHERE, BARRICADES HAVE BEEN PILED UP'. *The Confession of Mikhail Bakunin* [1851], trans. Robert C. Howes (Ithaca and London, 1977), p. 55.

66 RULING ÉLITES ... COULDN'T RELY UPON URBAN GARRISIONS TO SUPPRESS INSURRECTIONS. Jonathan Sperber, *The European Revolutions, 1848–1851* (Cambridge, 1994), p. 115.

66 ONLY SUCH REFORM AS WAS 'COMPATIBLE WITH THE LIBERTY OF CAPITAL AND THE SECURITY OF PROPERTY'. Quoted in G. Lowes Dickinson, *Revolution and Reaction in Modern France* (London, 1892, 1927), p. 161.

68 'ALL THESE PEOPLE WANT LAW AND ORDER'. Georges Duveau, *1848: The Making of a Revolution*, trans. Anne Carter (London, 1967), p. 185.

69 'AT THAT TIME, THE NATION SAW LEDRU-ROLLIN'. Alexis De Tocqueville, *Recollections*, trans. George Lawrence (New York, 1971), p. 138.

69 'I BELIEVE HE HAS A MIND MORE RICH THAN HIS HEART'. Leo A. Loubere, *Louis Blanc: His Life and Contribution to the Rise of French Jacobin-Socialism* (Westport, Conn., 1961), p. 60.

70 'IT IS THE NATURE OF SUPERIOR STATESMEN TO GIVE AN IMPULSE TO THINGS'. Ibid., pp. 79–80.

71 'IN MY EYES, AND IN THE EYES OF THE MEMBERS OF THE *GOUVERNEMENT PROVISOIRE*'. Alfred Talaudin, J. Domenge, J. Teyre, 'The Murderer Barthélemy', *The Times*, 17 January 1855.

71 BLANC WAS ABLE TO GET BARTHÉLEMY A JOB. 'Ein Kriegsgericht in Paris', *Rheinisches Echo* (Cologne, 1849), p. 85. Alexander Herzen, *My Past and Thoughts*, trans. Constance Garnett (London, 1925, 2008), IV, p. 253.

71 BARTHÉLEMY 'TOOK PART IN ALL THE MOVEMENTS'. Wilhelm Liebknecht, 'Karl Marx: Biographical Memoirs' in *Wilhelm Liebknecht and German Social Democracy: A Documentary History*, ed. William A. Pelz, trans. Erich Hahn (Westport: CT, 1994), p. 106.

71   SOCIALISTS WERE STRONG IN PARIS ... ORGANISING
        ABOUT 100,000 PEOPLE. Peter H. Amann, *Revolution and Mass
        Democracy: The Paris Club of 1848* (Princeton, NJ, 1975), pp. 34–5.

71–2   MOST SIGNIFICANT WAS THE CENTRAL REPUBLICAN
        SOCIETY. Proclamation of the Central Republican Society (March
        1848), in George Woodcock (ed.), *A Hundred Years of Revolution:
        1848 and After* (London, 1948), p. 225.

72   'BEHIND US WE HAVE THE PEOPLE'. Speech of L. A. Blanqui
        to the Central Republican Society on 26 February, in R. W. Postgate,
        Revolution from 1789 to 1906 (New York, 1920, 1962), p. 192.

72   BLANQUI ... DEMANDED COMPLETE FREEDOM OF THE
        PRESS. An address dated 1 March 1848, in Alfred Delvau (ed.), *Les
        murailles révolutionnaires* (two volumes: Paris, 1852), II, pp. 586–7.

73   'THE LIVING BARRICADES OF DEMOCRACY'. A statement
        of '*Le club des travailleurs libres*', 26 March 1848, quoted in Roger
        V. Gould, *Insurgent Identities: Class, Community, and Protest in
        Paris from 1848 to the Commune* (Chicago, 1995), p. 42.

73   ITS PURPOSE WAS TO 'STUDY THE FORMATION OF
        BARRICADES'. Alphonse Lucas, *Les clubs et les clubistes: histoire
        complète critique et anecdotique des clubs et des comités électoraux
        fondés à Paris depuis la révolution de 1848* (Paris, 1851), pp. 47–8.

74   THE GARDES MOBILES ... DRAWN FROM 'THE MOST
        TURBULENT SUPERFLUITY'. Alphonse Lamartine, *History of
        the French Revolution of 1848* (two volumes: Boston, 1849), II, p. 49.

75   'GOOD NIGHT, – AS USUAL, NOT TO SLEEP'. Marc
        Caussidière, *Memoirs of Citizen Caussidière: Ex-prefect of
        Police, and Representative of the People* (two volumes: London,
        1849), II, pp. 50–59, quotes pp. 53, 59.

75–6   'ALAS!' REPLIED SAINT-JUST. Alphonse de Lamartine, *History
        of the Girondists: or, Personal Memoirs of the Patriots of the
        French Revolution* (three volumes: New York, 1849), II, p. 131.

76   THE PRÉFET DE POLICE DESCRIBED BARTHÉLEMY AS
        'EX-FORÇAT'. Adolphe Chenu, *Les chevaliers de la république
        rouge en 1851* (Paris, 1851), p. 138.

76   'BARTHÉLEMY THEN PROPOSED THAT THEY SHOULD
        PLACE IN A HAT'. 'Further Particulars', *Windsor and Eton
        Express*, 30 October 1852.

7 – BLOOD AND SAND IN THE STREETS

78   PEOPLE DID NOT LIKE TO GET WEIGHED. Priscilla
        Robertson, *Revolutions of 1848: A Social History* (Princeton, NJ
        1967), p. 65.

78   WORKER REPRESENTATIVE, MARTIN NADAUD. Gillian
        Tindall, *The Journey of Martin Nadaud: A Life and Turbulent
        Time* (London, 1999), pp. 147–8.

78   IN PARIS ALONE, 300 COOPERATIVE ASSOCIATIONS.
        Starved of aid, markets and government contracts, most subse-
        quently collapsed. John M. Merriman, *The Agony of the Republic:
        The Repression of the Left in Revolutionary France, 1848–1851*
        (New Haven, 1979), pp. 67–8.

79   THEY 'HUMILIATED THE WORKING MAN'. Louis Blanc,
        1848: Historical Revelations Inscribed to Lord Normanby (London,
        1858), pp. 205–6.

79   'A PRAETORIAN ARMY IN WAITING'. Alphonse de Lamartine,
        Histoire de la révolution de 1848 (Paris, 1849), II, p. 120.

79   'THE DEATH SENTENCE OF THE REPUBLIC'. Samuel Bernstein,
        August Blanqui and the Art of Insurrection (London, 1971), p. 150.

79   LEDRU-ROLLIN DISPATCHED COMMISSIONERS AS
        'REPUBLICAN MISSIONARIES'. Robert Gildea, *Children of the
        Revolution: The French, 1799–1914* (London, 2009), p. 55.

80   MARCHERS CALLED FOR THE 'ABOLITION OF THE
        PROLETARIAT'. Marc Caussidière, *Memoirs of Citizen Caussidière:
        Ex-prefect of Police, and Representative of the People* (two volumes:
        London, 1849), II, pp. 23–4.

81   'THE BOURGEOISIE IS DETERMINED TO FINISH WITH
        THE PROLETARIAT'. Louis Antoine Garnier-Pagès, *Histoire de
        la révolution de 1848* (eleven volumes: Paris, 1869), IX, p. 66.

81   WORKERS' UPRISING IN ROUEN ... WAS BLOODILY
        SUPPRESSED. Roger Price, *The French Second Republic: A Social
        History* (London, 1972), p. 143.

81   'A VAST HOTBED OF INSURRECTION'. Ronald Aminzade,
        *Ballots and Barricades: Class Formation and Republican Politics
        in France, 1830–1871* (Princeton, 1993), p. 187.

82   BLANQUI'S PRISON PALLOR ... 'SUNKEN, WITHERED
        CHEEKS'. Alexis de Tocqueville, *Recollections*, trans. George
        Lawrence (New York, 1971), pp. 147–8.

82   DECREES ... FAVOURED DICTATORSHIP OF THE WORKING
        CLASS. Documents prepared for issue in the event of the success
        of the revolt of 15 May, in R. W. Postgate, *Revolution from 1789
        to 1906* (New York, 1920, 1962), p. 208.

83   'MANY OF THEM WERE ... SKILLED CRAFTSMEN'. Gustave
        Flaubert, *A Sentimental Education: The Story of a Young Man*,
        trans. Douglas Parmée (Oxford, 1989), p. 347.

83   'AT ABOUT 9 O'CLOCK THE CROWDS GATHERED AT THE
        BASTILLE'. Ibid., p. 347.

84   ON THE LEFT BANK. *Rapport de la commission d'enquète sur
        l'insurrection qui a éclaté dans la journée du 23 juin et sur les
        évènements du 15 mai 1848* (Paris, 1848), p. 213.

84   COMPOSITION OF JUNE COMBATANTS. Mark Traugott,
        *Armies of the Poor: Determinants of Working-Class Participation
        in the Parisian Insurrection of June 1848* (Princeton, 1985), p. 30.

84–5   ONE CAPTURED REBEL GAVE 'AS THE REASON FOR THE REVOLT THE DESIRE FOR A DEMOCRATIC AND SOCIAL REPUBLIC'. Excerpted in Roger Price (ed.), *1848 in France* (London, 1975), p. 111.

85–6   'THE INSURRECTION OF JUNE 1848'. Emmanuel Barthélemy, 'L'insurrection de Juin au faubourg du Temple', in *Les Veillées du peuple* (March 1850) [reprinted in *Les révolutions du XIXe siècle: 1848, la révolution démocratique et sociale. Tome 2.*], pp. 90–91. For a translation of this document, see CrimethInc. Historical Research Society, *Emmanuel Barthélemy: Proletarian Fighter, Blanquist Conspirator, Survivor of the Galleys, Veteran of the Uprising of 1848, Fugitive, Duelist, Ruffian* (online, n.d. [2016]), pp. 12–21.

87   THE INSURRECTION ERUPTED BECAUSE WORKERS ABANDONED THE BARRICADES, ACCORDING TO BARTHÉLEMY. This was also a conclusion drawn by many insurgents. Georges Bourgin, 'France and the Revolution of 1848' in François Fejtő (ed.), *The Opening of an Era: 1848 – An Historical Symposium* (London, 1948), p. 92.

87   EVERYWHERE HE WENT HE FOUND 'IMPROVISED FORTRESSES'. Emmanuel Barthélemy, 'L'insurrection de Juin au faubourg du Temple', p. 91.

87–8   REBELS BUILT THEIR DEFENCES 'BECAUSE THEY WANTED TO SEND THE WORKERS AWAY FROM PARIS'. Excerpted in Roger Price (ed.), *1848 in France* (London, 1975), p. 110.

88   'I INSPECTED THE FAMOUS BARRICADE'. Leonard de Vries, *Panorama, 1842–1865* (London, 1967), pp. 63–4.

89   IN THE TEMPLE DISTRICT THE ATMOSPHERE WAS MORE SOBER. Fifteen years later, some of these bronze workers were among the pioneers of the International Workingmen's Association, the first transnational socialist organisation with a mass basis. Georges Duveau, *1848: The Making of a Revolution*, trans. Anne Carter (London, 1967), p. 137.

89   THEY WERE THE ÉLITE OF THE JUNE 1848 INSURRECTION. Eric Hazan, *A History of the Barricade*, trans. David Fernbach (London, 2015), p. 88.

89   'YOU COULD SEE IN THE DISTANCE'. Victor Hugo, *Les Misérables*, trans. Christine Donougher (London, 2013, 2016), pp. 1054–5.

90   'THEY WOULD NOT LISTEN TO ME'. Louis Hincker, *Citoyens-combattants à Paris, 1848–1851* (Villeneuve d'Ascq, 2008), p. 154.

91   'THE STREETS OF PARIS HAVE A SINISTER AND DESERT ASPECT'. Anon., *Sanglante Insurrection des 23, 24, 25, 26 Juin, 1848* (Paris, 1848), p. 4.

91–2   BARTHÉLEMY TOOK COMMAND OF 'A LONG, STRAGGLING, MISERABLE STREET'. Quotation, John Frazer

Corkran, *History of the National Constituent Assembly, from May, 1848* (New York, 1849), p. 235.

92   BARTHÉLEMY 'MIRACULOUSLY ESCAPED ARREST'. Emmanuel Barthélemy, 'L'insurrection de Juin au faubourg du Temple', p. 93.

92   'HE HIMSELF SAID THAT HIS INFLUENCE WAS ZERO'. Ibid., p. 93.

93   'HE REPLIED BY GIVING ME A FALSE NAME'. Ibid., p. 94.

93   ALL PRISONERS WERE 'TREATED FRATERNALLY'. Ibid., p. 94.

94   'THE LINE, THE NATIONAL GUARD, AND THE MOBILE'. Percy B. St. John, 'France: The Revolution of June and July' in *Tait's Edinburgh Magazine*, Vol. XV (Edinburgh, 1848), p. 536.

94   'THE WHOLE NEIGHBOURHOOD WAS IN FACT ONE IMMENSE FORTRESS'. William S. Chase, *1848, a Year of Revolutions* (New York, 1850), p. 85.

94–5 'HEROISM ON BOTH SIDES'. Percy B. St. John, 'France: The Revolution of June and July', p. 536.

95   PROUDHON ADMIRED THE 'SUBLIME HORROR' OF THE CANNONADE. C. L. Lesur, *Annuaire historique universel ou histoire politique: 1848* (Paris, 1848), p. 260.

95   RED-HOT BALLS WHISTLED ALL AROUND. 'A Letter from Paris', *Hampshire Chronicle*, 1 July 1848.

96   ARRIVING BACK 'IN THE MIDDLE OF THOSE WHO HAD ABANDONED US'. Emmanuel Barthélemy, 'L'insurrection de Juin au faubourg du Temple', p. 95.

96   'IT WAS PROBABLY THIS THREAT'. Ibid., pp. 95–6.

97   BARTHÉLEMY RESOLVED TO USE EVERY HONOURABLE MEANS. Ibid., p. 96.

97   ARRANGEMENTS TO END THE FIGHTING. Cervelli considers it to be 'hardly credible' that government forces made the first move, but I can see no reason for his incredulity. It would obviously make sense to force a surrender rather than to storm a position. Innocenzo Cervelli, 'Emmanuel Barthélemy, in memoria', *Studi Storici*, Anno 41, No. 2 (Apr.–Jun. 2000), pp. 277–402, 292.

98   'I KNEW FROM THAT MOMENT' WROTE BARTHÉLEMY. Emmanuel Barthélemy, 'L'insurrection de Juin au faubourg du Temple,' p. 97.

98   'THE GENERAL RECEIVED US POLITELY'. A later version has it that the talks broke down when Barthélemy refused to remove his military cap. Innocenzo Cervelli, 'Emmanuel Barthélemy, in memoria', pp. 277–402, 293–4.

98   'WE TOO HAVE WEAPONS'. Emmanuel Barthélemy, 'L'insurrection de Juin au faubourg du Temple', p. 97.

98   THE REBELS BELIEVED THEMSELVES TO BE 'FIGHTING FOR THE WELFARE OF THE WORKING CLASSES'. Frederick

Chamier, *A Review of the French Revolution of 1848* (two volumes: London, 1849), II, pp. 106–10.

99   'THOSE WHO WERE ABOUT TO DIE SALUTED HIM'. Jules Vallès, *Le Cri du peuple* [28 February 1884], ed. Lucien Scheler (Paris, 1970), p. 345.

99   THE GARDE MOBILE COMMANDER BOASTED OF INFLICTING 'CRUEL LOSSES'. Jill Harsin, *Barricades: The War of the Streets in Revolutionary Paris, 1830–1848* (New York, 2002), p. 305.

99   'ALL THESE STORIES OF MEN SAWN IN TWO BY THE INSURGENTS'. Emmanuel Barthélemy, 'L'insurrection de Juin au faubourg du Temple', p. 97. For an example of the propaganda referred to by Barthélemy, see Mike Rapport, *1848: Year of Revolution* (London, 2008), p. 207.

100   'IT IS ALL OVER, GENTLEMEN, THANK GOD!'. Eric Hazan, *The Invention of Paris: A History in Footsteps* (London, 2010), p. 287.

100   'UNHAPPILY, I CALLED TO HIM'. 'Ein Kriegsgericht in Paris', *Rheinisches Echo* (Cologne, 1849), p. 84.

100   'NEVER HAD THE BATTLES OF THE EMPIRE BEEN SO MURDEROUS'. '*Témoin oculaires*', *Journées de juin, 1848* (Paris, 1848), p. 36. Seven generals perished during the June Days, more than had been killed at Waterloo. Henri le Lubac, *The Un-Marxian Socialist: A Study of Proudhon* (London, 1948), p. 11.

100   'FROM THAT DAY FORWARD'. René Arnaud, *The Second Republic and Napoleon III*, trans. E. F. Buckley (London, 1930), p. 29.

101   'WHICH IS BETTER? IT IS HARD TO TELL'. Alexander Herzen, *From the Other Shore* [1855] (London, 1956), pp. 46–9.

8 – ESCAPE INTO A STORM

102   'THE BLOODIEST INSURRECTION THAT PARIS HAD YET EXPERIENCED'. Frederick A. De Luna, *The French Republic under Cavaignac, 1848* (Princeton NJ, 1969), p. 149.

102   11,642 PEOPLE WERE ARRESTED. Pierre Lévêque, 'The Revolutionary Crisis of 1848/51 in France' in Dieter Dowe et al. (eds), *Europe in 1848: Revolution and Reform* (New York and Oxford, 2000), p. 100.

102–3   THE MILITARY PRISON ON THE RUE DU CHERCHE-MIDI IN PARIS. Paul Fromageot, *La rue du Cherche-Midi et ses habitants depuis ses origines jusqu'à nos jours* (Paris, 1915), pp. 517–18. Mrs. William Pitt Byrne, *Red, White, and Blue: Sketches of Military Life* (three volumes: London, 1862), III, p. 151.

103   HIS FIRST CELL WAS 'A KENNEL WITH OOZING WALLS'. C. Lacambre, *Évasion des prisons du Conseil de guerre, épisode de juin 1848* (Brussels, 1865), p. 14.

103 LACAMBRE WANTED THE TRUTH OF THE JUNE DAYS TO BE KNOWN. Maurice Dommanget, 'Blanqui, Historien de la Révolution de 1848', *L'Actualité de l'histoire*, No. 13 (Nov. 1955), pp. 6–25, 7–8.

104 'HIS FACE HAD A NOBLE AND ENERGETIC EXPRESSION'. 'Ein Kriegsgericht in Paris', *Rheinisches Echo* (Cologne, 1849), p. 82.

104 BARTHÉLEMY REFUSED TO BE SILENCED. Ibid., p. 82.

104 BARTHÉLEMY SHOT BACK. 'FORGIVE ME, YOU SPEAK OF MEN OF MY CLASS'. Ibid., p. 83.

105–6 'IT IS MY DUTY TO SAY ALL THAT I KNOW'. Appendix B, 'Extrait de l'audience du 8 janvier 1849 du Conseil de guerre de Paris — Afaire Barthélémy' in Auguste Vermorel, *Les hommes de 1848* (Paris, 1869), p. 413.

106–7 'AN OFFICER WALKING UP AND DOWN'. 'Ein Kriegsgericht in Paris', pp. 84–5. See also Henri d'Alméras, *La vie parisienne sous la République de 1848* (Paris, 1920), p. 479.

107 WHEN 'A WOUNDED MAN FELL INTO THE HANDS OF THE NATIONAL GUARD'. Appendix B, 'Extrait de l'audience du 8 janvier 1849 du Conseil de guerre de Paris. — Afaire Barthélémy', p. 414. Hippolyte Castille, *Les Massacres de Juin, 1848* (Paris, 1868), p. 110.

107 'I CANNOT ALLOW YOU TO CONTINUE IN THIS WAY'. 'Ein Kriegsgericht in Paris', p. 85.

107 BARTHÉLEMY HAD SUCCESSFULLY 'TURNED THE PRISONER'S DOCK INTO A PLATFORM'. Alexander Herzen, *My Past and Thoughts*, trans. Constance Garnett (London, 1925, 2008), IV, p. 253. Hippolyte Castille, *Histoire de la seconde République française* (four volumes: Paris, 1855), Vol. III, pp. 332–3.

107 HE WAS FOUND GUILTY OF 'HAVING TAKEN PART IN AN ARMED STRUGGLE'. Innocenzo Cervelli, 'Emmanuel Barthélemy, in memoria', *Studi Storici*, Anno 41, No. 2 (Apr.–Jun. 2000), pp. 277–402, 277.

107 'I HOPE THAT THIS CONDEMNATION MAY NEVER CAUSE YOU REMORSE'. 'Ein Kriegsgericht in Paris', p. 86.

108 NAPOLEON, 'THE CRETIN'. John Bierman, *Napoleon III and his Carnival Empire* (London, 1988), p. 71.

108 'I FOLLOW ONLY THE PROMPTINGS OF MY MIND'. James F. McMillan, *Napoleon III* (Harlow, 1991), p. 37.

109 LACAMBRE'S PLAN WAS 'SIMPLE BUT RISKY'. C. Lacambre, *Évasion des prisons du Conseil de guerre, épisode de juin 1848* (Brussels, 1865), p. 48.

111 HIS COMMANDER WAS NOT IMPRESSED: 'VILE CREATURE!'. Ibid., p. 72.

111 A VIOLENT STORM 'SMACKED THE SLATES LIKE CASTANETS'. Ibid., p. 71.

III   IT WAS A STORMY NIGHT 'AS BLACK AS THE BACK OF
          AN OVEN'. Ibid., p. 83.

II2   A SENTRY 'WRAPPED IN HIS WINTER COAT'. Ibid., p. 75.

II2   BARTHÉLEMY'S COMRADES HUDDLED IN THE
          'HURRICANE WHIRLING IN FURY'. Ibid., p. 75.

II2-3   'BARTHÉLEMY CONTINUED HIS TIRELESS WORK'. Ibid.,
          p. 82.

II3   'I CAN DO NO MORE'. Ibid., p. 84.

II4   'WE THREW OURSELVES'. Ibid., p. 85.

II4   'ON HIS RETURN, BARTHÉLEMY FOUND ME'. Ibid., p. 87.
          HE FOUND THAT 'THOSE DAMNED ROOFS'. Ibid., p. 88.

II5   'THIS IS THE WAY TO FREEDOM'. Ibid., p. 89.

II5   'WE ARE NOT CRIMINALS', HE WHISPERED. Ibid., p. 90.

II5   THE GLASS FELL INTO A 'THOUSAND PIECES'. Ibid., p. 91.

II5   'WE ARE DEVASTATED'. Ibid., p. 91.

II6   'CITIZEN, I HAVE BEEN FORCED BY NECESSITY'. Ibid.,
          p. 96.

II7   'ON THE SAME THOUGHT, WE STOPPED IN THE MIDDLE
          OF THE PONT DES ARTS'. Ibid., p. 101.

II8   ACCORDING TO THE PRESS, HE HAD BEEN 'JOINED' BY
          LACAMBRE. For example, 'France' in *Evening Mail*, 15 January
          1849.

II8   BARTHÉLEMY'S FLIGHT, ACCOMPLISHED WITH SUCH
          'ADMIRABLE ADROITNESS'. Wilhelm Liebknecht, 'Karl Marx;
          Biographical Memoirs' in *Wilhelm Liebknecht and German Social
          Democracy: A Documentary History*, ed. William A. Pelz, trans.
          Erich Hahn (Westport: CT, 1994), p. 106.

II8   THEY WERE 'JUBILANT' ABOUT THE ESCAPE. C. Lacambre,
          Évasion des prisons du Conseil de guerre, épisode de juin 1848,
          p. 106.

II8   THE VIRTUES OF 'NOBILITY, COURAGE AND
          INTELLIGENCE' HAD PASSED TO THE 'RACE OF
          PROLETARIANS'. Lejeune-Resnick Evelyne, 'Anjou, républican-
          isme et romantisme: les aspirations de Sophie Leroyer' in *Annales
          de Bretagneet des pays de l'Ouest*, Tome 99, numéro 4, 1992, pp.
          415–22, 420.

II8   BLANQUI DEMONSTRATED 'THE SUPERIORITY OF THIS
          ELITE MAN'. *Veillées du Peuple*, in *Les révolutions du XIXe
          siècle: 1848, la révolution démocratique et sociale*. Tome 2 (Paris,
          1984), p. 63.

II8   HIS LAWYER RECEIVED NUMEROUS LETTERS FROM
          'BEAUTIFUL LADIES'. C. Lacambre, *Évasion des prisons du
          Conseil de guerre, épisode de juin 1848*, p. 104.

II9   'I KNOW NOTHING MORE IMPOSING'. Frederick Engels,
          Condition of the Working Class in England [1845], MECW, Vol.
          4, p. 328.

119   HE HAD A RELATIONSHIP WITH MADAME BESSON.
        'Further Particulars', *Windsor and Eton Express*, 30 October 1852.

119   MADAME BESSON MAY HAVE BEEN A SPY. Gustave Lefrançais,
        Souvenirs d'un révolutionnaire: de juin 1848 à la Commune (Paris,
        2013), p. 198.

                    9 – A MANUAL FOR REVOLUTION

120   200,000 COMMUTERS WALKED INTO CENTRAL LONDON
        EVERY DAY. Liza Picard, *Victorian London: The Life of a City,
        1840–1870* (London, 2005), p. 32.

120   'A DISORDERLY CROP OF ... MEAN HOUSES'. Charles
        Dickens, *Dombey and Son* [1848] (Oxford, 1966, 2001), p. 503.

121   'CARRIAGES FLOUNDERING THROUGH POOLS OF SLUSH'.
        Frank E. Huggett, *Victorian England as seen by Punch* (London,
        1978), p. 51.

121   'COMMUNISM IS IN THE POSITION OF AN OUTLAWED
        DOCTRINE.' 'The new political heresy', *Spectator*, Vol. 22, no.
        1107 (28 July 1849), pp. 704–5.

122   SOME CHARTISTS PLANNED BARRICADE INSURRECTION
        IN LONDON. Report by a police spy on a Chartist meeting, 14
        June 1848, in F. C. Mather, *Chartism and Society: An Anthology
        of Documents* (London and New York, 1980), pp. 168–9; Edward
        Royle, *Revolutionary Britannia? Reflections on the Threat of
        Revolution in Britain, 1789–1848* (Manchester, 2000), pp. 123–53,
        quote on p. 135.

122   SPECIAL CONSTABLES. Malcolm Chase, *Chartism: A New
        History* (Manchester, 2007), p. 301.

122   'WE ARE A SERVILE, ARISTOCRACY-LOVING, LORD-
        RIDDEN PEOPLE.' Excerpted in Norman Gash (ed.), *The Age
        of Peel* (London, 1968), p. 179.

122   'HERE IS A COUNTRY, PART AND PARCEL OF ENGLAND'.
        Entry dated 9 February 1849, *The Greville Memoirs, 1814–1860*,
        ed. Christopher Lloyd (London, 1948), p. 186.

122   GLADSTONE ON THE FAMINE. 'Ireland is the minister of God's
        retribution.' Boyd Hilton, 'From Retribution to Reform' in Lesley
        M. Smith, *The Age of Revolution* (Basingstoke, 1987), p. 38.

123   LONDON A STRONGHOLD OF CHARTIST OPINION. David
        Goodway, *London Chartism, 1838–1848* (Cambridge, 1982), p. 225.

123   HAND-LOOM WEAVERS. Alan Ereira, *The People's England*
        (London, 1981), p. 187. Their social ideal had been 'a community
        of independent small producers, exchanging their products without
        the distortions of masters and middlemen'. E.P. Thompson, *The
        Making of the English Working Class* (London, 1965), p. 295. For
        French antecedents: Anonymous [Henry Morley], 'The Quiet Poor',
        Household Words, IX, 15 April 1854, p. 294.

123–4   COMPARATIVE WAGES. *The Family Economist: a Penny Monthly Magazine devoted to the Moral, Physical and Domestic Improvement of the Industrious Classes*, London, Vol. II (1849), p. 40.

124   WORKERS WHO WERE 'TREATED AS BRUTES, ACTUALLY BECOME SUCH'. Frederick Engels, *Condition of the Working Class in England* [1845], *MECW*, Vol. 4, p. 411.

124   'COMPARED TO WORKERS OF OTHER COUNTRIES THE ENGLISH PROLETARIAT IS CLEAR-EYED'. Georg Weerth, *Fragment eines Romans* [1846–47] (Berlin, 2013), pp. 48–9.

125   'INDUSTRY WOULD NOT HAVE MADE HALF THE PROGRESS.' Quoted in Sidney and Beatrice Webb, *Industrial Democracy* (London, 1897, 1901), p. 725.

125   A CITY OF DISTRIBUTION, MANUFACTURING AND SMALL BUSINESSES. See the census digest, *The Family Economist: a Penny Monthly Magazine devoted to the Moral, Physical and Domestic Improvement of the Industrious Classes*, p. 200.

125   NUMEROUS CARRIER PIGEONS. Francis Wey, *A Frenchman Sees the English in the 'Fifties*, ed. Valerie Pirie (London, 1935), p. 87.

125   'AMONG THEM WERE TO BE FOUND THE IRISH FRUITSELLERS'. Henry Mayhew, *Mayhew's London*, ed. Peter Quennell (London, 1949), pp. 29–30.

126   'MAY WE BEG AND BESEECH YOUR PROTECKSHION AND POWER'. David Snodin, *A Mighty Ferment: Britain in the Age of Revolution, 1750–1850* (London, 1978), p. 50.

126   'GREAT BLOCK OF STONE EATEN BY SLUGS'. W. Weir, 'St Giles. Past and Present' [1842], excerpted in Kate Flint (ed.), *The Victorian Novelist: Social Problems and Social Change* (London, 1987), p. 132.

126   'AN EFFORT AT SOCIAL RECONCILIATION'. E. P. Thompson, 'Mayhew and the *Morning Chronicle*' in E. P. Thompson and Eileen Yeo (eds), *The Unknown Mayhew: Selections from the Morning Chronicle, 1849–1850* (London, 1971), p. 22.

126   COST OF LIVING. Patrick Howarth, *The Year is 1851* (London, 1951, 1971), p. 70.

127   'THE EAGER CURIOSITY OF THE PRETTY WOMEN'. Letter from Barthélemy to Auguste Blanqui, 4 July 1850, Blanqui Papers, NAF 9581, fol. 206–7.

127   'THE BRITISH GOVERNMENT HAD ABSOLUTELY NO POWER TO BANISH OR EXCLUDE'. Bernard Porter, *The Refugee Question in Mid-Victorian Politics* (Cambridge, 1979), p. 143.

127   'THE CITY OF BLACK MUD AND SMOKE'. C. Lacambre, *Évasion des prisons du Conseil de guerre, épisode de juin 1848* (Brussels, 1865), pp. 108–9.

127   'THIS DREADFUL ANTHEAP'. Alexander Herzen, *My Past and Thoughts*, trans. Constance Garnett (London, 1925, 2008), IV, p. 142.

128   BARTHÉLEMY SECURED A JOB WITH MR COPTEL. 'Further Particulars', *Windsor and Eton Express*, 30 October 1852.

128   'THE GAIT OF AN ENGLISHWOMAN IS GENERALLY STIFF AND AWKWARD'. Quoted in Liza Picard, *Victorian London: The Life of a City, 1840–1870* (London, 2005), p. 213.

128   BARTHÉLEMY'S 'COUNTENANCE WAS VERY FORBIDDING'. James Stratton, 'The correspondence between the characters and heads of two murderers newly executed at Newgate', *Zoist*, No. L, July 1855, p. 208.

128   'CITIZEN BARTHÉLEMY, *OUVRIER MECANICIEN PROSCRIT*'. 'The Kossuth Mania', *The Times*, 10 November 1851.

129   'A SHORT WHILE AFTER MY ARRIVAL, A PARISIAN LABOURER CAME TO LONDON'. Wilhelm Liebknecht, 'Karl Marx; Biographical Memoirs' in *Wilhelm Liebknecht and German Social Democracy: A Documentary History*, ed. William A. Pelz, trans. Erich Hahn (Westport: CT, 1994), p. 106.

129   LIEBKNECHT'S MEMORY WAS UNCERTAIN. Barthélemy was a skilled worker rather than a labourer. He had first been sent to prison in 1839, not 1838, and he had not actually killed the policeman.

129   'ONE OF THE MOST ELOQUENT ORATORS OF HIS PARTY'. *Repertoire des Connaissances Usuelles*, supplement to *Dictionnaire de la conversation* (Paris, 1871), I, p. 415.

130   'WHOSE HEARTS WERE ON THE LEFT BUT WHOSE POCKETS WERE ON THE RIGHT'. Theodore Zeldin, 'The Myth of Napoleon III', in Eugene C. Black (ed.), *European Political History, 1815–1870: Aspects of Liberalism* (New York, 1967), p. 172.

131   'A FEW CRIES "TO THE BARRICADES!" MET WITH NO RESPONSE.' 'Personal Recollections about Ledru-Rollin', *Frasers Magazine*, Vol. XI, New Series, January/June 1875, p. 247.

131   LEDRU-ROLLIN IN LONDON. Thomas C. Jones, 'French Republican Exiles in Britain, 1848–1870', Cambridge PhD, 2010, pp. 48–50.

132   'CONVICTS OF THE GALLEYS ... MISERABLE BANDITS ... FILTH OF THE SEWERS OF PARIS'. Ledru-Rollin, *De la décadence de l'Angleterre* (Brussells, 1850), p. 3.

132   'ANOTHER REPETITION OF THE LESSON WHICH SAINT-JUST WAS POWERLESS TO TEACH'. 'The Trial at Versailles', in G. Julian Harney (ed.), *The Democratic Review of British and Foreign Politics, History and Literature*, Vol. 1, 1850, p. 269.

132   'JUNE INSURGENT AND COMMANDER OF THE BARRICADES'. 'Report on a banquet of Fraternal Democrats in

London', 23 December 1849', *Der Bund der Kommunisten: Dokumente und Materialien* (Berlin, 1983), Band II, p. 64. 'The French exiles of the 13th of June, at present residing in London, to the Fraternal Democrats of England' published in *Northern Star*, 22 December 1849.

133   'EUROPEAN CENTRAL DEMOCRATIC COMMITTEE'. Kossuth, Ledru-Rollin and Mazzini, *Manifesto of the Republican Party* (London, 1855), p. 10.

133   'NO, NO: THE REPUBLICAN FORM OF GOVERNMENT IS NOT THE OBJECT'. Louis Blanc, *Observations on the Recent Manifesto by Kossuth, Ledru Rollin and Mazzini* (London, 1855), p. 7.

134   BLANC 'THE GREATEST EXPOSITOR OF REPUBLICANISM'. George Jacob Holyoake, *Sixty Years of an Agitator's Life* (two volumes: London, 1892), I, p. 97.

134   'IT WOULD BE DIFFICULT TO DEPICT THE DESTITUTION OF THE PROLETARIAN EMIGRATION' Letter from Barthélemy to Auguste Blanqui, 4 July 1850, Blanqui Papers, NAF 9581, fol. 207.

134   GUSTAVE LEFRANÇAIS SLEEPING OUTDOORS. Fabrice Bensimon, 'The French Exiles and the British' in Sabine Freitag (ed.), *Exiles from European Revolution: Refugees in Mid-Victorian Britain* (New York, Oxford, 2003), p. 89.

134–5   '[FRANCIS GOUJON] WAS A POOR, INDUSTRIOUS MECHANIC'. 'Funeral of a French Refugee', *Illustrated London News*, 3 July 1852.

135   SOCIÉTÉ DE PROSCRITS 'ESSENTIALLY COMMUNIST'. Letter from Vidil to Auguste Blanqui, 19 July 1850, Blanqui Papers, NAF 9581, fol. 214.

135   DIRECTING COMMITTEE OF THE *SOCIÉTÉ DE PROSCRITS*. Georges Bourgin, '*Le procès des communistes allemands a paris en 1852*' in *Revue politique et parlementaire*, no. 238, April 1914, p. 118.

135   ENGELS OFFERS A TOAST 'TO THE INSURRECTION OF JUNE 1848!' Hal Draper, *Karl Marx's Theory of Revolution: Volume 3, The 'Dictatorship of the Proletariat'* (New York, 1986), p. 193.

135   BLANQUIST IDEAS 'LITTLE ESTEEMED' IN LONDON. Letter from Barthélemy to Auguste Blanqui, 4 July 1850, Blanqui Papers, NAF 9581, fol. 209.

135–6   'WHERE IS THE REVOLUTION NOW?' François Pardigon, *Épisodes des journées de juin 1848* (London and Brussels, 1852), pp. 66–7.

136   'THE FORCE OF THE MASSES DRIVEN BY NECESSITY TO HATRED'. August Willich, *Im preuszichen Heere! Ein Disciplinarverfahren* (Mannheim, 1848), p. 38.

137   'AN OLD REVOLUTIONARY RIGHT OF THE PEOPLE'. Marx
       and Engels, 'Freedom of Debate in Berlin', *Neue Rheinische
       Zeitung*, No. 105 [16 September 1848], *MECW*, Vol. 7, p. 437.

137   COMMUNIST LEAGUE'S MARCH CIRCULAR. Karl Marx,
       'Address of the Central Committee to the Communist League,
       London, March 1850', *The Revolutions of 1848*, ed. David Fernbach
       (London, 1973), see particularly p. 325.

137   'LOUIS BLANC OFFERS THE BEST EXAMPLE OF HOW YOU
       FARE'. Marx's gloss on the circular, quoted in Hal Draper, *Karl
       Marx's Theory of Revolution*, vol. II: *The Politics of Social Classes*
       (New York, 1978), p. 605.

137   'NO, TO BAR THE ROAD BEHIND YOU.' Suzanne Wassermann,
       Les clubs de Barbès et de Blanqui en 1848 (Paris, 1913), p. 46.

137   A '*DICTATURE PARISIENNE* SHOULD ASSUME DIRECTION
       OF GOVERNMENT UNTIL THE COUNTRY WAS RIGHT
       FOR DEMOCRACY. Blanqui quoted in Max Beer, *The General
       History of Socialism and Social Struggles* (two volumes: New
       York, 1957), II, p. 198.

138   FOR MARX AND ENGELS, THE PROLETARIAT SHOULD
       SEEK TO 'DICTATE' CONDITIONS. Karl Marx, 'Address of
       the Central Committee to the Communist League, London, March
       1850', *The Revolutions of 1848*, ed. David Fernbach (London, 1973),
       p. 325.

138   SOCIÉTÉ   UNIVERSELLE   DES   COMMUNISTES
       RÉVOLUTIONNAIRES (SUCR) PROGRAMME. *Cahiers du
       communisme*, Volume 8, Issue 1 (1977), p. 451.

138–9 'WITH THE GERMAN COMMUNISTS WE HAVE BEGUN TO
       DRAFT A REVOLUTIONARY MANUAL'. Letter from
       Barthélemy to Auguste Blanqui, 4 July 1850, Blanqui Papers, NAF
       9581, fol. 210.

139   SMUGGLED TO PARIS. Letter from Vidil to Auguste Blanqui,
       19 July 1850, Blanqui Papers, NAF 9581, fol. 217.

139   'FENCING SALON' IN RATHBONE PLACE. Wilhelm
       Liebknecht, 'Karl Marx; Biographical Memoirs' in *Wilhelm
       Liebknecht and German Social Democracy: A Documentary
       History*, p. 107.

139   'BARTHÉLEMY WAS AN INCESSANT CAUSE OF TROUBLE'.
       Maurice Dommanget, *Les idées politiques et sociales d'Auguste
       Blanqui* (Paris, 1957), p. 383.

139   THAT 'TERRIBLE WORD – *MOUCHARD*'. Charles Victor
       Hugo, *Les hommes de l'exil; précédes de Mes fils par Victor Hugo*
       (Paris, 1875), p. 31.

140   'BUT THE DISCUSSIONS HAVING BEEN EXTENDED TO
       FIRST PRINCIPLES; A SPLIT TOOK PLACE'. Letter from
       Barthélemy to Auguste Blanqui, 4 July 1850, Blanqui Papers, NAF
       9581, fol. 207.

140   'RICH FOUNDERS' AND 'POOR MEMBERS'. Ibid., fol. 207–8.

140–1   'HONOURED WILLICH AS THEIR GOD-THE-FATHER'.
           Letter from 'Schily' to Marx, 8 February 1860, in Karl Marx, *Herr
           Vogt* [1860], trans. R. A. Archer (London, 1982), p. 23.

141   'COMMUNISM COULD BE INTRODUCED ONLY AFTER A
           NUMBER OF YEARS'. Christine Lattek, *Revolutionary Refugees:
           German Socialism in Britain, 1840–1860* (London and New York,
           2006), p. 68.

141   'THROUGH THE POWER OF THE GUILLOTINE'. Ibid., p. 76.

141   'BROUGHT FORTH OF A GLOOMY EVENING'. Engels to
           Marx, 23 September 1851, *MECW*, Vol. 38, p. 460.

141–2   BARTHÉLEMY   AND   WILLICH'S   REVOLUTIONARY
           MANUAL. This is substantially reproduced in Ernst Drahn, *Karl
           Marx und Friedrich Engels ueber die Diktatur des Proletariats*
           (Berlin-Wilmersdorf, 1920), pp. 28–34, quotations 28, 29, 33, 30,
           34. See also *Annuaire des deux mondes, 1851–1852* (Paris, 1852),
           pp. 562–4.

142   'ACCRETION OF UN-DERIVED CRAZINESS'. Engels to Marx,
           23 September 1851, *MECW*, Vol. 38, p. 460.

142   'THIS BUSINESS OF THE PARIS DOCUMENT IS QUITE
           STUPID.' Marx to Engels, 23 September 1851, *MECW*, Vol. 38,
           p. 463.

143   'DRIFTED INTO THE COMPANY OF WILLICH AND THERE
           CONTRACTED   A   SPITE   AGAINST   MARX.'   Wilhelm
           Liebknecht, 'Karl Marx; Biographical Memoirs' in *Wilhelm
           Liebknecht and German Social Democracy: A Documentary
           History*, p. 107.

143   GÉROLSTEIN'S 'FEVERISHLY BURNING LUST FOR
           REVENGE'. See S. S. Prawer, *Karl Marx and World Literature*
           (Oxford, 1976), pp. 88–90.

10 – 'SNAKES WITH HUMAN FACES'

144   'THE WORKMAN DOES NOT SING'. Francis Wey, *A Frenchman
           Sees the English in the 'Fifties*, ed. Valerie Pirie (London, 1935),
           p. 5.

144   'PRINCIPLES! WHAT ARE PRINCIPLES?' Louis Blanc, *Letters
           on England*, trans. James Hutton and L. J. Trotter (two volumes:
           London, 1867), II, p. 52.

144   'THE BUSINESS MAN'S POINT OF VIEW IS ALWAYS THE
           ONE FORWARD IN THIS COUNTRY'. Francis Wey, *A
           Frenchman Sees the English in the 'Fifties*, pp. 75, 91.

145   'HARDLY A LESS BEAUTIFUL OBJECT THAN THE ELDERLY
           JOHN BULL'. 'From the English, French and Italian Journals'
           [1853] in William C. Spengemann (ed.), *The Portable Hawthorne*
           (London, 2005), p. 388.

145   WOMEN, TREES AND HORSES WERE 'MARVELLOUSLY
        BEAUTIFUL'. Francis Wey, *A Frenchman Sees the English in the
        'Fifties*, p. 189.

145   THE ENGLISH LOVED ANIMALS. Ibid., p. 232.

145   'UNLESS YOU HAVE SEEN RAGS IN LONDON'. Ibid., p. 106.

145   ENGLISH LIBERTY WAS NO MYTH, AND BRITAIN WAS
        EASILY THE FREEST COUNTRY IN EUROPE. True, free
        England ruled an unfree empire, but most British people paid
        little heed to the colonies, leaving them to members of the upper
        class who almost alone administered and exploited them.
        Bernard Porter, *The Absent-Minded Imperialists: What the
        British Really Thought about Empire* (Oxford, 2004), pp. 38–63
        and passim. For another view, cf. Catherine Hall, *Civilising
        Subjects: Metropole and Colony in the English Imagination,
        1830–1867* (2002). Ireland is too exceptional for easy inclusion in
        the imperial schema.

145   'HE HAS NEVER CHANCED TO GO UP THE STREET, HAT
        IN HAND'. Louis Blanc, *Letters on England*, I, p. 203.

145–6   '*GOD-DAMN!*' 'French notions of English Gentlemen' in *Chester
        Chronicle*, 25 April 1857.

146–7   EARL OF CARDIGAN'S DUEL. Margery Masterson, 'Pistols at
        dawn: duelling in the Victorian age' [2014], *Historyextra* http://
        www.historyextra.com/article/premium/pistols-dawn-duelling-
        victorian-age-guns-fighting.

147   'WILLICH AND HIS COMPANIONS WERE ALREADY AT
        THE SCENE OF THE DUEL'. Karl Marx, *Knight of the Noble
        Consciousness* [1853] in *MECW*, Vol. 12, p. 495.

147–8   '*SCHRAMM A UNE BALLE DANS LA TÊTE*'. Wilhelm
        Liebknecht, 'Reminiscences of Karl Marx' in *Reminiscences of
        Marx and Engels* (Moscow, n.d.), p. 113.

148   'KARL ABOVE ALL WAS PERSECUTED'. Jenny Marx, 'Short
        Sketch of an Eventful Life' [1865] in *Reminiscences of Marx and
        Engels* (Moscow, n.d.), p. 226.

148   LETTER TO 'CITIZENS MARX AND ENGELS'. Hal Draper,
        Karl Marx's Theory of Revolution: Volume 3, *The 'Dictatorship
        of the Proletariat'* (New York, 1986), p. 197.

149   'NAME THE TIME AND PLACE, MESSIEURS!' Ibid., p. 197.

149   'WE HAVE THE HONOUR OF INFORMING YOU'. Ibid.,
        pp. 197–8.

150   MARX 'PRICKLY WITH SOCIAL SUPERIORS, RUTHLESS
        WITH RIVALS, AND KIND TO CHILDREN'. Bertrand Russell,
        Freedom and Organization, 1814–1914 (London, 1934), p. 216.

150–1   MANIFESTO OF THE CENTRAL EUROPEAN DEMOCRATIC
        COMMITTEE, LONDON, 1850. Appendix in W. J. Linton,
        European Republicans: Recollections of Mazzini and his Friends
        (London, 1892), pp. 343–4.

151   'TO THE DEMOCRATS OF ALL NATIONS'. Reproduced in Marx to Engels, 2 December 1850, *MECW*, Vol. 38, pp. 246–7. Christine Lattek, the historian of the socialist emigration in London, convincingly speculates that the manifesto was drafted by Willich and Barthélemy. Lattek, *Revolutionary Refugees: German Socialism in Britain, 1840–1860* (London and New York, 2006), p. 134.

151   'WHAT BLUNT SPEAKING IS'. Engels to Marx, 17 December 1850, *MECW*, Vol. 38, p. 254.

152   'THE PARIS PROLETARIAT WAS *FORCED* INTO THE JUNE INSURRECTION'. Marx, *The Class Struggles in France* [1848–1850], *MECW*, Vol. 10, p. 69.

152   'WILLICH WRITES ME THE FUNNIEST LETTERS'. Karl Marx, *The Cologne Communist Trial* [1853], trans. Rodney Livingstone (London, 1971), p. 112.

153   'MARX SPEAKS LITTLE ENGLISH'. Engels to Ernest Dronke, 9 July 1851, *MECW*, Vol. 38, p. 380.

153   'HE WAS YOUNG, FEARLESS AND SELF-ASSURED'. Samuel Bernstein, *August Blanqui and the Art of Insurrection* (London, 1971), p. 235.

154   'THE MOST MISERABLE PALINODES'. Letter from Barthélemy to Auguste Blanqui, 9 March 1851, Blanqui Papers, NAF 9581, fol. 375.

154   BARTHÉLEMY MEETS LEFT-WING INTELLECTUALS IN PARIS. Christine Lattek, *Revolutionary Refugees: German Socialism in Britain, 1840–1860* (London and New York, 2006), p. 133; Letter from Barthélemy to Auguste Blanqui, 9 March 1851, Blanqui Papers, NAF 9581, fol. 375.

154–6   SCHOELCHER AND BARTHÉLEMY TALK. Juliette Drouet, *Souvenirs, 1843–1854*, ed. Gérard Pouchain (Paris, 2006), pp. 288–90. Drouet, who heard this story from Schoelcher in October 1853, dates the encounter to late 1848, but she must have misheard; Louis Blanc only left for London after the June Days, while Barthélemy was in prison. Evidence suggests that the meeting took place in late 1850 or early 1851. Victor Hugo was also present to hear Schoelcher's tale, and the impressions he received about Barthélemy's appearance informed the portrait he painted in *Les Misérables*. In the novel Barthélemy was depicted as scruffy and scrawny, but these were characteristics adopted by him as part of a disguise.

156   BARBÈS AND HIS FRIENDS REFUSED TO COOPERATE. Alexander Herzen, *My Past and Thoughts*, trans. Constance Garnett (London, 1925, 2008), IV, p. 254.

156   'PÈRE BARTHÉLEMY, BORN FOR THE GALLEYS'. Marx to Engels, 28 October 1852, *MECW*, Vol. 39, p. 224.

157   'STRIKING DOWN' THE 'ARISTOCRACY OF MONEY AND INTELLECT'. *The Friend of the People*, 15 March 1851.

157   MARX AND ENGELS OPPOSED INCOME REWARD FOR TALENT. 'In a society of private producers, private individuals or their families pay the costs of training the qualified worker; hence the higher price paid for qualified labour-power accrues first of all to private individuals ... the skilful wage-earner is paid higher wages. In a socialistically organised society, these costs are borne by society, and to it therefore belong the fruits .... The worker himself has no claim to extra pay.' Frederick Engels, *Anti-Dühring* [1878] (Moscow, 1959), pp. 277–8.

157   'COMBINED WITH THIS "SCUM" TO ARRANGE A BANQUET'. Marx to Hermann Becker, 8 February 1851, *MECW*, Vol. 38, p. 282.

157   'AN EXTREMELY GRANDIOSE EULOGY OF BLANQUI'. Karl Marx, *Heroes of the Exile* [1852] in *MECW*, Vol. 11, p. 295.

158–9   BARTHÉLEMY'S SPEECH. '*Le banquet des égaux. Londres, 24 février 1851* (Paris, n.d.)', in *Les révolutions du XIXe siècle: 1848, la révolution démocratique et sociale*, vol. VI, pp. 17–21.

160   'C'EST UN INFÂME! IL FAUT L'ÉCRASER.' Marx to Engels, 24 February 1851, *MECW*, Vol. 38, p. 298.

160   'COLLARED, AND CUFFED, AND SHOUTED AT'. Brenda Colloms, *Victorian Visionaries* (London, 1982), p. 94.

161   BLANC, WHOSE 'INTENTIONS HAD BEEN FAR BETTER THAN HIS DEEDS'. Samuel Bernstein, *August Blanqui and the Art of Insurrection* (London, 1971), p. 217.

161–2   'SINISTER NAMES, WRITTEN IN LETTERS OF BLOOD'. Auguste Blanqui, '*Avis au peuple (le toast de Londres)*,' *Annuaire historique universel pour 1851* (Paris, 1851), p. 56. See Neil Stewart, *Blanqui* (London, 1939), p. 180.

162   'FOR MY PART, CITIZEN, I DO NOT HESITATE TO TELL YOU'. Letter from Barthélemy to Auguste Blanqui, 9 March 1851, Blanqui Papers, NAF 9581, fol. 374.

163   'UNDOUBTEDLY, WE MUST THREATEN WITH POPULAR JUSTICE'. Ibid., fol. 375.

163   'REPUBLICANS WHOSE CHARACTER RESIDES ONLY IN THEIR BEARDS'. Ibid., fol. 376. It was fashionable for republicans to wear beards.

163   BARTHÉLEMY AS AN 'ENERGETIC REVOLUTIONARY'. Maurice Dommanget, *Auguste Blanqui à Belle-Île* (Paris, 1935), p. 78.

164   YES, THIS UNEXPECTED PUBLICATION IRRITATED ME'. Letter from Auguste Blanqui to Barthélemy, 16 May 1852, Blanqui Papers, NAF 9581, fol. 238.

164   'YOU CAN IMAGINE THE LAMENTATIONS'. Marx to Engels, 8 March 1851, *MECW*, Vol. 38, p. 313.

165   'WE HAVE OFTEN ASKED OURSELVES'. P. Mayer, *La Patrie*, No. 71, 12 March 1851. Marx to Engels, 17 March 1851, *MECW*, Vol. 38, p. 317.

165   30,000 COPIES DISTRIBUTED. Engels to Ernest Dronke, 9 July
       1851, *MECW*, Vol. 38, p. 381.

165   WHISPERING IN FIREPLACE INGLENOOKS. Engels to Marx,
       23 September 1851, *MECW*, Vol. 38, p. 460.

165   'BEWARE OF SNAKES WITH A HUMAN FACE'. Letter from
       Barthélemy to Sophie Blanqui, 26 March 1852, Blanqui Papers,
       NAF 9584–2, fol. 382–3, 386.

II – PLOTTING, TRAGEDY, FARCE

167–8 10 DECEMBER SOCIETY. Maurice Agulhon, *The Republican
       Experiment, 1848–1852*, trans. Janet Lloyd (Cambridge, 1983), p. 128.

168   'THE PRESENT IS NEITHER THE TIME NOR THE PLACE'.
       'M. Kossuth and the French Socialists', *The Times*, 8 November
       1851.

169   POLICE ALSO DESCENDED UPON MADAME ANTOINE.
       *L'Ami de la religion et du roi: journal ecclésiastique, politique et
       littéraire* (Paris, 1851), p. 368; 'Express from Paris', *Evening Mail*,
       14 November 1851.

169–70 THE *COUP D'ÉTAT*. Eugène Ténot, *Paris in December 1851, or
       the Coup d'État of Napoleon III*, trans S. W. Adams and A. H.
       Brandon (London, 1870), pp. 93–106, quotation p. 105.

170   *JEUNE MONTAGNE* GAVE LEADERSHIP. 'Express from Paris',
       Morning Post, 17 November 1851. Noël Blache, *Histoire de
       l'insurrection du Var en décembre 1851* (Paris, 1869), pp. 12–19.

171   IF THEY TRIED TO FIGHT IT WOULD 'BE DOING A CRAZY
       THING'. Victor Hugo, *History of a Crime* [1877], trans.
       Huntingdon Smith (New York, 1888), pp. 151–2.

171   'THERE MUST BE PEOPLE IN THE STREETS'. Ibid., pp. 151–2, 154.

171   'YOU WILL SEE HOW ONE CAN DIE'. Ibid., pp. 151–2, 183.

172   GRAPPLE OVER BAUDIN. Xavier Durrieu, *Le coup d'État de
       Louis Bonaparte: histoire de la persécution de décembre; événe-
       ments, prisons, casemates et pontons* (Brussels, 1852), pp. 80–86.

172   'SHOT DOWN WITHOUT WARNING'. Victor Hugo, *Napoleon
       the Little* [1852] (New York, 1909), p. 129.

173   'THAT BARRICADE AT THE FAUBOURG DU TEMPLE'. Victor
       Hugo, *Les Misérables* [1862], translated by Norman Danny
       (London, 1976), pp. 992–3.

175   RAGS ON FLAGSTAFFS. *Mot d'Ordre*, quoted in *London Evening
       Standard*, 18 November 1879.

175–6 'OH, I'VE HAD MY BELLY FULL OF THAT BUNCH'. Gustave
       Flaubert, *A Sentimental Education: The Story of a Young Man*,
       trans. Douglas Parmée (Oxford, 1989), pp. 401–2.

176   'THE NATURE OF DEMOCRACY IS TO PERSONIFY ITSELF
       IN ONE MAN.' Louis Napoleon Bonaparte, *Des idées napoléo-
       niennes* [1839] (London, 1860), p. 18.

177 SOLIDARITÉ RÉPUBLICAINE. Theodore Zeldin, *France, 1848–1945: Politics and Anger* (Oxford, 1979), p. 364.

177 'WHAT A DEPRESSING EXPERIENCE!' Samuel Bernstein, *August Blanqui and the Art of Insurrection* (London, 1971), p. 231.

177 'WHEN FRANCE FALLS BACK, EUROPE BECOMES LAX.' Ibid., p. 233.

177 'I DON'T DOUBT THAT HAD BLANQUI BEEN ABLE TO JOIN THE ORGANISATION'. Christine Lattek, *Revolutionary Refugees: German Socialism in Britain, 1840–1860* (London and New York, 2006), p. 133.

177–8 'IF I HAD BEEN ABLE TO EXECUTE THE PROJECT I INTENDED'. Letter from Barthélemy to Sophie Blanqui, 26 March 1852, Blanqui Papers, NAF 9584–2, fol. 383–4.

178–9 'BUT THE PEOPLE, THE PEOPLE!' Engels to Marx, 3 December 1851, *MECW*, Vol. 38, pp. 503–5.

180 'THE FIRST TIME AS TRAGEDY, THE SECOND TIME AS FARCE'. Karl Marx, *The Eighteenth Brumaire of Louis Bonaparte* [1852] in *MECW*, Vol. 11, p. 103.

180 FOR MARX, JACOBIN POLITICS WAS EXHAUSTED. See Margaret A. Rose, *Reading the Young Marx and Engels: Poetry, Parody and the Censor* (London, 1978), pp. 131–2.

181 GENERAL MAGNAN 'RESOLVED TO LEAVE THE INSURRECTION TO ITSELF FOR SOME TIME'. 'Report from the Commander-in-Chief of the Army of Paris' [9 December 1851] in A. La Guéronnière, *Napoleon the Third*, trans. Charles Gilliess (London, 1853), pp. 164–72, quotations 165–6, 168.

181–2 BARTHÉLEMY AND VASSEL ESCAPE. *Le journal d'Adèle Hugo*, ed. Frances Vernor Guille (four volumes: Paris, 1968), II, p. 332; Charles Victor Hugo, *Les hommes de l'exil; précédes de Mes fils par Victor Hugo* (Paris, 1875), p. 34. Adèle Hugo gives the name 'Venel'. I have assumed that this is the same man as 'Vassel', and have combined both mother and son accounts.

182 VASSEL RECAPTURED. 'The Trial for Conspiracy in France', *Spectator*, 19 July 1862, p. 799.

182 FÉLIX PYAT IN SWITZERLAND. William James Linton, *Memories* (London, 1895), p. 121.

182 BARTHÉLEMY'S PRACTISE FIRING. *Le journal d'Adèle Hugo*, II, p. 333.

182–3 BARTHÉLEMY'S GUN DESIGN. Alexander Herzen, *My Past and Thoughts*, trans. Constance Garnett (London, 1925, 2008), IV, p. 254.

183 'UNABLE TO RESIGN HIMSELF TO ALLOWING LOUIS NAPOLEON TO ENJOY HIS TRIUMPH IN PEACE'. A letter from Barthélemy intercepted and partly copied by the Marx party. Marx to Engels, 28 September 1852, *MECW*, Vol. 39, p. 199.

183   'SINISTER BARTHÉLEMY'. Engels to Marx, 6 July 1852, *MECW*, Vol. 39, p. 128.

183   'YOU CANNOT BELIEVE WHAT SORROW I FEEL'. Letter from Barthélemy to Sophie Blanqui, 17 September 1852, Blanqui Papers, NAF 9584–2, fol. 388.

183   'THE EVENTS OF DECEMBER HAVE HAD TO MODIFY A LITTLE THE ANTIPATHIES OF CERTAIN MEN'. Ibid., fol. 388.

183   BARTHÉLEMY'S 'BELOVED MARIA'. Letter from Barthélemy to Sophie Blanqui, 26 March 1852, Blanqui Papers, NAF 9584–2, fol. 385; Alexander Herzen, *My Past and Thoughts*, trans. Constance Garnett (London, 1925, 2008), IV, p. 256.

184   'WHAT A PITY THAT THIS MOST SOCIALIST OF SOCIALISTS'. Alexander Herzen, *My Past and Thoughts*, IV, p. 256.

184   BARTHÉLEMY'S MISTRESS A POLICE AGENT? 'The Warren Street murderer', *Sheffield and Rotherham Independent*, 13 January 1855.

12 – BARTHÉLEMY AND COURNET

185   'SO RIGID AND INTOLERANT AS TO BE INCONCEIVABLE'. Francis Wey, *A Frenchman Sees the English in the 'Fifties*, ed. Valerie Pirie (London, 1935), p. 43.

185   'I KNEW ENGLISH MEN WERE AVERSE TO KISSING'. Ibid., p. 280.

185   'SAUNTER AROUND FOR SEVEN CONTINUOUS HOURS'. Schurz quoted in Rosemary Ashton, *Little Germany: Exile and Asylum in Victorian Britain* (Oxford, 1986), p. 154.

186   'A COMMUNISTIC PEASANTRY STILL SLUMBERING'. Alexander Herzen, *My Past and Thoughts*, trans. Constance Garnett (London, 1925, 2008), IV, p. 244.

187   'HERZEN KEPT OPEN HOUSE'. E. H. Carr, *The Romantic Exiles: A Nineteenth-Century Portrait Gallery* (London, 1933, 1968), p. 123.

187   'GREAT SYMPATHY AND CONFIDENCE'. Alexander Herzen, *My Past and Thoughts*, IV, p. 271.

187   'CONTINUAL CONFLICT HAD AROUSED IN HIM AN INFLEXIBLE WILL'. Ibid., IV, p. 250.

188   'IN HIM I SAW FACE-TO-FACE'. Ibid., IV, p.251.

188   'BARTHÉLEMY'S ONE-SIDED LOGIC'. Ibid., IV, p. 251.

188   'BROUGHT UP IN THE STIFLING FOUNDRIES'. Ibid., IV, p. 252.

189   'THE KEEN, PASSIONATE BUT EXTREMELY COMPOSED FACE'. Ibid., IV, p. 251.

189–90 'I WAS SO TAKEN BY MY ACQUAINTANCE WITH THIS MAN'. Monte Gardiner, 'Malwida von Meysenbug's "Memoirs of an Idealist", translation of *Memoiren Einer Idealistin*', Thesis (MA), Brigham Young University Dept of Germanic and Slavic Languages, 1999, p. 212.

191–2 'WE SAW BEFORE US, THEREFORE, ONE OF THOSE FANATICS.' Carl Schurz, *The Reminiscences of Carl Schurz* (two volumes, New York, 1907, 1913), I, p. 393.

192 WILLICH, THE BRAGGADOCIO SOLDIER. Christine Lattek, *Revolutionary Refugees: German Socialism in Britain, 1840–1860* (London and New York, 2006), p. 152.

193 'ABOVE ALL THE PETTY CONSIDERATIONS'. Monte Gardiner, 'Malwida von Meysenbug's "Memoirs of an Idealist"', p. 229.

193–4 FRÉDÉRIC COURNET'S CAREER. *La Presse*, 28 September 1852; *Carlisle Journal*, 29 October 1852.

194–5 'INFLICTING VOLUNTARY WOUNDS'. *Gazette des Tribunes*, cited in 'Further Particulars', *Windsor and Eton Express*, 30 October 1852.

195 'THE STRANGERS, THEY SAY, ARE CERTAIN TO BEGIN A REVOLUTION'. J. R. C. Yglesias, *London Life and the Great Exhibition, 1851* (London, 1964), p. 25.

195 'ALL, HOWEVER, WERE RESPECTABLE AND DECENT PEOPLE.' Quoted in J. B. Priestley, *Victoria's Heyday* (London, 1972), p. 78.

195 'BARTHÉLEMY WAS A DISREPUTABLE CHARACTER'. 'The Fatal Duel near Windsor', *Examiner*, 30 October 1852; De Bussy, *Les conspirateurs en Angleterre, 1848–1858* (Paris, 1858), p. 132.

195 ACCUSED BARTHÉLEMY OF PIMPING HIS LOVER. After the duel there were also rumours spread that Cournet had believed Barthélemy to be a police spy. But if this was the case, he would hardly have made contact at all, never mind passed on sensitive information.

195–6 ARTHUR REEVES. Letter from Arthur R. Reeves, A. B., *Morning Advertiser*, 27 October 1852.

196 A '*RANCUNE* GRUDGE'. 'The late French duel', letter from Arthur R. Reeves, A. B., *Morning Advertiser*, 23 October 1852.

196 'WHAT THE FRENCH CALL A *BROUILLE*'. 'The late French duel,' *Morning Advertiser*, 22 October 1852.

196 COURNET CONTINUED TO SPEAK ILL OF BARTHÉLEMY. Alvin R. Calman, *Ledru-Rollin après 1848 et les proscrits français en Angleterre* (Paris, 1921), p. 138.

196 BARTHÉLEMY ISSUED A CHALLENGE. Lorenzo Sabine, *Notes on Duels and Duelling* (Boston, 1855), pp. 133–4.

196–7 COURNET ARRIVES IN ENGLAND. Charles Victor Hugo, *Les hommes de l'exil; précédes de Mes fils par Victor Hugo* (Paris, 1875), pp. 19–20.

197 'HIS VIOLENT AND QUARRELSOME DISPOSITION'. 'The fatal duel near Windsor', *Examiner*, 30 October 1852.

197 COURNET WAS A 'QUARRELSOME CHARACTER'. Gustave Lefrançais, *Souvenirs d'un révolutionnaire. De juin 1848 à la Commune* (Paris, 2013), p. 200.

197 'A KILLER, TALL, STRONG, SOLID'. *Le journal d'Adèle Hugo*, ed. Frances Vernor Guille (four volumes: Paris, 1968), II, p. 332.

197 RUMOURS SPREAD THAT COURNET WAS A BONAPARTIST SPY. 'The fatal duel near Windsor', *Windsor and Eton Express*, 13 November 1852. 'Confession of the murderer Barthélemy', *Reynolds Newspaper*, 20 January 1855.

198 'ACTED SAVAGELY WITH ALMOST EVERYONE'. 'The late French duel', *Morning Advertiser*, 22 October 1852.

198 'HE CALLED OUT TWO OR THREE OF HIS DEFAMERS'. 'The fatal duel near Windsor', *Windsor and Eton Express*, 13 November 1852.

198 COUTURAT UNABLE TO DEFEND HIMSELF. Gustave Lefrançais, *Souvenirs d'un révolutionnaire. De juin 1848 à la Commune* (Paris, 2013), p. 200.

198 'COURNET WAS ONE OF THAT SPECIAL CLASS'. Alexander Herzen, *My Past and Thoughts*, IV, pp. 254–55.

199 'COULD NOT BE CONSIDERED A RATIONAL MAN'. Ibid., IV, pp. 254, 255.

199 'FEW PERSONS IN ENGLAND KNOW HOW TO MAKE GOOD COFFEE'. Liza Picard, *Victorian London: The Life of a City, 1840–1870* (London, 2005), p. 193.

200 'HARBOURING SODOMITES'. Matt Houlbrook, *Queer London: Perils and Pleasures in the Sexual Metropolis, 1918–1957* (Chicago, 2005), p. 79.

200 'I DON'T FEAR THE FIRST COMER.' 'The duel near Windsor – suspected murder', *Daily News*, 27 October 1852.

200 WILLICH DELIVERS THE LETTER TO COURNET. 'The fatal duel near Windsor', *Examiner*, 30 October 1852.

201 WILLICH TELLS HERZEN OF HIS ENCOUNTER WITH COURNET. Alexander Herzen, *My Past and Thoughts*, IV, p. 257–58.

201 'TRIBUNAL OF HONOUR'. 'The late French duel', letter from Arthur R. Reeves, A.B., *Morning Advertiser*, 23 October 1852; Alvin R. Calman, *Ledru-Rollin après 1848 et les proscrits français en Angleterre* (Paris, 1921), p. 139.

202 'AVOIDING ALL STRONG LANGUAGE'. Andrew Steinmetz, *The Romance of Duelling in All Times and Countries* (two volumes: London, 1868), I, p. 95.

202 BURST COURNET'S BELLY. 'The Fatal Duel Near Windsor', *Morning Chronicle*, 27 October 1852.

202 FIXED PROCEDURE IN FRENCH DUELLING. 'The duel near Windsor – suspected murder', *Daily News*, 27 October 1852; V. G. Kiernan, *The Duel in European History: Honour and the Reign of Aristocracy* (Oxford, 1988), pp. 143, 146–8.

203 'THE COWARD WOULD NOT ACCEPT ME'. 'The duel near Windsor – suspected murder', *Daily News*, 27 October 1852. 'Further Particulars', *Windsor and Eton Express*, 30 October 1852.

203 DUELLING PROTOCOL. 'The fatal duel near Windsor', *Examiner*, 30 October 1852.

204 MADEMOISELLE GOLDSMITH TALKS WITH MAZZINI. *Le journal d'Adèle Hugo*, ed. Frances Vernor Guille (four volumes: Paris, 1968), II, pp. 334–5.

205 'SINISTER, BUT A MAN OF CONVICTION'. Charles Victor Hugo, *Les hommes de l'exil; précédes de mes fils par Victor Hugo* (Paris, 1875), p. 33.

205 'IN FRANCE WE FIRST LOOK FOR MATERIAL CLUES'. Jean Belin, *My Work at the Sûreté*, trans. Eric Whelpton (London, 1950), p. 170.

206 'SURROUNDED BY SPIES, WHO COMPLETELY BEFOOLED HIM'. John Ludlow, *The Autobiography of a Christian Socialist*, ed. A. D. Murray (London, 1981), p. 178.

13 – THE LAST DUEL

207 'MONEY IS THE SUPREME GOOD'. Marx, *Economic and Philosophic Manuscripts* [1844], *MECW*, Vol. 3 p. 324.

207–8 DUELLING EFFECTIVELY BANNED IN THE ARMY. Richard Hopton, *Pistols at Dawn: A History of Duelling* (London, 2007), pp. 27, 41.

208 'TO PROVE THE ABSURDITY OF THE DUEL IS NOT WORTH WHILE'. Alexander Herzen, *My Past and Thoughts*, trans. Constance Garnett (London, 1925, 2008), IV, p. 78.

208 'WEARS HIS HAIR TURNED BACK OFF HIS FACE'. 'The fatal duel near Windsor', *The Times*, 28 October 1852.

208–9 THOUGH MUTILATED, PARDIGON HAD SURVIVED. Alexander Herzen, *My Past and Thoughts*, IV, pp. 265–66.

210 'THEY BLEW DOWN THE MUZZLES OF THE PISTOLS'. 'The fatal duel near Windsor – final examination, and committal of the prisoners', *Morning Post*, 30 October 1852; 'The fatal duel near Windsor', *Examiner*, 30 October 1852.

210 'A STRANGE MASS OF UGLINESS IN ITS PRESENT FORM'. Charles Knight, *Knight's Cyclopaedia of London* (London, 1851), p. 854.

210 THE LONDONER 'NEVER IN ANY CASE KNOWS HOW TO FORM A QUEUE'. Alexander Herzen, *My Past and Thoughts*, IV, p. 263. As English sensibilities may be shocked, I had better include a second reference. Wey witnessed theatre-goers waiting for entry 'when a sudden movement of oscillation in the ranks was immediately followed by a hail of blows, elbow play and general scramble, irrespective of the age or sex of the

victims. This is the mode of entrance to a theatre generally practised by the natives of this island!' Francis Wey, *A Frenchman Sees the English in the 'Fifties*, ed. Valerie Pirie (London, 1935), p. 112.

210–11   *'JE NE SUIS PAS AGITÉ'*. 'The late duel near Windsor', *Morning Chronicle*, 22 October 1852.

211   'THAT SCOUNDREL BARTHÉLEMY, I'LL DO HIM IN.' *Le journal d'Adèle Hugo*, ed. Frances Vernor Guille (four volumes: Paris, 1968), III, p. 336.

211   FARQUHARSON WAS INDIGNANT. 'The late duel near Windsor', *Morning Chronicle*, 22 October 1852.

212   HERZEN THOUGHT THIS A PECULIAR PLACE FOR A DUEL. Alexander Herzen, *My Past and Thoughts*, IV, p. 260.

212–13   'LIKE BROTHER LINKED TO BROTHER'. Aleksandr Pushkin, *Eugene Onegin* [1833], trans. C. H. Johnston (London, 1977), p. 153.

213   'WELL, SIR, DO YOU INTEND TO REMAIN YONDER?' *Windsor and Eton Express*, 13 November 1852.

213   'THERE IS STILL TIME, MONSIEUR, FOR YOU TO RETRACT.' Beaumont School, *The History of St. Stanislaus' College, Beaumont: A Record of Fifty Years, 1861–1911* (Windsor, 1911), pp. 155–6.

213   'YOU CALL YOURSELF A GENTLEMAN'. *Windsor and Eton Express*, 13 November 1852.

213   'THE TRUE STYLE OF FRENCH RODOMONTADE'. 'The fatal duel near Windsor', *Examiner*, 30 October 1852.

214   'SACREBLEU! SIR, YOU LAUGH AT ME?' 'The fatal duel at Egham', *Manchester Times*, 27 October 1852. 'The fatal duel near Windsor', *Examiner*, 30 October 1852. 'The duellist murder at Egham', *Hampshire Advertiser and Salisbury Guardian*, 30 October 1852. Charles Victor Hugo, *Les hommes de l'exil; précédes de mes fils par Victor Hugo* (Paris, 1875), p. 37. Gustave Lefrançais, *Souvenirs d'un révolutionnaire. De juin 1848 à la Commune* (Paris, 2013), p. 199.

214   'AWAY WITH YOU, WRETCH!' *Windsor and Eton Express*, 13 November 1852.

214–15   'ONE OF THEM ASKED ME FOR THE ROAD TO WINDSOR' ... BARRONET TOLD DR HAYWOOD THAT HIS FRIEND. 'The late duel near Windsor', *Morning Chronicle*, 22 October 1852.

215   'IN GREAT DISTRESS OF MIND'. 'Assize intelligence', *Morning Post*, 22 March 1853.

215   'VOTRE AMI EST FOUT'. *Le journal d'Adèle Hugo*, ed. Frances Vernor Guille, III, p. 337.

216   'YOU WANT TO GO, THEN GO!' Veron was later taken into custody by the police as a suspect, but was quickly cleared. It seems certain that Veron had been the doctor at hand, no doubt

much closer than London, but that the English doctor and others covered up for him; Lefrançais gives him another, Italian name, but from the description it is Louis Veron: more a music critic than a medical doctor. Veron himself had fought a duel. *Le journal d'Adèle Hugo*, ed. Frances Vernor Guille, III, p. 337; Gustave Lefrançais, *Souvenirs d'un révolutionnaire. De juin 1848 à la Commune* (Paris, 2013), p. 199; William M. Reddy, *The Invisible Code: Honor and Sentiment in Postrevolutionary France, 1814–1848* (Berkeley and Los Angeles, 1997), p. 236.

216 'HE WAS SENSIBLE AT THE TIME I LEFT HIM.' 'The late duel near Windsor', *Morning Chronicle*, 22 October 1852.

216 'THEIR TROUSERS WERE COVERED WITH DIRT'. Ibid.

216 'A CLOAK UNDER HIS ARM'. Ibid.

217 IN HIS LAST EXTREMITIES OF PAIN. *Le journal d'Adèle Hugo*, ed. Frances Vernor Guille, III, p. 338.

217 'STRANGELY SHAPED CLASP KNIFE'. Beaumont School, *The History of St. Stanislaus' College, Beaumont: A Record of Fifty Years, 1861–1911* (Windsor, 1911), p. 158.

218 'HUMAN EXPERIENCES SIMULTANEOUS FOR THE FIRST TIME'. 'The First Word to Cross the Ocean', in Stefan Zweig, *Decisive Moments in History*, trans. Lowell A. Bangerter (Riverside: Cal., 1999), p. 156.

218 'I RECEIVED INTELLIGENCE FROM THE ELECTRIC TELEGRAPH'. 'The late duel near Windsor', *Morning Chronicle*, 22 October 1852.

218–19 'I'LL GIVE YOU A SOVEREIGN'. Ibid.

219 WILLICH TELLS HERZEN ABOUT THE DUEL. Alexander Herzen, *My Past and Thoughts*, trans. Constance Garnett, IV, p. 258.

219–20 UNDERWOOD SEARCHES AND INCARCERATES PRISONERS. 'The late duel near Windsor', *Morning Chronicle*, 22 October 1852.

220 'CONSTABLES DO NOT CARRY STAFFS NOR ENGLISH MEN SAY "GODDAM!"' Alexander Herzen, *My Past and Thoughts*, trans. Constance Garnett, IV, p. 261.

220 'THE RAG RENDERED IT NEXT TO AN IMPOSSIBILITY THAT THE POWDER SHOULD EXPLODE.' 'The duel near Windsor – suspected murder', *Daily News*, 27 October 1852.

220 RAG COULD NOT HAVE BEEN LEFT IN GUN ACCIDENTALLY. 'The fatal duel near Windsor', *Examiner*, 30 October 1852.

220 BRISSON ESCAPES TO BELGIUM. Alexander Herzen, *My Past and Thoughts*, trans. Constance Garnett, IV, p. 260.

220 POLICE REFUSE TO ACCUSE WITHOUT PROOF. Ibid., IV, p. 261.

220–1 LOUIS BLANC SECURED GOOD LAWYERS FOR BARTHÉLEMY AND DE MORNEY. Ibid., IV, p. 258.

221   'A YOUNG ENGLISH RADICAL WITH HIS HAIR DONE À LA JESUS'. Ibid., IV, p. 259.

221   MAZZINI AND LEDRU-ROLLIN PAID FOR ALLAIN AND BARRONET'S TRIAL DEFENCE. Innocenzo Cervelli, 'Emmanuel Barthélemy, in memoria', *Studi Storici*, Anno 41, No. 2 (Apr.–Jun. 2000), pp. 277–402, 390.

221   'ALMOST AS FINE AND STOUT AS YOU'. 'The Fatal Duel Near Windsor', *The Times*, 22 October 1852.

222   'STRIKING PROOF OF THE ALL-PERVADING INTEREST'. 'Further Particulars', *Windsor and Eton Express*, 30 October 1852.

222   'A REPORT WHICH, BESIDES BEING UNTRUE'. 'The late duel near Windsor', *Morning Chronicle*, 22 October 1852.

222   'A THING I CANNOT STATE'. Ibid.

222–3 'WHATEVER MAY BE THE CONSEQUENCES OF THE SEVERITY OF THE ENGLISH LAW'. 'The fatal duel at Egham', *Manchester Times*, 27 October 1852.

223   'IT IS TRULY TO BE REGRETTED THAT A CERTAIN CLASS OF EXALTED AND MISGUIDED MEN'. 'The late fatal duel near Windsor', *Morning Post*, 22 October 1852.

224   'IN THE EYES OF THE LAW ALL WERE EQUALLY GUILTY'. 'The fatal duel near Windsor', *Morning Post*, 27 October 1852; 'Assize intelligence', *Morning Post*, 22 March 1853.

14 – A BITTER MASQUERADE

225   'CIVIC' RATHER THAN RELIGIOUS FUNERALS. Hugh McLeod, *Secularization in Western Europe, 1848–1914* (Basingstoke, 2000), pp. 42–3.

225   'ALL SORTS OF COSTUME AND EVERY VARIETY OF BEARD'. 'The Fatal Duel Near Windsor', *Windsor and Eton Express*, 30 October 1852.

226   COURNET'S GHOST. Beaumont School, *The History of St. Stanislaus' College, Beaumont: A Record of Fifty Years, 1861–1911* (Windsor, 1911), pp. 163–6.

226   A ROYAL COACH AT COURNET'S FUNERAL. Beaumont School, *The History of St. Stanislaus' College, Beaumont*, p. 159.

226–7 'COURNET WAS A GREAT AND COURAGEOUS CITIZEN'. 'The fatal duel at Egham', *Manchester Times*, 27 October 1852.

227   ONLY ONE NAME ON THE LIPS OF THE GATHERING. *Morning Advertiser*, 25 October 1852.

227   COURNET LIES IN EGHAM CHURCHYARD. Beaumont School, *The History of St. Stanislaus' College, Beaumont*, pp. 160–61.

227–8 'I WILL ADD ONLY A FEW WORDS. COURNET IS DEAD'. 'The fatal duel near Windsor', *Windsor and Eton Express*, 13 November 1852.

228   'IT IS TRUE THAT SOME OF THE PERSONS ARE PERSONAL FRIENDS OF MINE'. Louis Blanc, 'To the Editor of *The Times*', *The Times*, 25 October 1852.

228   MR PARRY ENGAGED ON BEHALF OF BARRONET AND ALLAIN. A letter from the Clerk of the Petty Sessions at Chesney to the Home Secretary, 27 January 1853, National Archives, HO 45/4762.

228–9   'BARTHÉLEMY, WHO SPEAKS ENGLISH VERY WELL, IMMEDIATELY SAW THE FORCE OF THE ADMISSION'. 'Further Particulars', *Windsor and Eton Express*, 30 October 1852.

229   DESCRIPTION OF SIXMILEBRIDGE. T. W. Freeman, *Pre-Famine Ireland: A Study in Historical Geography* (Manchester, 1957), pp. 87, 217–18.

229   'ALTHOUGH I AM NOT EASILY MOVED, I CONFESS MYSELF UNMANNED'. David P. Nally, *Human Encumbrances: Political Violence and the Great Irish Famine* (Notre Dame, IN, 2011), pp. 141–2.

230   THE LAST STARVATION VICTIM. Ciarán Ó Murchadha, *The Great Famine: Ireland's Agony 1845–1852* (London, 2011), pp. 173–8.

230–1   SIXMILEBRIDGE AFFRAY. Patrick White, *History of Clare and the Dalcassian clans of Tipperary, Limerick, and Galway* (Dublin, 1893), p. 367. 'Slaughter of Unoffending Men at Six Mile Bridge', *Freeman's Journal*, 24 July 1852; 'People Killed at Six-Mile Bridge', *Dublin Evening Packet and Correspondent*, 4 November 1852; 'The Six-Mile-Bridge Tragedy' and 'The Affray with the Military at Six-Mile-Bridge: verdict of "wilful" murder', *Anglo-Celt*, 5 August 1852; 'The Homicides at Six Mile Bridge', *Dublin Evening Post*, 26 August 1852; 'The Six-Mile-Bridge affray', *Examiner*, 28 August 1852; 'The Six-Mile Bridge affray', *Waterford Mail*, 26 February 1853; 'The attack on Soldiers at Six Mile Bridge', *Dublin Evening Mail*, 18 July 1853.

232–3   'ABOUT 10 O'CLOCK THE FIRST MASQUERADERS, HERALDS WITH TWO TRUMPETERS, APPEARED'. Alexander Herzen, *My Past and Thoughts*, trans. Constance Garnett (London, 1925, 2008), IV, pp. 262–3.

233   'THE LAW, NO DOUBT, WAS THAT DUELLING WAS A CRIME'. *Crown Cases Reserved for Consideration* (London, 1853), p. 55.

233   'IN ACCORDANCE WITH THE FEELINGS OF THE CLASS OF SOCIETY TO WHICH THEY BELONGED'. Ibid., p. 56.

234   'I TRUST THAT THE TIME WILL SOON ARRIVE WHEN DUELLING WILL BE CONSIDERED NOT ONLY AS ILLEGAL, BUT AS ABSURD.' Ibid., p. 63. 'Law intelligence', *Reynolds Newspaper*, 20 November 1852.

234   'GOD GRANT THEM A GOOD DELIVERANCE!' *Crown Cases Reserved for Consideration* (London, 1853), p. 63.

234   'I CONFESS I DO NOT SEE HOW SUCH A MAN IN GOING INTO THE FIELD OF HONOUR'. *Life of Lord Chancellor Campbell*, ed. Hon. Mrs Campbell (two volumes; London, 1881), II, p. 140.

235   SIR JOHN F. FITZGERALD WAS SCATHING. *HC Deb*, 16 November 1852, vol. 123, cc. 201–5.

235   'EVEN THE LONGEST LANE HAS A TURNING'. *HC Deb*, 15 July 1853, vol. 129, cc. 292–306.

235   'SIXMILEBRIDGE ASSASSINS'. J. Redding Ware, *The Victorian Dictionary of Slang and Phrase* (new edition of *Passing English of the Victorian Era: a Dictionary of Heterodox English, Slang, and the Phrase*, 1909) (Oxford, 2013), p. 225. It is not likely to be a coincidence that Sixmilebridge was a hotspot in the twentieth-century War of Independence. The RIC, buttressed by British Black and Tans, suffered a significant loss nearby when they met a substantial IRA ambush party in 1921. Michael Hopkinson, *The Irish War of Independence* (Dublin, 2004), p. 131.

236   'AS A SAILOR, HE DID NOT WANT OF A CERTAIN DEGREE OF RESOLUTION'. 'The Late Fatal Duel Between Frenchmen', *Reynold's Newspaper*, 30 January 1853.

236   BAUDIN'S LETTER COULD BE 'SEEN BY THOSE WHO FEEL INTERESTED IN THE MATTER'. *Reynold's Newspaper*, 6 February 1853.

237–8 'KILLING IN A DUEL HAD NEVER BEEN LOOKED UPON AS AN ORDINARY MURDER'. 'Assize intelligence', *Morning Post*, 22 March 1853.

238   'THE OPINION OF BARTHÉLEMY'S CASE FORMED BY THE JUDGE'. Alexander Herzen, *My Past and Thoughts*, IV, p. 264.

239   JUDGE WAS SILENTLY LAUGHING. Ibid., IV, p. 267–9.

239   'THE LAW WAS THIS'. 'Assize intelligence', *Morning Post*, 22 March 1853.

239–40 'THAT PARDIGON HAS GOT OFF CLEAR'. Alexander Herzen, *My Past and Thoughts*, IV, p. 270.

240   'THE DUEL WAS CONDUCTED IN GOOD FAITH AND IN ALL HONOUR.' The Attorney for Mm. Barthélemy and Morney, 'The Egham Duel', *The Times*, 24 March 1853.

240   'HE WOULD REGALE BARTHÉLEMY WITH A STICK'. Marx to Engels, 22–23 March 1853; Marx to Adolph Cluss, 25 March 1853, *MECW*, Vol. 39, pp. 296, 299–300.

241   'DO YOU THINK A MISERABLE MAN LIKE BARTHÉLEMY CAN KILL ME?' *Le journal d'Adèle Hugo*, ed. Frances Vernor Guille (four volumes: Paris, 1968), III, p. 334.

242   'THE OBJECT OF THE DUEL IS NOT MURDER.' G. J. H., 'The duel between Cournet and Barthélemy', *The Reasoner: Gazette of secularism*, 4 March 1855, p. 129; Alexander Herzen, *My Past and Thoughts*, IV, p. 271.

242–3   'STERN TRANQUILLITY' OF ENGLISH LAW. Herzen to Carl Vogt, 24 March 1853, in Marc Vuilleumier, Michel Aucouturier, Sven Stelling-Michaud and Michel Cadot (eds), *Autour d'Alexandre Herzen: documents inédits* (Geneva, 1973), p. 111.

243   FRENCH REFUGEES SING 'RULE BRITANNIA'. Alexander Herzen, *My Past and Thoughts*, IV, p. 270.

15 – THE ROAD TO WARREN STREET

244   FRENCH EXILES LEAVE FOR AMERICA. Taxile Delord, *Histoire du second empire* (six volumes, Paris, 1870), II, p. 567.

244   COMMUNE RÉVOLUTIONNAIRE. A. Müller Lehning, 'The International Association (1855–1859): A contribution to the preliminary history of the first international' in *International Review for Social History*, vol. 2 (January 1938), pp. 201–12.

245   'WHEN A MAN RAISES HIMSELF ABOVE PUBLIC JUSTICE'. An 1857 pamphlet by Pyat, quoted in 'Imperial Manifesto', *Dublin Evening Mail*, 12 March 1858.

245–6   HENRI BEAUGRAND'S FUNERAL. '*Fragment du journal de Philippe [Fauvre]*' (London, 9 January 1853), in Philippe Faure, *Journal d'un combattant de février* (Jersey, 1859), pp. 218–19.

246   COMMUNE RÉVOLUTIONNAIRE ASSASSINATION ATTEMPT. Thomas Wright, *The History of France: From the Earliest Period to the Present Time* (three volumes: London, 1871), III, p. 739.

246   BARTHÉLEMY AND TONY PETITJEAN INVENT. Alexander Herzen, *My Past and Thoughts*, trans. Constance Garnett (London, 1925, 2008), IV, p. 272; Alfred Talaudin, J. Domenge, J. Teyre, 'The Murderer Barthélemy', *The Times*, 17 January 1855; *Newton's London Journal of Arts and Sciences* (London, 1854), vol. XLV, pp. 256–58.

247   MERCURY KILLED SCORES OF WORKERS EVERY YEAR. Henry MacCormac, 'On mercurial poisoning and its Prevention' in *The New York Medical Journal* (New York, 1867), IV, pp. 147–8. John Emsley, *The Elements of Murder: A History of Poison* (Oxford, 2005), pp. 53–4. Though in the end the process invented by a German chemist called Liebeg would come to dominate mirror production.

247   MICHAEL FARADAY NOTICES WORK OF PETITJEAN. Professor Faraday, 'On M. Petitjean's Process for Silvering Glass: Some Observations on Dividing Gold' (13 June 1856) in *Notices of the Proceedings at the Meetings of the Members of the Royal Institute of Great Britain* (London, 1858), II, pp. 308–12.

247   BARTHÉLEMY, WORKING LATE INTO THE NIGHT. Alfred Talaudin, J. Domenge, J. Teyre, 'The Murderer Barthélemy', *The Times*, 17 January 1855.

247–8   'THE CRIMES OF OUR ENEMIES'. 'Funeral of a French refugee
         – Oration Over his Grave', *Reynold's Newspaper*, 12 November 1853.

248   THE 'BLACK FLAG' OF VENGEANCE. *Le journal d'Adèle
         Hugo*, ed. Frances Vernor Guille (four volumes: Paris, 1968), II,
         p. 327.

248   HIS 'RULING IDEA, HIS PASSION, HIS MONOMANIA'.
         Alexander Herzen, *My Past and Thoughts*, IV, p. 272–73.

248   BARTHÉLEMY PLANNED TO SOAK DEER-SHOT IN
         SULPHUR. Wilhelm Liebknecht, 'Karl Marx; Biographical
         Memoirs' in *Wilhelm Liebknecht and German Social Democracy:
         A Documentary History*, ed. William A. Pelz, trans. Erich Hahn
         (Westport: CT, 1994), p. 107.

248   MOORE RESIDENCE. E. Beresford Chancellor, London's Old
         Latin Quarter: Being an Account of Tottenham Court Road and
         its Immediate Surroundings (London, 1930), p. 127. 'Latest intel-
         ligence', *Manchester Courier and Lancashire General Advertiser*,
         23 July 1886.

248   MOORE AN UPPER WARDEN OF THE WHEELWRIGHTS
         COMPANY. Eric Bennett, *The Worshipful Company of
         Wheelwrights* (Newton Abbot, 1970), p. 97.

249–50   'TWO GENTLEMEN OF LONDON, NO COMMON
         COCKNEY "GENTS"'. 'Mr George Moore,' *Gloucester Journal*,
         27 January 1855.

250   'MERE "OLD NOBILITY" IS LEAST IN WORTH'. George
         Moore and Family, *Commonplace Book*, A. R. Heath Rare Books
         (Bristol, *c.* 1850).

251   BARTHÉLEMY MOVES IN WITH WOMAN COMPANION.
         Alexander Herzen, *My Past and Thoughts*, IV, p. 271.

251   BARTHÉLEMY 'PASSIONATELY ATTACHED' TO HER. Carl
         Schurz, *The Reminiscences of Carl Schurz* (two volumes: New
         York, 1907, 1913), I, p. 393.

251   SARAH LOWNDES 'A PROFICIENT, IF NOT A PROFESSIONAL
         THIEF'. 'Windsor Epiphany sessions', *Windsor and Eton Express*,
         20 January 1855.

251   'NO MORE RELENTLESS FLIRTS IN THE WORLD THAN
         ENGLISH GIRLS'. Francis Wey, *A Frenchman Sees the English in
         the 'Fifties*, ed. Valerie Pirie (London, 1935), p. 184.

252   BARTHÉLEMY'S TRUE DESTINATION WAS PARIS. Alexander
         Herzen, *My Past and Thoughts*, IV, p. 272–3.

252   BARTHÉLEMY 'HAD OBTAINED AN ADMISSION CARD'.
         Wilhelm Liebknecht, 'Karl Marx; Biographical Memoirs' in
         Wilhelm Liebknecht and German Social Democracy, p. 107.

252   'WITH LITTLE WINDOWS LIKE GUILLOTINES'. Edmond
         Taxier, a French journalist writing of his visit to London in 1851.
         Quoted in 'Munchausen Modernised', *Household Words*, ed.
         Charles Dickens, London, 1853, Vol. 1, No. 23, pp. 533–8, 534.

16 – 'DOUBLY HORRIBLE AND HORRIBLY DOUBLE'

253   BARTHÉLEMY DENIED THAT ANY WOMAN HAD BEEN WITH HIM. 'Central Criminal Court', *Daily News*, 1 January 1855.

253   NEIGHBOUR SAW A WOMAN GO 'OVER THE RAILINGS'. 'The Double Murder in Warren-Street', *The Times*, 22 December 1854.

253–4   JOHN SLOMAN HERRING. Ancestry.com. England & Wales, National Probate Calendar (Index of Wills and Administrations), 1858–1966 [database online]: original data: Principal Probate Registry. Calendar of the Grants of Probate and Letters of Administration made in the Probate Registries of the High Court of Justice in England. London, England. *London Gazette*, 9 May 1854, p. 1470 and 16 May 1854, p. 1636.

254   HERRING SAW IN BARTHÉLEMY'S CASE AN OPPORTUNITY TO ADVERTISE HIS BUSINESS. Alexander Herzen, *My Past and Thoughts*, trans. Constance Garnett (London, 1925, 2008), IV, p. 279.

254   POLICE SUSPICION THAT BARTHÉLEMY WAS ATTEMPTING TO REPEAT 'THE BERMONDSEY HORROR'. 'The Murderer Barthélemy', *Norfolk Chronicle*, 23 December 1854.

254   'THERE IS NO LAW FOR ME.' Judith Flanders, *The Victorian Invention of Murder: How the Victorians Revelled in Death and Detection and Created Modern Crime* (London, 2011), p. 164.

254   A READY-MADE 'GRAVE'. 'The Late Murder in Fitzroy Square', *Sunday Times*, 17 December 1854.

255   *SUNDAY TIMES* ALLEGATIONS. 'The Late Murder in Fitzroy Square', *Sunday Times*, 17 December 1854.

255   GEORGE MOORE'S SON DENIES THAT BARTHÉLEMY IS HIS BROTHER-IN-LAW. 'The Double Murder in Warren-Street', *The Times*, 22 December 1854.

256   RUMOURS THAT PALMERSTON DID NOT WISH FOR TOO MUCH SCRUTINY OF MOORE'S DEATH. See the *People's Paper*, 27 January 1855.

256–7   'A MAN OF VERY REPULSIVE APPEARANCE'. 'The late atrocious murders in Warren Street, Tottenham Court Road', *Standard*, 14 December 1854.

257   'A REMARKABLY FINE LOOKING YOUNG MAN'. 'Horrible double murder', *Cheshire Observer and General Advertiser*, 16 December 1854.

257   BARTHÉLEMY 'ABOVE THE MIDDLE SIZE'. 'The double murder in Warren Street', *Morning Post*, 11 December 1854.

257   'BARTHÉLEMY'S VOICE 'WAS ABSOLUTELY MELODIOUS'. James Stratton, 'The correspondence between the characters and heads of two murderers newly executed at Newgate', *The Zoist*, No. L, July 1855, p. 208.

257 'THERE IS A CLASS OF PEOPLE WHO HAVE A MORBID PREDILECTION'. George Augustus Sala, *Twice Round the Clock or Hours of the Day and Night in London* [1858] (New York, 1971), p. 167.

257 'I NEVER KNEW MY FATHER TO LEAVE ENGLAND TO GO TO PARIS.' 'The Double Murder in Warren-Street', *The Times*, 22 December 1854.

258 'BARTHÉLEMY'S END IS A GLORIOUS ONE'. Marx to Engels, 15 December 1854, *MECW*, Vol. 39, pp. 505–6.

258–9 HERZEN'S V MEETING WITH TWO REFUGEES. Alexander Herzen, *My Past and Thoughts*, trans. Constance Garnett (London, 1925, 2008), IV, p. 273.

260 DESCRIPTION OF THE OLD BAILEY. 'The Old Bailey' in *London Society: An Illustrated Magazine*, Vol. 10 (London, 1866), pp. 399–405, quotation on p. 403.

260–2 BARTHÉLEMY'S TRIAL FOR COLLARD'S MURDER. 'Central Criminal Court', *Daily News*, 5 January 1855.

262–3 JUROR'S LETTER TO *THE TIMES*. 'The convict Barthélemy', *Morning Advertiser*, 8 January 1855.

263 'THE JUSTICE OR EXPEDIENCY OF CAPITAL PUNISHMENT'. Karl Marx, 'Capital Punishment' (written 28 January 1853), published in the *New York Daily Tribune*, 18 February 1853, in Karl Marx and Frederick Engels, *Articles on Britain* (Moscow, 1971), p. 150.

263–5 'I IMPLORE YOU ... TO REPENT.' 'The double murder in Warren Street', *Standard*, 5 January 1855.

265 'AS FOR BARTHÉLEMY, HE WAS IMPASSIVE'. *Journal des débats politiques et littéraires*, 7 January 1855.

265 'NO DOUBT HE WAS GLAD TO HEAR THE SENTENCE OF DEATH PASSED ON ME.' 'The double murder in Warren Street', *Standard*, 5 January 1855.

265 'REMARKABLE IMPENETRABILITY TO COMMON EMOTIONS'. 'Execution of Emmanuel Barthélemy', *Daily News*, 23 January 1855.

266 THIS MOST UNREGULATED OF MARKETS. The first Food and Drugs Act, regulating quality, was not passed until 1860.

266 'HE PREPARED THE UNFORTUNATE MAN FOR THE GRUESOME TORTURE'. Monte Gardiner, 'Malwida von Meysenbug's "Memoirs of an Idealist", translation of *Memoiren Einer Idealistin*', Thesis (MA), Brigham Young University Dept of Germanic and Slavic Languages, 1999, pp. 229–30.

266–7 'PANIC STRICKEN, HE RUSHED OFF TO NEWGATE'. Alexander Herzen, *My Past and Thoughts*, IV, p. 277.

267 'HIS PROUD SOUL SHUNNED THIS PROSPECT'. Monte Gardiner, 'Malwida von Meysenbug's "Memoirs of an Idealist"', pp. 229–30.

267   'PRESERVING THE EQUILIBRIUM OF THE CHAIR WITH THE DEXTERITY OF AN ACCOMPLISHED TUMBLER'. 'Barthélemy in Newgate', *Reynold's News*, 14 January 1855.

267–8 'THERE WAS NOT A SINGLE MITIGATING CIRCUMSTANCE'. 'Notice to correspondents', *Windsor and Eton Express*, 6 January 1855.

268–9 THE CASE OF LUIGI BARANELLI. *The Annual Register*, 1855 (London, 1856), pp. 4–10.

269–71 'WITH THE DREADFUL HEAD-ROLL STILL RINGING IN OUR EARS'. 'Notes of the week', *Durham County Advertiser*, 12 January 1855.

271   'BARTHÉLEMY … COULD NOT BE LEGALLY PUT TO DEATH IN FRANCE'. C.N., 'The Murderer Barthélemy', *The Times*, 11 January 1855.

272   'THE CUSTOM OF ENGLAND IS THAT MURDERERS MUST DIE ON THE SCAFFOLD.' 'The case of the wretched murderer Barthélemy', *The Times*, 11 January 1855.

272–3 'I CANNOT HELP FEELING THAT THERE HAS BEEN SOME ERROR IN THE CONVICTION OF BARTHÉLEMY.' A Lawyer, 'The Case of Barthélemy', *The Times*, 19 January 1855.

17 – 'NOW I SHALL KNOW THE SECRET'

274   'LIVING SKELETONS, DEVOURED WITH VERMIN'. Letter written in spring 1856 reflecting on January 1855 [incomplete], Lynn MacDonald (ed.), *Florence Nightingale: The Crimean War*, Vol. 14 of the *Collected Works of Florence Nightingale* (Waterloo, Ontario, 2010), p. 409.

274   '*WHOM SHALL WE HANG?*' Asa Briggs, *Victorian People: A Reassessment of Persons and Themes, 1851–67* (London, 1955, 1990), p. 69.

275   LEDRU-ROLLIN PARTY 'ALMOST GLAD' BARTHÉLEMY FACED THE ROPE. Monte Gardiner, 'Malwida von Meysenbug's "Memoirs of an Idealist", translation of *Memoiren Einer Idealistin*', Thesis (MA), Brigham Young University Dept of Germanic and Slavic Languages, 1999, p. 226.

275   JOSEPH DOMENGÉ AND HIS COMRADES DEFEND BARTHÉLEMY. Monte Gardiner, 'Malwida von Meysenbug's "Memoirs of an Idealist"', p. 226.

275–7 HOSTILE ACCOUNT OF BARTHÉLEMY'S LIFE ANONYMOUSLY PLANTED. 'The Warren-Street Murderer', *The Times*, 11 January 1855.

277–8 'NOTHING I HAVE GONE THROUGH AMAZES ME'. Monte Gardiner, 'Malwida von Meysenbug's "Memoirs of an Idealist"', p. 229; Arthur Koestler, *Darkness at Noon* (New York, 1941, 2015), p. 258.

278   SHE DID NOT CONFUSE 'SOCIAL PREJUDICE FOR VIRTUE'.
           Monte Gardiner, 'Malwida von Meysenbug's "Memoirs of an
           Idealist"', p. 229.

278-9   'IT IS HARD TO SUPPOSE THAT ANY MAN, BUT UTTERLY
           MAD'. Alexander Herzen, *My Past and Thoughts*, trans. Constance
           Garnett (London, 1925, 2008), IV, p. 272.

279   ALFRED TALAUDIN AND JOSEPH DOMENGÉ CLOSE TO
           HERZEN. Monica Partridge, 'Alexander Herzen; His Last Phase'
           in Chimen Abramsky, Beryl J. Williams (eds), *Essays in Honour
           of E. H. Carr* (Basingstoke, 1974), p. 48.

280   BARTHÉLEMY'S 'THREAT TO TAKE THE LIFE OF LEDRU
           ROLLIN ... WAS REAL'. G. J. H., 'The duel between Cournet
           and Barthélemy', *The Reasoner: Gazette of Secularism*, 4 March
           1855, p. 128.

279-81   'WE WILL NOT ADD A WORD ABOUT THE WARREN
           STREET TRAGEDY'. Alfred Talaudin, J. Domengé, J. Teyre, 'The
           Murderer Barthélemy', *The Times*, 17 January 1855.

281   'I HAVE ONLY SIXTEEN DAYS TO LIVE.' 'Execution of
           Emmanuel Barthélemy', *Daily News*, 23 January 1855.

282   'THE HARDEST CRIMINAL WITH WHOM HE EVER HAD
           TO DEAL'. 'Execution of Barthélemy', *Jackson's Oxford Journal*,
           23 January 1855.

283   'NOT A HIGH-FLOWN SENTENCE'. Alexander Herzen, *My
           Past and Thoughts*, p. 274.

283   'IT WAS A BRIEF, EMOTIONAL LETTER'. Monte Gardiner,
           'Malwida von Meysenbug's "Memoirs of an Idealist"', p. 231.

284   SARAH LOWNDES. 'Windsor Epiphany sessions', *Windsor and
           Eton Express*, 20 January 1855.

284-5   MR. DAVIS'S REPORTS ON HIS DISCUSSIONS WITH
           BARTHÉLEMY. 'Execution of Emmanuel Barthélemy',
           Coventry Standard, 26 January 1855; 'The double murder in
           Warren Street – execution of Barthélemy', *Berrow's Worcester
           Journal*, 27 January 1855; 'Execution of the murderer
           Barthélemy', *Cheshire Observer and General Advertiser*, 27
           January 1855.

285   'HE HAS THE GOOD TASTE NOT TO SPEAK TO ME ON
           MATTERS OF RELIGION'. 'The double murder in Warren Street
           – execution of Barthélemy', *Berrow's Worcester Journal*, 27
           January 1855.

285-7   BARTHÉLEMY'S OPINIONS ON GOD. 'Execution of the
           murderer Barthélemy', *Leicester Chronicle*, 27 January 1855.

287   'HIS UTMOST POWER WITH ADVERSE POWER OPPOS'D'.
           Paradise Lost, l1.104-11.

287-9   'I SUGGESTED TO HERZEN AND DOMENGÉ THAT WE
           THREE ASK FOR PERMISSION'. Monte Gardiner, 'Malwida
           von Meysenbug's "Memoirs of an Idealist"', p. 230.

289–91   BARTHÉLEMY'S EXCHANGE WITH THE SHERIFFS. 'Execution of Emmanuel Barthélemy', *Daily News*, 23 January 1855; 'The double murder in Warren Street – execution of Barthélemy', *Berrow's Worcester Journal*, 27 January 1855. Alexander Herzen, My Past and Thoughts, IV, p. 279.

291–2   DESCRIPTION OF WILLIAM CALCRAFT, THE EXECUTIONER. Ronald Pearsall, *Night's Black Angels: The Forms and Faces of Victorian Cruelty* (London, 1975), p. 183.

292   BARTHÉLEMY'S EXCHANGE WITH SHERIFF CROSLEY. 'The double murder in Warren Street – execution of Barthélemy', *Berrow's Worcester Journal*, 27 January 1855.

292   'I WISH TO BE PERMITTED TO HOLD THIS PAPER IN MY HAND'. 'Execution of the murderer Barthélemy', *Cheshire Observer and General Advertiser*, 27 January 1855.

293   'NOW I SHALL KNOW THE SECRET'. 'The double murder in Warren Street – execution of Barthélemy', *Berrow's Worcester Journal*, 27 January 1855.

293   'IN GENERAL, ONE OF THE VERY LOWEST EVER CONGREGATED'. 'The double murder in Warren Street – execution of the murderer', *Trewman's Exeter Flying Post*, 25 January 1855.

293   PRESS WAS EQUALLY FASCINATED. Rosalind Crone, *Violent Victorians: Popular Entertainment in Nineteenth-Century London* (Manchester, 2012), pp. 237, 240.

293   'THE EXECUTION WAS ... ONE OF THE MOST REMARKABLE IN MODERN TIMES'. 'Execution of Barthélemy', *Jackson's Oxford Journal*, 27 January 1855.

294   'THERE WAS NO EBULLITION OF FEELING'. 'Execution of Emmanuel Barthélemy', *Daily News*, 23 January 1855.

294   BARTHÉLEMY'S EXPRESSION 'CHANGED VERY LITTLE'. Wilhelm Liebknecht, 'Karl Marx; Biographical Memoirs' in *Wilhelm Liebknecht and German Social Democracy: A Documentary History*, ed. William A. Pelz, trans. Erich Hahn (Westport: CT, 1994), p. 108.

294   PROFESSION LISTED AS 'ENGINEER'. Newgate Prison, London: Register of Prisoners, PCOM2.

18 – BARTHÉLEMY'S CONFESSION

295   'IT BELONGS TO THE ALL-SEEING AND INFINITELY JUST GOD'. Editorial, *Belfast Commercial Chronicle*, 26 January 1855.

296   'O PITY ME, O GOD ON HIGH'. 'Life, Trial, Confession and Execution of Emanuel Barthélemy' (Whitechapel, n.d.).

296–8   ABBÉ ROUX'S ACCOUNT OF BARTHÉLEMY'S LAST DAYS. 'Execution of Emmanuel Barthélemy', *Era*, 20 January 1855.

298–9   'HE DIED IN A TRULY COURAGEOUS MANNER'. Monte Gardiner, 'Malwida von Meysenbug's "Memoirs of an Idealist", translation of *Memoiren Einer Idealistin*', Thesis (MA), Brigham Young University Dept of Germanic and Slavic Languages, 1999, pp. 231–2.

299   'ONE OF THE MOST NOBLY SIGNIFICANT MEN'. Letter to Gottfied Kinkel (24 January 1855), cited in Innocenzo Cervelli, 'Emmanuel Barthélemy, in memoria', *Studi Storici*, Anno 41, No. 2 (Apr.–Jun. 2000), pp. 277–402, 362.

299–300 BARTHÉLEMY 'WROTE SOME MEMOIR'. Alexander Herzen, *My Past and Thoughts*, trans. Constance Garnett (London, 1925, 2008), IV, pp. 277–8.

300   'WHEN HIS LAWYER CAME AFTER THE EXECUTION'. Monte Gardiner, 'Malwida von Meysenbug's "Memoirs of an Idealist"', p. 231.

300–1   'AND THEN THE PISTOL WENT OFF'. 'Confession of the murderer Barthélemy', *Reynolds's Newspaper*, 20 January 1855.

302   'NOTHING COULD BE MORE CERTAIN'. Carl Schurz, *The Reminiscences of Carl Schurz* (two volumes: New York, 1907, 1913), I, p. 395.

302   'SENT TO RUIN THE ENERGETIC REFUGEE'. Monte Gardiner, 'Malwida von Meysenbug's "Memoirs of an Idealist"', p. 227.

302   'SENT TO LONDON WITH INSTRUCTIONS TO WATCH BARTHÉLEMI'. Carl Schurz, *The Reminiscences of Carl Schurz*, I, p. 394.

302   'SHE HAD HEARD THIS AND THAT AND GAVE INFORMATION TO THE POLICE'. Wilhelm Liebknecht, 'Karl Marx; Biographical Memoirs' in *Wilhelm Liebknecht and German Social Democracy: A Documentary History*, ed. William A. Pelz, trans. Erich Hahn (Westport: CT, 1994), p. 108.

302–3   'BARTHÉLEMY WHO FEELS THAT HE IS THE WEAKER MAN'. Ibid., pp. 107–8.

                                  EPILOGUE

306   'WE ARE USED FOR ALL THE WORLD LIKE CAB OR OMNIBUS HORSES'. P. E. Razzell and R. W. Wainwright (eds), *The Victorian Working Class: Selections from Letters to the Morning Chronicle* (London, 1973), p. 127.

306   'SO AS TO ACQUIRE THE KNOWLEDGE AND SKILL REQUISITE'. 'Memorial to the Master Builders of London and its Vicinity', 18 November 1858, in *Labour's Formative Years: Nineteenth-Century, Vol. II, 1847–1879*, ed. James B. Jeffreys (London, 1948), p. 64.

306   A SOCIALISTIC 'ORGANISATION OF LABOUR' HAD BECOME A NECESSITY. John Ruskin, *'Unto This Last': Four essays on the First Principles of Political Economy* (London, 1862, 1893), p. 63.

306–7   CONCEPT OF 'LABOUR POWER'. This was a concept Marx first scribbled in the notebooks he composed in 1857–8 – the *Grundrisse* – and published in his *Contribution to the Critique of Political Economy* in 1859.

307   MARX PARAPHRASED THE LABOURERS' MEMORIAL. David Riazanov, *Karl Marx and Friedrich Engels: An Introduction to their Lives and Work*, trans. Joshua Kunitz (London and New York, 1927, 1973), p. 135.

307   'YOU AND I KNOW ON THE MARKET ONLY ONE LAW'. Karl Marx, *Capital* [1867] (New York, 1906), pp. 258–9.

308   'GREAT *RABBLE OF THE PEOPLE*'. Mikhail Bakunin, 'The International and Karl Marx' (1872), in Sam Dolgoff (ed.), *Bakunin on Anarchy* (London, 1971), p. 294.

309   'THE DAY OF JUSTICE APPROACHES'. John Merriman, *Massacre: The Life and Death of the Paris Commune of 1871* (New Haven 2014), p. 78.

309–10   FRÉDÉRIC COURNET JNR. Ernest Alfred Vizetelly, *My Adventures in the Commune, Paris, 1871* (London, 1914), pp. 101–2.

310   NO GRAVE FOR DELESCLUZE. Laure Godineau, *La commune de Paris par ceux qui l'ont vécue* (Paris, 2010), p. 218.

311–2   PHRENOLOGY OF BARTHÉLEMY. James Stratton, 'The correspondence between the characters and heads of two murderers newly executed at Newgate', *The Zoist*, No. L, July 1855, pp. 215, 216, 232.

312   BARTHÉLEMY'S MIND 'FROM A PSYCHOLOGICAL POINT OF VIEW'. Alfred Hutchinson Dymond, *The Law on Its Trial: Or, Personal Recollections of the Death Penalty and its Opponents* (London, 1865), p. 232.

312   BARTHÉLEMY DESCRIBED IN TUSSAUD'S CATALOGUE. *Biographical and Descriptive Sketches of the Distinguished Characters which compose the unrivalled exhibition and historical gallery of Madame Tussaud's and Sons* (London, 1866), p. 38.

312   ITALIAN ÉMIGRÉS WHO THREATENED TO BEAT UP TUSSAUD'S STAFF. *Die Lorette von einem Mitgliende der Emigration leben in London* (four volumes: Berlin, 1864), IV, p. 44.

312–3   'A BARTHÉLEMY IS NOT POWERLESS'. 'Red Republicans in Europe', reprinted in *Dublin Evening Mail*, 19 October 1855.

313   'LION-LIKE APPEARANCE'. 'Dramatic and musical gleanings', *Sportsman*, 16 January 1866.

313   THE PSYCHOLOGY OF VIOLENCE. See Aaron T. Beck, *Prisoners of Hate: The Cognitive Basis of Anger, Hostility, and Violence* (New York, 1999).

314   'SAVOIR-FAIRE, THAT SUCKING VAMPIRE'. Auguste Blanqui, 'Dispositions Immédiates' (1869–1870), V. P. Volguine (ed.), *Auguste Blanqui, textes Chosis* (Paris, 1971), p. 141.

314   'HEARTS WITH ONE PURPOSE'. W. B. Yeats, 'Easter, 1916', ll. 41–4.

SELECT BIBLIOGRAPHY

The following contains only those items that bear most closely on the details of Emmanuel Barthélemy's life. The endnotes contain all items explicitly cited.

MANUSCRIPT

Blanqui Papers, Bibliothèque nationale de France, 9581, 9584–2.

George Moore and Family, *Commonplace Book*, A. R. Heath Rare Books (Bristol, United Kingdom), c.1850.

Home Office Papers, National Archives, HO 45/4762.

Newgate Prison, London: Register of Prisoners, PCOM2.

Calendar of the Grants of Probate and Letters of Administration made in the Probate Registries of the High Court of Justice in England. London, England. *London Gazette*, 9 May 1854.

Ancestry.com. England & Wales, National Probate Calendar (Index of Wills and Administrations), 1858–1966 [database online]: original data: Principal Probate Registry.

'Old Bailey Online' Project, *Proceedings of the Central Criminal Court*, 1 January 1855.

'Life, Trial, Confession and Execution of Emanuel Barthélemy' (Whitechapel, n.d.).

OFFICIAL AND SEMI-OFFICIAL SERIALS

Journal du droit criminel, ou Jurisprudence criminelle du Royaume (Paris, 1840).

Bulletin des arrêts de la Cour de cassation rendus en matière criminelle (Paris, 1840).

Rapport De La Commission D'enquête Nsur L'insurrection Qui A Éclaté Dans La Journée Du 23 Juin Et Sur Les Évènements Du 15 Mai (three volumes: Paris, 1848).

House of Commons Debates, 16 November 1852, Vol. 123.

Crown Cases Reserved for Consideration (London, 1853).

The Annual Register, 1855 (London, 1856).

PRESS

'Nouvelles et Faits Divers', *La Presse*, 6 December 1839.

'Untitled', *Journal des débats politiques et littéraires*, 7 December 1839.

'Untitled', *La Presse*, 7 December 1839.

'Affaire Barthélemy', *Gazette des tribunaux: journal de jurisprudence et de débats judiciaire*, 21 December 1839.

'Tentative d'assassinat, par un coup de pistolet, sur un sergent de ville', *Journal des débats politiques et littéraires*, 21 December 1839.

'Untitled', *Morning Post*, 23 December 1839.

'France', *Evening Mail*, 15 January 1849.

'Ein Kriegsgericht in Paris', *Rheinisches Echo* (Cologne, 1849).

Veillées du Peuple, in *Les révolutions du XIXe siècle: 1848, la révolution démocratique et sociale*. Tome 2 (Paris, 1984).

Emmanuel Barthélemy, 'L'insurrection de Juin au faubourg du Temple', in *Les Veillées du peuple* (March 1850) [reprinted in *Les révolutions du XIXe siècle: 1848, la révolution démocratique et sociale*. Tome 2.]

'The French exiles of the 13th of June, at present residing in London, to the Fraternal Democrats of England', *Northern Star*, 22 December 1849.

'The Trial at Versailles', in G. Julian Harney (ed.), *The Democratic Review of British and Foreign Politics, History and Literature*, Vol. 1, 1850.

'The Kossuth Mania', *The Times*, 10 November 1851.

'Express from Paris', *Evening Mail*, 14 November 1851.

'The late French duel', *Morning Advertiser*, 22 October 1852.

'The late duel near Windsor', *Morning Chronicle*, 22 October 1852.

'The Fatal Duel Near Windsor', *The Times*, 22 October 1852.

'The late French duel', letter from Arthur R. Reeves, A. B., *Morning Advertiser*, 23 October 1852.

'Untitled', *Morning Advertiser*, 25 October 1852.

Louis Blanc, 'To the Editor of *The Times*', *The Times*, 25 October 1852.

'The duel near Windsor – suspected murder', *Daily News*, 27 October 1852.

'The fatal duel at Egham', *Manchester Times*, 27 October 1852.

Letter from Arthur R. Reeves, A. B., *Morning Advertiser*, 27 October 1852.

'The Fatal Duel Near Windsor', *Morning Chronicle*, 27 October 1852.

'The fatal duel near Windsor', *The Times*, 28 October 1852.

'The Fatal Duel near Windsor', *Examiner*, 30 October 1852.

'The duellist murder at Egham', *Hampshire Advertiser and Salisbury Guardian*, 30 October 1852.

'The fatal duel near Windsor – final examination, and committal of the prisoners', *Morning Post*, 30 October 1852.

'The Fatal Duel Near Windsor', *Windsor and Eton Express*, 30 October 1852.

'Further Particulars', *Windsor and Eton Express*, 30 October 1852.

'Untitled', *Windsor and Eton Express*, 13 November 1852.

'The fatal duel near Windsor', *Windsor and Eton Express*, 13 November 1852.

'Law intelligence', *Reynolds Newspaper*, 20 November 1852.

'The Late Fatal Duel between Frenchmen', *Reynold's Newspaper*, 30 January 1853.

'Untitled', *Reynold's Newspaper*, 6 February 1853.

'Assize intelligence', *Morning Post*, 22 March 1853.

The Attorney for Mm. Barthélemy and Morney, 'The Egham Duel', *The Times*, 24 March 1853.

'Funeral of a French refugee – Oration Over his Grave', *Reynold's Newspaper*, 12 November 1853.

'The double murder in Warren Street', *Daily News*, 11 December 1854.

'The double murder in Warren Street', *Morning Post*, 11 December 1854.

'The late atrocious murders in Warren Street, Tottenham Court Road', *Standard*, 14 December 1854.

'The double murder in Warren Street, Fitzroy Square', *Morning Post*, 15 December 1854.

'Horrible double murder', *Cheshire Observer and General Advertiser*, 16 December 1854.

'The late murder in Warren Street', *Daily News*, 16 December 1854.

'The Late Murder in Fitzroy Square', *Sunday Times*, 17 December 1854.

'The Murderer Barthélemy', *Norfolk Chronicle*, 23 December 1854.

'Central Criminal Court', *Daily News*, 1 January 1855.

'The Warren Street Murder', *Morning Post*, 9 January 1855.

'The Warren Street murderer', *Sheffield and Rotherham Independent*, 13 January 1855.

G. J. H., 'The duel between Cournet and Barthélemy', *The Reasoner: Gazette of secularism*, 4 March 1855.

'The Double Murder in Warren-Street', *The Times*, 22 December 1854.

'Central Criminal Court', *Daily News*, 5 January 1855.

'The double murder in Warren Street', *Standard*, 5 January 1855.

'Notice to correspondents', *Windsor and Eton Express*, 6 January 1855.

Journal des débats politiques et littéraires, 7 January 1855.

'The convict Barthélemy', *Morning Advertiser*, 8 January 1855.

'The Warren-Street murderer', *The Times*, 11 January 1855.

C.N., 'The Murderer Barthélemy', *The Times*, 11 January 1855.

'The case of the wretched murderer Barthélemy', *The Times*, 11 January 1855.

'Notes of the week,' *Durham County Advertiser*, 12 January 1855.

'Barthélemy in Newgate', *Reynold's News*, 14 January 1855.

Alfred Talaudin, J. Domenge, J. Teyre, 'The Murderer Barthélemy', *The Times*, 17 January 1855.

A Lawyer, 'The Case of Barthélemy', *The Times*, 19 January 1855.

'Execution of Emmanuel Barthélemy', *Era*, 20 January 1855.

'Confession of the murderer Barthélemy', *Reynolds Newspaper*, 20 January 1855.

'Windsor Epiphany sessions', *Windsor and Eton Express*, 20 January 1855.

'Execution of Emmanuel Barthélemy', *Daily News*, 23 January 1855.

'Execution of Barthélemy', *Jackson's Oxford Journal*, 23 January 1855.

'The double murder in Warren Street – execution of the murderer', *Trewman's Exeter Flying Post*, 25 January 1855.

Editorial, *Belfast Commercial Chronicle*, 26 January 1855.

'Execution of Emmanuel Barthélemy', *Coventry Standard*, 26 January 1855.

'The double murder in Warren Street – execution of Barthélemy', *Berrow's Worcester Journal*, 27 January 1855.

'Execution of the murderer Barthélemy', *Cheshire Observer and General Advertiser*, 27 January 1855.
'Execution of the murderer Barthélemy', *Leicester Chronicle*, 27 January 1855.
People's Paper, 27 January 1855.
'Red Republicans in Europe', *Dublin Evening Mail*, 19 October 1855.
'The Warren Street Murders', *Morning Post*, 1 December 1856.
'Dramatic and musical gleanings', *Sportsman*, 16 January 1866.

BOOKS

L'Ami de la religion et du roi: journal ecclésiastique, politique et littéraire (Paris, 1851).
Annuaire des deux mondes, 1851–1852 (Paris, 1852).
'Le banquet des égaux. Londres, 24 février 1851 (Paris, n.d.)', pp. 17–21, in *Les révolutions du XIXe siècle: 1848, la révolution démocratique et sociale*. Tome 2 (Paris, 1984).
Beaumont School, *The History of St. Stanislaus' College, Beaumont: A Record of Fifty Years, 1861–1911* (Windsor, 1911).
Blanqui, Auguste, '*Avis au peuple (le toast de Londres)*,' *Annuaire historique universel pour 1851* (Paris, 1851).
Cahiers du communisme, Volume 8, Issue 1 (1977).
Calman, Alvin R., *Ledru-Rollin après 1848 et les proscrits français en Angleterre* (Paris, 1921).
Castille, Hippolyte, *Histoire de la seconde République française* (four volumes: Paris, 1855).
Castille, Hippolyte, *Les Massacres de Juin, 1848* (Paris, 1868).
Caussidière, Marc, *Memoirs of Citizen Caussidière: Ex-prefect of Police, and Representative of the People* (two volumes: London, 1849).
Cervelli, Innocenzo, 'Emmanuel Barthélemy, in memoria', *Studi Storici*, Anno 41, No. 2 (Apr.–Jun. 2000).
Chenu, Adolphe, *Les chevaliers de la république rouge en 1851* (Paris, 1851).
CrimethInc. Historical Research Society, *Emmanuel Barthélemy: Proletarian Fighter, Blanquist Conspirator, Survivor of the Galleys, Veteran of the Uprising of 1848, Fugitive, Duelist, Ruffian* (online, n.d. [2016]).
De Bussy, *Les conspirateurs en Angleterre, 1848–1858* (Paris, 1858).
Drahn, Ernst, *Karl Marx und Friedrich Engels ueber die Diktatur des Proletariats* (Berlin-Wilmersdorf, 1920).
Drouet, Juliette, *Souvenirs, 1843–1854*, ed. Gérard Pouchain (Paris, 2006).
Dymond, Alfred Hutchinson, *The Law on Its Trial: Or, Personal Recollections of the Death Penalty and its Opponents* (London, 1865).
Faraday, Michael, 'On M. Petitjean's Process for Silvering Glass: Some Observations on Dividing Gold' (13 June 1856) in *Notices of the Proceedings at the Meetings of the Members of the Royal Institute of Great Britain* (London, 1858), II.
Gardiner, Monte, 'Malwida von Meysenbug's "Memoirs of an Idealist", translation of *Memoiren Einer Idealistin*', Thesis (MA), Brigham Young University Dept of Germanic and Slavic Languages, 1999.

Herzen, Alexander, *My Past and Thoughts*, trans. Constance Garnett (London, 1925, 2008).

Hincker, Louis, *Citoyens-combattants à Paris, 1848–1851* (Villeneuve d'Ascq, 2008).

Le journal d'Adèle Hugo, ed. Frances Vernor Guille (four volumes: Paris, 1968).

Hugo, Charles Victor, *Les hommes de l'exil; précédes de Mes fils par Victor Hugo* (Paris, 1875).

Hugo, Victor, *Les Misérables*, trans. Christine Donougher (London, 2013, 2016).

Lacambre, C., *Évasion des prisons du Conseil de guerre, épisode de juin 1848* (Brussels, 1865).

Lefrançais, Gustave, *Souvenirs d'un révolutionnaire: de juin 1848 à la Commune* [1902] (Paris, 2013).

Liebknecht, Wilhelm, 'Reminiscences of Karl Marx' in *Reminiscences of Marx and Engels* (Moscow, n.d.).

Liebknecht, Wilhelm, 'Karl Marx: Biographical Memoirs' in *Wilhelm Liebknecht and German Social Democracy: A Documentary History*, ed. William A. Pelz, trans. Erich Hahn (Westport: CT, 1994).

Lucas, Alphonse, *Les clubs et les clubistes: histoire complète critique et anecdotique des clubs et des comités électoraux fondés à Paris depuis la révolution de 1848* (Paris, 1851).

Madame Tussaud's, *Biographical and Descriptive Sketches of the Distinguished Characters which compose the unrivalled exhibition and historical gallery of Madame Tussaud's and Sons* (London, 1866).

Marx–Engels Collected Works (fifty volumes: London, 1975–2004).

Marx, Karl, *Heroes of the Exile* [1852] in *Marx–Engels Collected Works*, Vol. 11.

Marx, Karl, *The Cologne Communist Trial* [1853], trans. Rodney Livingstone (London, 1971).

Marx, Karl, *Knight of the Noble Consciousness* [1853] in *Marx–Engels Collected Works*, Vol. XII.

Marx, Karl, *Herr Vogt* [1860], trans. R. A. Archer (London, 1982).

Newton's London Journal of Arts and Sciences (London, 1854), vol. XLV.

Repertoire des Connaissances Usuelles, supplement to *Dictionnaire de la conversation* (Paris, 1871).

'Report on a banquet of Fraternal Democrats in London', 23 December 1849, *Der Bund der Kommunisten: Dokumente und Materialien* (Berlin, 1983), Band II.

Schurz, Carl, *The Reminiscences of Carl Schurz* (two volumes, New York, 1907, 1913).

Stratton, James, 'The correspondence between the characters and heads of two murderers newly executed at Newgate', *Zoist*, No. L, July 1855.

Tchernoff, J., *Le parti républicain sous la monarchie de juillet; formation et évolution de la doctrine républicaine* (Paris, 1905).

Vallès, Jules, *Le Cri du peuple* [28 February 1884], ed. Lucien Scheler (Paris, 1970).

Vermorel, Auguste, *Les hommes de 1848* (Paris, 1869).

Vuilleumier, Marc, Michel Aucouturier, Sven Stelling-Michaud and Michel Cadot (eds), *Autour d'Alexandre Herzen: documents inédits* (Geneva, 1973).

INDEX